BRIT(ISH)

The ache for home lives in all of us, the safe place where we can go as we are and not be questioned.

– Maya Angelou,
All God's Children Need Travelling Shoes

BRIT(ISH)

On Race, Identity and Belonging

AFUA HIRSCH

JONATHAN CAPE
LONDON

5 7 9 10 8 6

Jonathan Cape, an imprint of Vintage Publishing,
20 Vauxhall Bridge Road,
London SW1V 2SA

Jonathan Cape is part of the Penguin Random House group of companies
whose addresses can be found at global.penguinrandomhouse.com.

Penguin
Random House
UK

First published in the United Kingdom by Jonathan Cape in 2018

penguin.co.uk/vintage

A CIP catalogue record for this book is available from the British Library

ISBN 9781911214281

Typeset ii   n Keynes
Printec   Great Britain   Ltd,   S.p.A.

Pengui   ure for
our b   nade

For my grandparents, Paul Kofi, Ophelia Joyce,
John and Ann, whose stories have inspired mine.

In memory of Alexander, whom we called King, gone too soon.

To Naya Ketawa. This is for you.

CONTENTS

BRIT(ISH)

INTRODUCTION:
IDENTITY LESSONS

British sheet music cover, *c.* 1850. Minstrels were a popular form of
entertainment in Victorian music halls, and were broadcast
on the BBC until the 1970s.

The world is wrong. You can't put the past behind you. It's buried in you; it's turned your flesh into its own cupboard.

– Claudia Rankine, Citizen

On a Friday evening in October 2004, with the nights drawing in and the layers piling up over summer clothes, I was sitting cross-legged in the living room of my friend Miranda's house in east London. I had recently returned from living in Senegal, one of the last frontiers of Africa before it stabs into the Atlantic Ocean to the west, and melts into the Sahara Desert in the north. Two years earlier, I'd barely had time to say goodbye to these university friends – I'd given myself a few days to recover from the exhaustion of my final exams, packed two large suitcases, then boarded an Air France flight, twenty-one years old, impatient to begin the journey into my new, African identity. It was a journey that had been years in the planning.

The friends gathered round on this autumn night had treated my return much as they had my departure: curious, but unsurprised. I came bearing stories of unpredictable work in countries that most British people have barely heard of – Chad, Burkina Faso, São Tomé – of trying to hold meetings with government ministers in languages I could barely speak, of only just surviving cerebral malaria, of smuggling suitcases of cash into war zones. My friends, deep in the hustle of London's graduate job market, pointed out how fortunate I was to be able to decorate my CV with this kind of experience. But that had never been the reason for going. I hadn't left Britain to become an expat with a competitive advantage in the job scrum; I had left Britain to leave being British. I believed that relocating my future to one or more of Africa's many nations would solve the problems of belonging that had nibbled away at me, a mixed-race girl growing up in Britain, for as long as I could remember. I had not meant to come back, not after two years, not ever, but to settle in West Africa for good, and take up my place in the world as a proud African, in places where I thought I would fit in.

Exactly the opposite had happened. Living in Senegal I had discovered, to my endless confusion, how British I was. Returning to London meant the relief of familiarity, of home, but the painful reminder that home was a place that had surveyed me as alien, questioned me about my background, and expected me to provide explanations. Very little, it seemed, had changed.

Evenings like this, in the little house that marked the beginning of a steep staircase of Victorian terraces descending down to the River Lea and the bleak London marshland beyond, were different. These friends and I – a group of black, mixed-race and other misfit Oxford graduates, sitting in a loose circle on the carpet – were bonded by the fact that none of us had ever really fitted in. So we would congregate there, feasting on vegan food, painfully aware of the clichés and contradictions that we embodied, and trying to work out the point of it all. I'd longed for this companionship while I'd been away, and the rhythms of our London lives, the quirkiness of our homes and our clothes and our seasons, the cynicism and sarcasm of our humour. Now I was back in the midst of these traditions, and drinking them in like warm tea.

I was in love with a man I'd met not long before – Sam – who lived just a mile away from Miranda in Tottenham, a part of London he always described as 'the hood'. This environment had shaped him into a person unlike any I had ever met before, and having returned to it from a northern university where he'd spent three years getting a law degree, he now clerked at a solicitors' firm during the day, saving up money before starting the vocational course to become a barrister. He spent each evening after work on the athletics track near White Hart Lane, where he trained as a sprinter, lumps of lactic acid layering themselves onto his thighs hour upon hour. Unlike any other 24-year-old I knew, Sam had his own car, a source of independence for which he spent years working, and he was always on the move late at night, plugging away at the personal development books he credited with sparing him the same fates as his friends. It never ceased to shock me how many of the people he grew up with were in jail, or in and out of mental institutions, or stuck in minimum-wage jobs. And in his community, he seemed to know everyone.

That night, Sam was visiting a school friend who lived on a nearby council estate further up Miranda's road, a sprawl of decaying social housing at the top the hill. Neither of us could have known that this was the last time Sam would visit. Just a few weeks later his friend was dead, caught up in crossfire from a turf war. These weren't innocent times – his friend was already getting slowly drawn into the drug trade, the one industry that provided many local jobs. But for a few hours that evening it was like the old days, before Sam had gone away to university and left his friends behind; just hanging out with his boys on the block, catching up.

Since he was so close by, Sam offered to pick me up from Miranda's house, and drive me home to Wimbledon, where I lived, around seventeen miles across town. Just before midnight, he rang the doorbell. The scene had already played itself out in my mind – I was excited about introducing my friends to this man they had heard so much about. I pictured him coming in, joining our little circle, sharing some tofu cheesecake.

That, however, is not how it went down. Miranda opened the door, and Sam said hello to her, cautiously, as he stepped through that front door and into the room with the big bay window, the cluttered piano. Once inside, he stopped dead, as if in shock, and stared. He shifted from foot to foot, mumbling hello, and gazed around in bewilderment, taking it all in. Sam, so confident, so uneasily fazed, was quiet, and perplexed. In all his life, he told me later, he had never seen a scene like this – people talking so earnestly, almost conspiratorially, in low, hushed voices, even eating the way we were eating, an array of strange plant foods being passed around on little plates.

Thirteen years later, we still talk about that day.

'You lot, sitting there with your herbal tea, all round in a circle, nah!' Sam shakes his head. 'That blew my mind! And I mean I thought I'd seen it ALL!' What was so strange about it? I ask. 'You don't understand.' He shakes his head again. 'This area is hood, you know! People getting shot in the area, man, dem on the hustle. And you lot were sitting there oblivious, all huddled around. In Wimbledon, yeah, fine. But in my area, and you still behaving the same way? I would *never* in all these years growing up around here have known that that scene could have even existed in this area . . .'

There was something else that bothered Sam at the time. He had his own preconceptions about my group of friends. He knew we had been to Oxford, and that many of us were privately educated, some at elite boarding schools. Now we had our degrees in the bag, we represented everything he and his friends had never had access to, a kind of uniform privilege that, as far as he was concerned, meant that success for us was guaranteed with as much certainty as failure was for most of the people around him.

'Listen, in my brain, you lot went to Oxford, you are supposed to be the crème de la crème. You are supposed to be blitzing this life. And there you were, sitting there, so *tentative* like. So unsure of yourselves. Trust me, if man like me had the opportunities you all had, there would be no stopping me. We'd be up in this country making some serious *money*. We'd be running things! Instead of sitting round all quiet.'

Conversations with Sam still go like this. Where he thinks in terms of generating wealth and opportunity, I think in terms of identity and belonging. Where he imagined gaining access to elite institutions like Oxford as a road map to making money, I lived it as a crisis of confidence. We are like two people colliding at high speed, who then stop to scoop up bounty from the wreckage, to understand what is inside the other's head. He sees musing about belonging and identity as a luxury for someone who is privileged enough to not worry about where their next meal is coming from. I was profoundly shocked by the material deprivation he experienced growing up, but when it comes to identity, I tell him, he was born with the equivalent of a silver spoon.

Because when it comes to the *black* British experience, Sam's world is its epitome. He comes from Tottenham, one of the most diverse inner-city communities in Europe. Almost all of his peers have parents who are, like his Ghanaian family, first-generation immigrants from African or Caribbean countries. Those immigrants, as has so often been the case in European cities, worked long hours in low-income jobs – irrespective of the education or skills they brought from their home countries – and raised their families in substandard housing, with little support from the state. And while their children grew up amid a chaos of poverty and violence that filled the void left by working parents and disinterested, underfunded public services, a kind of confidence grew up too. Sam's generation created a subculture of almost unparalleled influence; a black, inner-city language and grime-music scene that has since the turn of the century been progressively taking on the world. It's a society with black roots, grounded in strong African and Caribbean influences, but transcendental in popularity, shaping identities that range from northern working-class Asian masculinity,[1] to white working-class youth culture in Glasgow.[2] TV series set in its streets and tower blocks have been marketed across the world.[3] The vocabulary and vernacular that have emerged along the way is studied by linguists, who've given it a name – Multicultural London English (MLE) – and variously praised it and accused it of subsuming other versions of our language, the length and breadth of the UK.

My childhood world was very, very different. Wimbledon: a plane- and oak-tree-lined London borough, with Edwardian houses, laid out methodically on the steep streets of this patch of high suburbia famous for the tennis championships, an annual celebration of typically British stoicism in the face of summer rain, strawberries and cream, and the ever-elusive fantasy of national triumph in global sport. My memories are filed under the botanical English seasons that thread through them; berry-stained rambles on Wimbledon Common, gathering crumble fillings for autumn puddings, sledging on snow days, nature trails in spring and picnics in summer. It was a soft and silky childhood, with treats, adventures, absorbing schoolwork and intense friendships, challenges that I embraced and seasons that I loved; tossing in bed on long summer evenings, listening to the sounds of older children still playing on the street, kicking up the leaves on the walk home as the autumn nights drew in, hot chocolate on stormy nights, fires in the hearth in winter, school uniform bulking and shedding as the planet turned away from and back towards the sun.

It was the perfect place to raise a family, in all but one respect. I had brown skin, an African name, hair that coiled tightly, knotted and frizzed when brushed, and never flopped around my face. I shared this with my sister, characteristics we inherited from our mother, who is black and African – from Ghana – and our father, who is white with a mother from Yorkshire and a father who came to Britain as a Jewish German refugee.

When I was young, my parents, who scrimped and saved from their own immigrant beginnings to create the middle-class lifestyle we enjoyed, often joked that I would rather have grown up on a council estate. Like all jokes, this one – still frequently rehashed – contained a grain of truth. I was not so spoilt as to take for granted the life we had – a lovely, spacious house, a garden with fruit trees and swings, summer holidays walking in the Alps, a private education. I knew its benefits, and had gleaned its cost by how hard my parents worked, and at times struggled, to provide it. But when it came to my identity, I felt impoverished. I longed to be around other black people, to have a sense of black culture and community, to see a flicker of recognition in a person's face when I told them my name. But everyone around us was white. Our neighbours were white. My school friends were white. The history I learned was about white people, the books I read were about white children; Jack and Jill, Peter and Jane – that was what childhood was meant to look like.

I'm not sure how many of my neighbours in Wimbledon, where I still live, would approve of this description. Most of the well-heeled residents of my home suburb prefer to say they do not see race at all. And because race allegedly did not exist, in this all-white world, the whiteness that made me so self-conscious was regarded as completely normal. It was *I* who was at odds with my environment – I did not conform. But, since there was no such thing as race, there was no space in which it could matter.

But it did matter to me. Even before I had a vocabulary to express it, race began to manifest itself in my life.

Take a look at my bookshelf. From the age of fifteen, I began to collect the works of Toni Morrison, Chinua Achebe, Ama Ata Aidoo, Caryl Phillips and James Baldwin. Maya Angelou's autobiographies, especially *All God's Children Need Travelling Shoes* – attacking the idea that Africans and Western people of African descent have nothing in common, based on her own time searching for her African identity in Ghana – affected me profoundly. 'The ache for home lives in all of us, the safe place where we can go as we are and not be questioned,'[4] she wrote. I hung on every word.[5]

Books about apartheid South Africa, like Alan Paton's *Cry the Beloved Country*, and the slave trade, like Alex Haley's *Roots*, awoke in me a sense of struggle far more profound than anything I had directly experienced. I somehow found my way to protest reggae, the Ivorian singer Alpha Blondy and Bristol band Black Roots, as well as the Wu Tang Clan, Tupac and Nas rap soundtracks that defined my generation. Like so many teenagers, the culture that I actually inhabited in the real world around me was not reflected in the sounds and words of my bedroom. But my intentions, consciously or unconsciously, were not about rebellion, or about discrimination; they were about balance. There was no danger of becoming isolated from the work of white writers and thinkers, I decided – because growing up in 1980s and 90s Britain, these formed the entirety of my formal education, as well as almost all of my day-to-day influences in the media, in the paintings and statues displayed in public places or galleries, in songs, in discussions with friends, colleagues and peers. I decided to create my own counter-narrative in secret, in my private spaces. I decided to seek the other voices out, and devour as much of their work as I could.

From a lifetime of reading these books, speaking to anyone and everyone I encountered with something to say about race and identity, and endlessly researching this subject, I learned how common my experiences were. And I learned something else, something that over time has come to crystallise the uniquely British problem we have with race and identity. In Britain, we are taught not to see race. We are told that race does not matter. We have convinced ourselves that if we can contort ourselves into a form of blindness, then issues of identity will quietly disappear. My sister and I were no different. My parents were, laudably, concerned with nurturing us with a happy childhood, full of opportunity. Race, heritage and identity did not rank among their priorities for raising their children.

But like the people in my books, being taught not to see race only heightened my sensitivity to the extent of my difference. I didn't find race, race found me; in the playground or the classroom, on the street, in the shops. I already knew that I looked different – kids work that out for themselves – but that there was something *bad* about my difference, something inherently undesirable about being black: that, I had to be taught.

The first teachers were my peers at school. From the age of seven to the age of eighteen, I went to the same school, where I was one of a minuscule number of children with brown skin. In primary school, my classmates' favourite name for me was 'troll' – more a reference to my hair than my skin colour. In the 1980s, the days before social media, high-budget Dreamworks movies[6] or Justin Timberlake songs, 'troll' described unglamorous little plastic key-ring toys with Day-Glo, gravity-defying hair. The comparison was obvious. My dark brown hair always started the day sensibly, only to push back against gravity in gradients. By the time school was finished, my head had inevitably released a gentle fringe that stood up vertically, a tiara crowning my difference.

Boys didn't see me, but aberrations of legs, breasts and face. They called me names. 'Thunder thighs', because of my strong, shapely legs, a feature I only found out years later was a typically West African one. At one point, they nicknamed me 'Shaggy', after the Jamaican musician whose song 'Oh Carolina' topped the charts in 1993. It's not obvious what resemblance I bore, aged thirteen, to a black, male dancehall artist from the Caribbean, but for private schoolkids in Wimbledon, he was probably the only other black person who sprung to mind.

By the end of my childhood, I'd learned that black people were ugly. It took a few more years to learn that we were criminals too. The younger children thought I was the 'scariest' girl in the school. I found this amusing at the time, it was so far-fetched. My most noticeable feature is probably my smile; the fine lines around my eyes testify to the fact that, if anything, I smile too much. I have never inflicted physical violence on another human being – or animal for that matter – in my life. My temperament is mild, friendly and unconfrontational. I'm not saying these are necessarily desirable characteristics – I don't like the idea that people, or especially women, should try to be mild and sweet. I would like to be fiercer. But I am who I am. A friend's little sister, the year below in the same school as us, later confessed that whenever I spoke to her, she began to shake. There is only one explanation for this perception. I looked 'scary', because I am black.

The harshest lessons came in my late teens, visiting my best friend at work at a boutique in Wimbledon Village. The manager told her I could not come in. 'It's off-putting to the other customers,' she said, 'and the black girls are thieves. Tell her she is not welcome.' It's one of the only times I was given the dignity of having my racial identity openly acknowledged. The sense that I was not welcome in my own local shops, in the place I had lived since childhood, had a profound effect. It was almost two decades until I had the confidence to shop in Wimbledon Village boutiques after that experience, and to this day I still find it requires psyching myself up. On the rare occasions I do go inside, I keep my hands visible at all times, to avoid even the possibility of suspicion.

I've often imagined myself encountering Sam as a teenager, just a few months older than me, growing up miles away in a place that was such a perfect inversion of mine. Tottenham: as far north as Wimbledon is south; as poor as Wimbledon is rich. As neglected, avoided and shunned as Wimbledon is pampered, preened and broadcast around the world as proof of the sophistication of English culture and sport. Where I took for granted a future of glittering A*s – 99 per cent of pupils in my year had top GCSE results, and most of them in ten or eleven subjects – only 21 per cent of the pupils at Sam's school would manage five GCSEs with those grades.[7] Where Wimbledon's residents enjoy a greater than average proportion of houses with gardens, Tottenham's residents are more likely than average to live in social housing and overcrowded, multiple-occupation flats. Where my local shops were boutiques and expensive grocers selling bread made from fine, imported flour, his were Poundshops, fast-food joints and money transfer outlets. And where I was light-skinned, female, posh and relatively – fellow pupils' perspectives aside – unthreatening, Sam was the ultimate villain in the eyes of a prejudiced society: a dark-skinned, muscular, working-class black man.

When we did meet, in 2004, it was at the unlikely setting of an event in Westminster. I noticed the shape of his shaven head – a familiar feature of West African heritage – a diamanté radiating from his otherwise sombre, suited silhouette, his physique – stacked with muscle – but his quiet, almost timid demeanour. I approached him. 'Who are you?' I wanted to know – a question he and his friend still laugh about to this day. They looked at each other, almost rolling their eyes, as if to say, *Here we go! Who is this character coming to interrogate us . . . ?* It later transpired that he was intrigued by me too, the mixed-race girl with natural hair, chunky Sahelian jewellery, but the clipped tones of a private-school education, striding so boldly towards him.

Both Sam's parents came, like my mother's family, from Ghana, speaking the same dialect of the same language as my relatives. He had just finished his law degree; I was studying to convert my philosophy, politics and economics degree into one. We both intended to become barristers, and were enrolled, by sheer coincidence, on the same course at the same school, to do our barrister training the following year. I said there were exceptions to the Afrocentric nature of my bookshelf, and it turns out Sam and I shared one of these exceptions: we both loved *The Great Gatsby* – albeit for radically different reasons. I saw it as magical realism, and for me it was the unreal glamour, extravagant prose and glazed-eyed emotion of Gatsby's unrequited love that made me return to it again and again. But Sam felt it revealed,

in stark detail, a truth he had learned growing up poor and marginalised. In the characters of Daisy and Tom, he saw a picture of how the
privileged in our society behave, exploiting the lives of others, using
and abusing them when convenient, leaving destruction in their wake.
We argued about this clash of perspectives – that was, and still is,
above all else, the basis of our relationship. We had both grown up seeing things in society that others around us didn't see; in my case
because I was black in a white world, in his, because he was reading,
voraciously devouring books, in a world where he was expected to be
stupid. We both read, questioned and challenged every stimulating
thing we could get our hands on, debating them with each other passionately, aggressively even, right from day one.

But in other ways, our behaviour was as different as our backgrounds. Sam spent his spare time on the track, and at the local
gym, coaching and mentoring younger boys from his area, teaching
them discipline and the art of life planning – skills he felt had saved
him. He prized discipline and planning above all else. Relationships
were a no. He did not drink or smoke, he was Buddha-like in his attitudes towards excess. His family relied on him heavily, he was forever
ferrying his mum around in his little black Vauxhall Corsa, to weddings, funerals and other events on the gruelling circuit of parties for
Ghanaian elders in Tottenham. The debt he owed her, he always said,
was his life. Whenever he had been tempted to follow his friends into
crime, find light relief in relationships, or just give up, he saw how
hard she was working, year after year, to put food on the table, and he
could not reconcile wasting the chance she had given him. Other than
taking her where she needed to go on Saturday nights, on weekends he
could be found studying in a motorway service station on the M1,
hoodie up, buried in a book on self-realisation, or algebra. 'Weekends,'
he was fond of saying, 'what's that? I ain't got time for weekends, I've
got one life, one shot.' Here we were, at a similar stage in our careers,
midway through our legal training. But I had got there by following
the path laid out for me. I put in the effort, but I was pushing hard at
doors that were already open, opened by my parents, my teachers, and

the general expectations of my environment as to what was normal for a child to achieve. Sam, on the other hand, had made it through school and university by becoming an extremist, in discipline, intelligence and drive.

I had never met anyone like Sam before. His life revealed to me that if you are poor, and black, with an African surname and a community of poor, black immigrants around you, parents who are not equipped to guide you, a school which expects nothing from you, except a life of crime or low-paid, unskilled labour – because of your race and class – and older children who offer you quick solutions to your safety, by joining gangs, then becoming a lawyer, say, takes something special. It takes a feat of endurance and strength. It takes being like Sam. 'Going with the flow', in Sam's world, is jail, death, or a life earning the minimum wage. In my world, in Wimbledon, all you had to do was coast. Show up at school, get through university, just don't screw up. If you were mediocre in my world, you wouldn't have the *best* job, but you'd have a job, a professional one at that, a home, a family, dinner parties on the weekends, holidays in the summer. These are things you could expect from life, more or less as a matter of course.

Understanding how our seemingly autonomous lives had been so greatly moulded by these unseen forces humbled me, and awoke me to the true scale of race and class prejudice in British society. I'd been so conscious of the racism and obstacles in my way, obstacles that complicated my path compared with that of my white peers, that I hadn't appreciated the extent of my privilege. Sam's life drove home to me that racism operates on a deep structural level in our society, bedded down in socioeconomic circumstances, migration and the labour market, so that the child of an immigrant, born here, as British as me, as clever as me – more so – was never going to have the same opportunities as me in the first place. The defining issue of my life had been feeling isolated in a world where everyone else around me was white. The defining issue of Sam's life had been working out how to escape conditions of poverty which trapped people, in his world, who were almost entirely black.

Becoming close to Sam wasn't without its tensions. From that first October night when I introduced him to my friends, he refused to slot into my world, to sit down and eat cake, to have Sunday brunch, or gossip over tea, and I found it infuriating. Dinner parties, friends' birthdays, even weddings, he refused to come. For a long time, I think many of my friends – those who had not been at Miranda's that night – believed Sam to be a figment of my imagination, because we had been together for three years or more before they even glimpsed sight of him. Sam had no choice but to incorporate me into his no-frills life, because we had formed this intense and addictive connection, in spite of his intentions to avoid relationships until he had achieved the long list of goals on his daily, weekly, yearly and five-yearly plans. But he didn't see why he should spend his precious time performing what were – in his mind – the superfluous and unnecessary rituals of middle-class society. Time-wasting was a luxury only the privileged could afford, disconnected as we were from the true brutality and urgency of life.

Birthdays used to be a particular source of grievance. Even now, thirteen years later, Sam has never been to one of my birthday celebrations. I eventually discovered that, as a child, Sam had learned to hide from his mother on his birthday, to avoid her feeling any pressure to buy presents he knew she could not afford. He has never lost his childhood perspective, that in celebrating your own life, you inevitably make someone else feel worse about their own. I began to feel self-conscious about my self-indulgent celebrations, drinks with friends, presents and cards, a sense of being special that I learned from my parents, who always treated both my sister and me like superstars on our birthdays.

Disputes like these only emerged in relation to others, when I wanted to involve Sam in some wider social gathering. We used to joke that if we were the only two people left in the world, our relationship would be perfect. But sometimes just the two of us, going somewhere to eat or shop, was enough to ignite another incompatibility in our world view. Sam would avoid going into certain shops, feeling it was not worth the inevitable frustration of being treated as a suspect. Large chains were OK, as were fast-food outlets and mainstream coffee shops. But I much preferred small, quirky boutiques, independent coffee shops with far more personality than the chains, 'whole food' places that sold the food I depended on for, what was at the time, my vegan lifestyle. Whenever I wanted to buy something from one of these, Sam would wait outside. And we'd stand there on the street, on the Holloway Road, or Stroud Green, north London neighbourhoods close to where I then lived in Islington and he in Tottenham, and we'd argue and argue. He was letting people's prejudice limit his life, I'd say. He was letting racism win. I *knew* what it was like to have a security guard follow you around a shop – it had happened to me on my own local high street growing up, and *I* hadn't let it put me off. 'You don't know what it's like to be a dark-skinned black man,' he would retort, not even remotely persuaded. 'I'm not going in.'

I realised that I had what Sam did not. Even when it's quite clear that people around me are conscious that I'm different, because of how I look, I know exactly how to reassure them. I've been conditioned in the art of English manners, politeness, harmless banter and casual charm my whole life; at the dinner table with my parents, in the classroom with my teachers, in my tutors' studies, dining at the Inns of Court, in training for the Bar, at chambers parties, newspaper after-work drinks, and countless other social settings where you learn to send the subliminal message: don't worry about the fact that I'm black, I won't make you feel uncomfortable. I may be brown, my hair is a texture you don't understand, I have a name you struggle to pronounce, but it's OK – I am completely non-threatening, I am brown, but safe.

I also realised that Sam had what I did not: absolutely zero desire to make himself appealing, non-threatening and safe. Sam and his peers spoke their own language, and had their own value system, their own subculture, their own music, their own aesthetic and fashion ideals. It had nothing to do with the white, middle-class world of Wimbledon and beyond, and it wasn't interested in making itself palatable to that world either. From where I was standing, what Sam had was a coherent, multidimensional identity which was unequivocally his. It was black, and it was proud. I dreamed of this certainty, and I was drawn to it, with a gravitational pull.

As well as growing up in a cultural hub of black Britishness, Sam had a Ghanaian identity that was equally strong. Whereas I had diligently studied Ghanaian history and culture, accumulated African novels, spent time in Accra conducting 'field research' for my thesis on the rule of Ghanaian women in politics, Sam had absorbed Ghanaian culture by osmosis. The books he read were about becoming effective, successful and transcending your environment. I don't think, when I met him, he had ever read a single book about Africa. He didn't need to; he was steeped in it, soaked in the stories circulated among the smells of deep-frying spiced plantain and okra stewing. He was, like most of his friends, second generation, British-born but fluent in his parents' culture, and he learned to navigate British institutions on their behalf – as linguistic or cultural interpreters for their parents' generation who never adapted and always intended to return 'home'.

The first time I went to Sam's family home, I wondered why I had travelled so many thousands of miles to experience Ghana, when I could have just gone a few miles across town. It even smells like Ghana – fermented corn and fried onions, dried shrimp and palm oil. On the weekends, Sam's mother, Joy, does not cook European food, but sits on a low Ashanti stool in the kitchen, just as women do in the village, pounding fufu or some other somniferous dumpling that will later be eaten by hand, scooping up spicy, oily, watery soup. Food always seems to be cooking, relatives showing up, unannounced, sometimes to sit and talk, sometimes to stay, the extended family undifferentiated from the nucleus. On Saturdays they go to weddings, christenings and funerals, on Sundays they go to church, 'holidays' are trips to Ghana, to inspect the house that their wages have been ploughed into building, each £100 saved up dispatched by Western Union to acquire another pile of bricks. Delivering on the bargain to the relatives that helped them to reach the UK in the first place is more important than spending money on themselves.

This is the mentality behind many of the immigrants I know who live in Britain; this is how many were able to come. Their families made sacrifices so that they could make the journey here; back home, you invest in your children, your siblings, your nieces and nephews by educating them, marrying them off or paying for their travel to the UK, then they are meant to return with their pounds, and take care of you. Sam sometimes describes his house as an 'underground railroad'. When he was young and there were three children living there, a good number of newly arrived relatives from Ghana seemed to end up on the sofa or living-room floor, filling up the precious little space there was with their visa struggles and remittance burdens. Money was scarce, but Ghanaian culture, heritage and chaos were abundant.

When I understood the reality of Sam's upbringing, I couldn't help but feel critical of the decisions made by the adults in his life. While I'd longed for the cultural certainty he took for granted, he experienced poverty I'd not even known existed. When I first met him, a 24-year-old graduate and semi-professional athlete, he could not sleep unless there was a packet of biscuits, or some other high-calorie food, by his bed. He was still traumatised from all the years when he had gone to sleep hungry, not knowing where his next meal would come from. When as a teenager he became a talented football player, taking buses across north London into the suburban areas where his team trained, he would have nothing to eat or drink on the cold winter nights. His football coach took such pity at the holes in his football boots that he paid for new ones himself. Sam's mother worked long hours so he had no parental supervision – no one to help with his schoolwork, to play with or nurture him on evenings and weekends, to go with him to parents' evenings, to make sure he had the basics. And yet – I would protest – his mother had money to spare to send to Ghana. How could she think of providing for so many others, when her own children were going hungry? How could she make space for distant relatives from Ghana to stay in the house, while her own children didn't have their own bedroom, or desk, or attention, or even toys?

Sam's response was not what I expected. He said that when he had learned about *my* upbringing, in pretty, spacious, orderly Wimbledon, he said he felt sorry for *me*. The hardship he experienced – which I found so extreme – taught him valuable lessons about the essence of society, seen with a clarity only available to those at the bottom: a black boy with a low-paid, single parent, in a violent area, at a failing school. He would describe my world – where everything is centred on expectation, achievement, politeness, and the talking rituals of dinner parties, Sunday lunches, where things are spoken in sophisticated code – as fake. He took my inability to understand the communal mindset which saw his mother make these sacrifices as evidence that I'd been cut off from the most fundamental aspect of Ghanaian culture: the village, before the individual. He thought I had been raised to be selfish, always putting myself and my immediate family first. He thought I was lost. I will never forget the first time I told him I was writing this book, and exactly what it was about. He laughed and said, 'You see – this is what I mean! What kind of black person feels they actually have to write a *book* about being black?'

I am the eternal outsider. In Wimbledon, I am the black girl. The more I asserted my black identity, the more of a threat I became to the prevailing order – that race is something unseen, unspoken of and unacknowledged in polite society. In Tottenham, I am the rich girl, who speaks 'like a white person', and has access to privilege and opportunity most people cannot imagine. For years I internalised this as a status that carried with it multiple rejections, because everywhere I went, I was other. But over time, it began to manifest as an opportunity to observe and question our attitudes towards race and identity, driven by a fascination that perhaps only an outsider can have, and, maybe, the ability to see things that only an outsider can see.

I envied Sam's confidence in his Ghanaian heritage, and the lack of interest in making himself something that mainstream, white society would find palatable. I was an expert in turning myself into what the world around me seemed to want me to be – black, but not in any way disruptive. I made myself as appealing as I could to the institutions I wanted to accept me – my school, my university, my workplaces – society had taught me that being black was a bad thing, a threatening thing, a thing that must be stamped out. I couldn't stamp it out, so I grew an alternative version of myself in secret, a version that yearned to be African – the blackest identity I knew – that sought out black culture, black stories, black wisdom, black role models. But I had to keep it secret because I thought it would alienate everyone in my white, middle-class world.

This was what had driven me to Senegal. In the months and years after that October dinner at Miranda's house, when I was still fresh with the adventure of return, I decided that my project of relocating to Africa had not failed, I had simply chosen the wrong country. Ghana, home to my maternal family, is a very different nation to the one where I had lived in the arid Sahel, a far more familiar land of dense forest and rich red earth. Through the rest of my twenties, I fixed on the idea that moving to Ghana represented the new solution. I had been to Ghana before; as a fifteen-year-old, as an undergraduate researching my thesis, on family visits and work trips when I was based in Senegal. I knew moving there would be a high-risk enterprise, possibly exposing me to ridicule. Ghanaians have never taken me seriously as a Ghanaian – not just because I am half white, but because, as far as they are concerned, I *am* white. '*Obruni!*' they call me, which literally means 'person from across the cornfields', but which over centuries of their dealings with Europeans has come to mean 'white person'. But, I reasoned, if I still did not feel British, then I *must* be Ghanaian, or at least capable of becoming so. It's not possible, I thought, that there could be no place in which I belonged. Moving to Ghana would allow this secret island in my sense of identity to become, at last, part of something whole.

'I discovered I was black when I came to the US,' the brilliant Nigerian writer Chimamanda Ngozi Adichie has said. 'I would say, "*I'm not black, I'm Nigerian*." I did that for maybe a year. And I realised even that, my reaction, was an indictment of American racism. Because obviously I'm black, but because I realised that America's understanding of black was so loaded with negativity, I thought, no, I don't want that.'[8]

Adichie's initial rejection of the label 'black' says something about American racism, but it also says something about African identities. 'Black' is as meaningless an identity in a country like Nigeria, where almost everyone is black, as 'white' is in a country where almost everyone is white. It's simply not how people see themselves – other identities have more significance instead, like ethnic group, faith, region, dialect. Listening to Adichie made me think of my mother, who moved to the UK from Ghana with an identity first formed in a country where to be black was the norm.

Unlike Adichie, as British people, ours are identities that have played themselves out in a nation where these things are not talked about openly. When I first started thinking about identity, which is when I first started thinking, it was something private. It wasn't the kind of thing you could talk about at school, or know the language with which to raise it at home. My mother never described herself – in front of me at least – as black. Which raised further questions. Was I black, like people said? How would my father, who is white, feel if I described myself that way? What was the black 'community', and was I a member of it?

The exact meaning of 'identity' has always been difficult to define.[9] To me, it encompasses two concepts. The first is a personal set of characteristics that make up an individual, the things we consider relevant in making us who we are. The second concept is a social one, denoting characteristics shared with others in a group, a sense of belonging, and membership to a social category, community, tribe, faith or nation.

It's the relationship between the two – the individual and the group – that makes identity such a fundamental part of being a successful human being. It's often said that you cannot do anything until you know who you are. As social creatures, part of knowing who we are is knowing what group we belong to, what characteristics, values or beliefs we share with others, which others, and why. Many thinkers have reflected on this. Some focus on the past: 'A people without the knowledge of their past history, origin and culture is like a tree without roots,' said the pan-Africanist pioneer Marcus Garvey. Others focus on the ability to build a new future. 'Know from whence you came,' wrote the great African American intellectual James Baldwin. 'If you know whence you came, there are absolutely no limitations to where you can go.' Ralph Ellison puts it best in his great novel *Invisible Man*. 'When I discover who I am, I'll be free.'[10]

Belonging is a foundational human need. For most people, throughout most of history, it was inherited from family, shaped by society, and contained within language, customs, religion, and nationhood, in an unconscious process of social conditioning. That's not to say that these identities aren't frequently disrupted, dispersed, updated – that's as much a part of the human condition as the need to belong. Our founding myths often feature identity crises – from Moses, the Israelite raised as an Egyptian royal, to Mahatma Gandhi, who went from prototype Englishman, with Savile Row suits and elocution lessons, to Hindu ascetic, both examples of individuals whose personal journeys influenced millions to reframe their own identities too. Even Harry Potter is as much a story of identity as anything else; the wizard child raised by Muggle relatives who could not nurture or tolerate his magical heritage.

The confusion I experienced, as a mixed-race girl descended from Jewish and African immigrants in a European country in the twentieth and twenty-first centuries, is no different from those that have gone before. It's not the muddled inheritance itself that is the problem. There is no such thing as racial purity in any event. It's the muting of the conversation – the fact that we cannot in Britain today cope with exploring and accommodating these identities in a healthy way – that is the issue. This failure is capable of turning both our individual and our national heritage from a rich and complex asset into an identity crisis of epic proportions.

Recent years have shown us that threatened identities don't fade away quietly; they become defensive, and fight back with new confidence, pride and desperation. Donald Trump represents a white, crude-talking, gun-owning hyper-masculinity to which I personally cannot relate. But I *can* relate to the concept of relating to him; it's the same impulse that made me passionate about Barack Obama. I'm not American and have no vested interest in its fate as a nation, yet I still felt Obama represented *me*. Here was a man whose parents were descended from immigrants, like mine, who'd lived abroad, like I had, who was mixed race, like I am, and who was obsessed enough with the nuances of his identity and the pitfalls of understanding and then owning it, that he wrote a book about it, not unlike what I am doing. I agreed with many of his policies, on health care, and closing Guantánamo Bay, but that's not really why I loved him. Watching Obama hand over to Trump, a president endorsed by a broad-spectrum, white nationalist movement, that either endorses or is forgiving of racism, misogyny and bigotry, feels like the ultimate backlash against a world that is more diverse, its identities more fractured and sophisticated.

Identities are shaping broad social and political change across the world. At the same time, they are an expression of an intimate relationship with oneself, something it's impossible to police, or dictate, from the outside. For that reason, I have used my own experience of identity to form this book. And so while the forces most visibly at work in shaping British identities are based on class, religion, region, gender, political tribe and nationality, I am writing mostly about racial and ethnic heritage. This is what I've learned from being a British person, with Yorkshire, Jewish and African inheritance. I'll let others with other identities speak for themselves. This is what I have learned from navigating a place for myself in a nation convinced that fairness is one of its values, but that immigration is one of its problems.

Perhaps Sam is right – I have no idea what it's like to be a dark-skinned black man. And perhaps he's also right that it's a strange thing to do, to write a book about being black. But I've written from this perspective only because it is my perspective, not because I think my identity is more important than anyone else's, or that people from my background have more to say than those from any other. It's just my experience. But I do believe that, as an example of an intense, unrelenting search for a kind of Britishness I can belong to, my experience may offer an insight into where we are headed as a nation.

Race and identity are difficult subjects to unpick. Does race even exist? It's a social construct, designed in relatively recent human history to artificially distinguish between members of the same biological species. Does that make it meaningless? Not in my view, since humanity has evolved to self-identify along cultural lines, and to discriminate based on visual differences. Our attachment to created cultural, racial and religious difference makes these things real. Can you be mixed race? It follows that you can.

Is there any point talking about race when class is the major basis of resource distribution in society? Yes, because race and class intersect and those disadvantaged by both face unique challenges, and because there is a specific baggage attached to race that is a very real factor shaping all of our lives. My life is not a story of the kind of prejudice that a young black person growing up in an aggressively policed, publicly neglected, negatively stereotyped and materially deprived inner-city council estate experiences on a daily basis. The unbelievable odds stacked against a person coming from such a background are as much about poverty as they are about race. I learned this from Sam, who had to become as abstemious as a monk, as focused as a CEO, as strong as a wrestler, to follow a path so conveniently laid out for me. I would have had to work hard to avoid it.

And yet, the fact that someone with my advantages has still experienced the full toxicity of a world in which prejudice is racialised speaks volumes. I have watched disadvantaged young black people, who are exceptional, defy the odds stacked against them to become the student, candidate or trainee that enters the middle-class professional world. And I have understood the sense of betrayal that then takes hold when they realise that, having done everything imaginable to prove their worth, dedication and ability, the racism they observed from the bottom of society will follow them to the top.

White supremacy is ever-present in British society. I'm not talking about hooded hillbillies in the Deep South burning crosses, or skinheads with Nazi tattoos – although they do exist – but the underlying ideology for a system where generations of people were conditioned to believe in the inferiority of non-white, non-Christian, non-Europeans. An empire was built on this idea; the enduring concept of 'Western civilisation' is an expression of this idea. It is not something that disappears overnight, especially when it has never actually been defeated or overthrown. You cannot get over a wrong without the wrong having been named, owned and acknowledged. You cannot change without articulating what needs changing.

The progress we have made is, in some ways, part of the problem. We live, the American academic Eduardo Bonilla-Silva has written, in an era of 'racism without racists'. It's an era of 'color-blind racism', of 'racism with a smiling face'.[11] Compared to what black people in Britain went through up until only two decades ago, being roughed up by the police regularly for no reason, being called 'nigger', and chased down the street by armed Teddy boys, it's 'racism lite'. It makes it so much easier for people to say these days that they 'don't see race', hoping perhaps that if they don't dwell on racial difference, then maybe that difference will go away.

The problem is, there is still race, and there is still racism. Denying it does not solve the problem, it creates two further problems. First, it assumes that seeing race is something bad, that perhaps to admit to seeing race is to embark on the slippery slope towards racism. Given that most of the prejudice and othering I've experienced in my life has come courtesy of polite, smiling people who claimed not to see race, I know that this is not true.

I remember very clearly a warm autumn day, sitting under the breeze of a horse chestnut tree, baked by the long weeks of the summer holiday, with my school friends aged fourteen. One girl looked at me, a slight tone of pity in her voice, and said, 'Don't worry, Af, we don't see you as black.' The others concurred. I remember their faces; kind, accommodating, distancing themselves proudly from any possibility that they could be accused of being racist, and at the same time willing to overlook the problem my very existence created.

This act of kindness is one of the most traumatic things that has ever happened to me. It taught me that being black is bad. It taught me that seeing race has sinister consequences. It implied that with recognition, racism inevitably follows. So much so, it's better to pretend there are no black people at all. It offered me a way out of blackness, a denial, on the condition that I abandoned any attempt to be proud of my black heritage, to forge any sense of community with those who shared its history and culture. It felt like my friends were erasing my very identity, all the while claiming to be doing me a favour. I relive this experience every single time someone tells me that they 'do not see race'.

The second problem is that as long as racism does exist – whether or not with a smiling face – 'not seeing race' shuts down analysis of the issue. Just because one individual chooses not to 'see race', it doesn't mean that the racialised nature of poverty, discrimination and prejudice in society at large disappears. That individual is simply refusing to acknowledge it. The effect of both of these tendencies is to deny people who do experience race – almost always members of ethnic minorities – a sense that they can have their own identity. Why can't their identity and heritage be acknowledged, without it compromising their belonging in Britain, which is, after all, their country too?

We have tied ourselves in knots attempting to become a post-racial society without ever truly understanding racialised identities. A deep-seated belief in whiteness, in the racial, intellectual and cultural superiority of white Britain, a sense that there is some inherent conflict between white British values and accomplishments and those of everyone else, remains in so many forms. These distortions are so ingrained in our historical narrative, so tangled up in our culture, that it's a challenge to tease them out, let alone hold them up to the light and examine them for what they are. The true failure of our nation is not the things that have happened in the past, but our failure to acknowledge this past, the prejudices, problems and hypocrisy that have – as a result – become woven into the fabric of everyday British life, everywhere. Most people just don't see this. But I do. I was born directly into it. And this book is my attempt to, in my small way, acknowledge, name and articulate it so that, one day, we can move on.

1. WHERE ARE YOU FROM?

My grandmother, Ophelia Joyce (right), and my great-aunt,
visiting relatives in Aburi in 2006.

I feel most colored when I am thrown against a sharp white background.

> – Zora Neale Hurston,
> *How It Feels to Be Colored Me*

I cannot pronounce my name.

I know it looks simple. Afua. Four letters, two syllables, almost a palindrome, so nearly a simple word. It should be my most uncomplicated label, the easiest description of myself. But instead, it has always been a word steeped in mystery and confusion, which makes encounters with new people fraught with potential strife. Each of its four, innocent-seeming letters has its demons. The 'A' is really more of an 'E'. Not the way 'E' sounds in 'eating' or 'email', but more of an 'eh', like in 'elephant' or 'exercise'. The teeth are meant to linger on the 'f', hovering over the lips for a split second too long. The 'ua' is like 'wah', not 'oooa'. The word as a whole needs to be said in such a sing-song, musical manner, descending gently at the end, that I sometimes think it simply cannot be learned.

Thirty-five years into bearing this name, I have failed to master it. In this, I am not alone. One of the less often appreciated consequences of Ghana's five centuries of mingling its people, and economic fate, with people from the British Isles, is that Britain is now littered with people like me; Ghanaians – many high profile – who either mispronounce their own names, or have given into other people doing it for them. There is Paul Boateng, once the most senior black politician in Western Europe when he was chief secretary to the Treasury under Tony Blair, who seems to have resigned himself to his name, which should be pronounced 'Bo-waat-eng', being changed to 'B-oh-teng'. Kwasi Kwarteng, permanent private secretary to the House of Lords, introduces himself as 'Kwaaasi', when, like my name, the 'a' in Kwasi should be pronounced more like an 'e' – 'Kwesi' – with, again like my name, a little sing-song rhythm from the first syllable to the second. And, on the world stage, there is Kofi Annan, former secretary general of the United Nations, whose name should be pronounced 'Koffie', but who settles for 'Koh-fey', and seems to have done so all his life.

When it comes to identity, names matter. When my father's father, a Jewish teenager in Berlin, boarded a train in 1938 that would carry him out of Nazi Germany, to safety in Britain, the first thing he did was change his name. 'Hans' became 'John', and with it, he sought to recraft his identity into something British. 'Hans' was buried forever, along with the blissful ignorance of not knowing what it's like to bear a heritage that is grounds, all on its own, to be put to death. When my daughter was born, we were not allowed to call her by name until the eighth day, until a gathering of clans could be organised – according to the Akan custom of Ghana – and herded to my parents' house in Wimbledon, wearing cloth and bearing traditions, so that her spirit could be fixed properly in time, place and title. And when she was finally allowed a name, there had to be five of them.

My parents named me Afua – which means girl born on Friday – to give me, the half-white, half-black, fully confused child, a connection to my mother's ancestral land and the practices of the Akan, Ghana's largest ethnic group, and the *Twi* (pronounced *tchwree*) language they speak. I thank my parents for this now; I think it worked. Names can do that; they plant a seed that influences how your sense of self will grow, and what it will become.

But what my parents didn't anticipate when they gave me this most Ghanaian of names, is that I wouldn't be able to pronounce it. Nobody in Wimbledon could pronounce it either, and knowing how it's meant to sound, I was forever trying to correct them. The blind leading the blind.

The effect of having a name that so clearly marked me out as African, without the cultural knowledge or certainty to back that identity up, was compounded by living in a place where everyone else was white. It was a magnetic one, a force powerfully pulling me towards Ghana. I needed to sharpen the blurry outlines of this African identity I felt, I needed to colour it in. To start with, I needed to learn how to say my name.

That journey begins in 2012, with five of us crammed into one car – my grandmother, my mother, my daughter and me, and our long-suffering driver Seth. Seth has defied the laws of physics to squeeze us into an old four-wheel drive the colour of mud, which guzzles fuel like a greedy god, even when not weighed down – as it is that day – by four generations of my family and ten pieces of luggage. It is definitely illegal, and when, driving away from the airport, we reach the first police checkpoint, the middle-aged officer now hailing us to pull over knows it. He's so skinny, I notice, as he begins to survey our crime scene, that he is swimming in his uniform. He flicks a jumpy beam of torchlight over us: my grandmother in front, then my daughter, reclining casually in a palatial baby seat, the plane tags still attached, and finally my mum and I folded into the small spaces on either side of her. Seth – himself hemmed in by suitcases and only just able to reach the gearstick – says nothing, but rolls down the window and hands over a grubby, yellow two-cedi note, Ghanaian money, crumpled deliberately between his fingers, as if making it almost invisible makes it less of a bribe. It's worth about seventy pence. The policeman beams and, with another flourish of his torch, wishes us on our way.

It's not the corruption that shocks me, but how little it costs. The price of turning an offence into a non-offence: one humble dollar. It's an early warning that the new world I am entering may not be the perfect motherland I've imagined, with all my writing, talking and proselytising endlessly about how badly Africa is misunderstood.

Africa *is* misunderstood, described in Britain as 'the hopeless continent',[1] patronised, caricatured in the press, in films and fashion. On the contrary, I know, Africa is rising. And I've told myself this over and over again, as I sold my little flat on a bleak estate of new-builds in a downtrodden part of London's East End, packed up our things – snow fluttering around the removal van on the January day when we left – and boarded a flight to the Ghanaian capital. Time to put my money where my mouth is. So there's corruption, I tell myself, so I have already broken my own rule against paying bribes on day zero, within thirty minutes of leaving the airport. Who am I to judge this still young

West African nation, one that has borne five centuries of draining trade and economic looting at the hands of European states – my country, Britain, foremost among them – and only sixty years of independent rule? It takes time for the rule of law to set in. Things are evolving in this country, the land of my ancestors, and I want to be there to see the change, to contribute, to grow with it.

I'm full of hope, but I am driven by disappointment too. As well as the long-term desire to be immersed in the Ghanaian heritage to which I felt so drawn, the truth is that Britain and I are not getting along well right now. Britain and I are done. I've given it everything – I am British after all – it's my home, my nationality, my frame of reference. I've spent almost all my life in England; there is no other culture with which I can claim anything like as much familiarity. I've spoken its language all my life – correct, middle-class, Thames Estuary English – have studied at Oxford, been called to the Bar, and at this moment, I am still a correspondent for one of its best-known newspapers. I've both aspired to be part of its institutions, and been institutionalised by its aspirations. And yet this country of mine has never allowed me to feel that it is where I belong.

If I were to single out the most persistent reminder of that sense of not belonging, it would be The Question. The Question is: *where are you from?* Although I have lived in five different countries as an adult, nowhere have I been asked The Question more than right here where I started, where I *am* from, in Britain.

It can be difficult to communicate to British people who innocently ask The Question, usually out of a harmless, well-meaning curiosity, what is wrong with it. It's rarely posed out of malice or with any ill will. In fact when I have met people who do actually feel hostile towards me because of the colour of my skin, or my 'foreign'-sounding name, they never bother asking The Question – they already know the answer, which in their imagination is a mythical 'darkie country'. When they tell you to 'Go back to where you came from!' they couldn't care less whether such a place actually exists. The Question is usually asked by a different kind of person altogether – the interested, curious, polite and open-minded.

But being asked where you're from in your own country is a daily ritual of unsettling. This is not to say there is anything wrong with getting to know people and their heritage, of course there isn't. I'm unfailingly curious about people's backgrounds and often draw people into conversations about it; some of the most interesting stories I have heard come from white British people, with Irish, Cornish or Celtic lineages, or Eastern European or Mediterranean immigration, or working-class city traditions that are rooted in places whose history we always live with vaguely, but whose family backgrounds paint a human picture behind the names.

But that's different. That is *a* question, it's not *The* Question. White people often look taken aback when asked about their background, it's never the first thing they get asked in a regular social encounter, it's not an upfront demand for information, it's not requested with such insistence, it becomes almost a condition of further interaction. Even the questions asked of people with foreign accents are not *The* Question, since The Question, as someone like me experiences it, is often posed before a single word has even been uttered. The Question is reserved for people who look different, and, thanks to it, someone who looks like me is told that they are different, and asked for an explanation, every single day, often multiple times.

The Question is both a symptom and a cause. It's a symptom of the fact that we don't really know what it is to be British. Is someone like me included? Don't know, people think, better ask. And there goes The Question. It's also the cause. The more you get asked The Question, the more confused you feel about the answer. I can't be British, can I, if British people keep asking me where I'm from? I must be something else. It could be Norway, where I was born; London, where I live; Ghana, responsible for my blackness; Germany, the reason for my last name – unmistakably that of a German Jew.

There are moments in my early memories that reveal to me the struggle of being brown, sharpened by the all-white background around me. I remember another little child reaching his hand out to my mother's face, and wiping, to see if the dark, smooth brown came off like paint, or melted chocolate. Even as a four-year-old I remember the child's mother scooping him up in a mortified panic, but she was not as mortified as me. My mother was different. So different that occasionally a child would reach out to touch, but often they simply stared.

I lied once, at Show and Tell on Monday morning at school, a private school I joined when I was seven, and where out of around one thousand pupils, I was one of only two or three black children. I'd spent the day before at Nana's house – my mother's mother Ophelia Joyce, who has helped raise me, and whom I love. But her house was a little dark, and smelt of jollof rice and fried fish. Visits like the one that weekend involved awkwardly greeting a stream of aunties wearing M&S cardigans and wigs, speaking Twi, relaying stories I didn't understand, then marinading in their own expressions. Mmmmmm. Eh! Ooooo. I told my teacher I had been at my father's parents' house instead, Grandma and Grandpa, who lived in a light brown brick house they'd designed themselves, set in half an acre of lovingly tended garden in Sevenoaks. It was so much easier to explain that world to my already critical schoolteacher, and the other little white girls whose houses smelt of high-end potpourri and roast dinners. I drew a picture of Ann, my blonde-haired grandma, standing in a flower-strewn garden, me skipping under the flowery vines that formed an arch over the entrance to their pond. My parents caught me out, having found that picture in my school bag. That's not what you did this weekend, they confronted me, you were at Nana's house. Why did you lie?

I remember the lie with the same precision that I remember myself at that moment. Seven years old, a plump little brown girl, a dimple funnelling into a round chin, a smile that came easily, and the alien hair that crowned my difference. My sense of difference plagued me. I tried, and failed, to change my name to Caroline, hoping that might erase the alien in me. It was not enough. Everywhere I went, and everything I did, I stood out, sensing that there was something inherently shameful about the brown skin that set me apart, so much so that people preferred not to talk about it directly, but hinted it was something they were willing to overlook. Burying my blackness was the ultimate goal.

Sometimes, burying my blackness was like burying me. Sometimes it was as if my body didn't exist. Children had blonde hair and blue eyes, and digressions were permitted in degrees – red hair and freckles, or chubby and brunette. But there were no images in which I saw myself reflected – I was off the scale of acceptability. There were no products to cleanse my scalp and untwine my grasping curls. There were European products, which only made my hair knotty and brittle, and, if a pilgrimage could be undertaken to a poorer, blacker part of London, Afro products for Afro hair – bright blue jellies that smelt of chemicals, and fluorescent yellow oils made of petroleum and lanolin, designed to smooth down hair that was coarser and thicker hair than mine. None were designed for me. My hair type was a fiction, and I was invisible. My friends tried to help by pretending I was the same as them in their imaginations, and that made me, for fleeting moments in which I existed only in their gaze, acceptable.

It's harder than it looked, as a parent now myself, to live up to the standard set by my own parents in creating a home where my sister and I could experience a family life we did take for granted, could grow our ideas and our friendships, and flourish like the fruit trees in the garden. But both of my parents have identities that are very different to my own. I've heard my dad describe himself as 'mixed race' before. He is white, but his surname, and mine, is easily identifiable as one of German Jewish origin, and even though he wasn't raised with Jewish faith or customs, he has a large family of Jewish relatives in Germany and Poland – the *Hirsches*, *Lesses* and *Irwigs*, those who survived the Second World War by fleeing just in time from their homes in Germany and Eastern Europe. When my dad graduated from university, he told me, his degree results were published in the *Jewish Chronicle*, along with all the other students whose names marked them out as the descendants of Jews. But most of his life has been lived as a white man in a country where that put him in the majority, albeit one who lived with three black women at home – my mother, sister and me. He told me that the first awareness of the prejudice that could be attached to race came as a young adult, visiting some of those

Jewish relatives, who had moved to apartheid South Africa. 'I felt very uncomfortable being treated as a white person, and therefore privileged, in that system,' my dad says. 'I couldn't wait to leave.'

When Dad met Mum, he fell for her right away. From conversations with his younger sisters, I don't think he appreciated how scandalous it would be for a white boy from Sevenoaks, a smart town in Kent, to bring home a stunning young black woman, with extravagant eyelashes, a miniskirt, Mary Quant make-up and an Afro, to his parents' house on the respectable, uneventful street, backing onto a wild forest, evocatively named Brattle Wood. My aunts still enjoy dining out on the shock in the household and the wider neighbourhood that day – *everyone* was talking about it. My mother was used to causing a sensation, but she had the confidence to pull it off. She was a beautiful, private-school-educated, nineteen-year-old artist with proud Ghanaian heritage and a remarkably enunciated version of the Queen's English that I've come to associate with those born in the British Empire, as she was. She had spent the first years of her childhood in the Gold Coast, as it then was, becoming independent Ghana when she was six. She moved to the UK when she was eleven, but not before those formative years of being black in a country where that put her in the majority. Identity is multifaceted, and shaped by so many factors. In my parents' case their social and political values – which I would describe as liberal – their belief in fairness and justice, in working hard and living well, are part of who they are, and characteristics they have passed on to my sister Ama and me.

One day, while writing this book, I was speaking to my parents about their identities. I said that it must be nice for them both, to know there is a country where they look like everyone else, blending in unnoticed. My parents froze when I said this, and then looked at each other in astonishment. It had never occurred to them that the experience of blending in was one my sister and I had never had. And it moved them. 'I wonder if there is something we could have done differently,' my mother said.

In fact I would say that, as parents, mine did everything right. They did not see things through the prism of race; they saw each other in the context of their loving relationship and regarded their children's futures with aspiration. They raised me to be British, and there is no reason, from their point of view, why this should have been problematic. English was my first language, Britain was unequivocally my home, I was being educated at a prestigious school and brought up in an affluent area. So why did I feel to the very core of my being that this was not a place I could ever fully belong?

One reason is that I didn't know what Britain was. I didn't know its true past, I was totally unaware of its secrets. And when it comes to race, Britain definitely has secrets. They lurk in the language, and the brickwork and the patterns of society, so that, for those who are silent or desperate enough to listen and search, clues gradually begin to reveal themselves. Some of these secrets relate to the days, turned years, turned centuries, in which British people mingled their destinies with the people and products of India, China, South East Asia and the Middle East for instance. Others would explain, if only we could hear them, why Britain and Africa are so closely linked. A link that was directly responsible for my existence.

We think of Africa as a remote, exotic, often alien place. Even the way Africa is referred to as if it is a country, rather than a continent, is a hint of our tendency to dismiss its fifty-four countries as 'all the same', the poor, corrupt, war-torn land of black people, far away.[2] Whatever the context, Africa's nations – and especially those south of the Sahara – are foreign, and as culturally and geographically other as it's possible, in the British imagination, to get.

But African stories are *part* of Britain – there are clues to it even in Wimbledon, a place seemingly devoid of any significant black presence. Take Wimbledon Common for example, the wide plateau of heaths and bogs that, along with Richmond Park, forms London's largest green space, a heaving city lung that begins right at the end of my road. At the centre of the common – spidery paths radiating out, like spokes on a bike – is an old, hollow-post windmill. It's here, beside this windmill, that Robert Baden-Powell wrote his famous book *Scouting for Boys* in 1908, a book which founded the Scouting movement, and

would go on to be the most successful post-war English-language publication after the Bible. A quintessentially British historical figure,
operating in a quintessentially British setting.

But in 1895, then a major in the British army, Baden-Powell was
chosen to lead a colonial war on Kumasi, the capital of the Ashanti
Empire, the Ghanaian kingdom where my third great-grandmother
and her family lived. That war turned them into refugees, sending
them fleeing through the dense forest for two hundred kilometres on
foot until they paused at a breeze-kissed, fertile and misty town named
Aburi, which still remains their home. The experience of my Ghanaian
ancestors and my life as a schoolgirl in Wimbledon were linked by
Scouting – which, as a Brownie, is a movement I too followed – a
movement which had the British army's adventures in Ghana at its
inception.

The origins of the Scouting movement were heavily influenced by
racist ideas. Baden-Powell's concern, in the era of turbulence and
change that accompanied the dawn of the twentieth century, was how
to restore white, British masculinity to its rightful glory, and paternal
leadership of inferior races. Ironically, he believed that some of the
practical, physical skills of Africans in places like the Gold Coast had
something to offer in this regard. He may have written of 'the stupid
inertness of the puzzled negro ... duller than that of an ox',[3] but
Baden-Powell was quite happy to borrow their tricks. Preparing for
the assault on Kumasi, Baden-Powell learned from Ghanaians how to
hack through 'the densest primeval jungle and forest, without roads
or paths of any kind to guard us', and was deeply impressed by how
his African men used skilful axemanship, pioneering and knotting,
and built hundreds of bridges from wooden poles, lashed together
with vines.[4]

Baden-Powell discovered what would become the most distinctive piece of Boy Scout kit – the Scout staff. 'Without a staff,' he wrote
of the forests of Ashanti, 'one could not have got along at all.' History
is written by the victors, as the saying goes – it's no surprise that the
endorsements I embraced, whose approval I sought so desperately as

a child, were not those of my ancestors, but those of Baden-Powell. Yet for someone like me, his ideology was not neutral. He drew on the experience of defeating, humiliating and ransacking the cultural heritage of the Ashanti kingdom to reinforce his confidence in the inherent supremacy of the white British male over inferior species like the African, an ideology which was, at its conception, at the very heart of the Scouting movement.

If this episode in British history – right on my doorstep, seemingly so removed from my African heritage but in fact so intertwined with my Ghanaian family's story – has been so hidden from my view, what other overlapping stories are all around us, just as secretively hidden away?

Had I known the true proximity of African stories to British stories, of black people to British people, of blackness to whiteness, it might have changed the way I saw myself. For most of my childhood, the way I saw myself was not kind. I have kept a diary since I was eight years old. From the very earliest entries these record a permanent and constant consciousness of feeling at odds with my surroundings, of being defined by skin, hair, an unpronounceable name, and the vague fact of a murky background from a place that was synonymous with barbarity and wretchedness. I was that awkward, highly noticeable outsider, and that is what I felt every day of my life, in my own street, my local shops, my school, my ballet and gymnastics classes, the birthday parties, everywhere.

In more recent decades, these experiences have been given a name: *otherness*. Unlike the alienation of being the only person with a foreign accent, say, or red hair, or the unusually tall child, mine was an otherness loaded with millennia of extra baggage that has accumulated to determine the way Britain has come to regard all things African. The powerful ideologies that persuaded otherwise good-natured and reasonable people that Africans were closer to animals, fit to be bought and sold, have left a stain that lingers. It's reinforced by the contemporary characteristics of an immigrant community that is both black and poor.

Growing up in Wimbledon in the 1980s, black people lived in the council estates clustered away from the affluent white hillside. Those I did encounter cleaned the streets and the toilets, or, like my grandmother, they served the wealthy at the tills, and nursed the mentally ill. They did jobs that the white people were willing to throw away. Occasionally they were victims too, of famine in Ethiopia or war crimes in Sierra Leone. These were not people who were beautiful, inventive or in control, unless they were Robert Mugabe, in which case power was conducted with an inhuman level of evil. Goodness, success, self-determination, affluence, intelligence, social mobility, desirability in all its forms, these belonged to white people, and I was, the world reminded me constantly, not one of them. Some of this I was able to articulate as a child. My diary entries record a miserable series of self-impressions, in which I compared my skin colour, hair texture, the shape of my thighs, to my peers and found them sorely lacking.

I was not familiar with deliberately, proudly black identities. My mother is black, and beautiful, and proud of her heritage, but these things were unrelated and de-racialised in her psyche, at least as far as I perceived it. She happened to be beautiful, and she happened to be African, and she happened to be black, which was not so much an identity I felt I could latch on to, as a personal coincidence of features unique to her. But for me, growing up as such a minority in a world so hostile to what it was that stood me apart, otherness was my identity.

And then, I fell into blackness. It happened overnight, it happened by accident. When I was thirteen, my mother allowed me to get my hair braided – a traditional African hairstyle that involves weaving synthetic extensions into long plaits that, the way I wanted them, fell all the way down my back. Shiva – a Caribbean lady from Tooting who regularly toiled at my mother's head – would do it, I just had to buy the hair. We surveyed the rows of plastic-wrapped hair, woven loosely into one fat plait – my mother knew what to do. She chose acrylic braid extensions, colour 2B – a light brown that matched my natural colour, two packs was enough, she explained. It took five hours that first time, the Ashanti stool, Shiva and me, her fingers clicking and weaving so fast sometimes it was hard to see them. When she'd finished, she burned the ends with a lighter, rolling the molten plastic into a hard cylinder, like the end of a shoelace. I was transformed.

The braids, which were thick and long, made me look older. But more importantly, they made me look blacker. This hairstyle was a cultural marker, it signified to others something the unmanaged frizzy fringe had not – I was a member of their community, I existed, I was there. It's no exaggeration to say that my hair gave me access to black people. Black boys saw me now, a heaving young bud of sexuality, and called out at me in the street. Black girls wanted to fight me, seeing me for the first time as a threat. I felt as though I became a woman overnight. Having begun puberty not long before, I already had curves, but now I had braids too, I went from being the ugly girl – deformed almost, in the sense that I did not conform to any of the norms of beauty in the world I inhabited – to the possibility that, for the first time in my life, I was attractive.

Being seen as attractive, and black, gave me confidence. I began writing at the *Voice*, immersing myself in the news and the challenges of the black community, ploughing my intellectual energy not into school, but into reporting for the newspaper on issues facing young black people. It was a coping mechanism, and a way of processing some of the struggles I knew so well. And it was a statement: I didn't want to try to be white any more, I was black now. And I was going to go all out.

The problem was, I knew very little about blackness. I had never been to a country where the majority of the people were black; I knew nothing of African history, hardly anything of its cultures, languages and legacies. All I knew was that Ghana existed, and that it was somehow in me. The otherness I felt in Wimbledon and the belonging I found in the black community both shared Ghana as their single source. And with the logic of a child, I thought that if the Ghanaian component of my physical inheritance was what made me so other, going to Ghana would solve the emotional problems of my inheritance too.

This was not without its flaws as an ideology. It was embarrassing to be African then, in the early 1990s. So loaded were perceptions of the continent with the colonial and racist notions of the 'heart of darkness' and 'savage' lands, I had on more than one occasion lied when teenagers I met asked me where I was from, telling them my family came from Jamaica, attempting to link myself to connotations of weed, reggae, jerk chicken and urban youth culture, not an African country, associated instead with unpronounceable names, famine and psychotic dictators.

But the more I embraced a black identity, the more it seemed that Ghana was ultimately where I belonged. When I read Barack Obama's memoir, *Dreams from My Father*, so many years later, I found this was not an isolated experience. 'I had been forced to look inside myself and had found only a great emptiness there,' Obama wrote of growing up mixed heritage in racially divided America, hoping this was an emptiness that going to Kenya, the land of his father, could fill. 'Africa had become more an idea than an actual place, a new promised land ... With the benefit of distance, we engaged Africa in a selective embrace,' he explained. 'What would happen once I'd relinquished that distance?'[5]

My first attempt to relinquish the distance came in 1995, when I was fourteen, a year after the braids had further flung open the door to my sense of black identity, without any particular content to give it meaning and sense. My mother had noticed the deterioration in my behaviour and well-being, the crisis of puberty colliding head-on with the crisis of identity, and decided to act.

It was a decision based very much on the dynamics within our family, and yet we were part of a flood of people in the Ghanaian diaspora who, in the mid-1990s, began returning to the country of their or their parents' birth. It was a diaspora that had fled Ghana in the 1960s, 70s and 80s, some of the country's darkest years when a revolving door of military dictatorships had brought atrocities, famine and repression. But in 1992, democracy began to return, and so did Ghanaians, bringing with them children who lived with the concept of Ghana every day in the sounding out of their names, but had never felt air so throbbing with heat, or red earth underneath their feet.

My sister and I were a classic case in point. By 1995, Ghana was stabilising at the same rate as I was unravelling, and the matriarchs swung into action, my mother and grandmother planning our first ever trip. I remember sitting on my perch on the bridge link above Wimbledon station's train platforms where my friends and I congregated, an unruly teenager with my Stüssy bomber jacket, long braids and Caterpillar boots. We passed the time, as the days grew shorter that autumn, going twos on Benson & Hedges cigarettes, monitoring the movement of boys, and taking phone calls from the payphones whose numbers – in the days before mobile phones – we knew by heart. And suddenly I had something new to say. I was bursting inside, tempted to shout out at the weary commuters, piling out of their overcrowded trains, or seize the station guard's loudspeaker and make an announcement over the tannoy. I was going to Ghana.

I have never forgotten the questions I was asked by friends about my forthcoming trip. 'Will they have phones there, if anything goes wrong?' 'Will you wear shoes when you're there?' 'Will you be staying in the jungle?' In all my ignorance about Africa, I was still surprised at the preconceptions misleading my peers. It was an early indication for me as to just how strong various stereotypes about life in Africa really were. And still are.

So there we were, my sister and I, standing at the door of a Ghana Airways plane, our mother and grandmother one step ahead, disembarking into a dense October night. The sensation of physically soaking in hot air soon faded under a sight so revolutionary it is cryogenically preserved in my memory. I saw the high-vis scurry of ground staff, bulky boots and bloodshot eyes, waving passengers enthusiastically along the tarmac. There was the airport lady, standing at the entrance to the airport, surveying us with vague curiosity, splitting the traffic and directing us to one side of the corridor, the side where a large sign said *Akwaaba*, 'Welcome', in wooden letters. There was the white of the immigration officer's shirt, luminescent against dark brown skin and in the thickness of the night, tucked into his too-large trousers, with an overly wide leather belt. 'The thing that struck me the most is that everyone is black,' I wrote in my diary, on 18 October 1995. 'It's so amazing, like nothing I've ever seen before!' Black police, black men in suits, black luggage boys. Everyone, everywhere, black skin, Afro hair, shocking. 'Have I ever even seen black people in uniform before?' I asked my diary. I was intoxicated. 'On the drive home, the dusty roads were lined with palm trees. Every so often you see little candlelit stalls which apparently stay open all night selling fruit and nuts and juice. It's beautiful, it's breathtaking. It's Africa.'

Reading back over my diaries, the week we spent in Ghana strikes me as the only period when I stepped out of self-obsessed adolescence and saw the world around me with wide-eyed wonder. My mother and grandmother took me to a healer by the sea, who carried out a ritual to guard us. I didn't understand what she said, it was in Twi, but I remember sitting in this little one-room shack, where the family slept at one end and an altar stood at the other. I remember this woman touching my head and speaking in rapid, tonal phrases. I remember my mother saying that we would be protected now. I remember feeling safe.

The experience that left the deepest impression on me, on that first trip, was the time we spent in Aburi, the town where my third great-grandmother found refuge, chased out of Kumasi by Robert Baden-Powell and his men, and where my grandfather P.K. lies buried in a graveyard of lovingly tended stones that is constantly at war with the encroaching wilderness. Aburi rises out of the slopes of a long, lateral range of West African mountains, where the earth has escaped the harsh exposure to the haunted shores of the coast. A bird flying north from those Atlantic beaches, congested with silent ghosts and noisy trade, would see the land begin to swell into lush hills half a kilometre high, then the town would appear like a sigh in the foliage, before the aerial view would be choked by the rainforests of the Ashanti kingdom, and north of that the savannah, growing drier and more sparse, with stubborn trees and thinner, taller people, into the sandscapes of the Sahara Desert.

These days it's just an hour's drive from the capital Accra on the coast to Aburi, and when you climb these hills to reach the town you can face outwards, and breathe in the blue of the Gulf of Guinea yawning out in the distance. On clear days, the space between the mountains and the ocean gapes with the relief of clean air, fresh water and mosquito-free breeze. Or you can turn inwards, to the heart of the town, to the house that my grandfather built, decaying now, its eaves used by hawkers of mobile phone SIMs and sugar bread, its walls painted with ads for laundry soap and cooking oil, or, these days, the neon of 3G network ads. By the time my family arrived in this town, the British had already begun planting a garden there, modelled on the botanical gardens of Kew in south-west London, just a few miles from Wimbledon. The plants are layered deep now, with mature bark and green foliage, a garden with thick, towering trees, and heavy, cool air that pulls you downwards. There's weight in the stones that scatter the earth, and a far older memory than when this garden was built 125 years ago. Its plants – gathered from the climatic extremes of the British Empire – are as perfect and unfamiliar as Eden.

On that first visit to the Aburi botanical gardens, in this alien yet familiar tropical land, I was fascinated by the unmistakably British creation at its heart. It had the sobriety of a Victorian construction, with its brick walls and methodical layout, its plaques of honour dedicated to the names of its curators – British men until the empire ended, after which the names began to be Ghanaian. This country, the motherland, seemed to capture all the mystery of this land of rich red earth and fragrant air, where my relatives spoke of spirits and ghosts as casually as they offered me water to drink. Yet it was recognisable, and it gave me a hint that things could be both British and Ghanaian at the same time – a message I was desperate to hear. A message I should have been able to hear in Britain, without travelling thousands of miles to find it.

2. ORIGINS

Unidentified woman photographed in Britain, 1881.

What can the England of 1940 have in common with the England of 1840? But then, what have you in common with the child of five whose photograph your mother keeps on the mantelpiece? Nothing, except that you happen to be the same person.

– George Orwell,
'England Your England'

'I'm not sure if these are real.' One of my friends is posting a frenzied stream of messages on a WhatsApp group chat that's never usually this lively on Monday mornings. I'm at work in the Sky News news-room, a barren start to a January week, and I'm trying to ignore the buzzing on my phone, but it's distracting. 'Wouldn't it be amazing if they were?' asks another. 'How would that have affected us differently psychologically, growing up?' A third friend says she is struggling to make sense of what she's seeing. 'My mind just can't process these,' she says, 'it goes against everything I believed about England.' The first friend chimes in again. 'Oh wow, you mean, these are English?' she asks. 'I had assumed they were American!'

The images my friends are discussing are sepia portraits of Victorian and Edwardian women. They wear bonnets, complicated bustles and layers of calico, starched cotton or silk, but – and this is the shocking part – it is brown skin radiating above their stiff chemisettes, and curly Afro hair swept up in flowery bonnets. These are black women, photographed more than a century ago. But in so far as I have seen images of black women from that era before, these are completely different. They are not dressed in the rags of slavery or plantations, the crude costume of prostitution or destitution on the sooty, inner-city streets, they are not toothless vendors in a hectic port. They are women who had the luxury of investing in their beauty and appearance, pro-jecting a look that's relaxed and confident, as if they enjoyed affluence and style. None of us has ever seen anything like it.[1]

If my experiences are anything to go by, most of us – apart from a few academics and historians – are unfamiliar with flattering, pampered images of black and brown people, residing in this country in the distant past. My friends – organised by my sister into this WhatsApp group for like-minded women with natural, Afro hair – are not reacting with mild surprise, however; they are going wild. We all have black heritage, and we are all on the long journey inherent to having alien hair. Alien because, after decades in which professional black women conformed to the unspoken rule that they must imitate European hair as closely as possible, with weave-on extensions and wigs, we are all experimenting in revealing our hair's true textures. Which may sound like a trivial thing. But one of the side effects of a society that claims not to see race is that anyone whose appearance is an excessive reminder of difference needs to conform. Failing to do so is frequently perceived as an act of radical politics, which threatens to upstage our other professional accomplishments. In an environment where being black places you in a tiny minority, proudly displaying black hair appears to be seen as a threat.

To the women in the natural-hair group, these sepia photographs – taken from an exhibition at a London gallery that focuses on themes of race and representation – have immediate and personal resonance, making us question our very idea of ourselves. It's as if they are prompting us to reset some old, deep insecurity about our exclusion from history, which – according to almost every other book, film, period drama we have ever read – is total. Until we saw these pictures, we had not felt particularly aware of their absence. I'd never consciously lamented the lack of women who looked like me in historical images, and who seemed in control of their bodies and destinies. It didn't occur to the members of my group to miss something we didn't know was available. It was only when presented with an alternative view that these buried parts of our psyches came spilling out. It made me wonder what other selective accounts of the past we might have absorbed, to create this apparent belief that the past was not about people like us. Why were we – even those of us who had most to lose from doing it – buying into a lie?

In the past, when my mother was growing up in 1960s Britain, for example, 'black history' simply did not exist. Neither events concerning black people nor information about Britain's relationship with majority black countries like Ghana – until a few years earlier Britain's 'model colony' – were part of the school curriculum. Now, thanks to the work of pioneering historians like Hakim Adi, David Olusoga, Imtiaz Habib, Miranda Kaufmann and Peter Fryer who over recent decades have tirelessly researched and revived the forgotten role played by black people throughout British history, aspects of this history is now taught in almost all schools, albeit usually for just one month – October – which has been designated Black History Month. I'm not sure which of these states of affairs – the 1960s attitude, which was to ignore it, or today's attitude, which is to marginalise it as 'black history' – is more dishonest. Maybe they're as bad as each other.

There is one aspect of Britain's historical relationship to people of African descent that we do love celebrating: abolition. As a nation, we obsess over the triumph of 1807, the year in which Britain abolished the transatlantic slave trade. In 2007 we held grand, international bicentennial celebrations commemorating it. We had special coins minted, activities and exhibitions across the length and breadth of Britain, a service in Westminster Abbey for the Queen. A wreath was laid at the statue of the famous abolitionist William Wilberforce.

I have always wondered how we have managed to contort our memories in such a way as to celebrate abolishing something, while forgetting how fundamental a prior role we played in developing it in the first place. We were not only one of the trade's major protagonists, but also one of its earliest adopters.

From 1562, when Sir John Hawkins began the industrial-scale exploitation of Africans, transporting Britain's first 'cargo' of five hundred slaves from West Africa to the Americas – a venture which so impressed Queen Elizabeth I she funded a return trip – every British monarch to George III gave his or her direct support to the transatlantic slave trade. The relationship between the monarchy and slavery was formalised in 1672 with King Charles II's establishment of Britain's first 'slave trading' corporation – the Royal African Company.[2] It's no exaggeration to say that the wealth of the royal family, much like the wealth of the nation itself, was built on the back of slavery and related trade, investment and industry.

In the seventeenth century, the 'discovery' of new parts of the world and the opening up of new trade routes provided the British consumer with new and interesting drinks – coffee, tea, chocolate and rum. But they were bitter, and this, given our national affinity for sweetness, placed a natural limit on their popularity.[3] The answer to that problem was another new import: sugar. It transformed these difficult flavours into delicious, And addictive, drinks. Sugar consumption in England increased fourfold between 1660 and 1700, and twentyfold from 1663 to 1775.[4] Britain's seemingly innocent cultural trait – the 'sweet tooth' still characteristic of the nation today – would, in the seventeenth, eighteenth and nineteenth centuries, play its part in the biggest atrocity of human history.

You could do worse than to begin the story of that atrocity on the Caribbean island of Nevis. Relatively few British people have heard of Nevis – a Leeward island in the eastern Caribbean, which forms part of a long volcanic arc that divides the Caribbean Sea from the Atlantic Ocean. The name 'Nevis' was dreamed up by Columbus, who first saw its volcanic peak on his voyage in 1493, and imagined the clouds above it to be snow. So he called it Nuestra Señora de las Nieves, or Our Lady of the Snows.[5] Now a sovereign state united with its larger neighbour to form St Kitts and Nevis, an elite selection of wealthy tourists venture to Nevis, where there are only a handful of mostly exclusive hotels, and where the easiest way to arrive is by private jet or yacht, since there are no direct international flights.

I stayed there in 2009 with my friend Amaki, invited by a Nevisian friend. I didn't realise then that this tiny island is where the modern British economy began. But it was here, and on St Kitts, that planters began to experiment with industrial-scale sugar production. They received an official mandate to do so from 1664, when Lords of Trade and Plantations in England legitimised sugar production. But while these English planters found their crop lucrative, it was also labour-intensive.[6] 'It is as great a bondage for us to cultivate our plantations without negro slaves as for the Egyptians to make bricks without the straw,' St Kitts planters told the Lords of Trade in

London in 1680.[7] It was more than 150 years since the Spanish had officially adopted the policy of replacing indigenous Carib labour with
imported African slaves – Spain's King Ferdinand having declared in
1510 that one African slave could do the work of four native inhabitants in Hispaniola.[8] The question of how hard the native population
could work soon became redundant in any event – they were wiped
out by European diseases, which only increased the certainty of
European colonists that it was Africans they needed. And Africans
they got.

In 2009, Amaki and I hopped back across the channel, known
locally as the Narrows, visiting some of the sights on St Kitts. At the
harbour in Basseterre, the nation's capital, you can still see the barely
ventilated cellars beneath the planters' buildings, where newly arrived
slaves were kept in holding cells until they were sold by public auction
in the square. Now it's cruise ships that frequent the harbour, their
cargo of European and American tourists seeking sun, sea and rum
cocktails. In Nevis, we walked a history trail around a sugar plantation, the steam mill and old brick tower still standing, along with the
ruins of the planters' Great House. The history is there for those who
want to see it, and we did.

This was my first ever experience of the Caribbean, and – having
lived and travelled in West Africa before – I found it an unsettling
experience. The people on Nevis bore such resemblance to the physical traits I was so familiar with in my own Ghanaian family or others
I had lived and worked with in West African countries. The meal I was
offered on arrival – a local dish known as *cook-up* – reminded me
exactly of *waakye*, one of my favourite Ghanaian meals. It's a form
of rice and beans, seasoned with pepper and cow skin. The texture of
the rice, the seasoning and the ingredients were quite specific, and
identical to what I had eaten in Ghana. Nevis is a minuscule island, its
population only around 12,000 – and within a few days Amaki and I,
both half-Ghanaian, half-white Londoners, seemed to be recognised
by chatty Nevisians wherever we went. They called us the 'African
princesses', seemingly referring to our Ghanaian names. It was a

bewildering experience, for two British girls, in a country full of people who looked to me like they had migrated from Africa yesterday, yet we were known as the exotic ones.

Of course no one 'migrated' from Africa to Nevis; the inhabitants are the descendants of people who were captured forcibly and shipped to the islands during the seventeenth and eighteenth centuries. Once the English planters' wishes to be put out of their own 'bondage' with the help of African slaves were granted, Nevis became the leading slave market for the Leeward Islands, handling 6,000 to 7,000 slaves every year. The days when planters had to beg permission for slave labour did not last long. By 1713, the collapse of the Spanish Crown led to the Treaty of Utrecht, often cited in British current affairs as the agreement that ceded Gibraltar to Britain; the fact that this document saw Britain acquire a monopoly on the slave trade to Spanish colonies in the Americas is far less well remembered.

Within fifty years, Britain became the leading slave nation in the world, the foremost supplier of slaves for the rest of Europe, and the financial heart of the triangular slave trade. Of the 12 million slaves abducted from Africa – a conservative estimate – 40 per cent were transported on British ships.[9] An estimated 15 per cent died on the notorious Middle Passage, and millions ended up in Spanish and Portuguese colonies – four million in Brazil alone. But well over one million were put to work, and often to death, in British colonies.[10] Britain made more profits from its slave-trading investments and extracted more wealth from the Caribbean than any other European slave-owning nation.[11] The economy could rise or fall on West Indian sugar – the single most valuable import to the British Isles – and by the end of the century, the security crises that Britain faced in the Napoleonic Wars had control of the West Indian colonies at their heart.[12]

Back in my neighbourhood in Wimbledon Village, ambling past grand houses towards the seductive green wilderness of the common, there is a house that has always stood out, with almost magical allure. It's long and low, a high wall masking some of the stock brick and jumbled outbuildings that reveal seventeenth-century origins, and it's wonky, in the way I think the best old houses are, its age suggested by an eccentric-looking bird coop built into its sloping roof. It was once the coach house to the grand 'Laurel Grove' that stood on three acres of manicured lawns and gardens on this site, where, in the 1780s, a young MP named William Wilberforce spent the summers with his friends, Prime Minister William Pitt the Younger among them.[13] They would lounge around, ambling away long afternoons, demanding peas and strawberries, cutting up clothes and strewing them around the flower beds, and alarming neighbours with their boisterous summer evenings.[14]

If I hadn't learned about Wilberforce at school, from the references periodically made to him by politicians, from the books – such as the high-profile biography written by former Conservative Party leader William Hague – and high-budget films – such as the 2006 production *Amazing Grace* – I would have learned about him from my local area, where he is remembered in street names, blue plaques and often relayed oral history. All these commemorations have cemented Wilberforce's legacy into a saintly staple of the national imagination. His is the face and the name synonymous with abolition.

Wilberforce, and the benevolent feats he accomplished for the wretched Africans, represents the sum total of the education I received growing up on Britain's centuries-old relationship with Africa. I could not have named a single slave, an African who campaigned for freedom, or any of the numerous families and businesses whose slave wealth has been handed down through the ages. But I knew Wilberforce, and felt proud that he lived in my town, and had been a benefactor to my primary school.

Like so many British people, I was a product of the Cult of Wilberforce – an obsession that has become as famous as the truth of slavery has become obscure. This is not to detract from the passion and commitment of Wilberforce, and the credit he is rightly given for a lifetime of persistently fighting for abolition. But there may have been 15,000 black people in Britain in Wilberforce's time, as well as hundreds of Lascars – sailors and militiamen from Asia and the Middle East, many of them Muslim, who helped fill gaps caused by the shortage of sailors at the peak of naval combat in the late eighteenth century. The authorities did not necessarily distinguish between these different groups of non-white men, calling them all 'negroes', treating them all as potential slaves.[15] They were not just there, they were active. Within that number was a highly politicised community – a select group that was mobilising and organising around the question of abolition, to great effect.

Imagine the scene. It is Westminster – the ancient village at the heart of what is now central London. I've often wandered, sometimes hobbled, these streets in the uncomfortable pencil skirts and impractical heels that are the non-negotiable female uniform of my trade, in breaks snatched from the aggressive appetite of a rolling newsroom. Westminster is now a sterile mix of government buildings, but in the eighteenth century it was home to a notoriously poor neighbourhood, so deprived it's where the word 'slum' was invented.[16]

As is often the case, this impoverished underworld was also the birthplace of one of the great social movements of British history. In the 1770s, a talented black man – born a slave, mid-Atlantic, on a ship – whose friends included the artist Thomas Gainsborough, the writer Samuel Johnson, and the Duke and Duchess of Montagu, set up a grocery store on King Charles Street. Ignatius Sancho's impressive address book didn't shield him from the worst that fellow Londoners had to offer. They frequently vented 'their prejudices against his ebon complexion, his African features, and his corpulent person'. But his talents did enrich his ability to defend himself. In one incident, a pair of passers-by, identifiable by their attire as 'a young Fashionable and his friend', said loudly, and rudely, as they encountered Sancho, 'Smoke Othello!' In response, a friend recalled, Sancho blocked the young Fashionables' path and 'exclaimed with a thundering voice, and a countenance which awed the delinquent, "Aye, Sir, such Othellos you meet with but once in a century," clapping his hand upon his goodly round paunch. "Such Iagos as you, we meet in every dirty passage. Proceed, Sir!"'[17]

Sancho's grocery opened with a push of a wicket door, and a little tinkling bell – a scene still familiar in so many independent and quirky retailers today. A customer walking in would have found a black couple – Sancho and his wife Anne, who came from the Caribbean – sitting in the corner, with some of their six children, Sancho writing or stocktaking perhaps, while Anne would chop sugar.[18] As a grocer, Sancho relied on products from the West Indies like sugar and rum, which has led some to discount his role as an abolitionist. But here was the first African writer whose prose was published in English, and who used his influential letters to assert a black British identity in writing. Like so many people with dual identities – Sancho was after all born to an enslaved African mother – Sancho commanded his mixed heritage expertly, to strategically position himself in an argument. When, in his letters, he needed to criticise African complicity in the slave trade, Sancho was not 'an African' but British, or 'a resident' of Britain. But when he wanted to insert himself in the thorny question of the American war of independence, he was anything but. Then he became an outside observer, deploying the signature 'Africanus', to distance himself from a British identity and sidestep accusations of partisanship. Confronted with a racist Londoner in an alley, he was 'an Othello' – the embodiment in the white imagination of a black man.[19] To have mixed African, Caribbean and British heritage in eighteenth-century Britain was to be in a precarious predicament – but that didn't mean it was without its opportunities, for a man sufficiently intellectually skilled to use it to his advantage.

Sancho would surely have known his own black contemporaries, some of whom would have been just as conspicuous for their high-profile political campaigning. One was Olaudah Equiano, who was baptised in St Margaret's Church, just in front of Westminster Abbey, only two months after the Sanchos got married there.[20] Equiano, author of *An Interesting Narrative of the Life of Olaudah Equiano, Or Gustavus Vassa, the African*, published in 1789, was perhaps the best-known black abolitionist of his time. *An Interesting Narrative* is now acknowledged – its original fame having been almost completely

forgotten for more than a century – as 'the most important single literary contribution to the campaign for abolition'.[21] It details his remarkable
life story, born in what is now Nigeria, kidnapped aged eleven, enslaved
in Virginia, taken to England while still a child, transported back
across the Atlantic to the Caribbean where he was finally able to save
enough money to purchase his freedom, before travelling around the
world – narrowly avoiding re-enslavement – and finding his calling in
the abolition movement gaining momentum in London.

Equiano and Ottobah Cugoano, another former slave originally
from Ghana, together founded the world's first pan-African organisation, Sons of Africa, in 1787. Sons of Africa was dedicated to securing an
end to the slave trade; but unlike other abolitionists, for these men it
was not a pastime, but a calling inspired by their own survival instincts.[22]
It was 'pan-African' because, as one scholar puts it, 'they organised
alongside other Africans, irrespective of their region or country of origin, to solve a common problem. They realised that theirs were shared
destinies, their fates bound together, and that by joining forces they
were more likely to change the fate of other Africans.'[23]

When its first letter was published in the *Diary* newspaper in 1789,
Sons of Africa had nine members – all former slaves evolving their
own black British identities.[24] They reviewed racist pamphlets by
members of the plantocracy, like James Tobin in Nevis, who exploited
a fear that lurked in the imaginations of the British – a technique that
still feels familiar today – that a flood of black immigrants could find
its way to Britain if slavery were abolished. Slavery was all that stood
between England as they knew it, Tobin argued, and 'the rapid increase
of a dark and contaminated breed'. If Africans were so toxic, Equiano
wanted to know, how come British planters and their overseers were
so keen on raping and impregnating female slaves? The Sons of Africa
disrupted the pro-slavery narrative and countered plantocracy propaganda at every available opportunity.[25] Despite their transformative
role in ending the slave trade, and all the symbolic and practical power
of this black community asserting its collective media and political
might, the influence of black abolitionists lay forgotten for more than

a century, obscured under the cult of Wilberforce. I wonder how many of the people so familiar with Wilberforce's name can with any ease recall the names or stories of those black abolitionists now.

Just as puzzling is the fact that we celebrate Britain's role in abolition but forget Britain's role in creating the slave trade in the first place. In 2010 the then prime minister, David Cameron, promoted, for example, as his favourite children's book, *Our Island Story* – a 1905 children's history book. His affection for the book was echoed by the then shadow education minister Tristram Hunt as his favourite history book of all time.[26] The book, written by Henrietta Elizabeth Marshall, was a staple for many of today's British adults, described by a review in the *Guardian* as 'feminist and progressive'[27] and reprinted in 2005 so that it could be distributed for free in all UK primary schools.[28] It's a classic example of our national amnesia. The first 460 pages mention nothing of slavery, until it finally appears in a chapter about the reign of William IV: 'another great thing which happened during the reign of William IV was the freeing of slaves'. There is then a brief discussion of what slavery was. 'In the old, rough, wild days no one cared about the sufferings of these poor, black people. They were only niggers, and made for work and suffering, and nothing was thought about it. But as time went on, people became less rough and more kind-hearted . . .'[29]

G. M. Trevelyan, a hugely influential historian whose book *English Social History* – written in a deliberately patriotic tone during the Second World War and then widely taught in schools – took a similar approach. He wastes little time on four centuries of slave trading – 'a horrible traffic'[30] – to which his volume devotes only one line. There is plenty, however, on abolition. 'The movement for the abolition of negro slavery aroused passionate popular enthusiasm sometimes excessive in its sentiment for the dusky brother,' British schoolchildren were taught. 'The sentiment of humanity was now a great political force in politics,' Trevelyan continues. 'In 1833 it abolished slavery in the Empire at a cost of £20 million cheerfully paid by the British taxpayer.'[31]

If abolition was a benevolent gift to passive Africans handed down graciously by posh white men, the companion myth is that black people forced into slavery just put up with it. This couldn't be further from the truth. There were frequent and often kamikaze-like slave rebellions, more than two hundred of them at sea, over the four centuries of slave trading.[32] Similar resistance manifested in countless acts of suicide by Africans who preferred death to enslavement, and in the establishment of whole runaway communities in islands like Jamaica. The first ever black republic – Haiti – was born out of a revolt led by former slaves, sometimes referred to as 'the Black Jacobins' for their pursuit of freedom and justice. The famous French abolitionist Abbé Henri Grégoire regarded the Haitian republic, not the United States of America, as the true custodian of liberty.

These developments did not go unnoticed in Britain. By the end of the eighteenth century, the tide was beginning to turn against the plantocracy, although the pro-slavery pamphleteers wasted no time in employing apocalyptic scenes from Haiti and Paris as a cautionary tale to anyone feeling tempted to rock the boat and free the slaves. The true reasons for Britain's decision to abolish the transatlantic trade are complex, and scepticism towards the traditional narrative – that it was a result of humanitarian concerns – is nothing new. As the great Trinidadian writer C. L. R. James put it, 'those who see in abolition the gradually awakening conscience of mankind should spend a few minutes asking themselves why it is man's conscience, which had slept peacefully for so many centuries, should awake just at the time that men began to see the unprofitableness of slavery as a method of production in the West Indian colonies'.[33]

Another Caribbean historian, Eric Williams, who went on to become first prime minister of Trinidad and Tobago, called the idea that abolition was achieved by an appeal to humanitarian principles 'one of the greatest propaganda movements of all time'.[34] More recent research by academics like David Ryden, for example, has renewed credibility in this 'decline thesis', showing that rapidly declining sugar prices from 1799 due to overproduction in the West Indies, as well as foreign competition and speculation, directly influenced Parliament's stance on the slave trade, tipping the scales in favour of abolition.[35]

The intersection of economic, socio-political factors and abolition is one of the most complex and protracted debates in modern historiography. What is not contested is that, when Britain did abolish the slave trade, the value of the 800,000 or so slaves still owned by Brits in the Caribbean was valued at £47 million. Of this sum, the £20 million so 'cheerfully' stumped up by the British taxpayer, after decades of black agitation, was not paid to compensate slaves for their abuse, loss of family, income, dignity, heritage, identity or life, but instead to compensate the slave owners for the loss of their chattels. The remaining £27 million – a colossal sum at the time – was paid for by none other than the slaves themselves, who had to work for another four years for free after abolition, in order to raise the funds.[36] The deprivation characterising their lives at the end of slavery, which left them illiterate, unskilled, psychologically traumatised and irreparably cut off from their African homelands, survives on an intergenerational basis to this day.

There was no clean break from slavery, no moment where those who had been slaves suddenly began to be prosperous owners of land or assets, highly literate and in a position to reverse the unhappy odds stacked against their ancestors at the moment of kidnap. The decline of slavery happened gradually, in fits and starts, at times going backwards. Britain's act of abolition in 1807 curtailed the supply of new African blood to slave owners in the Caribbean, worsening conditions for many of the slaves already there. Planters began to pay overseers a bonus for each female slave they impregnated, an obvious pecuniary incentive for rape,[37] to increase numbers through births. When slavery itself was abolished almost thirty years later, slaves were converted into 'apprentices'. The scheme, administered by former slave owners, is unlikely to have felt much different from the regime that preceded it. And in many cases the traffic in people from Africa continued regardless, more rebranded than significantly reformed. Britain still felt it needed to import African labour to its Caribbean colonies. Naval officers, deployed post-abolition on the Gulf of Guinea coast to intercept slave vessels, offered two choices to the Africans they liberated: they could settle in Sierra Leone, the West African nation established by Britain for freed blacks, or they could earn more as free labourers in the West Indies under an employment contract. The latter arrangement was optimistically called 'free emigration'.[38]

In fact, for those profiting from the trade in Africans, the greatest returns from slavery came after Britain's abolition. By 1840, there were more slaves crossing the Atlantic than there had been before,[39] and British investors and businesses were among those profiting. Conditions for slaves were becoming ever more hideous.[40] Illicit trading was only one part of the picture – the Acts of Parliament which actually abolished the slave trade were littered with loopholes, and banks, insurance companies, shipbuilders, merchants and their accountants wasted no time working out how to exploit them. British traders set up partnerships with traders in Cuba – where slaves continued to arrive until 1870 – and Brazil, where the transatlantic trade was only abolished in 1888.[41] There was nothing to stop Brits investing in the actual ownership of slaves in these nations, and in slave-worked mines and plantations, and they did, in significant numbers.

Perfectly legal actions saw Britain feeding the trade in ways that rendered it directly culpable for its continuation. Illegal slave traders, so effective at evading the poorly resourced British naval controls that were meant to intercept slaving along the West African coast, were using overwhelmingly British-produced goods to procure their slaves. About 80 per cent of the items still being exchanged for women, men and children on the African coast in the nineteenth century were manufactured in Britain, fuelling Britain's economic boom throughout the Victorian era. Cotton, which overtook sugar as the most important slave-produced commodity, linked the industry of Manchester with the slave plantations of Mississippi in one continuous economic loop.[42]

Britain's appetite for sugar continued to grow. In the 1840s, the import duties on free-grown and slave-grown cotton and sugar were equalised, despite campaigns pointing out that this would increase the trade in slaves. Much of the imported slave-grown sugar was refined and then exported, providing more jobs and earning even more money for Britain. Companies like Tate & Lyle – the quintessentially

British firm now also known as patrons of the arts, as well as for the sweet white stuff – were built on the proceeds of slavery. Decades after congratulating itself for abolishing its own direct role in the slave trade, Britain was still profiting richly from the unpaid labour of kidnapped Africans. It just let others do the dirtiest part of the work.[43]

Why does it bother me so much that we avoid and downplay the true legacy of slavery, and the extent of its contribution to modern Britain? It's quite possible – likely even – that among the Ghanaians trafficked across the Atlantic, there were those with whom I share a common ancestor. I may have distant cousins among the survivors of that terror, but I'm not descended from any – once they boarded that ship, their ties to my family were cut. I have no direct links to the Caribbean or other parts of the African diaspora created by slavery. If reparations were to be paid for the act of enslaving 12 million Africans, I would gain nothing personally.

During the course of writing this book I learned in fact that I am descended from a Dutchman who was in all likelihood a slave trader, and who found his way to the West African coastal fort of Elmina in the 1750s. I know only his last name – Welzing – he was my sixth great-grandfather. Of my sixth great-grandmother, I know nothing at all, except that she was a black African woman belonging to the local Fante ethnic group. Was she a slave, or was she free? And if she was free, how free in resisting the advances of a white man whose country controlled the trade? These details aside – I'll return to them later – my identity, and that of my Ghanaian family, unlike my African American and Caribbean friends, has never been one of a people who were aware of having experienced enslavement.

The reason I take issue with our relationship with our slave-owning past is that it goes against everything I value about Britain. We are a nation which prides itself on reason, on curiosity about history – you only have to look at the range and frequency of historical dramas, or the way history books climb to the top of our best-seller lists, or the popularity of our heritage tourism sites, stately homes, Stonehenge, cathedrals and Roman ruins. We are known for the world-class nature of our schools, universities, academics, writers and thinkers. Like many British people, during the course of my education, I was taught to prize intellectual rigour, academic excellence, reason and integrity above all else.

It's hard to reconcile these values with our approach to something that played such a crucial, and still relevant, role in building the nation we know and love. Our political leaders often tell us that transatlantic African slavery is in the past, and we should move on.[44] But there are people alive today whose grandparents worked as labourers on British-owned plantations; labourers descended from slaves, and employers descended from slave masters. There are nations whose inhabitants have little or no knowledge of their original ancestry, having been kidnapped by Brits and put to work on British plantations, to the enrichment of our nation, and whose surnames remain the surnames of their British enslavers. These psychological scars are long-lasting.[45]

Structural, deliberately orchestrated disadvantage is intergenerational, passed down through families, in just the same way as those born into privileged families inherit wealth. The impact of slavery on the African continent, from where so many millions – often the strongest and most able – were kidnapped, is harder to delineate. But it's widely acknowledged that slavery deprived huge swathes of Africa of its working-age people over four centuries, and that the trauma of industrial-scale kidnap and murder has been far-reaching. As the late Nigerian writer Chinua Achebe wrote, 'The victims of this catastrophe have been struggling for centuries now against their cruel fate on both sides of the Atlantic: on one side, scratching the soil of ruined farms in a devastated continent; on the other, toiling in the sweltering aftermath of captivity.'[46]

I knew nothing about it until I was at least thirteen, having learned nothing at school, nor seen anything about it in my local library, whose books I did my very best to exhaust. When I did first learn about slavery, it was as a result of a conversation with my mum, about the artist we all loved, Michael Jackson. 'Where is Michael Jackson from, Mum?' I remember asking, kneeling in the living room, leafing through the sleeves on the shelf where my parents kept their record collection.

'He's from America,' she replied. 'Yeah I know, but where's he *from*?' I insisted. 'You know, like how we are from Ghana? Where are his parents from?' So Mum explained. 'They don't know,' she told me. 'They were all slaves. They came from Africa originally, but they have no idea where, or when.' I thought *I* had identity problems reconciling my known sources of heritage; it had not occurred to me that there were people who didn't have that luxury. 'They,' my mum said, pondering this point, 'are completely cut off from their real heritage.'

My daughter's generation is likely to learn more about slavery, and Britain's role in it, than my generation did, at least from mainstream sources. If they don't learn about it at school, they will find films like *Twelve Years a Slave* and *Birth of a Nation* being made by Hollywood studios, and TV programmes like David Olusoga's *Black and British: A Forgotten History*, a 2016 BBC series that probed the untold history of slavery. The British context is important, because it relates directly to Britain's past in a way that the actions of British planters in North and South America, and the Caribbean, do not. Because it was not just the British royal family, aristocracy and banking and industrial classes who grew rich from slavery, fuelling the Industrial Revolution, the railways and other key parts of the physical and financial infrastructure that continue to serve us today. Preparing a vessel for a slave voyage, as Olusoga has shown, was complex, and expensive – the average cost of fitting one out to carry hundreds of humans, in the currency of 1790, was about £10,000. That's more than half a million pounds today. The cost was usually shared by anyone who wanted to invest, and frequently it was ordinary middle- and working-class people who ventured their savings – bakers, grocers, humble workers in cities like Liverpool, Bristol and London – who shared the risk, and the returns.[47] There's no easy defence of ignorance as to what was involved in the investment. It was said that Liverpool and other cities like it were always alerted to the arrival of a slave ship, as it was preceded by the smell of vomit, urine, faeces and sweat.[48]

Yet as a nation we are so desperate to forget. 'People somehow seem to not want to look at this particular time in history,' said Steve

McQueen, the black British Turner Prize-winning artist and Oscar-winning director of *Twelve Years a Slave*. 'I mean the second world war lasted five years and there are hundreds and hundreds of films about the second world war and the Holocaust . . . Slavery lasted 400 years and there are less than 20 [films].'[49] 'We can deal with the second world war and the Holocaust and so forth and what not, but this side of history, maybe because it was so hideous, people just do not want to see. People do not want to engage,' he said.[50]

And it's hard to understand, but maybe slavery was just long ago enough that we feel justified in disengaging. There are no photographs of Africans captured in shackles, or the horrific conditions on board slave ships – a rare picture of young boys chained by the neck in the Congo is easily dismissed as part of the unique horror that Belgium created. The banks in Liverpool and London and the columns at the base of Trafalgar Square contain images of black boys, with Afro hair, their hands in cuffs, but they are so often passed by, and rarely pointed out. 'Europe undertook the leadership of the world with ardour, cynicism and violence,' wrote Frantz Fanon,[51] and it's an uncomfortable reality that can't be addressed without existential questions about the most personal aspects of the conscience of people we prefer to think of as heroes.

How could so many people persuade themselves, over so many generations, into justifying a position of such evil? There is no easy answer. 'The devil was in the Englishman,' one contemporary observer in the Caribbean remarked, 'that he makes everything work, he makes the negro work, the horse work, the ass work, the wood work, and the wind work.'[52]

'English racism,' as one historian puts it, 'was born of greed.'[53] It takes a powerful ideology to ply the mind into a contortion as twisted as the idea that human beings could be intellectualised out of humanity, and racism provided it. Racism was able to square the circle of a people who regarded themselves as Christian, moral, polite, family-orientated, hard-working, sensible, and all the other values celebrated as quintessentially British, but enjoyed profiting from viewing people with black skin as not people at all.

A system that effective, is one that sticks. Saying we should 'move on' from the racism born of the transatlantic slave trade is like saying we should move on from class. We should, but it's not going to happen any time soon. And it can never even begin to happen in any meaningful way, until we fully address it, in all its complexity and breadth, and with an unflinching willingness to understand its legacy.

In 1995, back in London after my first trip to Ghana as a fourteen-year-old, I was hungry for more knowledge of the African continent. I searched eagerly for it – for more information, more images, more stories from my mother's ancestral land. I would read the TV listings in the newspapers – the only way I knew how to source them in the days before digital TV – and record any feature films that were explicitly about Africa on a blank VHS pilfered from my dad. In the days when there were only four television channels, with their Saturday afternoon and bank holiday habit of running old epics, I found precisely three films: *Zulu*, *Ashanti* and *Out of Africa*. These films were not about Africa, they were about white adventure with a tropical backdrop, and a few dark-skinned natives to complete the look.

Out of Africa in particular, of which I had the highest expectations because it had won so many awards, beautifully dressed, coiffed and glossed the African continent, skimming over the fact that this was a time when whites ruled Africa because, they argued, Africans were closer to children, in need of the paternal hand of European civilisation. Empire, according to this movie's world view, was flawed, but still glamorous. And in the absence of other information of equal prominence and appeal to counter that message, it's no surprise perhaps that, in a YouGov poll in 2014, the majority of British people thought the British Empire was something to be proud of, three times more than the number who felt it was something to be ashamed of.[54]

The situation is just as extreme when it comes to depictions of the Raj. In the 1980s, when I was growing up, Britain went through a frenzy of what novelist Salman Rushdie has called 'Raj Revival', with glossy depictions of the days of empire in India, including Richard Attenborough's Oscar-winning epic *Gandhi*, and the era-defining TV series *The Far Pavilions* and *The Jewel in the Crown*. Rushdie accused these depictions of reinforcing the view that the empire was something 'fundamentally glamorous',[55] while the veteran American film critic Harlan Kennedy wrote that 'all this Indian adulation', forty years after the end of empire, was proof that 'Great Britain has gone mad'.[56]

In Nairobi in 2013, covering the horrific terrorist siege of the Westgate shopping mall for the *Guardian*, I began to understand, for the first time, the origins of the British perceptions of Africa which I'd always found so mysterious. One of the first people I saw, touching down in the terminal at Jomo Kenyatta International Airport, was a British lady, who looked like she had just wandered off from an *Out of Africa* fancy-dress party. She wore fitted, high-waisted khakis, a safari hat, a leopard-print band around it, and a matching scarf draped around her 'safari-style' handbag. I was captivated. I had never seen people dressed like this in Africa before. The majority of foreign visitors to the West African airports where I usually lurked, people-watching while I tracked my flight delays, wore suits – on business missions to secure oil, gold and cocoa – or they had the uniform of humanitarian and development agencies – faded chinos and sensible shoes – or they were gap-year students, wearing harem pants, flip-flops and backpacks almost the same size as them. West African countries, anglophone ones especially, don't offer luxury safaris, and the idea that they can be places of leisure and tourism, rather than extraction, is still so new. But this was a different affair entirely. Something I had never understood began to make sense. Here in Kenya, this was where the 'Africa' of the British imagination really originates.

The more I observed Nairobi, the stronger this impression became. I stayed at the Fairview Hotel, a kind of colonial-style lodge, the walls decorated with photos of Edwardian Englishmen riding zebras, actually *riding* them, the rooms furnished with four-poster beds, images of the Serengeti sprinkled liberally around the interior. One night a private party was being held on the lawn in the hotel grounds – I wandered clumsily through on my way to the gym. All the guests, without exception, were white, and all the staff, without exception, were black. They wore white gloves as they served.

The next morning, three days after the Westgate siege began, I was invited to a press briefing at the high commissioner's house, where British journalists were graciously hosted at a small palace, tastefully built in English period proportions, with endless lawns and landscapes, tennis courts and terraces. Were it not for my presence – and I was only there by chance, since I was only covering East Africa for a colleague – there would have been a perfect white hierarchy: white British diplomats, white British journalists, black servants. We drank tea, and ate cupcakes and ham and cucumber sandwiches. The crusts had been cut off. A Ghanaian friend who worked for Britain's Department for International Development (DFID) was visiting Nairobi at the same time – on my last night we headed to a steak restaurant above a nightclub, recommended by some of her expatriate colleagues. There was no table available, we were told by the Kenyan front-of-house staff, who eyed us without interest. We'll wait, we replied, settling at the bar, surveying the empty tables. After an hour I asked to speak to the manager, who apologised and seated us at one of them, saying it had been a misunderstanding. We noticed that we were the only black people dining.

'I'm deeply saddened by a sense that whites are still superior in this country, in some sense, that if you sit at a restaurant, they're served before a Kenyan is served,' Barack Obama said, in a 1990 film depicting his first visit to his father's country as a young man. It's easy to see what he meant. This felt, viscerally, like a world in which the colonial hierarchy was alive and well. The effects are real. One Kenyan filmmaker described how it manifested in her, sitting at Amsterdam's Schiphol airport in transit on her first solo trip outside Kenya, aged sixteen. 'As I sat waiting for my connecting flight, a young, white busboy was clearing tables,' Ekwa Msangi recalled. 'The sight of him doing that type of work made me so uncomfortable – I literally had to leave the cafe in order to stop myself from jumping up to help him. It wasn't because the table was a mess, and not even because it was my mess to begin with, I just realised that I'd never seen a white man do that kind of work.' Growing up in Kenya, for Msangi, meant that she had 'only ever experienced white people in positions of superiority, as managers and bosses', she said. 'I left the cafe feeling frustrated and ashamed.'[57]

How could a Kenyan teenager, at a European cafe table for the first time, know that four centuries of work had gone into very deliberately cultivating those feelings of frustration and shame? It is hard-wired into the literary canon, the art, the music, the dance of Europe that Africans are inherently carefree, lazy and lustful, that where they do excel is in the physical, not the cerebral – they are good at sprinting and fighting, and have an irrational love of singing and drumming. As we'll see later, the notion that Africans have enormous penises, or strange libidos – messages that stem from four centuries ago when they were regarded as a subhuman, animalistic species – has even trickled down into our sexual fantasies.[58] In so far as Africans must be put to work, theirs is a destiny of menial labour. In the UK today, we complain about African immigrants occupying housing, school places and high street premises with their shops, but we never seem offended by the sight of them cleaning our toilets, sweeping our streets, or washing our dishes. This idea, tragically, is as alive in African countries, internalised in the notion that Africans should serve white people, and not the other way round.

When I read Msangi's account, it reminded me of something I'd experienced in childhood. I stayed at the same school from seven to university, and when we were eleven, new children joined. One of them was a black girl, whose parents were West African. I always got the impression that she was not used to being such a visible minority, in a school as un-diverse as ours. She was quiet and shy, quickly falling in with a group of girls I wasn't close to, and although we always said hello to each other, we never became friends. When we were twelve, we were both among a group of about thirty from our year who went on a school skiing trip to the Italian Alps. I remember the trip so clearly – the thrill of the slopes, which I'd never experienced before, even my favourite outfit, a soft, thick cotton blue-and-white Levi's lumberjack shirt that I'd persuaded my mother to buy me. Lumberjack shirts were very, very desirable for pre-teens in the early 1990s. I remember the dorm – with its log-cabin feel, single beds lined up against smooth wooden walls; about ten of us to a dorm. In the evenings, entertainment was put on for us – quizzes, movies, that kind of thing – but the first night, this girl did not want to come. She didn't feel like it, she said; I remember all of us trying to persuade her to join in. We went without her in the end, and she just stayed in the dorm.

When we came back, she had done something I found shocking. She had gone around the room, tidying it. She had made the beds, then folded the clothes we had left strewn around, and laid them out neatly on each person's duvet. There must have been a broom or dustpan and brush in the room, because, although I can't remember how, I distinctly remember that she had cleaned the floor. No one else seemed particularly bothered – they were vaguely amused, and very grateful – that this girl had done all our tidying up. But I was haunted. I never asked her about it, I felt so uncomfortable that she had performed these tasks and cast herself – consciously or not – in the role of servant. I wish I'd spoken to her about it, to ask her why, but I did not know how to deal with it at the time. Yet I sensed the rationale behind it. I too was conscious that this was the role carried out by the only other people in our environment who looked like us, back at school in Wimbledon; the dinner ladies, the porters, the cleaning staff were African, and black. It was as if she had got the message about how roles are distributed by race, and internalised it.

Where does this message come from? The idea that it's natural for people from Britain's former African colonies to clean up after us, that we should expect white-gloved black subservience on holidays in Jamaica, or – also remarkably persistent – that the savage tribes of West Africa exist in a state of nature?

As good a time, and place, as any to pick would be this: Wednesday 24 April, St George's Day, 1924. That was the day the biggest exhibition

Britain had ever seen, the Empire Exhibition, was launched in Wembley, north London. It was a display of unprecedented scale – a fifty-six-nation, 216-acre, £4.5 million (around £250 million today) bonanza of imperial propaganda – designed to immerse the British public in imperialist fervour, to teach them to 'think . . . and act imperially'. It was the defining national public event of its era, doing for the interwar generation what the Great Exhibition at Crystal Palace had done for the Victorians, and included a British Palace of Engineering, six times the size of Trafalgar Square, a statue of the Prince of Wales made of Canadian butter, newly possible thanks to the emerging refrigeration technology, a reconstruction of the tomb of Tutankhamen, Tibetan trumpeters, and . . . for Africa . . . a bunch of mud huts.

Or more precisely, a 'mud-baked walled town', home to the West Africa part of the exhibition, sandwiched between Palestine and the main stadium, where people from the Gold Coast, Sierra Leone and Nigeria were put on display.[59] King George V can be seen in silent Pathé footage from 1924 entering one of these humble huts, where 'tribesmen' are at work making arts and crafts – a task which they are described as undertaking 'untouched by trade with the outside world'. African women prostrated themselves before Queen Mary, dressed all in white, and the comedian and music-hall entertainer Billy Merson made no bones about their appeal in his musical tribute to the mud huts:

> There you will find me in a costume gay
> In charge of the girls from Africa.
> All they wear is beads and a grin;
> That is where the exhibition comes in.[60]

These images and words were unbelievably influential. There were a staggering 27 million visits to the Empire Exhibition during the 150 days it was open to the public – if those were all unique visits, that would amount to half of the entire population of Great Britain.[61]

Although colonies in other parts of Africa were also included in the exhibition, there was an emphasis on West Africa, which Britain wanted to showcase as an obscure and backward region where real progress was being made.[62]

The exhibits and publications explained to the British public that cannibalism and human sacrifice were entrenched customs in West Africa, reinforcing the message that Britain's presence in the region provided a much needed preventative benevolence.[63] The press allowed their imaginations to reach impressive new heights. The *Evening News* claimed that modern British rule had, within the brief space of twenty years, nearly abolished cannibalism, slave trading, and obscure black magic rites of almost incredible barbarity from Nigeria. The *Sunday Express* ran an article titled 'When West Africa Woos', including an interview with a 'Princess from Akropong' (a village neighbouring Aburi in Ghana) on the topic of marriage and lovemaking in Africa. The article was introduced by a drawing of two orangutans.

Ironically the blatant racial stereotyping of the Empire Exhibition radicalised a generation of Africans in Britain, led to the formal creation of the West Africa Students Union and played no small part in grooming the leaders who would precipitate the collapse of the empire in Africa. It was all the more ironic because colonial Africans, rightly or wrongly, had previously been kindly disposed towards the British Empire, in spite of its evils. Young men, like my maternal grandfather P. K. Owusu who travelled from the Gold Coast to Britain as a student two decades later in 1944, had been educated to look to Britain as the home of democracy, fairness and civilisation. They were told that the empire was benevolent, born out of a respect for Africans and a desire to help them, and they believed it. There was nothing to prepare them for the sense of betrayal they felt when confronted with the fact that they were being mocked by the same people who, they had been told, were part of their own imperial family, and at being treated as so blatantly inferior by the institutions they admired. If Britain had wanted to foster a spirit of rebellion in a generation of Western-educated

African intellectuals, they could hardly have come up with a more genius design than an exhibition like this.

It makes sense to me that these stereotypes, in the heyday of empire, would have affected my grandfather. My mother tells stories about the hurt he expressed to his own children at being heckled with gorilla noises and abusive language on the streets of London, a place he had until then regarded as the epitome of sophistication. It's hurtful but, with hindsight, not that surprising that British people in the 1940s held these views. Yet these stereotypes have also affected me. The mud-baked walled town of Wembley is still, I believe, alive and well. It's the reason why, whenever a black model manages to find her way onto a catwalk at a major fashion show, she is still often dressed up in animal print, 'exotic' patterns or 'tribal' accessories, like animal teeth. It's the reason why so many people still believe African women are hyper-sexual, as if they would really rather be walking around wearing, in the words of the song, only 'beads and a grin'. It's the reason why a senior British diplomat told me that he regarded Gambia – a tiny state that is literally an island within the Francophone state of Senegal, designed to give Britain access to the River Gambia – as a 'British penis thrust into the heart of Senegal'. It's the reason why, the first time I went to Ghana in 1995, my school friends asked the questions they did: *phones? shoes? jungle?* They imagined I was journeying to a mud hut, in the middle of nowhere, in a land where time stood still. It's the reason why I even believed that myself.

The idea of Africa as a bunch of mud huts is still surprisingly common; a static, 'traditional' land, a pre-civilised space. As Frederick Lugard, then governor of Nigeria, wrote in the opening lines of *The Dual Mandate* – a book of immense influence on the future of colonial policy first published in 1922 – 'Africa has been justly termed the "Dark Continent", for the secrets of its peoples, its lakes, and mountains and rivers, have remained undisclosed not merely to modern civilisation, but through all the ages of which history has any record.'[64] In other words, Africans had no history.

This differential treatment of Africans and all other races, from the British perspective, is cemented in language. Even the term 'sub-Saharan Africa', a standard way of differentiating black Africa from its Mediterranean counterparts in North Africa, symbolises this prejudice. The latter is recognised as a source of ancient civilisation – Carthage, in modern-day Libya, Alexandria and so much of Egypt, the biblical land and ancient home of the pharaohs. 'Sub-Saharan Africa', a term which replaced the more obviously racially loaded historic phrases like 'Tropical Africa' and 'Black Africa', on the other hand, is usually referred to in a context synonymous with material and intellectual poverty and underdevelopment. There is little other justification for the distinction embodied by the phrase 'sub-Saharan'. The World Bank's list of forty-eight countries that supposedly fit that category includes four countries that are on the Sahara, and Djibouti, which is further south, but considered more Arab than 'black African', is off the list. One US diaspora group found these distinctions so offensive it launched a petition to abolish the phrase 'sub-Saharan' in 2010, with little success.[65]

Branding black Africa as without history, culture or contribution towards human progress – the hallmarks of humanity – served an obvious purpose during colonial times. So half a century after the end of the empire, what are we saying now?

The answer is, silence. A silence that is rich and light and dwells in an old library, a place which smells faintly of dust and echoes. It's a place where the space has almost developed the texture of thoughts – or at least that's how I imagine it – filled with a kind of virtual ruin from centuries of invisible ruminating. It's peaceful, and it's intimidating. It's tucked away in a stony corner of Oxford University's medieval heart, at a college named All Souls. Since Oxford University has come, more than ever, to symbolise privilege and elitism, it's often forgotten that within the university itself, there are concentric circles of elitism and privilege. There are poor colleges and rich colleges, old colleges and new colleges, all jostling for recognition as the most prestigious, illustrious and best. At the apex is the College of the Souls of All Faithful People Deceased in the University of Oxford, or All Souls, a college that has something of a mythical status among students since you have to be invited to sit what is usually described as 'the hardest examination in the world' to study here. Those who pass are immediately propelled to academic stardom.[66]

It's here at All Souls that this silence lives, in a glorious library, an expanse of diamond-slated stone floor, coloured with puddles of light from the intricately crafted stained-glass windows at each end, thousands of books caged behind criss-cross wire: *The Imperial Factor in South Africa* and *The Cape Colour Question*, *A History of East Africa* in three volumes, *Mahdism and the Egyptian Sudan*, and *The Ashanti Campaign of 1900*, the final war in a century of British campaigns that turned my own family into refugees. From its founding, books and money were donated here in such copious quantities that by the early 1700s, All Souls was in desperate need of an upgrade.

The man who answered the call was Christopher Codrington, a former student who, when his father died, inherited his extensive estate of sugar plantations and slaves in Barbados. He donated £10,000, a vast sum at the time, as well as his own library of 12,000 books, £4,000 ring-fenced for buying new ones, and the rest for the construction of a new library. He maintains a steady presence in the library that bears his name. He stands in marble, hand on hip, looking towards the majestic window, styled as a Roman emperor, surveying the library that was paid for by the blood, sweat and toil of his slaves. He is not just remembered but exalted and memorialised.

There is something disturbing about the fact that, in order to research aspects of the Ashanti wars, you need to sit beside the statue of a glorious slave master; or during the time I was at Oxford, in order to research decolonisation, you had to walk respectfully past a bust of Cecil Rhodes at Rhodes House. Rhodes, the famous financier and founder of diamond company De Beers, and fanatical British imperialist, is described by one highly regarded historian of empire as 'a half crazed visionary who wanted the whole world British'.[67] Even in his own time, Rhodes was one of the most controversial imperialist figures,[68] giving his name to the states of North and South Rhodesia (now Zambia and

Zimbabwe respectively), describing the colonies as 'a dumping ground for the surplus goods produced in our factories', and earning the nickname, which persists today, 'the father of apartheid'. Knowing little more about him except that he believed passionately in the superiority of white people over black, I found it bizarre – as a student of decolonisation and African politics – that the only place to source my books was in a building dedicated to his legacy.

I found it even stranger that so many international graduate students, including a good number of Africans and African Americans, were 'Rhodes Scholars', supported in their studies by the funds he bequeathed and therefore, you could say, manifesting his legacy in their daily lives. The Rhodes Scholarship is one of the most prestigious scholarship schemes in the world, selecting the best of the best students from Africa, Asia, Europe, the Middle East, the Pacific and the US, based on their potential to become 'public-spirited leaders for the world's future'. It confers huge advantages to its recipients – fully funded study at Oxford University, alumni that include heads of state and major organisations, and, perhaps most importantly, training, retreats, internships and a rubber stamp that the recipients are destined for leadership themselves.

I was friends with a number of Rhodes Scholars at Oxford in the early 2000s. Although they were all overseas graduate students and I was a British undergraduate, in the minuscule numbers of the university's black student community, these boundaries were stripped away. I remember conversations about Rhodes and murmurings about the appropriateness of his memory being honoured so uncritically, and not just among those who were black. Long after our time at university, in 2015, murmuring gave way to protest. This happened first in South Africa, where the University of Cape Town is built on land which Rhodes bequeathed, a fact marked in a statue of him, seated in a chair, chin in hand, against a startlingly beautiful, mountainous backdrop. The statue was pulled down later that year. South African students had given their movement a hashtag – #RhodesMustFall – and argued that it was about far more than pulling down statues. It was, one former Rhodes Scholar said of the Cape Town monument, 'a metaphorical call for the transformation of the university's curriculum, culture and faculty, which many blacks feel are alienating and still reflect a Eurocentric heritage'.[69]

The question of pulling down statues has become a distraction, but the transformation that is really needed, as this Rhodes Scholar pointed out, is a deeper one. There is a pattern in our relationship with the past that I find increasingly difficult to ignore. We are still elevating the architects of 'scientific racism' – a theory that purported to use enlightenment reason to prove the physical and mental inferiority of Africans – as our cultural heroes. We do so without even acknowledging their enormous contribution to the creation of racism, even while we still struggle with its legacy today.

As a philosophy undergraduate, I was fascinated by the British empiricism movement. John Locke was its founder, and David Hume one of its most compelling protagonists. They argued that knowledge comes from sensory experience, a not entirely reliable source which should therefore be subject to scepticism and revision. I found this idea, and the men credited with it, far more lovable than the dogmatic rationalism of Immanuel Kant, which I also studied, but with far less enthusiasm.

I was in my thirties when I learned that both Locke and Hume were also important proponents of racism, pouring that same intellect they used to such great effect in epistemology – the theory of knowledge – into crafting a theory of African inferiority. Locke argued that both Native Americans and African 'negros' were subhuman. Native Americans had existed in a state of nature, or savagery, he argued, which justified colonisation by the racially and culturally superior English. Yet while these Native Americans had at least the potential to be educated, and should not be enslaved, the same was not true of 'negros', who had no such potential and so their enslavement was justified.[70] This was not just harmless philosophical musing. Locke was personally involved in the running of a plantation, and his theories found their way first into the constitution of the Carolinas in the US, which he drafted, and later into court cases that affirmed segregation, including the famous Supreme Court precedent *Plessy* v *Ferguson* – a milestone in judicially sanctioned Jim Crow practices.[71]

Hume's writings on the African race were, even in his time, one of the most controversial aspects of enlightenment thought, and became founding texts for the defence of slavery.[72] Even though Hume expressed disapproval towards the institution of slavery itself, he wrote, 'I am apt to suspect the Negroes, and in general all other species of men to be naturally inferior to the whites,' Hume wrote. 'There never was any civilized nation of any other complection than white, nor even any individual eminent in action or speculation.' When confronted with a black poet, Francis Williams, contrary evidence you'd expect an empiricist to at least take on board, Hume responded that Williams was 'a parrot, who speaks a few words plainly'.[73] Kant had a similar view – on hearing a report of something intelligent that had once been said by an African, he retorted 'this fellow was quite black from head to toe, a clear proof that what he said was stupid'.

The question I ask myself is how I studied these men, their philosophy and its legacy, at one of the best universities in the world, and yet neither this aspect of their work, nor its impact in legitimising slavery, not even its long-term influence in giving intellectual credence to racism, ever came up. Perhaps it was my own failure to read or research widely enough around the specific questions I was trying to answer. But I was studious, especially in philosophy, which I loved. I was also more interested, I think it's fair to say, than the average student in questions of race, racism and slavery. I never came across any of these references because I didn't know I was looking for them, and I didn't know I was looking for them because they were not part of the discourse about, or reputation of, these great thinkers. This aspect of their thought – profound as the consequences were, then and still now – had, in my world at least, vanished without a trace. Knowing this about them wouldn't have stopped me from studying their work, or admiring it, but it would have put it in an important context. Most of all, at a university that regards its intellectual integrity as second to none, it was a missing part of the picture, a gap too casually ignored.

I was probably the last year of undergraduate students who worked largely pre-Internet. I matriculated (Oxford-speak for enrolling) in 1999, and graduated in 2002. We had email, and Web portals and catalogues, but we used them to source physical books. Google had only just launched its first patent, and although I had a laptop, I still wrote most of my essays by hand. When I say this to undergraduate students now, they give me a look I can best describe as a blend of curiosity and pity. Along with greater access to information, this generation is a lot less tolerant of the kind of pre-packaged version of history that my classmates and I were dealing with then.

It's a summer's day in 2016, and I'm back at St Peter's College. I come here often these days – to give talks about identity among other things – and this time the college has generously lent me a conference room, a blank backdrop for what turns out to be the passionate conversation I'm about to embark upon with three female students. They all identify with the Rhodes Must Fall movement, and another rallying hashtag, #WhyIsMyCurriculumWhite, and they are vocal about the challenges of being minority students at Oxford. Yet they have all at various points distanced themselves from the most in-your-face elements of the protest, which they feel has become male-dominated and unnecessarily aggressive. For them it's not about ripping down statues either, but about questioning the history of racial exclusion, which translates – in their experience – into a very real sense of alienation for students from non-white backgrounds today, both in interactions with the university and in those with fellow students.

'It really disappoints me about my friends,' says Melissa, who is studying PPE, as I did. She is half Sri Lankan, her straight hair in a chin-length bob framing large, black-rimmed glasses. 'They organised a politics dinner, and it turned out that all the POCs [people of colour] were put at one end of the table. So it was the tutors and all these white boys all around them at one end, and all the women in the middle, and all the POCs at the other end. When I pointed it out, they said "but that's because you are all friends with each other". But we are not even friends! We are just not-white, that's all!'

'The amount of times I've heard *"Oooh, I've never slept with a black girl before"*,' says Jasmine, a tall, slim, black English undergraduate with ombré hair and full cheeks when she smiles. 'That sense of tokenism. When I meet guys, I'm never quite sure if I'm just some sort of fetish. Or if it's just like they genuinely like you.'

Interactions with college staff can be regular, if relatively trivial, frustrations, the women explain. They share the experience of my friends and me, when we were at Oxford, being refused entry into the colleges that all other students could enter freely, because the porters did not believe they were enrolled at the University. 'It's really small things,' says Jasmine. 'I'm the Junior Common Room welfare officer for our college, so I'm always popping into the lodge. There are only four black girls in our college, and I'm the one who's always there on welfare business. But the porter still always manages to get our names confused,' she says.

Similarly for my generation, discrimination was often subtle, and we lacked the confidence to take it on. Not so these students – it's clear from talking to Jasmine and her friends that they won't just tolerate 'microaggressions' – they have a word now for the regular acts, more often than not meant without any intended malice, that constantly serve to remind these students that there is something 'unconventional' or 'other' about their presence at a historic university.

These microaggressions often have a cumulative effect for young women already dealing with the loneliness of being away from home for the first time, and all the body consciousness, political awakening and insecurity that come with being a nineteen-year-old anywhere, let alone at a university such as Oxford which can be notoriously gruelling in the pressure of its academic demands. It's a combination that is crowned by an aggressively white, old-fashioned and sometimes stifling curriculum.

'We did a module on the Victorian era and the Industrial Revolution, and it wasn't even covered – the fact that a lot of the money for the Industrial Revolution came from colonialism,' says Jasmine. 'I discussed that with my tutor, and that fact that we weren't getting the full picture, and he was like *"Oh yeah, I didn't even realise"*.'

'With classics, I've kind of given up,' says Ella, an energetic mixed-heritage student with natural curly hair dyed blonde, referring to her degree on the ancient Graeco-Roman world. 'As a subject, it's inherently racist, it's inherently Eurocentric. Even the title "Classics", when you're only talking about Greece and Rome – it erases so many other cultures. And then there's the way they talk about "the East" or "the Turks" . . .'

'It's really interesting,' Jasmine interjects, 'that we are taught to think critically and be so intellectual. And yet when that results in us re-examining the institution that is teaching us to do that, it's kind of like "pipe down, just listen to what we are telling you".' And that is essentially exactly what the university said. When #RhodesMustFall confronted the then vice chancellor Chris Patten about the elevation of racists like Rhodes, and the erasure of black people from the curriculum, arguing they should be included not on the grounds of political correctness, but on the grounds of historical fact and academic integrity, his response was simple. If students don't like the 'generosity of spirit' shown to historical figures like Rhodes, Patten said, they should 'think about being educated elsewhere'.[74]

These experiences reveal the real power of British imperialism. It was not just controlling vast tracts of land, emptying precious minerals to fuel Britain's growth, nor even the official subordination of local traditions and governance. It was the mental regime, the intellectual brainwashing, inflicting upon Africans the belief that they were people who had no history, had achieved nothing, and contributed nothing to humanity, apart from their capacity to live in mud huts, make simple crafts, grow and extract from the land with ease – for the enrichment of Britain's coffers – have sex and reproduce. It was the idea that colonised people were no more than children, children that needed the firm hand of a British parent.

There have been some attempts to acknowledge the role of black people, African countries and diasporas as part of British history. It's just frustrating that this is being done in a way that subliminally endorses the view that it's only worth studying for one month of the year, each October, before reverting to 'white history' as usual. Britain has no 'white history'. British history is the multiracial, interracial story of a nation interdependent on trade, cultural influence and immigration from Africa, India, Central and East Asia, and other regions and continents populated by people who are not white, and before that, invasion by successive waves of European tribes most of whom, had the concept of whiteness existed at the time, would not have fitted into it either.

Even more irritating is Black History Month's indefatigably celebratory tone. The attempt to 'celebrate' black history echoes a worrying trend in the study of history generally. Michael Gove, education secretary in David Cameron's government, spoke of the role of history in schools as being to 'celebrate the distinguished role of these islands in the history of the world'[75] and portray Britain as 'a beacon of liberty for others to emulate'.[76] It's hard to see how framing British history as such a happy event could ever accommodate the truth of its relationship with the African, Indian, Native American, aboriginal and countless other peoples, in some cases entire races who barely survived it. Yet it's a position whose spirit – if not its content – is echoed by the growing Black History Month fan club.

Toni Morrison, one of the foremost storytellers of my lifetime, captured the futility of 'celebrating' black history, with a powerful speech in 1975. 'It's important to know . . . the very serious function of racism, which is distraction,' Morrison told students at Portland State University. 'It keeps you from doing your work. It keeps you explaining over and over your reason for being. Somebody says you have no language, so you spend 20 years proving that you do. Somebody says your head isn't shaped properly, so you have scientists working on the fact that it is. Somebody says you have no art, so you dredge that up. Somebody says you have no kingdoms, so you dredge that up. None of that is necessary. There will always be one more thing.'[77]

Acknowledging the presence of black people in history is not, and should not be, a celebration, or an attempt to *prove* that black lives have meaning and legacy. A version of history that includes black

protagonists is just fact. British history involves immigration stretching back thousands of years, and black immigration for at least two
millennia. Black people profited from the worst episodes of exploitation in British history. Black campaigners were also involved in some
of the most transformative social movements for democratic reform,
free speech and individual and collective rights.

Olaudah Equiano, the former slave whose work was so influential
in the abolitionist movement, joined the London Corresponding
Society and worked side by side with its founder, Thomas Hardy.[78] The
Society would emerge as one of Britain's strongest working-class
organisations at the end of the eighteenth century, and Hardy believed
that 'an advocate from principle for liberty for a Black Man will . . .
strenuously promote and support the rights of a White Man & visa
versa'.[79] William Davidson, a cabinetmaker born in Jamaica but sent to
Edinburgh as a teenager, was at the heart of the Spencean movement –
the ultra-left-wing group that was radicalised by the famine and deepening poverty suffered by the English poor during the Napoleonic
Wars. Davidson was hanged alongside his fellow conspirators after a
failed plot to assassinate members of the Cabinet, their heads then
severed from their bodies with a knife, in what turned out to be the
last public decapitation in England.[80] There was so much blood that
the coffins lined up nearby were strewn with sawdust to soak it up.
Robert Wedderburn, another black man at the centre of the Spencean
movement, had disagreed with the plot. Born to a slave mother in
Jamaica, Wedderburn was a tailor who emerged as a major radical
thinker, and who blended his calls for insurrection in the West Indies
with the redistribution of wealth in Britain.[81] He also spent time in jail
for sedition and blasphemous libel and, like Davidson had done, used
his trial as a soapbox, declaring 'there seems to be a conspiracy against
the poor, to keep them in ignorance and superstition'. The lord chief
justice complimented Wedderburn on the quality of his defence, but
he was still sent to jail – part of a movement that was instrumental in
the birth of free speech, a value so highly prized as fundamental to
British values today.

Black activists would continue to be an integral part of the radical left through the centuries. The famous Caribbean writer and poet Claude McKay thought the racism he encountered in Edwardian London intolerable, but found some brief respite in the solidarity of allies in the left-wing press. He formed a close relationship with Sylvia Pankhurst, the socialist and suffragette daughter of Emmeline Pankhurst, and the *Workers' Dreadnought*, her left-wing publication, was the only one to give him a platform.[82] Sylvia Pankhurst's beliefs about female suffrage and racial equality went hand in hand – as well as giving a platform to black voices in the *Workers' Dreadnought*, she was a patron of the International African Service Bureau, a group which saw pan-Africanism as 'an independent political expression of Negro aspirations for complete national independence from white domination'. But her mother did not concur. Emmeline Pankhurst, celebrated for her devotion to women's rights, was less interested in the rights of African and Asian women. She followed a path favoured by the suffragettes towards the political right, standing as a Conservative MP and becoming a staunch defender of the empire, extolling the profits Britain could reap from its colonies, which were, she said, 'great in territory, great in potential wealth'. It was an imperialism that suffused the suffragette movement, with the non-white women who did participate relegated to a supporting role.[83]

The true complexity of British history is beginning, for the first time, to enter the popular imagination. In 2016, Olusoga's BBC documentary describing the presence of Africans in Britain from at least Roman times brought some viewers to tears. 'I wish people learnt black Brit history,' wrote Charlene White, the black TV anchor for ITV news. 'The way we see our amazing country could be so different.'[84] It would certainly have been different for me.

The trouble with the British, observed Salman Rushdie, is that they don't know their history, because so much of it happened overseas.[85] But every British person has some personal connection to these hidden 'overseas' adventures. Living with this past has often been a lonely experience, like walking a quiet path, full of shadowy ghost sightings, and having to reconcile those with the popular version of Britain propagated through its mainstream historical narrative. I see a history of black contributions all over this country, almost never acknowledged, while the statues and buildings and books in the visible environment suggest a sanitised, even misleading facade.

Reassessing British history is not about race, it's about integrity. It's not about separating out who to celebrate for the good, and who to blame for the bad. It's about the fact that the past is linked to the present in a smooth continuity, from slavery, colonialism and the pillaging of resources to immigration and even today's waves of 'marauding' African migrants, the word chosen by the foreign secretary in 2015, to describe refugees from conflicts which Britain, in a number of cases, had a hand in creating.[86] Seeing things differently would affect reality for everyone.

It is *our* history, as British people. If we were able to see a different version of it – not a carefully curated, highly selective, politically convenient one, but an honest one, in all its nuances – it might give us all a chance to carve our individual and collective relationship with Britain in a more realistic way. That might allow Britain to evolve out of its current state of ideological conflict, in which white British identities are pitted against others, in spite of the shared past from which those identities have emerged. For people like me, born into the midst of this conflict which we played no part in creating, that might make Britishness an identity that we could more easily embrace.

3. BODIES

'Erosion', Imani Love and Daniel Stewart, 2016.

Beauty was not simply something to behold; it was something one could do.

– Toni Morrison, The Bluest Eye

It's past midnight, November 2016, in Dunstable – a small town in Bedfordshire, just outside Greater London's intricately veined and brightly lit web. It's the coldest hour of the coldest night of the year so far. The pubs have vomited staggering older women out onto the street, bent double after a long shift drinking. The newspapers say that this is a 'ghost town', a symbol of how ordinary provincial centres are still struggling to recover from the recession of 2008, shopfronts boarded up and closed down, like heavy eyelids shutting out the world.[1]

My friend Miranda has accompanied me here for moral support. We scale a no-frills metal staircase at the fag end of an alleyway behind the high street, where a weary blonde woman is ruling a domain of coats, cash, lists and tickets. Her wrinkles are heavily caked in too-orange powder, and she has a defeated manner, like the only sober person at a party when everyone is drunk. I look awful. I'm wearing a too-big red dress stitched together by a very mediocre tailor in Senegal more than a decade ago. I have no idea why I decided to make myself look quite so dowdy. Miranda is doing much better; she has obediently put on a basque, along with a skirt much shorter than mine, she's tall and the boots I've lent her have elongated her already long legs. She's calmer than me too. I've given fake names to come here, names that make us sound Jewish. It was the easiest way of manipulating our actual names without revealing the fact that we are both black. If we'd have sounded black, I'm not sure we would have been allowed in.

As it's our first time, Eddie – a solid black man, dressed in the standard-issue suit and armband of a bouncer – has been asked to show us around. His presence is a comforting one; he seems like an island of sanity in a sea of grotesque chaos. The first thing I see, once Eddie has led us past the dance floor and the bar, is a shaven-headed black man on his knees on a large bed, pumping himself into a white woman on all fours, doggy-style. He is wearing an unbuttoned shirt, and nothing else, but she is more or less fully dressed in her basque, suspenders and boots. He seems to have just brushed her underwear aside to enter her from behind. Another man is kneeling next to him, waiting for his turn. To the left, on the same sateen-effect mattress, a woman is kneeling with her back to us, clothed on top but naked from the waist down. A man has his hand on her ample butt cheeks, and is rubbing them vigorously. Other men hover around the bed, perched on the end, or just standing up at the edge of the room, beers in hand, watching. 'This is one of our playrooms,' Eddie says helpfully. 'It's not too bad now, but it gets very busy later on.'

Arousals is like no place I have ever been before; part nightclub, part seedy brothel and part all-out orgy. As Eddie continues his tour, we turn through a dark maze of cheaply lit corridors, their walls decorated with tacky art – a pair of breasts with leather tassels dangling from exaggerated nipples, a masked, topless woman sucking her fingers, half-hearted pop-art prints of pole dancing. We pass endless private rooms – locked, for couples who aren't in the mood for an audience – and toilets, a shower, a cinema where five white men are sitting at the back, drinking, half talking, half watching a large, erect, veiny black penis entering a woman's mouth in slow motion.

We venture further into the recesses of the building, into what Eddie describes as 'the dungeon'. There is a gold-effect throne at the end, with red upholstery, and a series of skulls that belong in a toddler's Halloween party. In pride of place is a swing, with a series of red ropes and buckles from which suspends a reclining black leather seat. 'The sex swing is very popular,' Eddie suggests. Some men reach out to touch us, but retreat when they see Eddie following behind. 'A pair of unicorns,' they exclaim, surprised. There are no phones allowed inside Arousals, so I look this up later, and realise it's a swingers' thing; the term they use to describe single women at swinging events, because single women are 'rare, precious and very welcome'.

At the end of the tour, Eddie gives us some words of advice. 'People are usually respectful, but it can get hairy by the end of the night. You know, by then some of the guys who maybe haven't seen any action start to feel like they want their money's worth.' The risk of being grabbed increases, he warns, so we should stay alert.

Welcome to the Black Man's Fan Club – a monthly swingers' night for white women who want to have sex with black men, and their white husbands or partners who want to watch. In the ethnically un-diverse world of swingers – couples and individuals who like to have sex, and watch their partners have sex, with other people – the BMFC is marketed as a community of people who 'appreciate the extras black men bring'. The promotional material tends to depict white women, albeit young, slim, porn-star-like white women – who bear very little resemblence to the real-life guests at Arousals – having sex with dark-skinned, clean-shaven black men with perfectly defined abs and huge cocks. Tonight's flyer features an intensely fake-tanned white girl wearing briefs that read in large letters across her crotch 'I heart black . . .'; the previous month's showed a pale-skinned woman, her legs crossed around a black man's torso, digging her nails into his mus-cular back. The contrast in skin tone was exaggerated, for effect. Members of the community – both white women and black men – are active on Twitter, where they share pictures of exceptionally large, erect black penises and rough sex, in which a black man clearly, powerfully dominates. Hashtag: #blackdick.

BMFC, the punters tell me, is one of a kind, but of course the sen-timent doesn't end in Dunstable. In an era of mass porn consumption, black male porn actors having sex with white women is a specific and popular subgenre, and BMWW (black man white woman) erotic novels specifically cater to the fantasy of crudely stereotyped black male aggression and sexual domination. It's as if the online commer-cialisation of sexual fantasy has globalised racial stereotypes and sent them freewheeling backwards; it doesn't take any imagination at all to surmise exactly what swingers mean when they say they so appreciate the 'extras' black men bring.

'There are three reasons why the women come here,' explains Leslie, one of the black men who are here to be, in BMFC parlance, 'appreciated'. Leslie has just come out of a playroom when he approaches me, and has barely bothered to put his clothes back on, his flies low, shirt open, sticking to his sweaty chest, and tie a mere gesture, hung nonchalantly around his neck. He's a good-looking guy, with a toned physique and neatly twisted locks, pulled back into a half-ponytail. 'One [reason is] black men have bigger penises.' That's a stereotype, I argue. 'It's not a stereotype!' he replies. 'Black men are built differently. You have to acknowledge nature . . . Number two,' Leslie continues, 'black men have better rhythm in bed. That's also a fact. And thirdly, they are just more dominant. You know a lot of these women are not satisfied by their husbands who want them to do all the work. They want to feel a strong man inside them, dominating them. They want an alpha male. That's what they get here,' he smiles at me, knowingly.

Leslie is leery, having drunk too much cognac, and has a tendency to lean precariously towards me when seeking my agreement. It's just one of any number of factors that make this experience so unsettling. I know it's a sex club, but surely there are inexperienced guests too, uncertain about how far they want to go, surely not everyone wants to have sex with everyone who asks. It doesn't feel that way in this dingy club, where it's clear just having walked through the door is interpreted by everyone I meet as some kind of giant leap towards sexual consent. The boundaries are scarily absent. I can see Miranda out of the corner of my eye, looking as if she feels similarly unnerved.

She's speaking to Leslie's friend Darren, who – she later relayed – is telling her he works as a carer for elderly and disabled people in a nursing home. He describes himself as a 'freak' and says BMFC is where he comes to indulge his sexual fantasies. Both men are surprisingly happy to answer my increasingly probing questions. I *want* to understand. I knew there would be white couples, I foresaw their characteristics; older, suburban. But I assumed the men would be sex workers, strippers, or otherwise paid or incentivised guests, whose role was to perform the required services. But these are unremarkable, middle-class black men. Leslie is friendly enough, even though it's probably dawning on him gradually that I'm not going to be doing any playing. Or maybe he thinks this is my idea of foreplay.

When I ask both men if they feel fetishised because of their race, they vigorously deny it. 'Black men *do* have extras,' they laugh. Later, speaking to Leslie alone again, I say, 'Why do you come here?' He shrugs. 'I come for the sex. Where else can you go and have sex as many times as you like? Plus, it's a nice vibe; there are no pretences. Everyone is here to get laid, have a good time, it's really friendly, you can walk up to anyone, everyone wants to meet people. It's not like a normal club where everyone has a poker face on. No one's judging.'

Swinging is not my thing, but I couldn't care less what consenting adults get up to behind closed doors. It's not the sex at the Black Man's Fan Club that bothers me, it's the racial stereotyping. It feels so regressive. It feels as if it's just the latest chapter in a history of sexual stereotyping towards Africans – a history so long and loaded, it stands apart from other contemporary fetishes, such as redheads or blondes, MILFs or body types.

Why are black men willing to actually embrace the myths of hyper-sexuality and abnormally large endowment? 'The number of things that have been said about black men in this country for the most part have been about as negative as you can possibly get,' Professor Herbert Samuels, relaying the African American experience, offers as one explanation. 'If someone says that you are good at sex or that your penis is bigger than anyone else's, that's about the only positive that you can get out of all those negatives to a certain extent. And I think some black men have bought into the myth that they are hyper-sexual, that their sexual prowess and the size, the physicality is greater than others'.'[2]

And this is what really unsettles me about the Black Man's Fan Club. Not just the fact that black men's self-esteem could be so low that this would be a welcome boost, but the fact that everyone in Arousals is, one way or another, unquestioningly complicit in a set of beliefs that have ancient and horrible roots.

When Europeans first came into contact with the African continent, they indulged in an imaginative riot of fantasy. Elizabethan travel books contained a heady mix of fact and pure invention, which confused English readers and popularised wildly fictional versions of the place and its people.[3] For example, *A Summary of the Antiquities, and wonders of the Worlde* published in 1566 reproduced, matter-of-factly, Pliny-era myths as if they were contemporary realities. It revealed tribes with no noses, others with no tongues, others ruled by dogs, some which were cannibal, and some who had eyes and mouths in their breasts. 'Like animals,' one account reported, Africans would 'fall upon their women, just as they come to hand, without any choice'. African men had enormous penises, these accounts suggested, and naked figures depicted on contemporary maps further popularised the belief.[4] In Guinea, reported one writer, the people were 'very lecherous',[5] while another described the 'extraordinary greatness' of their 'members' and the black men that bore them as 'very lustful and impudent'.[6] One writer went so far as to claim that African men were 'furnisht with such members as are after a sort burthensome unto them'.[7] Othello's embraces were, unforgettably, the 'gross clasps of the lascivious Moor'.[8]

Stereotypes about the sexual prowess of black people have been a constant feature of history ever since the first European contact with Africa, and have an equally illustrious presence in literature, journalism and art. The Mandingo Warrior, for example, immortalised by the slave rebel leader Dred in the 1852 novel *Uncle Tom's Cabin*, represented the ultimate African alpha male, dark, muscled and bristling with phallic weapons. It was a hugely influential image. Author Harriet Beecher Stowe lived to see her book become the best-seller of the century, after the Bible, and many of its stereotypes were absorbed by popular culture: the affectionate, dark-skinned mammy; the piccaninny children; and the Uncle Tom, or dutiful, long-suffering servant faithful to his white master or mistress.[9] Britain's left-leaning publications like the *Daily Herald* – which by 1920 had a circulation of more than 300,000[10] – ran front-page stories with headlines like 'BLACK SCOURGE IN

EUROPE: SEXUAL HORROR LET LOOSE BY FRANCE ON THE RHINE'. The author of that splash in 1920, E. D. Morel – who incidentally played a major role in bringing down the murderous rule of Belgium's King Leopold in the Congo, and who was also editor of *Foreign Affairs*, the respected journal still published today – complained that the 'barely restrainable bestiality' of black troops stationed in Europe after the end of the First World War had led to many rapes, which was particularly serious because Africans were 'the most developed sexually' of any race – a 'terror and a horror unimaginable'.[11]

Black men are still unfairly portrayed as rapists – not least by US President Donald Trump who in 1989 called for the death penalty for five black teenagers, the so-called 'Central Park Five' convicted of raping a female jogger in New York. Their convictions were later overturned and the miscarriage of justice these young men had suffered exposed. But in 2014, Trump still refused to accept their innocence. He told a journalist this stance would 'help' in his campaign for the presidency,[12] and he found many receptive audiences for his racially loaded claim, campaign in full swing, that Mexico was sending its 'rapists' to America. Stereotypes of black men and other ethnic minority men as sexually threatening on the one hand, and sexually desirable on the other, are two sides of the same hyper-sexuality myth. The former continue in inaccurate data spreading virally on social media, pointing to the false statistics about the prevalence of sexual assaults by black men. The latter have filtered into popular culture, such as the sayings, widespread when I was at school and university, that white women who have sex with black men have 'jungle fever', and that 'once you go black, you never go back'. They are implicit in the belief, internalised by Leslie at the BMFC, that black men have 'extras' in bed.

Knowing that the black men I saw in Dunstable were enthusiastically embracing these age-old stereotypes about black male sexuality – internalising, even celebrating them, reinforcing them with every thrust – only made the experience more upsetting.

My friend Sarah has a far less diplomatic way of putting it. 'Black man's fan clubs are where stupid black men act like a bunch of

Mandingos, and these highly unattractive white housewives go with their husbands, and get tanked out by them,' she declares. Sarah knows a lot about the swinging scene because, together with her husband, she has been a keen and devoted swinger for a decade. If there is a stereotype of your average British swinger, Sarah is not it. She is black, so is her husband, in a scene that is known to be predominantly white. Throughout their years of marriage, they have frequented swinging parties, and as their age and earning power have increased, they've developed a taste for high-end events, which require expensive annual memberships and rigorous vetting of one's appearance, income and personal background.

Sarah loves these parties. She describes the pleasure – you can see her mouth savouring the words – of pampering and preening, slipping on expensive underwear and a cocktail gown, looking and smelling exquisite, knowing that every ounce of effort will be explored and appreciated by imminent numerous sexual partners of both sexes. She talks about arriving, the breathtaking impression of the venues – imposing stately homes in beautiful, landscaped gardens, her husband in black tie by her side, being served champagne and oysters, and talking, mingling, meeting other like-minded and often impressive couples. Then, she explains, the lights – or is it just the inhibitions? – are dimmed, people begin retreating to a series of decadent playrooms, and the 'playing' begins.

Sometimes Sarah and her husband notice, when they arrive, a sharp intake of breath. 'We don't tend to have issues with people of our generation – the ones who went to the same schools as us, and probably had girlfriends who were black or white, and for whom race wasn't such a thing,' she explains. 'But when it comes to the older generation who are probably racist by day – the CEOs, the managing directors – we have walked in and felt those people, I mean literally felt them, looking at us and thinking "*uuuhh . . . will I get a chance with them?*" It's gross.' Sarah shakes her head. 'We are not here to be fetishised.'

But a risk of being fetishised is more or less a hazard of the hobby. 'We have had weird experiences,' Sarah admits. 'I remember there was this one French couple; the woman was all writhing against the wall in her Agent Provocateur underwear. And her husband was the one who found people for her. He came up to me and was like "Your husband . . . can we? My wife loves black men." And I was like *"no, he's not available"*. When people say to me "I love black men", instead of saying that you just love men, that tells me it's a fetish you've got, like it gives you like a shuddering orgasm just the thought of a black person. It's a shame black people actually capitalise on that. Because it makes me feel so dirty afterwards.'

In contrast to the Black Man's Fan Club, at Sarah's high-end swinging parties, where men and women are almost all white, black women have just as much exotic appeal. 'They look at me as if they are thinking *"Oh my God, what's she gonna do, backflips?"* I keep telling people, we all have the same anatomy. I have a vagina, you have a vagina. What, do you think it's got a flipping motor in it?

'I've had guys, me and my husband laugh, these people are so repressed.' Sarah chuckles. 'You just have to talk to them sometimes, and they're like, shaking. They just can't believe they are going to touch a black woman. I know as a black woman I am always gonna be fetishised to an extent – and the darker you are, the more you are.

'They think we are naturally very sensual,' Sarah continues, 'all of us are Rihanna; we are very raw, and so in touch with our sexuality . . . we can make a man come just by looking at him.' She laughs at the absurdity of the perception. 'The way that we move our bodies . . . they are very threatened by us. But secretly, they want to be with us, they want to be like us, they want to taste us and touch us. If they could, they would have one of us in their houses in a room, just kept there, for when needed. That's exactly what they did do not that long ago! And they'd love it again. There's so much about us that they love.'

It's weird to hear an educated, sophisticated British person speaking in such crude racial stereotypes, 'us' as these forbidden black fruits that 'they' are salivating with repressed appetites to sample. But then all the evidence I've seen suggests that sex and relationships are one of the last remaining bastions of naked, unreconstructed racial prejudice. Listening to Sarah is eerily reminiscent of seventeenth-century accounts, which described African women as sexual predators; 'if they meet with a Man they immediately strip his lower parts, and throw themselves on him . . . and use all their little Arts to move the darling Passion,' claimed one account.[13] We are doubly unlikely to confront this openly – hampered as we are by awkwardness around speaking to others about both race and intimacy. But it's not just about sex. Sex is, in some ways, a very tangible example of the deeper currents of prejudice and stereotype that have colonised our individual and collective psyches, through inherited beliefs.

As a brutally self-conscious teenage girl in suburban London, one of my earliest experiences of having a black identity was the way boys behaved towards me. We can laugh now, but twenty years ago, it felt very cruel. Teenagers from the neighbouring boys' school – one of the most elite and privileged private schools in the country – were among the most merciless. They made jokes about rumours they'd heard, that black girls 'give good head', and have 'more pussy'. It was a lot for a fourteen-year-old girl, just waking up to her sexuality, as well as her increasingly confusing racial identity, to bear.

My experience is less surprising when you consider that there were straight-faced academic attempts to normalise these sexual stereotypes well into the twentieth century. It was perfectly understandable that 'most young Southern men doubtless had their initial sexual experience with a compliant slave girl', explained historian Charles Page Smith, an award-winning emeritus professor whose book on the subject was published in 1970. 'It was not unnatural that many of them should continue to indulge themselves after their marriages . . . there was undoubtedly the attraction of the perverse, of the taboo, the association of darkness with pleasant wickedness . . . Moreover there was the tradition of Negro sensuality which may well have worked to make the white wife a more restrained sexual partner.'[14]

Black women were hyper-sexual, but not beautiful, and that is an important distinction. Beauty was, in some respects, the first racism. European chroniclers of Africa were keen to cast the African body as the darkness that contrasted to the light of whiteness, the supposed ugliness of its women as proof of the beauty and superiority of the white female form. 'Black skin was . . . used to highlight the presumed superiority and beauty of whiteness,' writes Olusoga in his important book *Black and British: A Forgotten History*, 'in an age in which both women and men whitened their skin with lead powder, which slowly poisoned them and ironically resulted in the slow blackening of their skin.'[15] Like their audacious claims about African male sexuality, writers, historians, diarists and intellectuals presented the black body as proof of Africans' greater proximity to animals, as part of a pseudo-scientific, intellectual justification for slavery.

No body part was exempt from this analysis. The hair of black people was, historian Edward Long wrote in the eighteenth century, a 'covering of wool, like the bestial fleece'.[16] The 'thick projection of the lower parts of the face, and the thick lips evidently approximate [the black person] to the monkey tribe', claimed Swiss anatomist Georges Cuvier. Black women had breasts which were, wrote French anthropologist J. J. Virey, 'large, flaccid and pendulous',[17] or, in the words of English merchant and politician William Towerson, 'very foule and long, hanging down like the udder of a goate'.[18] The sum total of the experience was that, early travellers said, Africans were 'dreadful to look upon'. Their perceived ugliness made it easier to deprive them of humanity, or the same interest in decency, integrity or complex emotional experiences which were accepted as part of white women's experience.

The African American feminist writer bell hooks dissects these dynamics like no one else. I remember reading her book *Ain't I a Woman* as an undergraduate student, and feeling like I had spent my whole life up until that point underwater, and was then experiencing, for the first time ever, the sensation of coming up for a gulp of air. A huge, loud, life-saving, relief-pumped gulp. Hooks explains how the dynamics of slavery and colonialism devalued the black woman's body with permanent effect. 'In the Victorian world, where white women were religiously covering every body part, black women were daily stripped of their clothing and publicly whipped.[19] Writing more than thirty years ago – the book was published in 1981, the year of my birth – hooks grounded her polemic in the US, a country in which the black woman's body was fundamental to economic growth; they had to be used to breed future generations of slaves, and then as labour to pick the cotton and sugar on which income depended. But she could equally have been writing about Britain, whose imperial ambitions depended for so many centuries on African slavery. 'White women and men justified the sexual exploitation of the enslaved black woman by arguing that they were the initiators of sexual relationships with men,' hooks writes. 'From such thinking emerged the stereotype of black women as sexual savages, and in sexist terms a sexual savage, a non-human, an animal cannot be raped.'[20]

For most of its history, mainstream feminism did a bad job of accommodating the specific experiences of black women. Early suffragettes in Britain were often pro-imperialist as we've seen was the case with Emmeline Pankhurst; some of America's most favourite campaigners for female suffrage were famously pro-segregation. The scale and shamelessness of slavery-era sexual violence towards black women may have died down by the twentieth century, but it left behind a complex and painful legacy.

Take dating, for example. The vast majority of people, in all countries and from all cultural backgrounds, enter into relationships with people from the same racial, ethnic or cultural-linguistic group. That applies as much to everyone – Chinese Americans, Muslim West Africans, Indian Hindus. In Britain, as we'll see, black people are far more likely to enter into interracial relationships than other non-white groups. That simple fact belies, however, some quite distinct patterns. It's not black *people* entering into a rainbow of interracial relationships; on the whole, the statistics show it's black *men* entering into relationships with white women.

That creates, in simple terms, a shortage. For black women, doing what most people do and seeking a partner of the same ethnic background as them, the odds are not in their favour. One consequence is that there are many black women in Britain with no prior experience of interracial relationships, now seeking them, only to find their new-found open-mindedness is not reciprocated.

One anecdotal example of this is my friend Yvonne. Frustrated at being single in her late thirties and hoping to find a serious long-term partner, Yvonne invested several thousand pounds in an expensive matchmaking service in Mayfair. She's a strikingly attractive black woman and impeccably groomed – hair and nails always freshly done – with a well-paid job in banking. She decided it was an invest-ment worth making to find a partner who, like her, works in the City and would share her ambition and outlook in life. With two black par-ents, and a mainly black social circle, she had always imagined herself with a black partner. But the paucity of single black men with similar lifestyles led her to consider dating someone of a different race. The problem was, she never received any apparent expressions of interest from the single white men she knew. She was frustrated at feeling invisible next to her male colleagues. Perhaps she wasn't giving off the right vibes, she told herself. In the hands of a bespoke matchmaking service, she decided, which spent hours eliciting intimate details of her personality, interests and views on relationships, a good deal of time-wasting would be stripped away. At least she *thought* that's what would happen. In the end, the service ended up refunding her money because, they told her apologetically, they could not find her a date – not one single match. None of the men on their database was willing to seriously date a black woman. Some were open to casual romance, but had stated that they would not consider one as a long-term partner, or a wife. 'Most of the men have homes in the country and do rural activities on the weekend,' Yvonne said, repeating to me what the matchmaking company had told her. She was matter-of-fact, as if it was somehow obvious that a black woman might dissolve when exposed to a non-'urban' environment, a bit like Dracula in the light of the sun.

Studies suggest that this is happening on a wider scale. Online matchmaking services, for example, have been becoming more aware of the prejudice alive on their sites. A study of Yahoo! Personals profiles revealed only 7 per cent of men on that site were willing to date black women. OKCupid, after studying the messaging patterns of more than one million users, concluded on its official blog that, with online dating, black women got the 'cold shoulder' and 'racism is alive and well'. The reason, according to one study, is that black women are 'too bossy'.[21]

The problem with these kinds of stereotypes – other than the fact they originate in racist ideology – is that they both repel and attract people for the wrong reasons. Yvonne didn't want a boyfriend who would feel hostile to a fictional, perceived 'bossiness', based on her race, any more than she wanted a boyfriend deliberately seeking it. The seminal writer Frantz Fanon famously declared, 'when people like me, they tell me it is in spite of my colour. When they dislike me, they point out that it is not because of my colour. Either way, I am locked into the infernal circle.'[22] To Fanon's thought, I would add: when people desire me, they tell me it is *because* of my colour. Many black women are aware of being seen through this stereotype-laden lens, in turn making them feel suspicious of the motives of the men who do approach them, making a genuine connection even harder, another of Fanon's 'infernal circles'. I remember this suspicion as a teenager, feeling that white boys and men, for whom I was often the first black woman they had ever met, did not see *me*, but whatever it was – exotic, freaky, supernatural, strong or otherwise – that they were projecting onto my blackness.

This is an experience that has transcended generations. Women who arrived in Britain as part of the Windrush generation of post-war Caribbean migrant workers, recruited by the government to work in the public sector after the war, were met with hurtful sexual expectations. 'The white men in Cambridge didn't want us as girlfriends, they just wanted to sleep with us,' said Barbara McLeod, who arrived in Cambridge from Jamaica in the 1950s as a seventeen-year-old nurse. '[They] would say: "I'm sure you're good in bed" because there was this false assumption that black women were sexually voracious.'[23]

McLeod was interviewed for a *Guardian* article in 1999, in which a black journalist, Omega Douglas, spoke to three black women from different generations about the way they felt perceived by white society. Aged eighteen and having just finished my A levels, I was the youngest to be interviewed. 'I've never dated a white guy,' her report quotes me as saying. 'Certainly when I was younger, I was very suspicious of white guys who dated black women. It seemed to me the forbidden fruit syndrome – wanting what was considered taboo. I didn't want to be an experiment, so I stayed well away from them.' It was true, but naively revealing it in a national newspaper wasn't necessarily the best of strategies. When I joined the *Guardian* as a senior correspondent almost exactly ten years later, a resourceful reporter had scoured the internal archive, looking for my name, and circulated that article around the newsroom in an email titled, *You won't believe who our new legal affairs correspondent is!*

And so as a professional, the observations have continued. A senior male boss at one broadcaster, with responsibility for keeping things presentable on screen, commented, 'I'm not being racist, but I do think that an Afro takes up too much of the screen,' referring to my curly, non-straightened hair. Another senior consultant, also a middle-aged white man, shared his concerns that my legs were too muscular for TV. There was a time when I would internalise these remarks; scrutinise myself under the gaze of those who made them, and find myself coming up short. My diary entries aged fourteen make for painful reading.

'I have had enough of my figure, it is so disgusting,' I wrote. 'I must have the biggest arse in existence. I WILL lose weight.' There was never anything wrong with me. I was just curvier and stronger than my white friends. It was so unbearable that I began retreating from my body altogether. 'When I look in the mirror, I can't feel anything, I can't even read the eyes. I feel no recognition, no passion, no love, no hatred, just nothing. I don't like the girl in the mirror. I want her to bugger off, I want her to go away.'

There is nothing original about a fourteen-year-old girl experiencing self-disgust, nor am I suggesting it's in any way limited to teenagers of ethnic minority or mixed-race heritage. All I know is my own experience, and the fact that in my case, all my self-hatred was centred on this sense of otherness. My appearance was the opposite of every single image of beauty that passed before my eyes. Where my school friends, films, pop stars, magazines, advertisements, even packaging, showed me fair skin or suntanned beauty, I was irredeemably brown. Where they were slender, I had curves. Where they had button noses that complemented their faces, I had a large one that dominated mine.

And most of all, where they had straight, floppy, feathered hair, I had frizzy, tightly coiled curls. I had that hair, in an area where there were no Afro-hair shops for miles around, in an era – the mid-1990s – that was the heyday of Pantene, of Jennifer Aniston's iconic smooth and feathered cut, of John Frieda Frizz-Ease. I remember the endless advertising campaigns for these products, promising as they did that they could immediately and miraculously solve the problem of frizzy hair. I can only infer that what was on my head was outside the realms of what they considered 'hair'. I saved up my pocket money for each of these products the moment I caught wind of their release, and embarked on a pilgrimage to my local Boots, anticipating some kind of healing from the disease of being black. And I cried each time the truth revealed itself under the harsh light of a bathroom mirror. They did nothing for me. They were never designed with me in mind. People with hair like mine were so invisible that the manufacturers didn't even acknowledge us in their acts of exclusion.

My hair defined me. It was too frizzy to be European hair, this my school friends pointed out with endless curiosity. Can I brush it? Why does it stand up straight in the air? How often do you wash it? What's that stuff you put in it? Why don't you ever wear it loose? But my hair was too flyaway and fine to be Afro. The black hairdressers struggled with it, it couldn't take the grease they wanted to use, it straightened too easily under the torment of hot tongs, and sprung back too readily under the influence of nothing less than fresh air, the kinks setting in the minute the blow-dryer or hot tongs or straightening irons went cool. My hair refused to be obeyed by all except my mother's firm, plaiting hand. And even her hair discipline was not enough to tame my halo for a whole day. Eventually my two plaits, or the ponytail she had resolutely twisted into the shape of an upside-down Mr Whippy swirl, to control the frizzy ends, had unravelled, staking its place in the atmosphere.

Being black is like having beauty special needs. The hairdressers on the high street have no idea how to do your hair – asking them to is a humiliating experience in which various white stylists are summoned, finger your tresses and mutter to each other shaking their heads, until someone tells you, forced smile creasing the corners of their eyes, 'I'm sorry, we can't do hair like yours here.' The shampoo and conditioner for sale in supermarkets and chemists on the high street assume European hair, so do the little bottles provided in hotel bathrooms – even, infuriatingly, in hotels in Africa. European beauty needs are normal, assumed default; everything else is 'other'. It's ironic given that black women outspend any other ethnic group on beauty products, by a significant margin.[24]

Try a Google search of 'most beautiful women', and with the exception of Indian film star Aishwarya Rai and music icon Beyoncé, only white women come up.[25] Magazine rankings of the most desirable women in the world, like Men's Health '100 Hottest Women' survey, routinely feature only a handful of women of colour, all except one of them fair-skinned.[26] Our beauty is often invisible. Yet our alleged ugliness is highly visible, and evolving. New make-up trends, and social media platforms where they are shared and copied, have led to a mushrooming of techniques like contouring, which black women apply to diminish the African dimensions of their noses, using concealer to shrink their lips, and highlighter to brighten their eyes. The inevitable, and nasty, by-product of these efforts is 'make-up shaming' – in which the pre- and post-make-up transformation of black women is revealed, opening them up to relentless abuse and ridicule online. Women of all races have suffered from this abuse, but black women have been particularly targeted, for example by the hashtag

#takeherswimming – a proposal by men to strip a woman physically and expose her true appearance. It seems to have tapped into the age-old idea that black women are essentially and fundamentally unattractive, and that anything they do to alter their true appearance is a kind of sorcery, designed to trick the unsuspecting male. That black women join in, shaming each other on social media, is a stunning reminder of how the self-loathing of black women has seeped into our own minds, staining our view of ourselves, and the world.

In 2016, Facebook hosted images from an *Esquire* article, in which Kim Kardashian was photographed, totally nude, sitting with her head tilted back, her hands behind her and her feet stretched out in front, in the heat of an anonymous desert. Streaks of white body paint marked her fingertips, shoulders, breasts and sides. The same year, an image of two elderly Aboriginal women, naked from the waist up with white, ceremonial paint adorning their breasts as part of a protest, were removed as violating the network's 'decency standards'. 'Stories and images of famous women's nudity are celebrated – while the cultural histories of other women around the world are erased as "inappropriate",' one commentator pointed out.[27] There still is something scary about them, apparently.

All bodies are not equal, all hair is not equal. My WhatsApp group members still share experiences of being given unwarranted feedback, in a manner that is careful to avoid any mention of the words 'black' or 'Afro', that we looked 'more professional' when we wore our hair 'the other way', i.e. straight. We share first-hand dilemmas about life at the Bar (can you reasonably place a barrister's white horsehair wig at high altitude over a voluminous natural hairstyle?), as a teacher (told you look too 'young' with natural hair), or stories we observe around us, like the woman who wore her hair in braids to a job interview in 2015, and was told that it was not a suitable hairstyle for selling 'high end' products.[28] We noticed when, the following year, the fashion website ASOS announced that box braids, which have been loved by black women for thousands of years, were having a fashion moment – they had become a 'thing' – because the model Cara Delevingne, who is white, had decided to wear them.[29]

This is the often misunderstood context for the debate around 'cultural appropriation'. Defined as 'the act of taking or using things from a culture that is not your own, especially without showing that you understand or respect this culture',[30] the term now reappears every time a white celebrity unveils braids, or dreadlocks, or a dance routine with strongly black roots. In 2017, for example, the Braid Bar – a business which offers African hairstyles to, its marketing suggests, white, female Selfridges shoppers – launched a campaign starring supermodel Kate Moss's daughter Lila Grace. The teenage Moss featured on the front cover of the *Evening Standard* magazine in a prominent ad for the salon, wearing cornrows, a style that women with Afro hair use to protect their hair and stimulate growth, and as a decorative style in its own right.

Black women still experience a penalty for wearing their own hair in traditional, natural styles, one reason why they spend billions of pounds globally on straightening or covering their hair with European hair-textured extensions. Black children in Britain – and around the world – have been told they cannot wear their hair in cornrows or Afro styles to school.[31] When white-owned businesses, such as the Braid Bar, or white celebrities, such as Delevingne or Lila Grace Moss, embrace these styles as mainstream fashion, they often do so on platforms that neither reference nor credit the black originators of the craft, the black women who continue to remain invisible in mainstream fashion and beauty marketing. It's no surprise therefore that 'cash-crop cornrows', as the actor Amandla Stenberg described them,[32] feel to many black women like a further pilfering from the best bits of the black experience. A white child penalised for wearing cornrows to school can just revert to their natural hair again. A black child has to mould themselves into something else, something their institution deems appropriate, at the expense of their cultural identity. Taken together, these experiences leave many black people feeling that their ingenuity is ignored but its creations appropriated when it suits. This doesn't feel like an exchange, but an ongoing kind of exploitation.

There is nothing wrong with exchange – cultural ideas and identities are forever cross-pollinating, merging and evolving. Black people do not wish to be the 'gatekeepers' of black hairstyles,[33] policing the imagined borders between races, monitoring the exchanges that do occur. The debate about cultural appropriation is not about the hairstyles themselves, or Jamaican jerk chicken, now commonly served in restaurants with no black owners or staff, or African print clothes, often seen on the catwalks of European designers who continue to show little interest in black models.[34] It's about power. As long as black women feel the critical, even disgusted gaze of white, mainstream beauty standards, telling them that their hair, skin, bodies and clothes are strange, primitive or ugly, not worthy of styling, modelling or celebrating, or that their look is unprofessional, or associated with poverty, then the sight of these cultural markers in a white context is never going to feel like cross-pollination. It's going to feel like an act of theft, with the sting of a double standard.

In the prejudiced world of beauty, even becoming a top model is not enough to escape. 'Black models don't sell magazines,' Jourdan Dunn, one of the most recognisable fashion faces in the UK, was told when she enquired about the absence of other black women from a high-end fashion magazine. In 2013, Dunn caused a sensation by tweeting that she had been cancelled from a fashion show because she didn't fit the clothes. 'I'm normally told I'm cancelled because I'm "coloured" so being cancelled because of my boobs is a minor,' she wrote.[35]

There is no escape from the idea that beauty is whiteness, and whiteness is beautiful. Nowhere have I been more conscious of its global reach and toxic power than in West African countries like Ghana. Living there with my daughter, then aged one, it was a neighbour who first shattered the illusion that this spiritual home to the black diaspora might also be the heartland for black beauty. 'Oh,' said my neighbour in our smart, residential estate off the evocatively named, once industrial Spintex Road. She was shaking her head, inspecting my daughter's deep skin tone, the drama of her almond-shaped eyes and the familiarity of her Afro hair, pulled unco-operatively into little bunches with brightly coloured bobbles. 'This is your child? You didn't do well. She's supposed to be whiter than you.'

The myth, rooted in colonial education, that European men had a monopoly over the inventions that led to technological advancement links white skin to sophistication. The dominance of the global beauty and advertising industry by white models, and Hollywood movies by white actors, links white skin with beauty and talent. As a result, in Nigeria 75 per cent of women use skin-lightening creams; in South Africa, the figure is 1 in 3. The number of black British women lighten-ing their skin is unknown, but it's been reported as a billion-dollar industry globally, predominantly among women of African and South and East Asian descent.[36] One manufacturer of British-made skin-lightening creams claimed in 2014 to have 100,000 clients across the UK alone.[37] I can't count the number of young black or mixed-race girls I've known to, like I once did, take to their skin with a Brillo pad, hoping to scrub the darkness away, or rip their hair out of their scalp, hoping to make it thinner and floppier, which is – according to the films, music videos, fashion shows, adverts and magazines – to make it objectively more beautiful.

We are still recovering from the long centuries of colonialism and slavery, the worst period of racism in Britain's history. But those days are not so far in the distant past as we might think. There are many heartbreaking things that have been done to black people to amuse European audiences. The last recorded image from a human zoo – a hugely popular form of entertainment for white audiences from London and Stuttgart to North America and France – was taken in 1958. It shows a little black girl in the 'Congolese Village' at a human zoo in Brussels, no more than four or five years old, being fed by a member of the crowd who reaches an outstretched hand into the enclosure, dozens of others watching in amusement.[38]

Another of the most haunting examples of this unique kind of tor-ture is that of Saartje Baartman, the South African Khoikhoi woman who was enslaved and put on display in the early nineteenth century in London, Paris and Ireland – naked, and caged. Her genitals, dissected after she died, were displayed floating in glass jars of formaldehyde at the Musée de l'Homme in Paris until the 1970s. Her remains were not returned to South Africa for a proper burial until 2002. Baartman, who became known as the Hottentot Venus, was a woman reduced to her sexual parts – a pronounced backside and genitals which were paraded as an example of the sexual extremities of African woman-hood. Ultimately it was further evidence, in an empirical era, that black people were a separate and lower race.[39]

It was the pain of Saartje Baartman's story that prompted one of the most heated flashpoints of how the black body is used in art and culture that I have witnessed in my lifetime. On a September even-ing in 2014 underneath the Victorian railway arches near London's Waterloo Station, the summer finally dredging away from the world in a mournful blast of damp, South African artist Brett Bailey is about to launch *Exhibit B*. The exhibition intends – its sponsors say – to 'con-front colonial atrocities committed in Africa, European notions of racial supremacy and the plight of immigrants today'. It includes a black woman topless on a bed, her lower half wrapped in a dirty cloth, her neck shackled and chained, a black man with his head clamped in irons, and a couple, marked with serial numbers, standing semi-nude in grass skirts among stuffed animals and other exotic relics.

The guests arriving at the exhibition's opening night seem affluent and are almost all white. Their interest in it suggests a willingness to engage in questions of race and perception, I suppose, but that is of little comfort to the swelling crowd of mostly black protesters outside. The hushed awkwardness of the guests, ushered quickly behind the damp brick into the gallery, could not have contrasted more with the almost euphoric rage of the crowd outside. I am there to file a neu-tral news report, but there is no denying something uplifting in the air; like carnival; drums, whistles, dancing – an Afrocentric and multi-racial throng united in the colourful chaos of protest. 'This exhibition is fundamentally racist and it's disrespectful to the memory of our ancestors, and the great pain and suffering they went through to this day,' enthuses Sara Myers, a lithe and energised black woman in her thirties with locks and a silver hoop in her nose. 'You don't challenge racism by creating racism. I think it's deeply disturbing that to look at the atrocities of colonialism, you need to go back and look at black people in chains, with tape measures around their heads. There are better ways of doing that.'

The protesters had their way, and the exhibition was pulled from London altogether. A tragedy for freedom of expression and the essential power of art to cause controversy and debate, the organisers said, and I sympathised. But they were too dismissive of the pain that informed that protest. It was not about an abstract political principle, it was real. Many black people are outside their comfort zone every day in the way they feel their bodies are still perceived by their colleagues, or passers-by, or those in our society in charge of dictating what is beautiful. They don't need a live installation of shocking images from slavery to tell them what they instinctively suffer from in real life. It didn't help them, and it wasn't for them. They were upset.

One of the most upset was Chantal Loïal, a Guadaloupe-born French dancer who performed in *Exhibit B* as one of the live installations when it was exhibited in Paris. She had hoped it would help garner interest for her own art. But she had found it so degrading, she said, being eyed up and down, naked, chained, by the same white French, elite urban crowd whose unloving eyes she felt so frequently upon her in everyday life, that she had pulled out after a few days.

It's a damning indictment because Loïal, more than anyone, appreciates the sensitivity of the subject matter. Her proudest achievement is *On t'appelle Vénus – They Call You Venus* – a one-woman show in which she uses dance to strip away the layers of time and thought between Saartje Baartman and the contemporary black woman.

It begins with Loïal standing under the harsh glare of a spotlight, wearing loose clothes that cling to the contours of her stomach and her generous thighs. Think of the clavicle- and ribcage-protruding frame of a bony, sinewy white ballerina, and then imagine the opposite, and you have Chantal Loïal. Hers is the fleshy, pliant body of a dancer who has both muscle and fat, honed into the classic African model of beauty – a pinch at the waist, buttocks that swell and move as she does, and shapely legs that power her, gracefully. Her head is wrapped in fabric in a style reminiscent of Caribbean women during colonial times. But there the expected ends; hers is also a show that is uncomfortable to watch. She begins by cackling, crudely, without context, her make-up-free face harshly lit as she emits loud, coarse laughter in bursts. Then she moves slowly and silently, making out the exaggerated figure of a larger stomach, more protruding bum, with her hands. Slowly she begins to thrust her body violently, in a parody of African dance, her headscarf unravelling with the force of the movements. '*On t'appelle Vénus*,' she begins to declare. She bears a skull on her head, encased in a glass cube, and pulls down her trousers, standing with her back to the audience, revealing the true contours of her large, dimpled bum.

The modern-day Venus, strangely enough, popped up on my road in Wimbledon in July 2000. My little sister, just fourteen at the time, was walking down that hill, the gradients of which so defined our childhood, when she saw a black girl, sitting on a wall. It was Serena Williams, a newcomer on the Wimbledon tennis scene at the time, who had just taken the tournament by storm, making it all the way to the semi-finals. She had lost, at that stage, to her sister Venus, also – obviously – a black girl. It was unimaginable, it was unreal. Wimbledon – the whitest suburb in London, during its whitest fortnight of the year. Wimbledon – which had always felt like Britishness commodified; lawn tennis, strawberries and cream, unaffordable champagne. And here were two girls from Compton, LA, with their hair in braids and beads – the most visual signifiers of an assertive and confident black culture – beating every single player that came before them, except each other. They were not just black, but they wore their blackness proudly. They beat everyone, and changed the game. The impact on my confidence, my sense of visibility, and my pride, was profound.

It took a force of nature of the magnitude of the Williams sisters to change my world, because no one, apart from me, seemed to want it to change. There is an unspoken rule in neighbourhoods with a particular character, I think, that will tolerate families who are visibly different moving in, so long as they make an effort to 'fit in'. We were welcome in Wimbledon; we kept our house looking pretty, like all the other houses, with roses and a neatly mowed lawn. We didn't throw loud parties, move around at unusual times of the day or night, my parents got plugged into the local bridge and dinner-party circuit more or less as soon as they could. This is what you're supposed to do, to be accepted – do what everyone else does, and avoid standing out, causing a commotion, and certainly don't try to take over. I may not have fitted in growing up – and lived in a state of inner turmoil as a result – but as a family, we did the expected thing: we played by the rules.

This is not what the Williams sisters did. Their arrival upset the delicate balance, and they made no apology for it. They came from nowhere, played differently, dressed differently, wore their hair differently and, most of all, they won. Wimbledon – apart from us, my whole family relishing this moment – may not have been thrilled about it. But their talent, their discipline, their sheer athletic, strategic and skilful brilliance could not be argued with.

Or so I thought. It turned out that I overestimated Wimbledon. There was no way that the 'genteel sport',[40] meant for the upper-class white elite, was going to give way gracefully to not just one but two talented geniuses from the hood. I remember listening to the BBC commentary and being incandescent at the description of the Williamses, who used 'brute force', 'intimidating' their opponents. In the US, American radio personality Sid Rosenberg commented that Venus and Serena Williams were too masculine. 'I can't even watch them play any more,' he said. 'I find it disgusting. They're just too muscular. They're boys.' Venus, he added, was an 'animal', and taken together the pair of them had more chance posing for *National Geographic* than *Playboy*. Rosenberg insisted his comments were 'not racist'.[41]

Venus and Serena became more and more unbeatable. I felt their incredible accomplishments, battled and won right on my doorstep, and I felt equally wounded, personally, by the way they were perceived by the public. Was this how people saw all of us? I grew up with Athena's iconic poster, the Tennis Girl, in which a blonde and knicker-less woman, tennis racket in one hand, places the other on a fully exposed butt cheek.[42] I remember that when Maria Sharapova accidentally recreated it, revealing more than a little of her own butt cheek, it was celebrated as a stunning homage to the poster. But when Venus wore an outfit on court that involved a lace corset-inspired outfit, worn over flesh-coloured shorts, revealing none of her actual bum but daring to suggest its shape, people reacted with disgust. 'Ooh la la!' cried the *Daily Mail*. 'Too much!'[43] More than 40 per cent of Americans consulted by the newspaper *USA Today* thought she should 'cover up'. The message was clear: a white woman's sexuality is cheeky, fun and tasteful; a black woman's offensive, off-putting and indecent.

But Serena, stronger and ultimately even more successful than her older sister Venus, has faced a singularly relentless, racist barrage of abuse. 'Williams, 33, is the more physically powerful, with a ferocious temper and the mindset of a battling champion,' wrote Alison Boshoff in the *Daily Mail* in 2015. 'However, she cannot compete with Sharapova's media-friendly combination of blonde Siberian beauty.' In other words, this tennis goddess, who at the time of writing has won 23 grand slams – and more open titles than any other player in history – is permanently handicapped by the unfortunate fact that she is black. Players joined the press in mocking her; both the Danish player Caroline Wozniacki and the Serbian Novak Djokovic made fun of Serena's physique, stuffing towels down their tops to imitate her breasts and, in Wozniacki's case, her bum too.[44] Annabel Croft, the former player and broadcaster, told guests at a corporate lunch at Wimbledon during the 2013 championships that Serena's dresses were 'very carefully designed to hide her bulk', that she had a 'huge backside' and one had to wonder what on earth she would look like in a wedding dress. Croft later dismissed her comments as 'banter'.[45]

Serena's breathtaking accomplishments have not turned her into a national treasure in the US. In 2003 when she was already scaling dizzying heights, an American commentator revealed a widespread hope when a blonde American teenager, Ashley Harkleroad, won a second-round match at the French Open, exclaiming perhaps America had found the women's champion it was looking for. 'And the Williams sisters, pray?' asked an exasperated reporter in the *Guardian*, one of the very few to point out the blatant racism staining the coverage of the sisters. 'Sorry, wrong colour.'[46] An influential magazine claimed Serena 'runs women's tennis like Kim Jong-un runs North Korea: ruthlessly'[47] – a description so telling in conveying the underlying fear, danger and instability associated with her success in sport. This, despite the fact that, as far as many commentators are concerned, Serena Williams is the greatest athlete of all time. In Wimbledon, I have watched her phenomenal dominance come to be accepted with grudging defeatism. I remember Steffi Graf, I remember Boris Becker, I know what it feels like when a player is loved by the tennis world, and I remember Martina Navratilova, the Czech and American player who was for years hated. But for Venus and Serena, there was never any love. Black writers have described Serena, a powerful black woman in a sport dominated by all things white, as 'the spectacle of hyperblackness'.[48] Serena, another has said, is the new Saartje Baartman.

Serena is just the best example of something happening on a far greater scale. Misty Copeland, the first black principal ballerina for American Ballet Theatre, one of the three major ballet companies in the US, describes being rejected from ballet schools as a child, told 'you have the wrong body for ballet'. Even now that she is a global star, ballet enthusiast social media sites regularly denounce Copeland; a recent post, for example, dissects an image that simply depicts the ballerina – hardly surprisingly – in a leotard, under the title 'Another Controversial Photo'. On the thread, ballet fans complain that Copeland's muscular form 'doesn't really fit with my idea of a ballerina', or is 'not my cup of tea, it looks like a rugby player's legs'. American talk-show hosts had a field day with Michelle Obama's physique, saying it was indistinguishable from Oprah Winfrey's, or, even less subtly, that it is simply too big.

Serena is reluctant to talk about this, when I've asked her over the years. It's hard not to notice when any other black woman arrives in Wimbledon Village, let alone the greatest female athlete of all time. In 2015, by coincidence, it ended up being my parents' house that she stayed in during the championships, a year in which she won both the singles and doubles titles at Wimbledon. A pre-dinner photo she posted online shows her and her family dressed for the champions' ball, posing in my parents' little garden; a fitting symbol of how intimately her journey has affected mine.

Serena has been an important figure to me because in some ways I see her as the ultimate black woman. At her peak, no one can compete with her talent. And when a hostile commentariat throw racially tinged insults at her body, claiming she looks like a man because she is strong, insulting her femininity, she responds with defiance, her red-carpet poses in the most revealing, sensual outfits seemingly only emboldening her further. As someone who has experienced slurs about my muscular frame my whole life, and called names because of it, she represents a woman and a black woman who owns her own image, and her own sexuality, and has helped redefine what it means to be beautiful. But she doesn't perform the caricature of the 'strong black woman' – the cartoon-like figure invented during slavery to justify working black women like farm animals, or separating them from their partners, children and families, the idea that a black woman, on her subhuman broad shoulders, can carry the world without flinching. Serena is shy, she is vulnerable, and she is human, which only makes her more endearing, more unlike the caricature of a tyrant that the press uses to describe her. But it's clear that portrayal has affected her. 'It was a tough crowd out there,' she said after one match, in which she was jeered by fans, and her every fault celebrated. 'The story of my life.'[49]

Before I witnessed what happened to Serena, there were only a handful of instances when I'd experienced overt racism in Wimbledon, a place, after all, where people prefer not to see race. I've been physically threatened by racists elsewhere – most notably once on a Tube when a white man took his belt off and threatened to beat me with it, because 'you people are out of control' – and I've been told to 'fuck off home' more times than I can count. But not in this part of town. Wimbledon is like a microcosm of how Britain sees itself, polite, wholesome, home to what we imagine to be 'British culture' – an obsession with the weather, picnics and deckchairs, umbrella in hand, eating strawberries and cream, cheering the underdog, forming endless orderly queues.

Wimbledon is a perfect example of how racism has evolved. The things I have experienced here that have rocked me most deeply, the comments about my body, being seen as 'scary' or 'criminal' because I am black, were meted out by people who would have been aghast if I'd accused them of being 'racist'. But they were interactions with people who would never see themselves as racist, and would be offended by the claim. The era of racism without racists is the story of my life.

It's the same racism that my sister experienced for the first time in 2016, when she introduced her newborn baby – a babbling, chubby bundle of pure light, with a round puff of curly black hair, deep dimples and the sweetest temperament of any infant I have ever known – to the world. One response: 'He looks like a little gangster!' A gangster! 'Another said he looked like a bouncer. It was a shocking, painful wake-up call to what life is going to be like for a black boy growing up in this country,' my sister told me afterwards. 'If he is being stereotyped that way before he can even sit up, or eat solids, or talk, imagine how people will look at him when he is a teenager.' The originators of these comments would be mortified if you accused them of racism. They meant well, they said it with a smiling, cooing face. The image is seemingly a hard one for black people to escape. I too was told at work by a colleague, returning from a trip to South Africa in 2015, that I looked 'gangster'. It was meant to be a compliment about the fact that I had had my hair done in traditional, African braids.

This is the racism that meant, when my mum used to take her assistant, who is white and half her age, out for lunch to thank her for her hard work, the restaurant staff would unfailingly bring the bill to the assistant. 'They just could not get their heads around the fact that I was the boss,' my mum recalls. It's the racism that, as a guest at drinks receptions in the City or Westminster, still sees me sometimes confused with the waiting or cleaning staff. 'Excuse me, we've got a spillage here' or 'Are you able to take my coat?', when you are a guest just like any other. They don't mean to offend you; the person making these remarks just assumes you are there to feed them, or clean up after them, because it is the role they are used to seeing black people perform in their lives. Statistically, it's a fairly safe bet – I cannot count the number of times I've been to a professional event at which I am the only non-white person apart from the servers.

At my school, my chambers, my newspaper, my TV station, my gym, the vast majority of black people in the building are janitors, mailroom staff, security or kitchen staff. In some cases, they have been the only other black people. I know this because I inevitably get to know them. At least one of them is always Ghanaian. They tell me, often at length, how they are using the money from this, and often another minimum-wage job to boot, to build a house back in Ghana. They complain about their housing problems and I help put them in touch with a charity or write a letter to their MP. One of their children would be born on a Friday, and share my name; sometimes they bring in food for me, if they've made *kenkey*, my favourite – a bun made out of fermented corn – or *achimon* – little deep-fried spicy biscuits that my daughter and I both love. I thank them in Twi – that much I can muster in my mother's language – and continue my eternally doomed quest to learn a few more words. Colleagues look at me askance when it emerges I have so much in common with the cleaners. It makes them feel uncomfortable, this traversing of the boundary between race and status. I've broken the rules.

There are rules, when it comes to being black at work. Unspoken, unwritten ones, which many obediently follow, but which are hard to define because they are understood only so quietly. There are things that cannot be said, for example, for fear of making colleagues feel uncomfortable. Overt references to being 'black' are to be avoided; many people I know have learned to code their otherness. Instead of saying their parents are 'immigrants', they call them 'expatriates', which is a lot less threatening. Not 'being black', for example, but 'having family from the Caribbean'. Not forming friendships or obvious associations with other black or minority staff members is another rule – it might intimidate white colleagues who often feel as if you are bound together by some secret allegiance. BME (black and minority ethnic) networks or societies at work are precarious, and in some cases actively discouraged. 'Where's the white society?' I've been asked, defensively. The answer could so easily be 'the rest of the company'.

'Time has moved on. And racism has evolved,' said the poet Benjamin Zephaniah. 'We don't really see gangs of racist thugs roaming the streets like they did back in the day. They now wear suits and ties. Some form political parties. Some build websites. And some of them . . . are academics.' The political left are often among the first to condemn racism, genteel or otherwise, but they have their own history of microaggressions. A friend of mine, let's call her Femi, ran as a Conservative parliamentary candidate in a staunchly Labour part of London. It was an ambitious first foray into politics for a young black woman, who has found since migrating here from Nigeria as a teenager that the Tories speak most to the pull-yourself-up-by-the-boot-straps, socially conservative and Republican values that have such resonance in West Africa. Femi had no idea how residents of this once run-down but now desirable borough, with its period terraced houses and well-established social housing, would respond to her.

What Femi found was that Conservative voters expressed surprise at the appearance of a young black woman, with her long braids and faint Nigerian accent, on their doorsteps. They were taken aback, but would quickly collect themselves and wish her well. But the Labour supporters were furious. 'How dare you!' they would say to her, their faces contorted by the spectacle of a betrayal. 'After everything we've done for your people! This is how you repay us?' Femi was shocked. 'It was as if, because I am an immigrant, they own me,' she said. 'I have never experienced that kind of racism from Conservatives.'

Microaggressions and unconscious bias pattern our world in ways most of us don't notice, pampered as we are by the soothing language of diversity and acronym. 'BAME' now rolls off the tongue, obviating the need to grapple with those thorny words 'black', 'mixed heritage' or 'Asian' – words that the British have never enjoyed deploying and never been sure they are allowed to say out loud. There is something uniquely British about this squeamishness. In the US, for example, for all its chronic problems of racism, segregation and the so recent legacy of slavery, there are agreed terms for black people, which Americans of all races are conversant in using. Black people in America are 'black' or 'African American'; the majority of people are confident in the appropriateness of this language and when to use it. By contrast, British people have rushed to embrace BAME – an irritating acronym which is so broad as to be meaningless, encompassing as it does every single group that does not have white skin. I find it even more grating when turned into a word pronounced 'bayme' – as a tool for avoidance.

The days of openly racist imperialist Britain – 'no dogs, no Irish, no niggers' – have blended into our modern world with no appraisal of what has passed, except a vague sense of skeletons in the closet that we would rather not disturb. This has created a lack of confidence in our language – an uncertainty as to which parts of our inheritance are tainted. Many choose the easy option, declaring that they 'do not see race' at all, an opt-out which obscures their understanding of the diverse heritage, identity and inequalities so closely linked – in our society – to ethnicity and race.

Others admit to seeing race but flounder on how to describe it. I'm often asked at work what the correct terminology is, and I have reluctantly – not without a sense of slight fraudulence – accepted the mantle of being some kind of expert, simply because I have had to work out during my life what is offensive to me. My perspective is simple. I am black; I am also mixed race – although some people I know dislike this term, for its implication that racial 'wholeness' or purity exists in others but has eluded them. I don't expect to be called 'coloured' – a term which definitely is tainted by the colonial era in which it was used. I don't expect to be called 'half-caste' – a derogatory phrase implying the 'caste' or social status I would usually enjoy has been diminished by the black half of my heritage, which still comes my way every so often. I do feel like a black person, and I identify with the phrase mixed race, but I will never wake up in the morning, look in the mirror and find a 'bayme' woman staring back at me.

I'm not the only one frustrated by the general lack of consensus as to what people like me are called. I've noticed more and more frustration among white colleagues, for example, who feel bound by confusing rules about what they can and cannot say, especially when it comes to race and immigration, which intersect right at the heart of the most toxic and powerful political debates of the day. The growing rebellion against the supposed repression of free speech is most commonly expressed as a resentment at 'political correctness gone mad'. Maybe they've forgotten the days before so-called political correctness, when people like me were simply referred to as 'nigger'. What those who see political correctness as the problem in our society also undoubtedly don't realise, is that black people are the most self-censoring group of all. We are the ones with our own self-originating, self-policed rules.

For example, a friend of mine, Nicola Rollock – who in 2015 was one of only seventeen black female professors in academia in the whole of the UK – has a ten-point 'survival strategy' for getting through life in a white world. The plan includes avoiding anything that could ever be interpreted as accusing a white person of racism, avoiding shows of emotion – especially anger – maintaining a lowered tone of voice on debates about race, and, when such debates are absolutely necessary, acting as if simply exploring some abstract idea.[50] I've never met anyone else who has articulated these rules so well, or even written them down, but I can't help but suspect their use, probably subconscious in many cases, is widespread.

The supposed triumph of unwelcome political correctness hasn't done anything to prevent one of the most irritating hazards of being one of very few minority women at work: the frequent reminder that we are all, apparently, very difficult to tell apart. Another ethnic minority female colleague may be a different height, shape and, in fact, from a different race to me, but these differences can be too subtle for people unused to discerning non-white features to work out. At the *Guardian* I was Jo Adetunji – an extremely tall and slender woman, also of mixed heritage, already a reporter of several years when I joined the newspaper. Apparently her colleagues had paid so little attention to her appearance, year after year, that I was immediately indistinguishable from her from day one. In fact, Jo and I did have similar heritage. In most cases, there aren't enough other mixed-heritage people for me to get confused with another one of those. At Sky News I was Darshini David, a woman of South Asian heritage with long straight black hair against my short light brown curls, smaller than me, and who had anchored the channel as a business presenter for six years. In a rapid metamorphosis I was mistaken for Gillian Joseph soon after, a well-established news anchor of Afro-Caribbean descent with a completely different look, hairstyle and skin tone.

There is almost no limit to the absurdity this can produce. In 2015, ITV paid tribute to the knighthood awarded to comedian and actor Lenny Henry, illustrating the package with footage of TV chef Ainsley Harriot.[51] Here was the usual, daily difficulty in distinguishing one black face from another, but this time, broadcast to the nation by some soon-to-be mortified producer. My most memorable personal experience took place in the spring of 2009, when I met David Davis – the libertarian Tory MP and minister – for lunch at Quirinale, an overpriced and politician-saturated Italian restaurant in Westminster. It was just a few months after Obama's first election victory, and the president and First Lady were in the UK to attend the G20. A famous columnist – a middle-aged white man who then wrote for broadsheets and current affairs magazines – walked into the restaurant with another lunch party, and headed straight over to our table. 'Michelle!'

he said, looking right at me, hand on heart, sounding humbled, and entirely serious. 'Can I just say, it is *such* an honour.' I checked behind me on both sides, but . . . yes. He was talking to me. It was as if the prospect of there being two distinct black females in Westminster at any one time was too implausible. I had to be the First Lady.

If our physical appearance is confusing, our background is assumed with certainty. One of the things that large organisations, in their rush to embrace diversity, tend to do these days is send staff members out to give talks at schools with disproportionately high numbers of children from disadvantaged backgrounds. This is laudable. Scouring the office for anyone non-white and assuming they went to such a school them-selves, however, is not. 'We'd like you to go into schools and tell kids from tough backgrounds your inspirational story about overcoming poverty,' I'm told, as if I grew up in a crack house. The last time I was asked to do this, I discovered it was a suggestion made exclusively to me and one other colleague, who is half Asian and went to boarding school in Cornwall. 'They'll really relate to that,' she joked. Both of us go into schools and do these kinds of talks anyway, it's a privilege and a responsibility, I feel, even if ours was a race-based, rather than class-based, adversity. We just didn't appreciate being singled out and channelled that way based on crude assumptions.

Here, too, the concept of BAME has a lot to answer for, creating as it has the impression that as long as the minority box can be ticked, the job of improving diversity is done. But BAME encompasses people of Chinese or black African heritage, who are outperforming others in school exam results for example, as well as those of black Caribbean backgrounds, who – for a complex assortment of race- and class-based reasons – are more likely to be significantly behind.[52] It includes Indian doctors, considerably over-represented at consultant level in the NHS,[53] as well as Africans and Eastern Europeans, who make up a dis-proportionate number of hospital cleaners, in some cases paid below the living wage.[54]

Achieving diversity in British society is meaningless without addressing the class inequalities that remain such a relevant indicator of our life experience, determining universities we are likely to attend, even determining the very length of our life – while 91 per cent of baby boys in affluent East Dorset will live to the age of sixty-five for example, only 75 per cent of boys born in far poorer Glasgow City can expect to live that long.[55]

At the same time, I would expect a black person to be just as likely to experience racism, prejudice or microaggressions growing up in East Dorset as they would in Glasgow. There are so many layers in the daily texture of feeling othered in Britain; for a black man at work, for a mother protecting her little baby from perceptions of gangsterism, for a promising student, unable to shake the sense that something unspecified about her is culturally incompatible with one of the oldest academic institutions in the country. These experiences are often delivered by people who would be aghast to hear themselves described as racist, who regard themselves not only as not racist, but not even conscious of race. By someone who will tell you: 'I don't see race.' The intention is a rejection of racism. That's fine, rejecting racism is standard, rejecting racism is what we should all expect. But claiming 'not to see' only serves to further delegitimise the experiences of those of us who are faced with the reality, and baggage, of our racial difference every day. It operates powerfully against a sense of belonging in this country. In my case, the combination of experiencing race, while being encouraged to ignore race, created a pressure to downplay the experience, or risk being disliked, seen as paranoid, a troublemaker, or simply raining on the post-racial parade.

It's absurd really, because racial prejudice is alive and well. Unlike the other disadvantages that are so deeply entrenched in our society – especially class – ours is often detected on paper, from our name alone, before we have appeared, or if we appear, with our visible otherness, before we have opened our mouths. It's remarkable that things are still this bad. But it's even more astonishing that as a nation we seem content to just live with it, commission the occasional report, make the occasional token policy change, host the occasional debate, and then, as if nothing ever happened, keep calm, and carry on.

Britain is not unique in these problems, Western European nations have all been changed by people from their former colonies, alongside the ideology of racial superiority that had those people as colonial subjects in the first place. Other societies colonised by Europeans at the expense of indigenous people, such as the US and Australia, are gradually coming to terms with the highly structured, and until recently state-perpetrated, racism delivered at the birth of their nations. But what *is* unique about Britain is the convoluted lengths we are willing to go to, to avoid confronting the problem. We will not name it, we avoid discussing it and, increasingly, we say we can't see it. We want to be post-racial, without having ever admitted how racial a society we have been.

4. HERITAGE

Liverpool street children, 1954.

It is a peculiar sensation, this double-consciousness, this sense of always looking at one's self through the eyes of others ... One ever feels his twoness, – an American, a Negro; two souls, two thoughts, two unreconciled strivings; two warring ideals in one dark body, whose dogged strength alone keeps it from being torn asunder.

– W. E. B. Du Bois,
The Souls of Black Folk

You can slice London in two jagged halves, taking the District Line as your knife, cutting a horizontal green line from west to east, before gently sloping upwards in a diagonal stagger of track. This line is one of the oldest commuter railways in the world, dating back to 1868, but these days it's always reinventing itself, its open-plan carriages a new design on an old theme, patriotic red, white and blue livery.

The views from this line are the landscapes of my life. The back gardens of south-west London's Victorian houses, lined up calmly, their kitchen extensions jutting out, offering vivisections of wood and chrome to passers-by, through floor-to-ceiling glass doors. Then we slide down into tunnels concealing the pastel streets of Chelsea, and in the blackness we hug the river, on a tour underneath the line of power. It takes us beneath St James's Park, the seat of royalty; Westminster, the seat of government; Temple, the seat of law; Mansion House, Monument and Tower Hill, the City of London, the seat of money. As the Tube shudders east, the rich and powerful disembark, the white men in suits become white men in tracksuits, clutching plastic bags in the slow hours that stalk those out of work in the mid-morning. Eastern European mothers with buggies travel into the East End; at Whitechapel there are schoolboys from the East London Mosque's madrasas, head to toe in white, with crocheted Muslim prayer caps and nascent, struggling beards. Further east, black boys get on, their hair barbered into high tops, mixed-race girls with full curly hair, middle-aged white ladies, sitting neatly, in jeans with elasticated waistbands. All seem blind to the sparkling towers of Canary Wharf or the overhyped design of the Olympics Stadium on either side of the line; this Tube is something forlorn.

My destination today is Elm Park, a downtrodden high street, with broken promises of regeneration, a place built cheaply as 'a healthy environment for working class people', the government said in the 1930s, clearing the East End of its slums.[1] Like many of the districts in this area, Elm Park was initially dreamed into the shape of a future garden city, but – interrupted by the war – was turned into higher-density social housing instead. No one aspires to live here now, except immigrants, who will take what they can afford. The last time I was in this part of town was during the 2015 general election, to monitor the rise of UKIP, whose share of the vote rose by 25 per cent that year, and still competes here for votes with the BNP.[2]

But there are pockets of affluence here too, cul-de-sacs of brand-new town houses, with pale brick walls, white stucco, little slate porches and royal-blue garages. The worlds it evokes are ads from daytime TV: new double-glazing, affordable kitchens, home alarm systems, capable plumbing. It is proud and aspirational. The house I've come to visit is exactly like the others, and when I step inside, the December air is assaulted by a wall of warmth. The whole place is perfumed with machine-spun, heated and drying laundry, fabric softener and starched shirts – distilled into the smell of cleanliness. It's addictive and comforting.

I've never been inside a care home of any kind before, and it's nothing like I thought it would be. It feels warm, it feels welcoming. It belongs to Lola, a woman in her mid-thirties like me. Technically not a children's home but 'supported, semi-independent living' for children transitioning out of care, this place is her passion, her business, her project and her hobby. I tell her it's more homely than I was expecting.

'Most of them are not this nice, to be honest,' Lola tells me, stretching out her long, slender legs on the black faux-leather sofa in the front room. She has the rich dark skin so characteristic of the country of her heritage, Nigeria, and wears her hair long and straight, woven on with a centre parting. There's a vitality to her body, a warmth and energy to the way she moves and speaks, but a self-consciousness too, and something ever so slightly withdrawn. 'I had to go the extra mile,' she explains. 'That's the whole point.'

Lola's path to owning her own care home began when she was four years old. Her Nigerian parents had met at university in north London, and had six children in total – four born during their marriage and two from her mother's previous relationship. When Lola's father left, her mother struggled to finish her studies, get a job, and raise the children alone. Lola and four of her siblings ended up in care.

'I've had to unpick this myself as an adult – why I was in care,' explains Lola, who is in touch with her mother now. 'From my perspective my mother had a bit of a breakdown, she couldn't cope. She had six children, and five of them in five years, in a three-bedroom flat. [We] got fostered at different times.'

The three older girls were sent to a foster-family in rural Oxfordshire, Lola and her brother went to a separate foster-family in Ware, a small town on the River Lea twenty miles north of London, in the Hertfordshire countryside. It was a rocky journey, one that has shaped Lola in so many ways. One outcome is her resolve to spend her adulthood working in the same system that had so much power over her own life, and do right by other children left at the mercy of the state.

Lola saved up her money over the years, working as a drug and alcohol worker for a large children's charity, and squirrelling away her salary, fostering children on the side, a way of helping more children and earning more money after work, at home. In her spare time she does extra, paid work sitting on foster panels, vetting prospective parents, helping more children, saving more money. Every part of her week and every hour of her day is spent earning. Because this house – the home she has created for children in care – had to be this way; a new building, a clean, light, welcoming house – and that costs money.

'It was a long journey to save the money for this place,' Lola says, looking around her. 'I had to put down £18,000 and I didn't borrow any of it. But I'm a saver, always have been. That's something my foster-carers taught me; to save my £5 pocket money every week.'

Homes like this are lucrative business. There are far too few publicly run children's homes to meet the demand to place children in care, and privately run homes have made up the shortfall. The possibility of earning thousands of pounds per child, per week, has attracted some people with questionable motives into the sector. And while homes for younger children are heavily regulated, inspectors I have spoken to, reporting on the issues as a journalist, are perfectly open about their concerns about the variation in quality. Meanwhile homes for older children like the ones Lola is caring for, aged between sixteen and eighteen, are, astonishingly, not regulated at all. It's up to local councils to inspect them, and they too are open – Lola says – about their dissatisfaction with some facilities they have no choice but to use. Because they are run for profit, it's rare to find such an attractive property – there are incentives to keep costs to a minimum. 'The more you spend on a property, the more you spend on your staff, the less profit you make at the end of the day,' Lola says. 'But for me [the home] was number one. These children have been let down and rejected. With me they know I genuinely care about them, and I want them to be happy here. And it has to be a high standard of home. Once you bring young people into a high standard, they keep that standard.'

I was taken by Lola's ambition and passion, but at the same time I was struck by her own insecurity around her identity. I first met Lola through Sam's younger sister, who also works with vulnerable children – they were both helping me with an investigation into a school where permanently excluded children were being abused and exploited. When I told Sam I'd met his sister's friend Lola he said, 'Which Lola? She's got two friends called Lola. Was it White Lola or Black Lola?'

This made no sense to me at the time – I knew both Lolas to be black, although this Lola was the only one I'd met. I asked her about this, and, laughing, she explained that *she* was White Lola – taking the nickname in her stride as one of many clumsy shorthand references to the cultural conditioning she has had. 'I didn't know any black people until I was eighteen,' she explained, in an undeniably cockney lilt with wide-open vowels. 'People say that the way I speak makes me sound white. And to be honest, I didn't know anything about black culture. Way into adulthood, I thought Nigerian food was Nando's.' In spite of their nickname for her – which had horrified me when I found out its rationale – it was clear how fond Lola was of Sam's family. 'That lot are always making fun of me. To be honest I've learned a lot about black people by hanging around with them, and I think I'm becoming more confident in my identity now.'

Lola's life manifests so many of the dilemmas involved in questions of race, culture and identity. Her foster-family, a loving, white, retired couple, already in their sixties when Lola and her brother arrived, had adopted five children who were by then grown up. 'They were an older generation,' Lola recalls. 'We actually called them "nan" and "grandad".' It's clear they cared for Lola and her brother, deeply. But it was still not a straightforward path.

'I had a lot of difficulties around being black – for me that was a massive issue. I was the only one who was black in the world it seemed, when I was four,' Lola says. The only outside reference to her race came, as is so often the case, from hostility and aggression. 'There was quite a lot of racism. We had our car bricked, we had people shouting abuse. It was probably worst when I was about nine or ten – we used to live up a hill then. I remember walking up the hill, and kids fighting with us, taunting us, then they would just come up and start punching and kicking us. Sometimes they were with their parents and their parents didn't say anything, didn't do anything to stop them. It just made me think we are different, that it was our fault.'

Lola would tell her foster-parents about the attacks, but they just told her to ignore the other children, and to walk home from school a different way. 'My foster-parents would tell me that I was lucky to be here, because I could be in Africa, where there was no water or food. They didn't have a clue to be honest, it's not really any fault of their own. Just the other day I went to a training for supported lodgings and foster-carers, and people were saying similar things. Two ladies were saying that they've got Eritrean young men staying with them, going "you should see the grease around the bath . . . it's because of their skin". A lot of my staff are not accepting of that, but I'm used to that kind of thing because of my own upbringing.'

When Lola was seven, it became clear to social services that her identity issues were affecting her well-being. 'I think I portrayed being depressed,' she says. 'I think it was apparent that I wasn't comfortable in my own skin, or with my hair – no one knew how to do my hair. I had really bad eczema because my skin not being cleaned or creamed properly. I think social services noticed I wasn't doing well.'

The system kicked into action. Lola and her brother, aged seven and six, were told they were going away for the weekend. Their foster-parents bought them each a new pair of pyjamas, a detail Lola has never forgotten. 'One minute we were with our white foster-parents in a completely white environment in Hertfordshire, and then suddenly we were in Tottenham, with this African family,' Lola recalls. 'After a few days I asked, "When are we going home?" And we weren't.'

It was the mid-1980s, and social services were increasingly experimenting with 'race-matching' policies, which emphasised the importance, for the first time, of matching ethnic minority children with families from similar backgrounds. Lola thinks her placement in a white family – so radically at odds with this policy – would have continued were it not for the visible deterioration in her outward happiness. But partly because of the way in which she and her brother were moved, without being consulted or even informed, and partly because of the conditions at their new home, it turned out to be a disaster.

'I remember loving the food with the new family, and they did my hair straight away, they plaited it,' Lola says. 'But they hit us, which in care you're not supposed to do. And the foster-dad would drink on occasions when he hit me; one time I remember him hitting me so that I fell and cut my eye, and I remember smelling alcohol on his breath when he did that. I only realised later on, when I was older, that that was what it was.

'My brother used to get hit a lot, and that was very emotional for me,' Lola continues. 'I remember him getting hit, for having holes in his trousers, because he played a lot of football – my brother loves football – that might have saved him in a way because he was always playing football and things like that. I remember being in the top bunk, it was rocking, because they were hitting him. And that was quite trau-matic for me. My brother knew how much it affected me, so he was always trying to downplay it.'

Not surprisingly the two children tried repeatedly to run away, until one day they made it out onto the streets of Tottenham. 'I don't even know how I planned that, at that age,' Lola says. 'But I remember us, in our duffel coats that our foster-parents in Ware had bought us. I remember us running out the house and going onto the main road, and going into a sweet shop, and saying, "We live in Ware, and we've just got lost." It was night-time, and I remember the shopkeeper phoning the police. And when the police arrived, an officer bought us Smarties – I remember it all – and they phoned our foster-carers, because we knew the phone number, and said, "These two kids are lost, and they are saying that they come from Ware." And obviously our foster-carers told the police that we had been moved, and we were taken back to the family in Tottenham. And as soon as we got there, we were sent to our room straight away. It was only a little box room, and we were made to just stay in there, as a punishment, on our bunks.'

But Lola's foster-parents in Ware, having received the phone call from the police, realised that all was not well. They applied to take the children back into their care, and when their application was refused, they were prepared to fight. 'Our foster-parents went to the High Court and fought to get us back,' Lola says. 'It took them a long time. Then one day, we were back in Ware. It was almost as if nothing had happened. All our friends had moved from the infant school to the junior school, and we had been away a year, but now we were back.'

It's clear, from the way Lola talks about her foster-parents' legal battle, that she cherishes the fact that they were willing to go to such lengths to fight for her brother and her to come back into their care. It's as if this is one of the defining acts of love shown to her in her life. But it was a mixed blessing. 'There were certain things I missed about Tottenham – the food, and having my hair done. My eczema had com-pletely cleared up, just from having it washed and creamed properly, and now that I was back, all those problems came back. And I think for me, more than anything, I felt that I needed to belong. Growing up and feeling that because I was black and I stood out . . . I know my self-esteem was very low.'

It was a choice of two extremes for Lola. On the one hand, an abusive family, who were yet able to cater to her sense of identity as a black girl, and all the markers of a culture that resonated with her. Things that may seem superficial, but which hugely affected Lola's sense of self – seeing others who resembled her, being able to style her hair, eat food she enjoyed, and respite from the torture of eczema's itching and burning, literally feeling uncomfortable in her own skin. And on the other hand, a loving family who offered her stability and safety, but who didn't understand or relate to her cosmetic or cultural needs, or her identity.

Aspects of life in Ware had a powerful, negative effect on Lola, and disabled her from the normal experiences of a teenage girl. 'I never had a boyfriend as a teenager,' Lola says. 'I just felt that no one would want to go out with me. I yearned for acceptance. I remember going round to this boy's house, and one of the mums who was there saying, *"There was this black girl with them – she was as black as the ace of spades."* And comments like that really affected me deeply. I just wanted to be in an area where I didn't have to stand out all the time. As a teenage girl I wore my hair in an Afro this short' – she puts a thumb and forefinger together to indicate an inch in length. 'From behind you couldn't tell the difference between me and my brother. I felt so self-conscious. Now I have to wear my hair long. I have never not worn it this way since I started earning my own money and been able to pay to get it done.'

When Lola left home and eventually went to university, she noticed clear patterns in the way students were congregating. 'I remember looking around. The African students were sitting together. The Caribbean people were sitting together. And I was sitting with the white people,' Lola said. 'I always gravitated towards white people, because that's what I was used to. And I know this sounds funny, but I used to pray for black friends.'

Now Lola has black friends, including Sam's sister and her friends, an entrepreneurial, energetic generation, supremely confident in their African heritage and their black and British identities. And they are not the only ones who use humour to unpick the complicated story of their friend 'White Lola' and her past. 'It's funny that I work in social care because it's an area where there's a lot of black staff,' Lola muses. 'And when I started, black people wouldn't accept me as black. Even the kids here say "you sound white". And when I'm around all black people, I do feel like the white person. I do speak different. But when I'm around all white people, I gravitate towards black people. I guess I am, maybe I will always be, in between.'

Sometimes, the discussions of race, heritage and identity come across as rather abstract. Academics have come up with impressive debates about the 'ontological status' of race, the fact that it's so clearly a social construct, whether it 'arises out of intersubjectivity',[3] but all this can seem far away from the clumsy reality of navigating race and identity in the real world. Even those most determined *not* to see themselves in terms of race, sooner or later come face-to-face with the fact that others do see them that way. They discover the racialised nature of social interactions one way or another; through a series of unwelcome assumptions, crude names or simply never fitting in. Dry intellectual discussions, public policy documents, think-tank publications never quite capture the lived experience of navigating these problems.

At its best, living with multiple heritage is an asset. It's a bit like being multilingual. But if speaking languages allows you to swim expertly, expanding the surface of the ocean you can navigate, having multiple cultural identities offers the possibility of full-body immersion, deep-sea diving; an experience that is difficult to pin down, but that feels mystical and profound. That's the best case scenario. But at its worst, having multiple identities can feel like being helplessly adrift, unable to embrace the beauty in any one place, fearful of the water, awkward on land.

When it comes to adoption, the stakes are high. The state is responsible for determining which, if any, of these experiences of identity a child with minority heritage will have. This has been the case ever since race became an issue determining the fate of children in care – which it has been since there *were* black children in care. The questions of what race is, whether there is such thing as 'mixed race', and how much it matters, have held the destiny of vulnerable lives in their grip.

This began to be a significant issue in Britain at the end of the Second World War, when a growing number of women who became pregnant outside marriage were pressured into giving up their children. Right up until the 1970s, potentially willing mothers surrendered their infants, making many newborn, developmentally normal white babies available for adoption – babies regarded by their future parents as highly 'adoptable'. It was a tragedy in itself, and it also did nothing for the prospects of the growing number of black and mixed-race children in the care system, who were, by contrast, regarded as 'unadoptable', undesirable additions to 'respectable' white families, who wanted adopted children who could blend in, or who had their own hostility towards those from other races.[4]

It wasn't until the 1960s that interracial adoption was officially endorsed. Attitudes towards black children began, very gradually, to change, and a generation was taken in by white families. Many had positive and enduring experiences of being part of an unconditionally loving family. But many, like Lola, also expressed a sense of cultural alienation at having been raised in white communities, isolated from their peers, too conscious of being 'other' to truly thrive, and lacking access to the culture or identity of their birth heritage, and these factors began to be taken more into account. The policy of race-matching that had such a dramatic effect on Lola's life crept into government thinking and became a legal requirement by 2002, the idea being that despite losing their ethnic or religious minority parents, adopted children should not also lose their identity.

But by 2011 black and mixed-race children, historically disadvantaged in the care system, had become three times less likely than white children to be adopted. The blame for this inequality was placed very squarely at the foot of race-matching policies. In 2012 then education minister Michael Gove, who had himself been adopted as a baby, was particularly blunt. 'It is outrageous to deny a child the chance of adoption because of a misguided belief that race is more important than any other factor,' he said. He went on to invoke a story not unlike Lola's – of a black child being taken away from a loving white adoptive parent on grounds of race-matching – to illustrate his point.[5]

The belief that race-matching has left black children languishing unnecessarily in care has weighed very heavily, and very personally, on the hearts of some of those who now regard themselves as to blame for allowing this policy to continue. 'It's hard to talk about this without getting into slightly difficult emotional things,' says Trevor Phillips, the former chair of the Commission for Race Equality (CRE) from 2003, and then of its successor, the Equality and Human Rights Commission. 'When I became chair of the CRE, one of the policies that was really current, was about race-matching and adoption. I had a decision to make about whether we should try to stop local authorities insisting that a black or mixed-race child couldn't be adopted unless you found a parent that was exactly the same. And I was persuaded that there were other things that were more important, and we never did it.

'That's a matter of great shame for me,' Phillips continues, 'because what it means, and meant, is that there are thousands of children that could have had a happy home that didn't. And that, more than anything else in my whole career, made me think that the whole idea of what people call "multiculturalism", which is about essentially my tribe, the left, imposing an idea about how the world should be, was making the people we were supposed to help, suffer.'

It is a striking confession. And the human stories behind it, like Lola's, are harrowing. Except that's not what really happened. The evidence that race-matching was actually the source of the delay was patchy. The House of Lords accused the government of missing the point, and said that the real cause of delay for black children was not race-matching, but poor practice by social workers, who were pessimistic about black children's likelihood of being adopted, and were therefore failing to promote them as available for adoption. Peers also pointed to the fact that many of these children were older and had more complex needs, making them generally harder to place.[6] Another report by the schools and care system inspectorate found that the greatest cause of delay for adoptive children was not race-matching, but repetitive and bureaucratic court proceedings, and understaffed social services.[7]

The government abandoned race-matching altogether. 'Left-wing' and 'misguided nonsense', Gove said in 2011, sweeping it happily away.[8] The decision was greatly influenced by professionals like former Barnardo's chair Martin Narey. 'An Asian, black or mixed-race adult born in the UK is accepted as being just as British as a white British adult,' Narey wrote, also in 2011. 'Mixed-race marriage and other permanent relationships are common and mixed-race children have long ceased to be a novelty. The UK has moved on. But not in the case of adoption where there is, in my view, a continuing, unjustified obsession with ethnicity.'[9] Like the claims of other people who say they 'don't see race', there is something appealing about this perspective, the idea that we have somehow got over race, and reached the promised land.

This is not as attractive as it might sound. It suggests that the cultural and emotional heritage that goes along with minority identities be written off as 'stereotyping'. It implies that there is nothing positive about these identities, they are simply an inconvenience, and preferably could just be made to go away. It seems to me a highly naive appraisal of how race in Britain really works.

Multiculturalism is, I think, partly to blame here. Even though Narey praises our 'multicultural society', he is explicitly rejecting – as almost all mainstream public figures now do – the political multiculturalism of New Labour in the 1990s, which regarded ethnic identities as cartoonish cultural traits, these days satirised as 'saris, steel bands and samosas'. In the nineties and noughties, our mainly white political class thought ethnic minority people could be lumped into distinct 'communities', represented by self-appointed community leaders who could now tap into rich pots of state funding, and follow their own distinct identity-orientated paths to success.

We'll look at the fallout from the political project of multiculturalism later on. But now that it has been rejected as roundly as it was once promoted, the pendulum has swung to the other extreme, and we have begun to lose our nascent understanding that identity does matter. Away from the politics of community funding and immigration statistics – both of which lay at the root of the downfall of political multiculturalism – there are children like Lola, desperate to address the fact that the society around them does not reflect who they feel they are, that the people around them do not have the language or insight to discuss it, and that there is no space in which to explore their anguish.

Of all the people who have a legitimate critique of race-matching, Lola stands out. Her story could easily be used as an example of 'race-matching gone wrong', since she was placed with an abusive black family simply on the grounds of achieving more ethnic continuity. Yet even she feels strongly that abandoning the importance of race and identity in adoption is a mistake.

'I think race-matching should be a priority,' she tells me. 'If it means a child is going to be kept in a children's home rather than being adopted or fostered, then I'm not saying it should override everything, if a child has an opportunity to get cared and looked after in a lovely family setting. But it should be prioritised as a criterion. I don't think people realise,' Lola continues, sitting on the edge of the sofa now, at the warm house in Elm Park, 'how important this is. From my experience, I think growing up with a black family would have been a massive part of me being comfortable in myself.'

Providing children with the cultural identity they need to thrive is an art, not a science. As a parent, I'm loath to lecture others on how to get it right, although there are some cases which quite obviously – as far as I can see – got it badly wrong. My friend Louise, for example, who is mixed heritage, was adopted by a white family in a comfortable county not far from Lola's east London home in Elm Park. Her adoptive mother, in particular, understood the concept of identity and alienation, and wanted to try to help Louise explore her blackness, even though – having lived all her life in an un-diverse area – she had never actually interacted with any black people before.

Despite her good intentions, Louise's mother could not have done more harm to her daughter's identity if she'd tried. She knitted herself a wig out of black wool, which was supposed to resemble an Afro, and insisted on wearing this wig when out in public, on the bus, in the supermarket, walking around the town centre, believing it would make her daughter feel less alone as a visible 'other'. Far from helping Louise to feel confident in her surroundings, the effect was a kind of real-life golliwog, which simply added an element of freak show to the already challenging experience of being adopted, being a visible other in an all-white environment, and the insecurity of adolescence. As an adult and parent herself now, Louise still finds questions of race, heritage and identity too painful to discuss.

Joseph Harker, on the other hand, can barely be restrained from speaking on the subject. A journalist at the *Guardian*, he is one of the few people who has been willing to voice his concerns about the changes to adoption rules, and has repeatedly criticised the complacency with which race-matching has been swept aside.

Joseph was never in the care system, although he was partly adopted. His mother, a white Irish migrant to Hull, became pregnant by Joseph's Nigerian father, who left her soon after. She later married a local white man who formally adopted Joseph as his own son. Joseph would for the rest of his adopted father's life refer to him as his 'dad', taking his last name, but differentiating him from the biological parent he calls his 'father', whom he eventually traced in Nigeria. As a mixed-race child raised by white parents, Joseph had – not unlike Lola – parental love, but at the same time a sense of identity deprivation which also left him deeply scarred.

'Hull was a white city,' Joseph remembers. 'I'd be walking down the street and someone on the other side of the street would just shout "nigger", sometimes "Paki" even . . . enough reminders to know that you are different and you are outside.'

Joseph's real racial awakening, as is so often the case for black and mixed-race children, came courtesy of the playground. 'When I was six or seven, I don't know what happened, at school, suddenly the kids got into a racist taunting thing daily,' Joseph remembers. 'It was literally every break time, they would surround me singing "wog nigger" and they would form a circle around me. They would just repeat the pattern daily.'

There is something so matter-of-fact in Joseph's account of these devastating memories, delivered, after decades of living in London, in what is still a distinctive Yorkshire accent. He's a tall man whose light brown skin speaks of his Irish heritage, while his features speak strongly of West African traits – a high forehead, strong jaw and broad nose. His face twinges with a faint shadow of pain as I probe deeper into the taunting and its effects. It must have been traumatic, to go through that every break time, every single day, I suggest. Joseph nods. 'And it wasn't the nasty kids, these were actually my friends,' he says. 'One moment you would be talking about the football with them, but then the next it was like taunting me would become that day's sport, and they would do it for however long, until they got bored.'

Eventually, Joseph told his parents about his daily ordeal. 'Their response was just *"don't react to it"*,' Joseph explains. '*"They know you're getting angry and upset, just ignore it and it will go away."* Which as a tactic is possibly a good tactic. But it didn't tackle the basic point that at the end of it you still feel inferior, an outsider, undesirable. You know in that period, in the sixties and seventies, there was no kind of race awareness,' he continues, educating me, spoilt as I am to have been born two decades later. 'There was no diversity agenda. It was just like you were stuck on your own and made to feel like shit.'

Joseph was looking for more than just a coping strategy. He was looking for a solution. 'I was never short of love . . . but if there is one tangible thing I can say about the way having white parents and a white family affected me, they didn't understand that basic thing that you are black and you [should be taught to be] proud of it,' Joseph says thought-fully. 'As a black child, you have a history. They could have told me about Nigerian history, there is so much to it that I could have learned about. But all I knew is that I was an outcast, and that I was inferior.'

'Wog' may be a word that echoes in the nightmares of Joseph and other mixed-heritage people growing up a decade or two before me, but the first time I encountered it, in my twenties, I had to look it up on Google, so remote was it from the world and time that I grew up in. Racist abuse has continued against non-white people in Britain, and appears to be dramatically on the rise since the 2016 vote to leave the European Union, but mixed-race people are often regarded as privileged relative to dark-skinned black people – a phenomenon known as 'colourism'. A legacy of the divide-and-rule tactics of pseudo-scientific racism and the categorised madness of the slave trade, light-skinned people are still perceived as the acceptable face of blackness, rewarded for their proximity to European beauty or parentage.

When I first met Sam, he was reluctant to introduce me to his friends and family, predicting – accurately – that they would see me as evidence that he had rejected black women of his own complexion, and bought into society's messaging that lighter-skinned women are more desirable. The beauty and fashion industries, so influenced by the colour-caste culture of America, have always promoted mixed-race women as closer to whiteness and, hence, more beautiful. Americans sometimes refer to this as the 'brown paper bag test' – the idea that to have a desirable shade of black skin, you need to be at least as fair as the colour of a brown paper bag. I was intensely aware of this as a teenager on the club scene, when black men would say to me, *'I like your skin. I want a light-skinned girl like you.'* I was conscious that I, or my colour at least, resembled the girls in American R&B music videos, the Beyoncés, the Mariah Careys, the Aaliyahs. It was a confusing message for someone who was coping with racism and otherness by desperately trying to be as black as possible, and at the same time getting to grips with the privileges that come with being fair.

While African American and Caribbean people have such a wide range of skin colours as a result of mixing – often through rape and violence – during slavery, many of the people in Britain who look this way are the product of an inter-racial relationship, often between one black and one white parent. And as diversity has become more in vogue, it's hard not to notice that advertisements, from M&S underwear, to sofas, family holidays, mobile phones and bank accounts, in their nod to diversity, have embraced a very specific type of black person. The one-white, one-black parent family, with mixed-race children, their blonde ringlets and vaguely Afro features. Or the woman modelling the new kitchen or in the clothing catalogue. She is ethnically indeterminate; she is fair-skinned but not pale, she is tanned but not black. She has something of all of us in her – black or white – only she is prettier, with freckles and rosy cheeks, strong bone structure and blue eyes, light brown skin and richly auburn, voluminous curly hair – long, the curl pattern loose, and not kinky. And that, I suppose, is why she is loved by those with something to sell.

Britain imported the same colourism so prevalent in the Americas from its own plantation societies in the Caribbean, but it has its own specific brand of prejudice as well. 'Mixed-race' may be inherently sellable now, but just a few decades ago it haunted modern Western thought, its offspring viewed with an almost unique suspicion. Black people were inferior, but mixed-race people, they were inherently corrupting, they were born depraved. For many of Europe's most famous philosophers, the emergence of 'mixed race' children was an ominous symptom of the genetic deterioration of the nation, and the human race itself.[10] In 'crossed races', wrote Nietzsche, 'together with a disharmony of physical features, there must also go a disharmony of habits and value concepts'.[11] A century earlier Immanuel Kant, whom I as a philosophy undergraduate was encouraged to venerate, was happy to divide the world into the 'good' races (white) and the 'bad' races (non-white), and thought mixing would degrade the good.[12]

These concerns have been incredibly persistent. It's within living memory after all that the great and supposedly philanthropic organisations of the world – the Carnegie Corporation, the Rockefeller Foundation, the British Colonial Office – were among those backing studies into the presumed social anarchy that would be caused by 'the mixing of the races'.[13] It was racism with a smiling face, couched in the patronising terms of concern for everyone's well-being, both black and white, which of course required keeping the races separate. 'Every one of us has, probably, many friends among the coloured people, whom we bear in kindliest remembrance,' insisted a former colonial administrator, Sir Ralph Williams, in a letter to *The Times* in 1919.[14] But, he went on, it was quite proper to have an 'instinctive certainty that sexual relations between white women and coloured men revolt our very nature'.

In the atmosphere of the intense class and race prejudices that flourished during these interwar years, dire warnings declared that mixing white with black would lead to the 'deterioration of the white race'. In the eyes of the white, upper-class elite, deeply attached to the idea of white supremacy, the mixing of dominant black genes with white represented a nightmare – the irreversible degrading of the white race.

The class implications were equally abhorrent. As far as the establishment was concerned, the white people – and white women in particular – guilty of this racial mixing were, by the very nature of their willingness to engage sexually with blacks, morally bankrupt working-class whites,[15] necessarily the lowest of the low.[16] As if this were not bad enough, once exposed to black men, these women became 'immoral' and 'over-sexed', notions which were inextricably linked to the colonial stereotypes of Africans as savage and sexually voracious. As one Home Office official put it crudely: 'the negro is said to be more largely developed than the white man and a woman who has once been with a negro is said to find no satisfaction with anything else'.[17]

The demobilisation of servicemen at the end of the First World War, and the resulting influx of soldiers and seamen returning home, created a unique set of pressures in British towns and cities: a surplus of labour, and housing shortages, not helped by the fact that the materials and labour needed for homes had been diverted to the war effort. In towns like Liverpool, the presence of significant numbers of African, Afro-Caribbean, Chinese, Arab and South Asian sailors provided a highly visible alien 'other' all too easily demonised as the cause of the problems. These ethnic minorities represented unwelcome competition in a period of intense recession – taking up precious resources and, as far as struggling young white men were concerned, 'stealing' the jobs that should belong to them and, perhaps even more emotively, providing sexual competition too.

In 1919, white ex-servicemen rioted, attacking and in some cases killing black men – many of whom had also fought for Britain in the war – in violent sprees fuelled by poverty and sexual jealousy. Yet the violence in what came to be known as the 'race riots' of 1919 was blamed on the black population. 'It is naturally offensive to us that coloured men should consort with even the lowest of white women,' explained the *Sunday Express*; 'racial antipathy is always present, the sex jealousy inflames it to a violent, unreasoning wave of emotion'.[18] The police took a similar view. 'The trouble,' said Liverpool's assistant chief head constable, 'was mainly on account of black men interfering with white women.'[19] Into the mix, complicating matters, was the influence of drugs, which were then beginning to gain favour with young women in the new, interwar culture of music halls. Cocaine, which was becoming increasingly popular, was thought to dissolve boundaries between the races, positively encouraging sexual contact across the colour line.[20]

The product of these sexual unions – Britain's mixed-race children – were tracked, measured and interrogated during the interwar years, in research backed by the eugenics societies of the time.[21] They were found, not surprisingly given the attitudes of those studying them and the poverty in which they were living, to be tragic human manifestations of degeneracy and immorality. A 1920 study of mixed-race children in Liverpool by a young social-work graduate named Muriel Fletcher – so influential in its time that it is credited with cementing the concept of 'half-caste' in the popular imagination – found that these children

were the cause of intractable social problems. Influenced by the eugenics movement, their physical dimensions were carefully studied, in
much the same way as Jews were later documented by the Nazis – for
signs of their genetic inferiority and abhorrence. Liverpool's 'half-
castes' were condemned for their 'bluish brown negro eyes', 'everted
lips', 'broad flat negro nose' and 'half-caste appearance'.[22] They were
pronounced to be frequently sickly, and intellectually inferior, with
intelligence 'below the average [of the "low type of white child"]'[23]. It's
said that the ghost of Fletcher's report, deeply ingraining as it did a
taboo around mixed-race people and prejudicial views of their potential, haunts perceptions of Liverpool's black population to this day.[24]

It didn't matter that the black population in many of these towns
was relatively small. In Liverpool, for example, the black community
was about 500 strong, compared with a Jewish population of 9,000,
and 6,000 new Irish migrants arriving each year.[25] It was the black
community that was most singled out, viewed with fear and suspicion,
and not just in Liverpool. At all of Britain's port communities where
there were black sailors and mixed-race children, there were similar
levels of alarmism. In Cardiff 'hundreds of half-caste children with
vicious tendencies' were growing up 'as the result of black men mating
with white women', warned the *Daily Herald* in 1929.

In east London in 1944, a report titled 'Condition of the Coloured
Population in a Stepney Area' adopted a similar tone. White women
consorting with black migrants were 'prostitutes', as far as the report's
author was concerned, their children growing up in an 'atmosphere
overcharged with sex'.[26] Marie Stopes, now feted for her work on con-
traception but in fact motivated by eugenicist beliefs, advocated that
'half castes' be 'sterilised at birth'.[27]

It was a grim view of the future, applauded by the press. 'Menace
of Mixed Unions,' exclaimed the *Daily Telegraph*, citing the report
with approval.[28] And it was widely reflected in literature. You notice
these details, as a mixed-race child educated in a canon which, during
my school life at least, was entirely composed of white writers. The
insanity of Rochester's wife in *Jane Eyre*, Creole, and therefore by

implication lacking white racial integrity, was a hint of what was to come. The description of one of the opium dens, frequented by Oscar Wilde's Dorian Gray, in which he encounters 'a half-caste, in a ragged turban and shabby ulster, who grinned a hideous greeting',[29] resonated with me as soon as I read it. 'Mixed race' was almost a byword for immorality and the grotesque. In the absence of other depictions of people who looked like me, it was all I had to go on.

There is a widely held belief that the UK did not experience segregation in the form of the Jim Crow-era Southern United States. It's true that racial mixing was never prohibited by primary legislation in twentieth-century Britain. But it was officially, and vehemently, discouraged. Apart from the diabolical warnings about the depravity of mixed-race children, Home Office guidance issued in 1925 openly sought to deter white women from relationships with non-white men, warning them of a litany of other, dire consequences.[30] The National Union of Seamen successfully lobbied for measures that gave police extra powers over black sailors, and required them to carry extra documentation. Meanwhile philanthropic organisations like the Liverpool University Settlement, ostensibly helping black communities by providing accommodation and services for them, were also attempting to keep them separate from the rest of the population.[31] The national and local authorities, along with the press, did their best to enforce the stigma that, it was hoped, would stop at least respectable whites from contemplating unions with blacks.

These views were still widespread in the decades after the Second World War, in the reactions to the influx of immigrants, from the Caribbean and Africa, from India and Asia, of many British people who voiced the opinion that Britain should remain 'white'. Enoch Powell's infamous 'Rivers of Blood' speech in 1968, warning that immigration would destroy Britain as the British knew it, was as much concerned with the descendants of immigrants as it was with the immigrants themselves. African, Asian and mixed-race children born in Britain, he predicted, were like 'the cloud no bigger than a man's hand, that can so rapidly overcast the sky'.[32] And there is still hostility in mainstream public opinion to the spectre of an increasingly mixed society. When the director Danny Boyle cast a mixed-race family in the opening ceremony of the London 2012 Olympics, many celebrated its inclusivity, its vision of an open and multicultural future. *Daily Mail* columnist Rick Dewsbury, on the other hand, described the depiction of a happily suburban white mother and black father as 'absurdly unrealistic', citing with approval the Tory MP Aidan Burley who called it 'a load of leftie multicultural crap'.[33]

Concepts of white purity and the dark forces that threaten it have not gone away; they have shifted and changed shape. The Irish, who were once regarded as almost as inferior as black people, have become 'white'. 'Black' has become inextricably linked with class to assume 'urban' identities, with undertones of an uncontrollable inner-city threat. 'Mixed race' has switched from the face of depravity to the most palatable, and eminently marketable, version of black.

One of my most revealing personal experiences came observing a rally with the English Defence League, the on-off face of the extreme far right. The EDL's popularity has waxed and waned since it sprung up in 2009 in towns with large Muslim populations, ostensibly in protest at Muslim extremism. Whatever subtle distinction there is in standing against Muslim extremists, as opposed to Muslims in general, appeared to be lost the day I was among this group of beer-soaked protesters, under a poster-paint blue-and-white clouded sky in Colchester. We stood outside the local police station, in marching distance from the town centre, men and their pit bulls draped in England flags, women and children with St George's crosses on their T-shirts or painted on their faces. Jaunty young women streamed out of pubs that had opened early for the occasion in pairs, swelling the crowd, and once a critical mass had assembled, the chanting began: '*Allah! Allah! Who the fuck is Allah?!*' and '*Muslim paedos off our streets!*'

I was reporting on the march for Sky News, as part of a documentary I was making into the reaction of people around the country to the arrival of Syrian refugees in 2015. As the size of the group grew into the hundreds, I felt conscious that for my colleagues – three bald-headed white men who in all honesty could, superficially, have otherwise blended in quite easily – my mere presence was turning what would have been a fairly straightforward job into a complicated one. It reminded me of reporting on the war in Mali, where local contacts warned me that I was a liability, at heightened risk of being targeted for kidnap or killed, because I was too fair. Here in my own country, I felt at risk for being too black.

But when I spoke to Gary Head, the local spokesman for the EDL movement, he wanted to make me feel at ease. There was nothing offensive about my presence at the march, he explained. He was a tall, upright man, whose shaved head revealed a soft halo of blond hair. He spoke with a kindly tone, reassuring me; it's not like I was wearing a hijab or anything. 'You're all right,' he told me. 'You have a good job. You speak English well. You probably have a white parent . . . do you?' His question surprised me. I nodded. 'You,' he continued, 'have integrated. It's the ones who come here and refuse to accept our culture that we have a problem with.'

When I met the EDL's original founder Tommy Robinson some months later, at an obscure pub in Buckinghamshire where he was attempting to launch a new movement, he told me that he had no problem with black people. 'Blacks are all right,' he said. 'A lot of them act like white people, they are becoming more and more like us. You know, we have Sikh members too. They love this country. It's Muslims that are the problem.'

With those words, Robinson could not have offended me more if he'd tried. But quite apart from the damning suggestion that black people are becoming more aligned with Robinson and his friends on the far right, his views showed who is perceived to be a threat and who is not, in the eyes of the modern far right. They have found a new bogeyman in the Muslim community, many of whom are experiencing abuse reminiscent of the treatment of black people five decades ago. 'Religion has become the new race,' said Sayeeda Warsi, the first Muslim woman to become a Cabinet minister in the UK. 'I could not have predicted that Muslim was slowly to become the new black.'[34]

Unlike the fascist and eugenics movements of the past, the modern far right are not so concerned about racial purity and interracial unions, in fact the anti-immigration, anti-Muslim EDL are relaxed about it so long as it represents evidence of non-white people becoming 'more white'.

And British people are intermarrying, in significant numbers. By the 2011 Census, 2.3 million people – almost one in ten people in England and Wales – described themselves as cohabiting or married in an inter-ethnic relationship. That figure is likely to have increased significantly in the years since that census, and in any event tells us nothing about young couples who are dating or not living together. One study gave Britain the highest rate of interracial relationships in the world, ten times the European average.[35]

But a closer look reveals that smaller sections of the British population are doing a disproportionate amount of its intermarrying. The vast majority of people overall enter into relationships with people from the same ethnic group as themselves. The number of white British people in interracial relationships is small – only 4 per cent. After white Brits, the next least likely groups to form a relationship with someone of a different ethnic group are people of Bangladeshi, Pakistani and Indian heritage. The Office of National Statistics says that's because of 'cultural, racial and religious differences' between these communities and the majority.[36]

But don't all ethnic minorities have such differences from the majority, and from each other? After all, the very definition of 'ethnic group', according to the ONS, is 'a putative common ancestry, memories of a shared past, and a cultural focus upon ... kinship, religion, language, shared territory, nationality or physical appearance'.[37] It may explain why Bangladeshi and Pakistani minorities are not marrying people of different races, but it doesn't explain why other ethnic minorities are.

One group stands out for having by far and away the biggest number of interracial relationships: black British people. People from both black Caribbean and black African backgrounds are forming interracial relationships, predominantly with white British people, in some cases in greater numbers than they are forming relationships with each other. For example, one study found that 90 per cent of black men aged twenty and in a relationship have a partner who is not black.[38] And as we've already seen, it is black men, more than black women, who are likely to marry or partner a white British person. Studies have found half of all black Caribbean men to be in a relationship with a woman from a different ethnic group, compared with one-third of black Caribbean women.[39]

I've always been curious as to why black people, and especially black men, are so much more likely to enter into interracial relationships than other ethnic minority groups. Not because there is anything wrong with this – after all, I'm the product of an interracial relationship myself. But the patterns in who is doing the mixing suggest there is some kind of logic at work – what is that logic? One theory is that it's seen as an act of 'integrating', and integration is associated with upward social mobility; an 'intermarriage premium', academics call it. And for some groups that does exist. For example, when South Asian women married white British men, they became more likely to be in managerial or professional occupations.[40] But black people, who were more likely to enter into these relationships, were less likely to enjoy those benefits. There is an intermarriage premium for black women, but it's smaller than for anyone else. And as for black men, the most likely to intermarry, they received no premium at all.

The more intangible benefits of 'integration' and 'assimilation' – two terms which I explore in more detail later on – are valued as a social good in themselves. Interracial unions are heralded triumphantly as evidence that Britain is successfully becoming a multicultural, integrated and post-racial society. As Martin Narey said, in suggesting race-matching adopted children was no longer a relevant idea, this is an 'increasingly multicultural society and one where, quite properly, the stereotyping of people because of their race is discouraged . . . the UK has moved on'.

But it can't be said that black people are intermarrying for the socioeconomic benefits. And when it comes to the children of these relationships, the figures are even starker. Mixed-race people with one black and one white parent are actually experiencing downward mobility. One report found that those who identify as black Caribbean and white are less likely to be in professional occupations than either 'non-mixed' black Caribbean people or white British people.[41] Again, this appears to be a special penalty for black people. The progeny of other mixed marriages have quite the opposite experience. Children of South Asian and white mixed marriages, by contrast, are more likely to enter the professions than either their white or South Asian parents.

Yet the mixed-race offspring of all these relationships are arriving anyway, and lots of us. I may have grown up feeling a total anomaly, but it's become more and more apparent over my lifetime that I'm part of a population that has grown dramatically and will continue growing. In 1991, when I was nine, 'mixed' categories didn't even exist as options on the census – you were supposed to be White, Black-Caribbean, Black-African, Black-Other, Indian, Pakistani, Bangladeshi or Chinese.[42] But over the following decade, the number of mixed-race people would increase by 150 per cent.[43] By 2001, when I was in my second year of university, there were 660,000 people ticking one of the 'mixed' boxes, and by 2011, when I gave birth to my daughter, that figure had doubled, to 1.2 million.[44] It's a very young population – 45 per cent of the mixed-race population was under sixteen in 2011, whereas only 19 per cent of the overall population is that age. There are now more mixed-race black Caribbean and white children in England and Wales under the age of five than there are children of this age with two black Caribbean parents.[45]

How does this unprecedented level of mixing, for the ethnic groups that are likely to form interracial relationships, affect their sense of Britishness and identity? Different subgroups within 'mixed race' have very different experiences. People who are classified as South Asian white, East Asian white and Arab white, for example, have been found to place little emphasis on their ethnic minority heritage, often describing their identity as 'British' or 'white', regarding 'British' as a term which is 'inclusive', 'race neutral', or denoting 'cultural belonging'.[46] And another survey of mixed-race people from a wide range of backgrounds found that only 17 per cent ranked their skin colour as an important factor in their lives.[47] But for mixed-race people with black heritage, the picture is completely different – 63 per cent of them chose skin colour as an important factor in their lives.[48] Hardly any of them chose 'British' as a term that describes their identity.[49]

Part of the reason is obvious. These black-white mixed-race people lacked what academics call 'ethnic options' – or the ability to make a genuine choice as to how they identify themselves. 'If I told a white person I was white, they would be confused, but if I said I was black then that's OK,' said one respondent to the survey. Another, 'Keith', who was mixed Jamaican British, had once told a white bank teller he was 'English', only to elicit the response 'You're not English!' The incident had upset him and he had never categorised himself as 'English' again.[50] 'Lisa', who has a white Scottish mother and a black Nigerian father, said she identified as 'black' because: 'this is how society sees and judges me, and this has shaped my perception of myself. I'm also accepted fully by my Black family, whereas this hasn't been the case with my White family. I also look more Black than I do White.'[51]

This phenomenon is widespread. A study in the US by Harvard University using face-morphing technology found that mixed-race people were regarded not as mixed, but as members of the ethnic group of their minority parent. Black-white or Asian-white mixed-race people are almost never identified as white, and had to be more than 60 per cent white before they were perceived as mixed, or 'biracial' in the American terminology. It described its findings as confirmation that 'the centuries-old "one drop rule" . . . appears to live on', a reference to the principle – codified into law in slavery-era America – that sought to enslave the fair-skinned children born after slave masters and overseers impregnated slaves, so long as they had 'one drop' of black blood.[52] A UK study of three hundred mixed-race people in 2013 found what it described as 'racial misrecognition' for many mixed-race people, whereby their self-claimed racial identities were rarely accepted by others. This was particularly salient for individuals with both black and white heritages.[53]

But what about me? I found that these studies resonated heavily with my own experience. My childhood could not have been further removed from the hardship of growing up in the care system, or the daily abuse of racist bullies in a northern town. I had an endlessly nurturing and stable family life, within the boundaries of one of the most diverse cities on earth. But a child's world is small. In the streets surrounding our suburban house, and the classrooms and playgrounds of my school, it was the sense of otherness and the consciousness of standing out that plagued me; it was feeling demonised and exoticised in equal measure because of the colour of my skin. I felt deeply confused as to where I belonged, living in a world where my two halves were drawn from identities supposedly in friction, both threatened by each other in different ways. What did that make me? How could I reconcile the ideological conflict within my genes from a battle neither created by me nor understood by anyone around me?

Now I realise that my struggle was Britain's struggle. The way Britain has coped with a Manichaean past and a multicultural future has been to ignore these intractable questions of identity. A new, mixed-race generation is often hailed as evidence that race and identity are no longer relevant at all, a message that I took to mean – grappling with identity as I was – that black culture, the history and struggles of my ancestors, the battles contained within my dual heritage, can be simply wished away.

It's a very British problem. While it's increasingly clear not everyone in Britain subscribes to the official image of Britain as a multicultural nation, with a pluralistic tradition of tolerance, it's still part of the official British brand. Interwoven into this branding is the idea that we don't see race, that this is a good thing, it represents the ability to transcend prejudice. But this has become part of the problem. It is denial, avoidance and obfuscation. You cannot just paint everyone in the families of the future a pleasant shade of light brown, and expect questions of identity, racial difference and histories of oppression to disappear.

If I'm rejecting this branding exercise now, I do not do so out of hand. There is a path I once followed, one I've seen reflected in so many other people I have interviewed, in which you begin life unaware of race. You 'don't see race' – the blindness that is now becoming so popular – but being thrown against what the Harlem Renaissance writer and anthropologist Zora Neale Hurston called 'a sharp white background', you become acutely aware of being a visible other. You are left alone to shape this difference – at first it is given sharp angles by the taunts of bullies or by prejudiced remarks – then you discover there is beauty in it, and depth, and you embrace it as a heritage to wear proudly. You say, as I did, that you are a black person, and you say it with dignity. And then comes the inevitable question: 'But why do you call yourself black, when really you are half white?'

I remember, clearly, the first time I said that I was black. I was fifteen years old, in my GCSE year, and I had started working at the *Voice*. A school friend asked me what the *Voice* was, and how come she had never heard of it. I wanted to tell her it was a black newspaper, but I felt embarrassed, worried it would make her feel excluded. Plus, the word 'black' had never been spoken between me and my friends before, except that one time, when one of them had told me not to worry, because they didn't really see me as black, and I was OK. Over time, I developed the confidence to call the *Voice* what it was. But that was the newspaper. It was different to apply that name to myself.

One Saturday lunchtime, I was helping my mother lay the table in the kitchen. Earlier that day, I had called up Choice FM, a black radio station based in Brixton, like the *Voice*, which had phone-in discussions on Saturday mornings. The DJ Jeff Schuman was having a discussion about mixed-race people, and I decided to contribute, sitting on the wooden Ashanti stool in our hallway beside our landline, the phone receiver cradled between my ear and shoulder as I waited my turn to speak on air. 'As a mixed-race person,' I said, on live radio, 'I think the problem is we don't fit in anywhere, black people don't see us as black, white people don't see us as white.' My parents had been listening, and as we got lunch ready, my mother challenged my view. 'I don't see why it matters,' she said. 'People are just people, why this obsession with fitting in with black or white people?' I was emboldened by now, and by calling myself mixed race on the radio, I was already halfway there. 'I see myself as a black woman,' I told her. 'Society sees me as a black woman – don't you realise?'

'We never raised you to be black,' my mother replied. My sister, who was eleven at the time, was listening intently. 'We just raised you to be yourselves.'

'It doesn't work like that, Mum! Can't you see?' I told her. 'You raised us in a society where people look at us and see our skin colour. We –' I looked hesitatingly at my sister '– are black.'

As soon as the words left my mouth, I was conscious of their powerful, and uncomfortable, potential. 'How do you think that makes your father feel?' my mother asked. And it was exactly what I had been thinking. What must it be like, as a white man, for whom race has never been a defining issue, to have a wife that you love, who just happens to be black, and then to have a daughter who turns round one day and tells you she, too, is 'black'; an identity which, in all its symbolism and meaning, erases you?

It's an intergenerational question. My dad often looks after my daughter, the two of them pottering along quite happily hand in hand, on an errand to the supermarket, or a trip to the library or the nearby city farm. One time, my dad told me, a black lady stopped him outside Sainsbury's, asking if the little girl he was with was lost. 'No,' he replied, 'she's my granddaughter.' The lady looked at him suspiciously. My daughter, with a mixed-race mother and black father, betrays no visible evidence of white heritage at all.

It's been something of a relief to read that, far from being the lone race-obsessed identity crisis personified, I'm fairly typical of people with my parentage. But this has important implications for identity.

While we are busy trumpeting the 'post-racial' implications of the rise in the mixed-race population, many mixed-race children themselves will self-identify in some way as 'black', either through choice or as a result of the racial misrecognition of others. Often this begins as the consequence of the negative, surprising, experience of racism, but then grows into a more positive phenomenon, which you might call 'black consciousness'.

Many mixed-race people are entering into relationships with people whose ethnic backgrounds are different from their own. But others are avoiding it – seeking instead partners whose ethnicity reflects the one part of their mixed background they most identify with. They are particularly concerned about what academics call 'racial dilution'. 'I'll see a mixed-race couple, and there's still part of me that feels funny,' a mixed-race woman called 'Kate' told researchers, in examples of concerns about 'racial dilution' they quoted on Radio 4. 'I don't know why but it's like [I can't] accept this . . . I feel like people are trying to stop the black line. I feel like I fight with myself because it's politically incorrect to have those thoughts. But there's part of me that still feels funny. And so I try to be really smiley, and just ignore it.'

Miri Song, the professor who has done so much research on this subject, found it was a specific preoccupation of black-white mixed-race people. 'The black-white participants seemed particularly racially conscious of the implications, the social political implications . . . [of racial dilution],' Song said. 'This idea of dilution and grappling with these often contradictory emotions, with the head saying hey, . . . it's almost racist to think this way, but at the same time [a mixed-race person] is also really fighting with herself about how she feels . . . This is a particularly live issue for the black-white participants.'[54]

It's a complex sentiment, but it's one I recognise well. There are several things going on. One is that, as a mixed-race person, you feel lost between worlds that seem – for all the modern talk of 'fluidity', and race being a 'social construct' – miles apart. In Britain, people see you, when you are mixed race, as 'black'. In majority black countries, certainly the West African ones I have spent time in, someone of my skin colour, and my British conditioning, is seen as 'white'. You are stateless. There is nowhere you belong. That spawns a desire, deep-rooted, subconscious sometimes, to have an ethnic and cultural identity that you can really, authentically, claim as your own. It's probably too late for you. But it's something that – depending on your own choice of partner – you might be able to offer your children.

Another is that being half black is not a neutral place. Blackness is a loaded heritage to have in a country like Britain. Most of us discover that we are black through acts of racism and prejudice – the taunting in the playground, the lewd sexual remarks, or the everyday acts of othering. Blackness is still associated with negative ideas – with crime and violence, poverty and underachievement, or migration from a dark continent. There's a whole separate realm of negative association just for the African continent itself – a place of starving babies and deranged, savage warriors. If you have swum through the sewage that the world has thrown Africa's way, and reached the other side, where you own your blackness, and are proud of it, where things are clear and old and smell good, you can't help but feel a little suspicious of other people of African heritage who embrace white identities. As if they saw the same rubbish floating in the water, and jumped out of the way to avoid getting dirty.

Ron, a mixed-heritage half-black-African half-white man I interviewed, told me a story. There used to be a show on the BBC, after the news, called *Nationwide*. It's not something I remember, but from 1969 until 1983, it was on every day – a current affairs magazine show, a bit like *The One Show*, and, according to Ron, just as popular. One day it featured a report about a black couple – immigrants who had moved to Birmingham in the 1960s. Ron can't remember what this couple were talking about, only the fact of them, and the way that this black man and his black wife were sitting there, in their front room, being interviewed by the BBC. 'I remember seeing that black couple,' Ron told me, 'and thinking "what a shame, he can only have a black wife. There are all these white people out there, and you can only have a black wife." I feel ashamed of that now, but I feel like that is what is still going on in the heads of a lot of black people. And it's not surprising. I remember at that time, I felt undesirable for being black. Every representation of blackness was negative. I didn't want to be black, and I remember wishing I would go to bed at night not being black, so that I could fit in.'

Ron suspects 'racial dilution' is something that black people are unconsciously seeking. Much like the literary figure of the 'Tragic Mulatto' – the doomed light-skinned character in American fiction who crossed the colour line and held themselves out as white – the assertion of 'mixed-race' identities is interpreted as a desire to dilute, or somehow escape black heritage, and seek the privileges of whiteness.

Discussions about race, and especially mixed race, are difficult to get right. Not least because race, as it's increasingly popular to point out, is a scientifically meaningless concept. The list of reasons for disregarding race is long and persuasive. It's now uncontested that humanity originated in Africa, and as a result 'it has been shown that we are all Africans under the skin', as one expert in mixed-race theory (this actually exists as an academic discipline now) has pointed out. 'Our differentiation into Eskimos, Bushmen, Australians, Scandinavians, and other populations has merely been a coda to the long song of human evolution.' Genetic difference between racial groups is negligible, and is far overshadowed by the range of ethnic difference *within* groups.[55]

Blackness and whiteness are both shifting. Identities the British once regarded as non-white, like the French – considered an indulgent and effeminate race inferior to the robust and logical British – and the Mediterranean nations of Southern Europe, have become white.[56] Jewish identities in the UK and the rest of Europe have been studied for their fluidity – subject to some common cultural and religious ties, but also increasingly secular, and highly differentiated, depending on national experience and influences. The only definitive identifying factor, it has often been said, is 'the propensity for a "Jewish" person to self-identify as such'.[57] Muslim identities since the late 1990s have been heavily influenced by the rising rhetoric of a perceived 'clash of civilisations' between Islam and the West. The demonisation of Muslims as part of an existential threat to the West has powerfully resurrected their status as 'other', in theory irrespective of their ethnic descent but in reality mainly synonymous – in Britain at least – with people of Bangladeshi, Pakistani, North African and Arab heritage. Black people are mixing with white people in unprecedented numbers, giving birth to a generation for whom, in theory, race should be an even less meaningful concept than it has been already.

In the constantly evolving landscape of racial, religious and ethnic minority identities, language carries real significance. The use of the term 'Islamism' to describe the ideology cited by terrorist groups is, for example, a source of anger and resentment among many Muslims, who perceive a tendency to conflate politicised Muslims on the one hand with criminal extremists on the other.[58] A number of people have cast similar doubt on the use of the term 'mixed race'. 'Mixing evoked for me visions of watering down on the one hand and racial purity on the other,' remarked broadcaster and professor Kurt Barling, writing about his experience of growing up in Britain with English, Irish, Nigerian and German heritage in his book The 'R' Word. 'Neither of which seemed to me to have the slightest credibility.'[59]

Several of the mixed-race people I interviewed had similar objections. 'I don't like "mixed",' said Ron. 'Above all, it implies that everyone else is pure, which means you, as a mixed person, are some kind of mongrel as opposed to the pure races of the earth. It says nothing about your history,' he added. 'It has no roots. It has no historical meaning. There's white history, European history, Asian history, whatever . . . there is no mixed-race history.'

There is the history of mixed-race *communities*, of course, like the Cape coloured community in South Africa, the mestizos, who now form so much of the population of Latin America, the Afro-Brazilian Saro and Tabon communities in Nigeria and Ghana and so on. But those are histories rooted in certain times and places, places where the need to classify mixed-race communities as 'other' arose in the oppressive conditions of the transatlantic slave trade, American segregation, South African apartheid. And when you broaden history out, so-called racial 'mixing' is nothing new – it is quite simply the history of the world.

But unlike Ron, a younger generation is comfortable with the language of 'mixed race', embracing it as an increasingly common identity that for them has social meaning. It's not unusual, in more diverse parts of south London than the patch where I live, to hear as I did one autumn afternoon in a playground, a teenage girl, curly Afro hair scraped into two buoyant puffs, arguing with a friend with a similar complexion, bellowing the catchy yet devastating insult: 'You're a *disgrace* to mixed *race!*'

It is also the future. Nearly one in sixteen children under five is mixed race; in London it's one in eight.[60] These children are the future – at least so said *Time* magazine, back in 1993, with a memorable cover of a light brown woman. Her skin is a warm shade of peachy tan, her hair is straight but a little textured, eyes wide but a touch almond, nose linear but ever so fleshy at the nostrils, lips generous but not too much. This 'beguiling if mysterious visage', *Time* managing editor James R. Gaines explained, was 'the product of a computer process called morphing ... to create the kind of offspring that might result from seven men and seven women of various ethnic and racial backgrounds'. In other words, this woman did not exist, but in the future, hers might become the only ethnicity that exists. She was 'The New Face of America'[61]: 15% Anglo-Saxon, 17.5% Middle Eastern, 17.5% African, 7.5% Asian, 35% Southern European and 7.5% Hispanic.[62]

What will such people call themselves? It's curious that the English language of the British Isles has, so far, spectacularly failed to come up with any linguistic solutions to the full-bodied, multilayered, many-textured world of mixed and multiple identities. There has been very little progress in resolving the unsatisfactoriness of our current vocabulary. When ethnicity options first appeared in the 1991 Census, it essentially boiled down to choosing whether you were 'white', 'black', 'Asian' or 'other'.[63] Now you can be a mixture of any of these, including special black, white or Asian varieties of 'other', or 'mixed' with white and any of these, including 'other'. You can be Irish, Roma or Sikh. But it still seems offensively crude. Given the now notorious fact that the Inuit people have fifty words for 'snow', and the Sami people of the Arctic fringe a thousand words for 'reindeer', should we expect languages to, as one scientist said, 'find a way to say what they need to'?[64]

I don't mind declaring my ethnic heritage per se. There is so much race-based inequality in society that I think the data needs to be collected, and monitored. I feel the lack of this information in areas where it doesn't exist. For example, reporting for the BBC in 2017 on the fact that black people are disproportionately unlikely to vote, I was reliant on exit polls, since no one collects information on turnout broken down by demographic factors including race and gender. Voter registration numbers and exit polls suggest strongly that there is a particular problem concerning the apparent alienation of black British people from the electoral process.[65] But without the hard facts, it's difficult to do anything about it. There *are* reasons for investigating the ways in which our society is becoming more ethnically diverse, but until we achieve a more open and sophisticated approach to identity, it will never be a pleasant experience. It feels as if the only time my identity is acknowledged in this not-seeing-race country of ours is when it serves some official, and often opaque, statistical purpose. It reminds me of the great writer Toni Morrison's words, referring to the extreme state of official callousness towards African Americans in the US. 'No group has had more money spent on it to have its genetics examined. I would like to know who are these people who know our sperm count, but they don't know our names.'[65]

The British unease at acknowledging identity is at its most visible in the tendency to celebrate the rise of interracial relationships and mixed-race people, as evidence that race and identity has somehow 'gone away'. People with mixed heritage aren't less interested in defining their identity, as some people have mistakenly assumed, but are often more so. They need to be allowed to define the way they see themselves, so that they can define themselves as British as well. Many will choose white partners, and have children who are fairer and fairer with each generation until the memory of a black ancestor all but disappears. Many will enter into relationships with other people of mixed heritage, and regardless of the ethnic background of their partners or their parents, they will not necessarily choose to align themselves with the struggles of black people, and will direct their energy to other pursuits, rather than the existential dilemmas of 'otherness'.

But this should be a choice, not an assumption, or it's just yet another episode in a long history of identity vandalism, carried out by others blindly, in plain sight.

5. PLACES

A family photograph showing my great-great-grandmother Betty,
a.k.a. Maama Welsing (centre back).

I was not leaving the south to forget the south, but so that some day I might understand it.

— Richard Wright, *Black Boy*

I am not African because I was born in Africa, but because Africa was born in me.

— Kwame Nkrumah

Africa was born in me. My upbringing could hardly have been further away. But the continent of my mother's birth was calling me, and the distance between us created a sense of emptiness – I believed – a chasm between worlds. And over time, as I gazed into the void, I began to see a bridge that could be built. Identity became a place.

In August 2002, just a few weeks after packing up my little room in a shared students' house in Oxford, I found myself sitting on a plastic chair in the middle of the tiny, tiled balcony of an aparthotel, sweat gluing my skin into my clothes, in what I then thought was *the place*. Or at least close to it. In my mind, Ghana was the epicentre of my belonging. But here I was in the Senegalese capital, Dakar – I figured it would do for a start. I would make a life here, make friends with Senegalese people, learn how to live and be part of a country like this. I was brimming with optimism. I was here to stay.

My job was a new graduate's dream. George Soros, the billionaire Hungarian philanthropist with one of the biggest non-profit foundations in the world, had decided to expand his grant-making organisation, the Open Society Foundation, into West Africa, and I was part of its founding team. My work was fascinating, demanding and rewarding; supporting journalists in the height of war, funding legal aid clinics for women in conservative Muslim societies in the Sahel, creating new plans for transparency in petrodollar-fuelled dictatorships.

By now, aged twenty-one, I was convinced that if I found the right place, my broken sense of identity could become whole. This was the real reason I had moved to the far western tip of Africa, a search for fertile soil in which to plant and grow a new identity for myself, an African identity that would allow all my other branches to flourish too; female, westernised, independent, ambitious, Afrocentric and optimistic. I found a common sense of purpose with young Senegalese people who had abandoned the Europhile ambitions of their parents' generation, and were hell-bent on spending their productive years in their home countries, rather than contributing to the French economy, as had previously been the case under French colonial rule, and ever since for those who could afford a visa.

People like Ibou and Assane, two cousins from a well-to-do Senegalese family who were working for global IT companies, having graduated in France, but who now planned to create their own businesses in Dakar, banking on the promise of rapidly transforming communications infrastructure. They and their friends, also educated in France and sharing the perspective young Africans often refer to as 'Afro-optimism', took me under their wing. As did Clédor, the only one of the group whose life resembled the poverty of the vast majority in Senegal, and it showed. Clédor's eyes were bloodshot red, and he had more teeth missing than you would expect from anyone in their early twenties. He had these straggly dreadlocks, his remaining teeth were a deep shade of yellow, and his speech a slurry deep soup of Wolof and French, the result of copious weed smoking and having never finished school.

I remember nights perched behind Clédor as we whizzed on motorbikes in convoy up the magical hill at Ngor, past the airport, spinning suddenly off the road into a mountain of complete blackness, broken only by a murky green blur of trees. Then a vast, flat, crystal plate of light rose up in front of me – a lighthouse casting chandelier beams over Dakar's dense coastal fringes, the lovely dark ocean and the painted suburbs stretching across the land. I wanted to gulp down the energy as if I were dying of thirst. It was like a dream come true then; the Gulf of Guinea ushering a vast open blackness that was in my mouth now, a salty taste and the rush of fresh, West African air. Years later, when I was back in London and that night a distant memory of everything else that happened in Senegal, I learned that Clédor was dead. He had made it to France, his lifelong ambition, by hook or by crook somehow, only to be killed in a car accident – a tragic end to his dreams.

My friends were versatile. One minute, they were partying with the grandson of a Senegalese king – more palace party than house party – skinny and scantily clad Senegalese girls, all bones and boobs, whisky and cigars, the backdrop a splurge of marble, crystal and gold; a kind of Senegalese Trump Tower meets hip-hop music video. The next, they were sitting behind the night guard's hut in their parents' gardens, getting high, and eating *dibi* – delicious chunks of fatty, spicy mutton that were roasted on the bone and sold in greasy brown paper by street vendors in obscure pockets of the city. And at heart these Senegalese twenty-somethings were deeply religious, steeped in the local blend of mystic, Afrocentric Sufi Islam.

I was mesmerised by the confluence of these lifestyle choices, and whiled away the hours of some of my best afternoons in Senegal this way, under the cool shade of a baobab tree in Assane's garden, arguing with his friends, drinking *bissap* – the red drink of the hibiscus tree – or *ditakh* – a thick, green juice from a fruit related to the kiwi, that is brittle like a nutshell and sweet and powdery inside. Like all Senegalese drinks, they were laced with so much sugar that marijuana seemed superfluous in inducing a high. We talked about religion, the triple sense of oppression at being black, African *and* Muslim in the weeks following 9/11, and the war in Iraq, which back then in the winter of late 2002 and early 2003, everyone knew was coming, international legal mandate or not. It was stirring extreme feelings of persecution and anger in even the most laid-back of this gang of aspirational, French-educated Dakarois.

But over time all of these international, intellectual Senegalese friends of mine just began to disappear. There were no opportunities in Senegal for them, no matter how idealistic their outlook and determination to contribute to their African homeland. The lure of careers and jobs and the push of parental pressure to make good on the investment in their education, saw them – one after another – boarding one-way Air France flights back to Paris, the old imperial centre.

Other friendships were hard to find. Local women were family-orientated, living at home until they married, and involved in large and complicated extended family obligations. Expats were there for completely different reasons to me. I made friends with Viki, the Hungarian woman who was married to my Malian colleague, whose little children had the same skin colour and hair type as me, as well as familiar issues with their identity, having been the only mixed-race children in their Budapest neighbourhood until they were moved to Dakar. I taught Viki, who had never encountered a single black person before meeting her husband in Budapest, how to care for her children's skin and hair, explaining how you never brush our hair from the root to the tip, you begin at the end, coating the tangles in coconut oil to separate the curls gently, then teasing out the knots with a wide-tooth comb. I took her shopping for detangling shampoos to help end the torture of her poor daughter's hair-washing nightmares.

But our friendship had its limits. The only saving grace that Viki could find in life in Senegal – which she quickly came to regard as an unbearably hot, dusty backwater with an alien religion and greasy food – was a relatively luxurious expat lifestyle. After all, Saturdays in Budapest did not offer mornings at a swish tennis club, lunch at a French fish restaurant on the Corniche, gently brushed in the ocean breeze, or evenings at waiter-served cocktail parties on the palm-fringed lawns of other parents at the American school. I did not belong to this world – young and single as I was, with no children at the American or any other international school, no lawn on which to host cocktail parties. I found myself always defending Senegalese culture, as if I were some kind of expert on this country I'd known for only a few months. It was as if, confronted with any sentiment anti-African, or any stereotypes, however subtle, that seemed a variation on the old theme of a 'dark continent', a backwards place, with primitive habits, I slipped into the role of the defender. I refused to see myself as an expat living in a white, European bubble; I came here because Africa is in me, and I wanted to be in it. And being the only black person in the tennis club is not what I had in mind.

And far from bitching about our Senegalese colleagues – the favourite pastime of expats, I noticed – I seemed to have swiftly become the butt of the local staff's daily jokes. Their favourite gag involved mimicking my voice; not so much the English accent that unavoidably shapes the contours of my French, but the soft airiness that filled out my words. Their voices seemed to me like walls of sound, strong and solid, but mine was clouds, porous and light. It lacked authority, it lacked certainty, it lacked density, and – in contrast to the level of responsibility with which they perceived my role – it did not command respect. It took less than one full week at my new job for the staff to work out that I was this soft British girl with pretensions of being African, vulnerable to tugs at my sense of communality, and they began asking me for money. I lent money to Agnes, the office cleaner, a short woman with deep brown skin and beautiful eyes that drew the gaze away from the set of large white teeth arranged at phenomenally haphazard angles in her mouth, who lived with her mother and father, her brother and sister, and her three children. Out of all of them, she was the only one who had any work. It was a common story, and I found myself bailing her out regularly. Word got around, which was not a good thing. I was the youngest and lowest-paid professional in the office and, somehow, the one with the biggest outgoings.

I was digesting the reality of the burdens Agnes bore when a ferry, *Le Joola*, carrying almost two thousand people from the southern province of Casamance – plagued by a war of succession that had made the roads impassable for years – sank on its way to Dakar. 'Africa's *Titanic*', as it eventually became known, is now regarded as one of the worst maritime disasters in history. Only sixty-four people survived, most of the two thousand dying in the ocean, many of them schoolchildren on their way back to the capital for the beginning of the school term. The boat was loaded with three times the safe number of passengers. Everyone I knew knew someone who was affected. 'We are not free,' one colleague at work would tell me, determined to educate away my naive ideas about the desirability of life in a struggling, African country. 'We can die at any moment – on the roads because of the war, or because people drive cars which don't even have brakes and are falling apart.' She whispered these words, her voice trembling with anger. This was her warning to me, and she would only deliver it once.

I had gone to Senegal to find the place where my identity could become whole. To reinvent myself as the African I had long been convinced I was. But it was a flawed project, doomed to failure. I never did feel at home in this hot, French-speaking, Sahelian land. One bright December day, I went to the Mali Market – one of my favourite places to shop, where Malian women sold raw shea butter by the kilogram, and chunky wooden bracelets with intricate ink patterns from the north. The market was configured as one long strip of stalls, and as I approached it, I felt the force of a man's whole body weight, descending on me from behind, wrestling me to the ground, holding me down and gyrating into me.

I couldn't see him, but as I struggled, I could see the attack playing out on the faces of the stallholders – their faces a slow motion of disfigurement from amusement to horror. But no one came to help me, for long minutes it seemed, until I began to scream, and eventually one of the men at the market scared my attacker off. I got a look at him then, and recognised him – he was the local crazy man. He wore an intricately designed outfit of rags straight out of *Mad Max*. This was accessorised with various pieces of trash, carefully arranged into belts, calf-length boots that had the same effect as the gladiator or fringed boots in the boutiques of London and Paris at the time, but his were made of shreds and various bands of fabric. His nose had multiple home-made piercings with sharp metal objects, and he had thick dreadlocks decorated with yet more trash. He was terrifying to look at but strangely compelling; fascinating, and unreal.

He was real now though. Slowly hauling myself to my feet, I watched him as he sauntered back to the lamp post that seemed to be his lair, smirking and then rapidly, mockingly, going through the motions of a Muslim prayer. I was shaken and shaking, stuck on the spot where I had forced myself up. Still no one asked if I was OK. Unsure what else to do, I continued walking towards the market, on a kind of autopilot. Then, they came; young men from the stalls. They offered no comfort or consolation, but said that, if I paid them 500 CFA – about 50p – they would accompany me while I finished my shopping. The sense of having being violated hit me then, with the same level of force my attacker had used to pounce on me moments before, and I began to cry. I had never felt so unloved – despised even. I realised these people didn't care if I lived or died. They were struggling, hustling and surviving, and as far as they were concerned, the most I had to offer was a bit of cash. How deluded I had been to think they could ever see me as one of them. I was just another privileged *métisse*, another *étranger* – stranger, foreigner – enjoying a lifestyle that for most people was far out of reach. And people like me were their only likely source of income.

My job involved exhaustive, and exhausting, travel around the West African subregion, but the inequality I came home to in Senegal was as extreme as it got anywhere. Lebanese diamond dealers fleeing the war in Liberia had moved to the relative safety and security of Dakar en masse, erecting breathtaking mansions and injecting even more foreign currency into the Paris-standard suite of fine-dining restaurants along the coast. Foreign-based Senegalese saved long and hard to build their own palatial retirement and family homes, and these dominated the dignified, tree-lined streets of the area where I lived, Dakar-Fann. Yet metres away from these homes, on any main road, armies of tiny rag-clad children stalked the cars in their stationary traffic with empty cans, begging for pennies. These *talibés*, as they were known, had been sent to Islamic residential schools by their impoverished parents, and lived there in a kind of bondage, taught the Quran by marabout teachers in the morning, in exchange for begging on the streets in the afternoon, and returning the money to the marabouts. These little children, some as young as five, were visibly malnourished, mistreated and often sickly; some were known to have been beaten severely, or kept chained together in shackles, and some were found dead.[1]

There was unfathomable poverty, and there was beauty too. Driving out of the overcrowded, polluted city, whenever I could get away, I would speed through the scorched plains – the gnarled, ancient baobabs and the delicate savannah trees dotting the parched, sandy scrubland, and the sun the hottest pale, perfect disc in the sky. I would pass village after village, little walled settlements – the peaks of each home's straw roof poking above the crude wall. Every three or four villages, a proud concrete mosque punctured the pattern, and a make-shift bus stop with ten or twenty villagers gathered in a shady spot waiting for a bus to take them to the market, or one of the Mourides religious festivals, like Magar, in the pilgrimage city of Touba. On grand days like that, the women would wear their finest *bubus*, dangling down their slender bodies from way off the shoulder, and boys would wear their crisp, pressed baggy jeans, 2Pac T-shirts and Tommy Hilfiger skullcaps, as if they had come straight out of the Bronx, or Brixton, and into the village somewhere in desert-like northern Senegal. The familiarity of it only highlighted how foreign, to me, this landscape really was.

It was in the loneliness and exhaustion of this period of my life that I began looking back for the first time. A rebellious and strong-willed child, I had spent the years until that point chasing some prize; the fantasy of being free from the rules and regimes of affectionate but strict parents, liberation from the all-white environment of Wimbledon where it seemed nothing I could do would ever allow me to feel accepted, leaving Oxford, which felt in many ways like a continuation of school. Moving to Africa became the answer; one upon which I was fixated. I had been sprinting towards this moment, and now – for the first time – I was on pause, stranded, it seemed, in a living reality check. In this dry land with its unfamiliar sounds – wide-vowelled Wolof, marabout chanting, slow French, the pouring of sweet, black tea, Muslim prayer calls and drumming, to which I could not dance – here on the outskirts of the Sahara, there was no avoiding the fact that the dreams I had had of finding a place of belonging were dissipating into the heat like a desert mirage.

I realised then, alone and strung out in Senegal, that the world I'd inhabited at Oxford had slipped away before I'd been able to appreciate it. When I was there, I'd felt as if I did not deserve to be. I was convinced that I had somehow tricked the wise and aloof old dons who had interviewed me into seeing intelligence where there was none. I had what a younger generation – with their knack for naming these things – call 'impostor syndrome'.

Years later, reading letters from my grandfather, I realised how many of my own experiences echoed his, sixty years earlier. P. K. Owusu, my mother's father, had studied at Cambridge in the 1940s – the son of a cocoa farmer plucked from a village in the Gold Coast, and sent to Britain on a colonial scholarship.

My grandfather is a titanic figure in our family, his journey from humble, illiterate origins to Cambridge the subject of huge pride. I never met him – he died a decade before I was born – but in 2015, the letters he had written as a student were diligently prised from the Queens' College archive by my judicious and persistent cousin Kesewa. They were subtle letters, gracious and modest in tone, but they had a subtext. And it was one which I recognised.

'We have all come to regard the College as our home, as we have learnt to value it as such. We are perhaps the most troublesome lot in the College, but you have always managed to help us,' P.K. wrote to his tutor apologetically in 1948, at the end of his time at the university. 'I will always cherish pleasant memories of the College, its dons and its beautiful surroundings. I am looking forward to the time when some of my pupils will come up and redeem the good name of Africa.' Why, I wondered, did my grandfather, who had defied so many odds – the boy from a poor family in a rural African colony who became a graduate in English literature at Cambridge University – feel the need to apologise?

The more I learned about P.K.'s story, the more I understood its implications for my own. Paul Kofi, the name that came to be always shortened to 'P.K.', was born on 13 December 1917 in Konkonuru, a village to the south of Aburi – the cool mountain town that provided refuge for the family fleeing Baden-Powell's war on Kumasi. His father, Owusu, died when he was still young, and his mother, Mary Addo, was a woman who had no formal education, who traded and worked the land. My grandmother told me that initially P.K. was set to follow in his father's footsteps, and become a cocoa farmer himself, but the ambitious boy was riding an unstoppable current towards another destiny. According to the stories the children in my family are told, the young P.K. sat up late at night in Konkonuru, toiling at his schoolbooks, swatting mosquitoes, sometimes battling perennial malaria, straining his eyes in the candlelight, when everyone else was sleeping, determined to have a better life. To keep himself awake late at night, he would plunge his feet into a bucket of cold water, and he worked, worked, worked.

Each year in those days, the British government awarded scholarships to a handful of Gold Coast students to study at Cambridge, and in 1944, my grandfather was one of them. The Second World War still staggering on, P.K. boarded an Elder Dempster boat sailing due west along the Gulf of Guinea, all the way to London, escorted by submarines. It must have been a treacherous voyage – Elder Dempster lost twenty-four of its ships in the war,[2] including a passenger mail boat similar to P.K.'s, torpedoed without warning en route to West Africa.[3] The fate of the imperial motherland was far from clear too.[4] My grandfather got stuck into the war effort immediately, his first destination an agricultural camp in Basingstoke. It sounds cold, and grim – 'It is a great change for me; for we live in tents a few yards from the town and have to queue up for food and our bath,' he wrote to the master of Queens', describing conditions he had never had to endure even with the basic, impoverished facilities of life in the rural Gold Coast. 'On the whole life over here is interesting,' he added, trying to put on a brave face. I can hear his Ghanaian accent in the letters. 'Please I beg,' is how he begins one sentence, a classic Ghanaian turn of phrase. 'I will be coming to the College on September 16th.'

Four years later, my grandfather had graduated with not only an English degree, but a new identity too. He had become, in his own words, 'a Cambridge man'. Yet he was under no illusions as to his status. Almost from the very beginning of his time at Cambridge, he had taken up the role of informal advocate for the small group of other

African undergraduates – lobbying first the college and ultimately the government to increase the stipend they lived on, to an amount on which it was actually possible to survive.

That P.K. left Cambridge with strong, loyal, pro-British conditioning was neither a surprise nor an accident. The scholarship he'd received was a deliberate component of British colonial 'indirect rule' – a system which involved educating 'natives' to perform much of the administrative work of running colonies on Britain's behalf. In spending scarce public money in the midst of a conflict that threatened Britain's very future, shipping young Africans like him to British universities across 7,000 kilometres of war-ravaged ocean, the government was deliberately inculcating loyalty to British culture and establishing a future generation of colonial officials. They chose only the best and brightest for this privilege, and P.K. was – by all accounts I have heard – a brilliant man, whose life was a remarkable testament to triumph over adversity. But reading his letters, it seems like he was always apologising.

This, I feel, is still the gift of an Oxbridge education for a black person, or someone who is visibly 'other'. An Oxbridge degree offers an institutional stamp of approval that opens doors to the establishment and the professions that otherwise remain sceptical of those with brown faces, and foreign-sounding names. I knew that it was a privilege to be a student at Oxford, and I was grateful for the opportunities it gave me. But entering this world can test your self-confidence to the core. I felt undeserving, and I felt too that my personal triumphs and failures would somehow have consequences for every other black student. If my college had made a mistake in taking me on, would they feel they had taken that risk, and it didn't work out, the next time they were faced with someone like me? Why did we feel it was our job to, in my grandfather's words, 'redeem the good name of Africa'?

Eventually, I thrived at Oxford academically. I managed to work out how to get through a reading list and write an essay, with not a little help from classmates and college friends – still some of my closest companions – and I came to enjoy the intellectual challenge of sitting alone in the Bodleian Library, under the light of a bronze-and-green banker's lamp, or sinking into the enveloping folds of an ancient armchair in an eccentric tutor's room, arguing about the Cuban Missile Crisis or the philosophical underpinnings of the social contract. But emotionally, things went from bad to worse. I performed convincingly in tutorials, but internally, the atmosphere at Oxford destroyed my confidence. It was like being back in my early adolescence – surrounded by privileged white peers, constantly face-to-face with my sense of otherness. There was no equivalent to the *Voice* in its Brixton community down the road, only the spectacle of some of the Eton boys I knew occasionally venturing to Cowley – then a working-class neighbourhood with a significant black population – where they would go to buy weed.

My coping mechanisms did more harm than the experiences they were designed to protect against. I starved myself, harnessing my new-found willpower and seriousness in an attempt to conform, finally, to the standard of beauty I felt I would now never be able to escape. I shrank into my sparse room with my expansive desk, telling myself that focus and silence were the new me, the adult me – the parties, and turbulence, and emotion of past years were gone with my childhood. The quiet, suffering despair that I went through in those three undergraduate years scares me still; it was the closest I ever felt to my spirit choking. I felt like I was becoming another person, and I had no idea who that would be. It was only later, wandering the streets of Dakar-Fann under an Atlantic, African dusk, or driving the long, empty highways that hugged the blustery coast late at night, that I came to understand my behaviour at Oxford as an experiment in suppressing myself.

If it sounds like my whole world was defined by race and racial difference when I was at Oxford, it was at first. By the time I had finished eleven years of a school where I was so conscious of standing out, I had vowed never to put myself in that position again. I didn't know then, as I know now, that the world of business, the legal profession, the establishment and especially the media would be more of the same. And I was aghast to find that, in going to Oxford, I'd extended the sentence I felt I'd already served in the social environment of my school. Of course this was a narrow and blinkered perspective. The college system at Oxford, and especially St Peter's, my small, poor and unpretentious college, made me socialise with other students whether I liked it or not. We shared PPE tutorials, we ate two or three meals in our college hall every day, since we had had to pay a fixed kitchen charge for it up front at the beginning of each term, we rescued each other from our frequent essay crises. Having run away from my friendships at school, I had to overcome the deluded notion that I had nothing in common with people just because they were white. It forced me to grow.

But for my black friends and me, Oxford could be an especially hostile place. We were forever rubbing against people who had never come into contact with black people before, coming as they did from elite boarding schools and privileged pockets of the country. Or if they did have an idea of black people, it was a very specific one. The *'Got any weed?'* question inevitably followed us around at student nights – after all, where there are black people, someone must be selling drugs. On the other end of the spectrum, I remember being asked by an undergraduate at Trinity College whether I was a 'Nigerian princess' – apparently the only type of black female student he could reconcile having made her way to the university.

There was a strong theme of rugby and rowing culture in my and many other colleges, as well as aggressively white and male social clubs like the Bullingdon Club and Piers Gaveston, in which public-school-educated men drank together and loudly promoted a certain ideal of female beauty. When an especially laddish rugby player won a college election, putting him in charge of divvying out college accommodation in the third year, he allocated these to female students not according to the official 'ballot' system, but in order of how attractive he found them. I came so far off the scale that I wasn't even offered a room in college, and had to find one outside the system altogether. Incidentally, I bumped into that student in 2016; he has moved to

Wimbledon with his family, and become a born-again Christian. He apologised to me, his room-allocation rankings one of many transgressions he felt the need to atone for, having spent his time at Oxford – he now explained – in a haze of rugby, drunkenness and general chauvinism. At the time, it had just served as another of many reminders that I was wrong: an ugly, unintelligent impostor – ideas embedded in so many ways in society, which he was parroting rather than originating, and which festered in my personal insecurity. By 2016, he had overcome his thoughtless cruelty and I had outgrown my insecurity, so the apology was not really necessary. But I appreciated it all the same.

The Oxford undergraduate student body was in those days, and still is, exceptionally un-diverse. In 2013, for example, after more than a decade of supposed progress since I graduated, twenty-three students of black British African heritage were given places to study at the university. Their success rate relative to the number of applications was 13 per cent, making them half as likely to be accepted as white applicants. The same year nineteen students were from black mixed-race backgrounds.[5] In 2011 then prime minister David Cameron created a media flurry by criticising Oxford for having given only one black student a place in 2009 – a figure which was not quite correct, but which did accurately describe the number of students from a black British Caribbean background admitted that year. For that one student, thirty-four others with similar ethnic heritage had unsuccessfully applied.[6]

When in my third year I began going out with a black American student who was studying for his masters, I found myself in a social group dominated by Africans and African Americans. As, often, the only British member of this group – which was surprisingly segregated from the mainstream undergraduate student realm – I acted as a kind of cultural interpreter, especially for these Americans, baffled as they were by the extreme Britishness of Oxford as an institution, and isolated from any actual British people. I had spent my teenage years idealising the world created by African American movies like *Love & Basketball*, *The Best Man* and *Love Jones* – films that revealed middle-class communities, and whole universities, where everyone was black. That was the closest thing I knew to a world where you could be both black and a graduate, black and living in a nice house, or black and in a well-paid job. It was the only societal example I had.

But now, as cultural interpreter to African Americans trying to decipher Oxford, it crystallised for me that I was definitely, unambiguously not American, but British. One difference was our tolerance threshold to ignorance and prejudice. The Americans were speechless not so much at the kind of racism we were used to encountering – most of which they recognised from back home – but by how normalised it had become and how pacified they thought we were in its face. They baulked at practices that ranged from those I'd considered harmless, such as white students dressing up in blackface and Afro wigs for fancy-dress 'bops', to more overt acts of hostile racism, such as black students being refused roles in student plays on the basis of 'image', or being singled out and required to provide ID to gain entry to colleges, where white students came and went freely. My college's decision to hold a 'slave auction', in which students put themselves up for sale to raise money for charity, annoyed me, but utterly incensed my African American friends. And they were particularly exercised by an experience I recounted, of a black friend who came to visit me at my college, prompting a usually kind and attentive college porter to say, 'You should have let us know in advance if you were expecting someone who looks like a criminal.'

My American friends couldn't understand why we put up with this, but ours was a different context. They had numbers on their side – even as a group of foreign, graduate students, they lived together in certain colleges, and were closely organised through their scholarship programmes. They had names, inherited from the civil rights movement, for acts of oppression and prejudice, and for their very identity as African Americans. When racism affected them in Oxford, they would not hesitate to call it out.

We, on the other hand, were fragmented and vulnerable. We were distributed throughout Oxford's forty-plus colleges, one here, one there; when we did meet, it was often by chance. Most of our friends were white, obviously, and we felt conscious of offending them, if only by highlighting our difference, or attracting any more unwanted attention than we already had. Some mixed-race students I met weren't even sure if they were 'allowed' to call themselves black – 'I'm only half!' one said apologetically.

I wish we could have been more organised, more together, bolder. We all had our subversive ways of trying, in some small manner, to change the system. Almost all of us informally mentored younger students, taking part in schemes during the holidays to encourage more black pupils to apply to Oxford, sensing instinctively that only a critical mass of ethnic minority students could ever really alter the atmosphere. Some of my friends used their creative pursuits – plays, songs and articles – to change perceptions, and we have carried a sense of responsibility with us throughout our careers, to bring others up behind us as we go. But confrontation, the kind of protest, organisation and publicity I see today's generation of Oxford students achieve with movements like Rhodes Must Fall – the call in 2015 for Oriel College's statue of Cecil Rhodes to be removed – was unimaginable in my time. These students are demanding an immediate acknowledgement of the white supremacist underpinnings of the intellectual and even physical foundation of the university. And they are achieving some success. In 2017, the university announced that for the first time, history students would have to take a compulsory paper on black, Asian or Middle Eastern history, in recognition of the need for diversity in its curriculum.[7] Whatever your views on the activism of students through campaigns like Rhodes Must Fall or #WhyIsMyCurriculumWhite, the simple fact of their existence as movements is evidence to me of how far things have come.

For all its social backwardness, Oxford – once I got the hang of the studying part – gave me a love for academic pursuit that I had never tapped into at school, where I'd had far more enthusiasm for writing about Puff Daddy for the Voice than I had, really, for my A levels. I threw myself so wholeheartedly into this – partly as a coping mechanism I think, but partly because I loved it – that I became a scholar. This was my first opportunity to study race and gender, colonialism, theories of politics and African societies as a subject, and I was hungry to learn, choosing every possible option on my PPE syllabus that moved me closer in that direction. Some of these papers were taught by African scholars whose political ideology was rooted in both the African countries I so romanticised and the dreaming spires of British academia. That changed my life.

Truths about my identity have tended to dawn on me in the negative. Oxford had highlighted my awkwardness and unease in the face of a version of elite, privileged, traditional Britishness. Living in Senegal made me realise, very decisively, that I was not Senegalese. In fact, it left me disillusioned that I could ever really be African. But I wasn't ready to give up, the dream did not die. Senegal was not my country after all, and its only connection with my heritage was the fact that it is technically considered the same part of the world as Ghana. But the two countries have as much in common as the UK and Poland, and roughly the same distance between them. The next time I packed up my things, said my goodbyes, and moved to West Africa, it was to Ghana itself. I still thought I could find my identity in a place.

The experiences of parents – their dreams, their pain, their hopes and disappointments – shape the lives of their children. In 1962, my grandparents left Ghana under painful circumstances. They had four – soon to be five – young children, and their future had been dramatically called into question. Later, my grandfather would learn just how much his life would have been in danger if they had stayed in Ghana – his name would appear on a 'blacklist' of 'enemies of the state'. Their dreams of a future in their country were over, and they were fleeing, not knowing when they would come back. My grandparents thought that by taking their family to the UK, they would not only be safe from the terror that they suspected – rightly as it turned out – was approaching in Ghana, but also that their children would find new identities. British identities. For the most part, they were right. My mother and her siblings do have ties to Ghana, but they all live in the UK, and have tended to have British partners. And yet here I was, exactly fifty years after they left, moving in the opposite direction, obsessed with the prospect of making a life for myself and my family in Ghana, convinced that Britain was not for me. What circle was I trying to close? What spaces was I trying to fill in? What silences was I trying to probe?

The answer begins, I think, with my grandfather's return to the Gold Coast. On 5 August 1948, one Cambridge degree completed, he boarded another Elder Dempster passenger vessel – this time West Africa-bound, heading towards a Gold Coast that had changed for good. Decades of export boom had turned the nation into a prosperous economy and, increasingly, a financial and transport hub attracting aspirational Africans from other countries as well as traders from Lebanon, India, Europe and America. These were imperial people in an international world, products of the globalising forces of the British Empire, with modern expectations of life and leisure. They were connected to the imperial centre in London; they read African-owned newspapers and visited African-owned clubs; they wore European fashions and entered into monogamous marriages.[8]

The cocoa farmer's son was now a member of this club. Four years of Cambridge undergraduate immersion had left him westernised, and energised about the prospects for his own country's future, perhaps in equal measure. He saw a future for himself in the modern polity of an independent African state – India had achieved independence a year earlier, and African nations would surely follow. Under self-rule he expected his country to modernise and develop. And modernity, in his eyes, had certain Western features – how could it not?

African 'returnees' like my grandfather were part of a tiny elite. Yet they still entered the rural African village society of their parents, a place that had moulded them, nurtured them and laid the foundation for the privileges which they now enjoyed. But they did so with the perspective of a colonial education that had taught them to regard their village relatives as synonymous with backward tradition, illiteracy, ethnicity, tribalism and polygamy.[9]

One of these traditions in particular was starkly at odds with Western culture. The Akan people of southern Ghana are one of the world's few traditionally matrilineal societies – following a system of inheritance through the mother's line. Daily life in traditional Akan society centres around compounds where men, women and children live with their maternal family, their allegiances to the descendants of their siblings, rather than the children they bear with a spouse, in a communal home. Boundaries are loose and family members, united by this common bloodline, pool their resources and energy. Marriages are matters of reproduction and diplomacy, rather than companion-ship or cohabitation. This is the Akan way.

This might all have been relatively straightforward if – as he ini-tially expected to do – P.K. had finished school and returned to the village as a farmer himself, joining the communal family home. But now P.K. was a Cambridge graduate, and not just a graduate, but a graduate in English literature; a force of cultural influence which he had passionately embraced, and which had affected not just his polit-ical, but also his more intimate desires. P.K. would marry for love, and live with his wife and provide for and raise his own children – a 'Cambridge man' was not about to return to the polygamous, matrilineal system of his family's tradition in Aburi. When Kwame Nkrumah – the audacious pan-Africanist who would become Ghana's first president – met my grandmother for the first time, he said to P.K., 'Well done! She's a beauty! So where did you find her then?' To which my grandfather, with his Anglophile sensibilities, took great and long-lasting offence.

Nkrumah had a background not unlike my grandfather's. He was born into a poor, rural family in western Ghana, but through scholar-ships and sponsorships had studied in London, where he became a leader among the already agitating West African students. Returning to the Gold Coast, on the very same ship as my grandfather, one year earlier, he had instigated a revolution.[10] 'Seek ye first the political king-dom, and all else shall be added unto you' was Nkrumah's battle cry, one which became victorious on 6 March 1957, when 'Ghana' was born – the Gold Coast renamed after the ancient African empire in the Sahara, emphasising Africans' contribution to world history and civilisation, and its pre-colonial roots. Nkrumah is still feted by many as a prophet, one of the most influential thinkers of the twentieth century, and the most influential African of the last millennium.[11] My mother remembers, aged six, celebrating Independence Day with P.K., and ushering in the birth of the new nation. The joy and pride she expresses is echoed by everyone I have ever spoken to who witnessed that day.

There was no love between Nkrumah and my grandfather, but they did have a functional working relationship. My grandfather was put in charge of teacher training – an important role for a country whose transformation had been visualised by Nkrumah as depending on high-quality, free universal education. But the vision was tempered by reality. Ghana's industry and commerce were still under foreign control. Britain accounted for one-third of cocoa exports, and a lack of manufacturing left the economy heavily dependent on imported consumer goods. The Cold War powers kicked the vulnerable young African states around like footballs, openly tussling for influence and trade ties, while simultaneously orchestrating coups from behind the scenes. Ghana was no exception. Nkrumah, with his socialist brand of pan-Africanism, formed ties with the Soviet bloc and China, attracting the attention of the CIA, who began to see the nascent Ghanaian regime as a threat to American interests in Africa.[12] Global cocoa prices collapsed, from £250 per ton in 1961, to £91 per ton in 1965, sending the economy into freefall.[13] As dissent and opposition among Ghana's elite mounted, Nkrumah retreated into an increasingly closed and powerful inner circle, silencing critics by force.

P.K., well known for his pro-Western, Anglophile views, was starting to be seen as a threat. As Ghana's first president became increasingly authoritarian, that perception began to carry new, sinister implications. P.K. triggered an exit strategy for his family, ultimately securing a posting at the Ghanaian High Commission in London. I believe he left Ghana with a heavy heart – the Cambridge graduate who had returned home bursting with energy to play his role in the emergence of the first African black nation to free itself from colonial rule. It was a decade later, in 1971, that P.K. finally went back, to a country which was by then in the full grip of military dictatorship. And he had gone back to die. He lies buried in a graveyard thick with foliage, close to his childhood home.

Ghana's flag is one of the most distinctive, and I think, most emotive, in Africa. Its horizontal tribune of red, yellow and green stripes are the traditional, pan-African colours: red – representing the blood of those who died in the struggle for independence from British rule; yellow – the gold of its rich mineral wealth; and green – symbolising its forests, and natural beauty. These colours appear again and again in the nations of Africa and its diaspora. But the centrepiece of the Ghanaian flag makes it stand apart from all others. A five-pointed black star – the emblem of African emancipation. It was an iconic symbol in 1957, as the world looked upon the first black nation to be unshackled from its former masters' colonial grip. It remains a powerful, and unique, symbol to this day.

But the journey has been a deeply troubled one. On 24 February 1966 Nkrumah, en route to Hanoi, was toppled in a *coup d'état*. It was not just Nkrumah's world that had crumbled. The descent of Africa's black star into violence and fear – a nightmare that would last for three decades – left many shattered dreams in its wake. The repercussions of P.K.'s exile were widespread. The family members he had taken with him to London were his wife and children, a choice which represented another break away from the matrilineal clan, alienating them, provoking the suspicion that he had also abandoned the values of his heritage. His livelihood, by now as education attaché to the Ghanaian High Commission in London with a salary paid by the central government in Ghana, was under threat.

A few years later, he was dying. His wish was now to return to Ghana, and he and my grandmother travelled together, but when they arrived, P.K.'s relatives prevented her from being with him, even in his last days. They blamed my grandmother for P.K.'s - in their view - incomprehensible adoption of a way of life in which he prioritised her and his children, his nuclear family, over the extended one. When she returned to London, Ghana was still on its descent, and the nucleus of the family – unable even to visit back home – shifted more and more towards its British base. Nothing was resolved. This conflict between British and Ghanaian values, unfinished business in the extended family and resentments that festered over decades, became a puzzle that formed the basis of my cultural inheritance. And in the absence of anything more solid to cling to, I found it puzzling indeed.

My own family's tragedies were not dissimilar to those of many others, broken apart, made destitute, and forced into exile during that period of turbulence in Ghana. It was not until the mid-1990s that the Ghanaian diaspora, having toiled to rebuild itself in new European and American homes, began returning, bewildered children in tow. I wrote a poem about this, as a teenager; I called it 'Like a Heartbeat that Stopped Dead'. The day I touched down in Ghana, I felt as if some dormant pulse had begun to beat again, and I vowed that one day I would make this land my home. In February 2012 – exactly fifty years after my grandparents had fled in the opposite direction – I fulfilled the promise.

The Ghana I found in February 2012 was a changed country from the one I remembered from 1995. The nostalgia I felt for Accra, the emotion I remember seizing my soul on that first teenage trip – the red earth seducing me as soon as I left the airport, the candlelit tin shacks along the roadside, the intensity of the smells in the air – back then they had been magical and radical to me all at once. There was no red earth now, just concrete, white lines, traffic lights and desolate but important-sounding hotels. The candlelit roadsides where vendors sold sweet, fatty fried plantain doused in ginger and chilli are gone, purged from the route to give the impression of order. I couldn't reconcile these changes because the poverty I saw beneath the glimmer of high-rise towers was the only thing that seemed familiar. You only had to travel a few metres before the chaos set in. But now chaos came strip-lit, roadside sellers had solar bulbs that illuminated stalls of pirate DVDs and chewing gum with a brutal white glow. They slowly crept back into view after the airport, as if a thin veneer of international swank has been posted over the most lucrative and visible patch of the same old city, with its same old hardship.

The opportunity to live in Ghana had come when I was appointed West Africa correspondent for the *Guardian*. We were like tourists, in a way. I don't know any other Ghanaians in London who stay in a guest house when they come back to Ghana – if they haven't built a house of their own, they have an endless stream of relatives whose homes they can stay in. But my daughter, my mother and I were like strangers, and my grandmother, accompanying us, almost a refugee in her own country. There were many traumatic memories for her here, things that happened in her past affecting her deeply, not least the painful year spent burying her husband, finding herself the target of his family's wrath, which pushed her away from her own people. And she had been gone for so long.

That's why we are here, I thought. *To build a bridge.*

This audacious emotional construction project begins in the most unlikely of settings: McCarthy Hills, a suburb to the west of Accra distinguished from the building site that is the rest of the city's vast, suburban sprawl only because it is at a gradient. The rugged hills twinkle unevenly with the lights of those homes which are both inhabited and have generators, as we appear to have arrived in the middle of a power cut, then fade impossibly far into the distance, swallowing up land that only a few years ago was green farms and pristine bush.

Despite the personal significance of this project, this is first and foremost a professional relocation. My employers would have paid for a hotel – have to, in the end, when my mother and I eventually veto the guest house my grandmother has chosen – but for now we lack the knowledge or energy to enter into combat with her cast-iron resolve. The owners are her friends, and she has convinced herself that it would be a good place for us all to stay.

It is not. The floor is a permanent bed of dust, no matter how many times a day it is swept, such is the nature of living in an area of intense construction on top of a windswept hill. The richly red earth I have been romanticising in poems and diary entries since I first came to Ghana in 1995, is less lovable, it turns out, when caked onto my crawling baby's hands and laboriously hand-laundered clothes in dirty orange patches. There is power in McCarthy Hills for a couple of hours every morning and evening, at which point the generator goes for another hour until its fuel ration runs out. And these magnificent hills are a gradient too far for the water company – the shower is a trickle on good days, and in a theme that will become familiar in the months to follow, sometimes it offers no prospect of getting clean. Water, it turns out, really doesn't flow uphill.

The people that run the guest house are kind enough, a sweet elderly couple with whom my grandmother remains friends five years later. Belinda, who is German, and her husband Jan, who is Ghanaian, rely on their core business hosting 'German tourists' – at least this is what my grandmother believes – who have come to Ghana to meet 'dates' they've found on the Internet. This turns out to be a polite way of saying that these pot-bellied, balding German men have found beautiful young Ghanaian women online willing to have sex with them, and are planning on doing it at this guest house.

The whole state of affairs awakens a sadness in me with which I was already familiar from my time in Dakar. It's hardly unique to Africa, or poor countries in general, to see women's bodies commoditised. But here it seems stained with the legacy of colonialism, where the colonised were brainwashed into believing, with the fervour of religious faith, that the white man is king. What hope does a young, beautiful girl from Ghana's slums have of obtaining the fruits that the developed world dangles before her now, in Accra's new shopping malls and five-star hotels, if not from a German 'tourist'? What does she have to give that can be cashed in for school fees, money for her family, or a plane ticket to the land where the streets are paved with gold? She has her body.

And these European men, not content with having enjoyed the spoils of Ghana's gold, land and bodies over the centuries, slurping up their space at the top of the food chain like beer, trample all over these young bodies, tossing them some make-up and new clothes in exchange, and the unfulfilled promise of a visa. It feels to me like a race, gender and power imbalance that is unchanged since Europeans first began stepping foot on these shores, ogling at black women's genitals – in some cases putting them on display back home for others to marvel at – raping them, torturing them, enslaving them and turning them into crude caricatures of licentiousness and sexual desire. It's a perception that is never very far from home. I remember my parents visiting me in Senegal, and going out alone with my dad, only to realise with horror that the immediate assumption of all around was that I was a local girl who had hooked up with a white man twice my age. It's probably, ironically, the only time I ever blended in.

Living in Ghana was, of course, an exercise in coming to terms with my Britishness. I remember following my grandmother to an intense Saturday-morning market in Batsonaa, sick of paying import prices for substandard foreign fruit and veg at Lebanese- and Syrian-run supermarkets, and realising how closely I resembled the expats I'd been so disdainful of in Senegal. I put the baby in the sling and followed my grandmother around as she chose a bunch of green plantains, a huge bucket of tomatoes, yams, garden eggs, onions and smoked fish – our meals for the week. It nearly broke my heart, this short, sweaty outing. I could have been an American tourist, with my daughter on my front, while other women at the market had babies tied snugly to their backs with cloth. I stood behind my grandmother awkwardly, trying to insist on paying for our groceries, unable to speak to the market women, except for the odd '*me de wasi*' – 'thank you' in Twi. Anyone with a copy of the Lonely Planet could have done just as well and, without the insecurity of feeling ashamed at their failure to fit in, probably would have looked a lot less awkward.

I vowed to learn Twi, and I did. At least I tried. My mission was to be able to say my name properly, and much else besides. I was determined to be at home in this country, to find a way of feeling less other, less like a legacy of the white man, as if I had some stake in the fabric of this land. I dreamed of being able to call a young boy, the way my grandmother does, and command him to fetch me a coconut just so, using short, staccato Twi words, moulding my hands in the shape of a coconut so that you could almost eat the instructions themselves. So that when I go to the village where my grandmother's brother has a nursery school, and there is a crowd of a hundred tiny children, barely able to speak yet able to yell at me in unison '*obruni, obruni!*', I can tell them, authoritatively, as Ghanaians speak to little children, that I am not *obruni*, I am a black woman. I am a Ghanaian.

I began taking lessons from a teacher named Chambas with my friend Feyi – who is Guyanese, with the mixed African, white and Indian heritage shared by so many in South America – and who is also a fellow south Londoner. I soon realised that all those notebooks I'd filled with expressions I couldn't pronounce properly over the years had left more of a residue than I'd thought. I already knew how to say '*me kɔ*' (I'm going), '*me ba*' (I'm coming), '*ahein*' (yes), '*yen kɔ*' (let's go), '*wo frɛ wo sen?*' (what's your name?) and '*wo hun ti den?*' (how are you?). It was basic, but it was something. When Sam arrived in Ghana a few months after our daughter and I had settled in with the help of the matriarchs, he began taking classes with the same teacher. We found ourselves practising together eventually, and it was a rude awakening.

Sam may not have learned how to speak Twi growing up, but he was raised deep in the cultural nuances of a large and important Aburi family, and he does know how to *think* like a Ghanaian. He has grown up fully exposed to the specific Ghanaian way of knitting your brows together and making your already-almond-shaped eyes narrow, while dismissing something authoritatively, with a muscular flick of the arm. It's in his hardwiring; it's the way he was raised.

As I practised my Twi exercises, sitting on the sofa, my legs crossed, saying '*wo firi hen?*' – which means 'where do you come from?' – he accused me of speaking in exactly the same way I would enquire after a neighbouring mum's origins in the middle of a London

NCT class. 'What's wrong with that?' I asked. 'What isn't wrong with that!' he retorted.

First, he criticised my pronunciation. 'It's "*haoeu*" not "*hen*",' he said, somehow managing a word that is every vowel at once, in a deep, hooting sound. Then he criticised my demeanour and tone. 'You can't be all flowery and gentlemanly like an English person when you're speaking Twi,' he said. In fact, he went on, my whole mentality was completely hopeless. 'You're acting like some kind of debutante,' he declared. 'You have to be bush! You have to screw up your face. You have to stand close to the person you're talking to, or squat hunched over a bowl of fufu, scooping it up with your hands. You have to be rough, dismissive and direct. Your whole mentality of polite inquisition just does not cut it. It's not authentic at all!'

He's exaggerating but there is truth in jest. I realise you have to learn Twi through role play, through assuming the character of one of two roles Ghanaians tend to fall into when dealing with each other. Either you are heavily exerting your authority or you are subservient, humble and bullied. There's so often nothing in between. Relationships are domineering or deferential. This, I know, is a highly hierarchical society.

Chambas teaches us an Anansesem – a story of the famous Ghanaian spider Ananse, whose parables have become folklore around the world – and it's a gorgeous, smouldering tale, rich in the oral tradition I have always understood comes from this place, but never experienced as it is meant to be heard. Chambas, on the other hand, tells us of evenings in the village as a child, sitting under an old tree, a fire burning in the centre, while his grandparents told these stories. Chambas was shocked to learn that Feyi was raised on these stories too, in her town house in Guyana – the slaves carried them with them in the diaspora to the Caribbean and the Americas. These stories go very deep into the culture, Chambas says. And this is what I love about Ghana; a sense that this culture lurks in my own past, and it goes deep.

Is it absurd to be nostalgic for a culture I know only in fragments, things half heard and half forgotten from my mother? If so, I'm not the only fantasist. You can't move in Accra for encountering people around my age – children of the 80s and 90s – who grew up in the UK and the like, in the era of Live Aid, of famine and war, images of Africa so irreconcilable with what we knew of our own families' intellectual and cultural heritage. Riled by the superiority and racism drummed into our everyday surroundings, even into the mentality of our own parents, so many others like me were trying to retrace the steps of the generation that left this continent. There were enough of us that people began to talk of reversing the long-established 'brain drain' – which saw the best and brightest seeping from Africa like blood from an open wound, living out their lives in the developed world, enriching it with their talent and energy, while their already downward-spiralling countries sank further into the mire.

Not us. We were 'returnees' – we had a name, and a purpose – turning our backs on the recession in the West and joining the oil rush of West Africa, the tech boom of East Africa, the flurry of start-ups, inventions and finance companies. Or creating charities, non-profit projects and development consultancies, intended as a non-patronising alternative to the mainstream. Many have felt the cold glass surface blocking off the pinnacle of their careers or professions in the UK because of their brown skin, yet in Africa, a British accent and education only accelerates their chances. And all the while correcting a historical injustice in the process.

There is almost no better evidence of the pernicious effect of subtle British racism than the thousands of people born and raised in Britain who leave in search of something that truly feels like theirs. There are no official figures monitoring the number of British Chinese people moving for the first time to China or Hong Kong, for example, of British Pakistanis moving to or returning to Pakistan, but their communities are full of stories, of blogs offering relocation tips, and citing racism and a sense of being limited by perceptions of race as the motivating factor for leaving.[14] I found so many British Ghanaians who fit this description starting new lives in Ghana. Like my friend Kofi, with whom I overlapped at Oxford. He left his respectable McKinsey job to become the founder and director of one of Africa's most successful private equity firms. Or Mustafa, an economist who worked as an administrator at an immigration charity in Zurich, and is now a multimillionaire gold dealer, transporting gold and packaging it into attractive financial products for Swiss banks. John worked as an estate agent in Richmond, and now owns a chain of restaurants, bringing the still exotic tastes of jerk chicken and pizza to Ghanaians, a venture which he runs after hours from his main business as a property developer, catering to the residential and business real-estate needs mainly of the other returnees. There is Eric, who worked as a consultant for London's investment banks, and now has an oil marketing company that turns over $150 million per year. And another Kofi, a mid-level accountant in London whose career was advancing far slower, he felt, than his white, British counterparts, and who returned to Ghana where he founded and runs one of the country's most successful retail banks.

There are Americans too, hundreds of them. Stacey, one of my closest friends in Accra, is Bronx born and raised but visually as close to the Ghanaian feminine ideal as you can get – which shows in her perfect almond eyes, cheekbones rounded like the stones in the mountains, full lips and generous wide smile. She is something of a serial entrepreneur since leaving her job in banking, and determined to start a business in Ghana that will allow her to cash in on Ghana's rapid economic growth but also build something that adds value in the country, where jobs are in short supply. There is Nicole, who quit her job at the World Bank to write incredibly successful TV dramas reflecting the lives of modern women in African cities.

What they all have in common is the fact that their families went to great lengths to raise and educate them in Europe or America, eyes firmly fixed on the associated material advantages but myopic to the physiological and social barriers their children would face in countries where even middle-class Africans are far, far more likely to be cleaning the toilets in a financial institution than running it.

These friends of mine were thriving in Accra. I, on the other hand, began to understand for the first time in my life why so many Ghanaians had been willing to tolerate the hostility towards 'African economic migrants' – an increasingly pejorative category to belong to – moving from African countries to Europe, rather than the other way round. The paradox is hard to ignore, even as it manifests within my own family. My grandmother – who gave up three months of her time to help me settle into Ghana before going back to her home in London – could never understand me for constantly seeking Ghana, since she sacrificed so much to get her descendants a chance at British life. She was watching me unravel her efforts in real time.

Part of my grandmother's motivations were unquestionably feminist, although I can't imagine her calling them that. Like her husband P.K., Ophelia Joyce came from humble beginnings. She spent much of her childhood living with her grandmother Betty, known as Maama – a baker still remembered in Aburi and the surrounding villages. My grandmother would go out selling the freshly baked loaves into the evening, from a tray she balanced artfully on her head, swaying through the green valleys in the fading light. When she neared the end of her final school exams, there were three professions open to her – telephonist, teacher or midwife. There was a midwifery post at Korle Bu, the Gold Coast's main teaching hospital, which her father had seen advertised in the newspaper. My grandmother applied, and was invited to Accra along with 120 other young women to sit the entrance exam, followed by an interview before a panel of six professionals, including a doctor, a lecturer, a matron and a nurse. It must have been – for a young woman from Aburi far more used to selling bread to villagers than conversing with medical professionals – seriously intimidating. I still detect the pride in her voice when she recalls hearing, in 1947, that she was one of twelve Ghanaian girls awarded a place – fully funded by the colonial government, which meant fees paid, lodging paid, three meals a day and uniforms provided, plus £1.50 a month for spending, rising to £2.50 a month in the second year.

Two years later, in 1949, my grandfather – recently returned from Cambridge – had been at a wedding in the Aburi botanical gardens. He had obviously been one of those bachelors at weddings that everyone notices. A handsome, single, young, local man with a Cambridge degree doesn't come along every day at weddings anywhere, especially not in a small town in the mountains. The women were not about to let this one go. *'Why aren't you married yet?'* one of the aunties asked him. In a story he relayed to my grandmother, and she repeated – and still enjoys repeating – to me, P.K. replied: *'I haven't found anyone yet that I like.'* The auntie was determined to fix that. *'I've got a niece doing midwifery training at Korle Bu,'* she said. *'You should go and look her up.'* She gave him a name, which he wrote down on a piece of paper. The name was Ophelia Joyce.

My grandparents had their wedding reception in the sweeping, low green of the same botanical gardens. As a couple, they stood out: they were educated, monogamous, idealistic. When Queen Elizabeth visited Ghana in 1961, P.K. was put in charge of organising the occasion. They sent their children – my mother and her siblings – to international schools where black children were in the minority, wanting them to have the same education that the white children of British expats were receiving. They socialised comfortably with foreigners and expected their children to feel as equals with the white children of their friends and acquaintances. At least, that's how my grandmother sees it. My mother tells a story of visiting a white family on a Sunday, my grandparents sitting by the pool with the other couple, in their Sunday best. 'Go and play with the other children,' my grandmother told my mother. The other children, white British kids, were playing in the swimming pool, and my mother dutifully jumped in, nearly drowning in the process. It hadn't occurred to my grandmother, apparently, that knowledge of swimming was a useful prerequisite.

I sometimes think my grandparents were so ahead of their time that their attitudes are still more progressive than those of many Ghanaians today. Moving to Ghana in 2012, around four months before Sam arrived, exposed me to attitudes I'd never directly encountered before. My neighbours in Accra were obviously scandalised by the way I had been gallivanting around town in my professional capacity, investigating corruption allegations and interviewing ministers, with no male guardian visible. They gave him a piece of their mind when he finally did arrive. 'You need to control your wife,' they said, right in front of me.

There is no escaping these views of gender roles; it's a small mercy when at least they provide some comedy. One afternoon, sitting under a palatial tree with at least a dozen other customers, a circle of women clicking their fingers as they weave long braids into our hair, a preacher descends on us – taking advantage of the fact that here lies a captive audience, tied to the spot by our scalps. She delivers, apparently, the word of Jesus as it relates to Ghana's plague of cheating husbands. 'Let there be change! Varieties . . . men need varieties, that's why they keep chasing other women,' she explains. 'After palm nut soup, make garden egg stew. Clean your mosquito nets. Clean your fans! Every man wants a woman who will be neat, even though most of them don't bath . . . I'm showing you the way! Hallelujah!' It's entertaining. But it is not home.

So many other British people are coming to Ghana, hoping to find identity in a place. In as many different ways as people in the African diaspora feel the pain of separation, a sense of having been ripped away from countries like Ghana, there are as many different experiences of 'returning'. After we had been in Ghana for about a year, my friend Lee – a black British man of St Lucian heritage, whom I had known since my days writing for the *Voice* – came to visit. Lee, a tall, dizzyingly energetic man who talks, drinks and smokes with equal rapidity, was once my editor at the newspaper. It was he who gave me my big breaks, nurturing my ideas and encouraging me to do bigger and better interviews despite being just a teenager at the time. Back then it was my urgent need to find a way of making myself a useful member of the black community that drove me to write for him, yet under his guidance, the work I did at the *Voice* gave my career early momentum. But as more and more opportunities came my way – with my private-school education and then Oxford degree – Lee, almost ten years my senior, found doors closed to him. These days, he told me, the heat bearing down through the windscreen as we cruised due west on a burning afternoon, he functioned back home in Derbyshire, where he lives, on 'a combination of anger and caffeine'.

Lee's visit to Ghana was motivated in part by the hope that he could scout the country out as a potential place for his own journey as a future returnee. In 2001, Ghana became the first African nation to enact a Right to Abode Act, giving people from the African diaspora – those descended from the millions of slaves taken from the continent to the Americas and beyond – the right to live and work in Ghana, even if they could prove no direct Ghanaian heritage. As a result, thousands of Caribbean, African American and other black people had been moving to Ghana, either tracing their original heritage to the country through the centuries of slavery, or regarding it as a symbolic home in the motherland.

We drive west for five hours, along the windswept coast; palm trees praying to the land to rescue them from the ocean, craning away from the relentless Atlantic. The gentle hills are sprinkled with the ruins of European forts from the days when the Portuguese, Swedes, Spanish, Germans, Danes, Dutch and finally the British treated this place as a sinister playground – seizing each other's property, arming local rivals, plying them with alcohol and ammunition and taking advantage of the chaos to load gold, ivory and millions of Africans onto their ships. Time and disinterest have reclaimed the land in the centuries since; these days the forts punctuate the coast like teeth in an old, rugged mouth.

Some, however, have been preserved. At the slave forts of Cape Coast and Elmina Castle, the holding cells that kept Africans in captivity until they were loaded onto ships for the middle passage are still intact. They offer the closest experience to understanding what it must have been like to be sold away from your African homeland into a new world, a deathly voyage away, your integrity, identity, language and family – even your name – left behind. For many diasporans, these castles are especially sacred places. They are not only incredible historic monuments, and vital relics of world history, memorials to perhaps the most grotesque and prolonged suffering in human history.

They are also personal graveyards – people's great-great-great-grandparents were trafficked through these walls, lived memories that have been handed down, remembered in culture and trauma alike.

Elmina is the most haunting, and haunted, place I have ever known. Unlike many of the other slave forts that litter the West African coast, time has almost stood still inside Elmina, preserving the sight, the sense, even the smells of the era of transatlantic slavery. The dungeons where slaves were held, before being pushed through a squat door into boats below waiting to ferry them onto the middle passage, are still stained with the stench of human suffering. The first time I went inside the male cell, the ceiling was lined with bats, a disarming blanket of writhing black coating it, as if to prove the suffering of the spirits that lurk there. In the dungeon where female slaves were held in filth and anguish for up to three months, a trapdoor leads directly to the master's luxurious bedroom above, where they would be washed before he raped them. It's estimated that at the peak of the slave trade, 10,000 people a year were transported onto the boats from its haunted cells.

My connection with Elmina is different. I am descended from someone who once lived within Elmina's walls – not as a slave, but as a slave trader.

Elmina is the oldest European building south of the Sahara Desert. It's hard to believe now that the great fortress was a kind of medieval prefab, built from ready-cut stones and lime shipped from Portugal, and assembled in just twenty days. Five hundred and fifty years later, it's still standing, and still bears the name given to it by the Portuguese, unsubtle as they were about the significance of the region they had 'discovered'. The land was literally lined with gold, and they named it Mina, or Mine,[15] while the castle – São Jorge da Mina – became known simply as 'Elmina'.

In 1637, at the peak of its traffic in slaves, the fort was seized by the Dutch, in whose hands it would remain for two and a half centuries. The Dutch had expanded the fort, which was sometimes described as being like a ship at permanent anchor, with work and leisure conducted inside, and a bell rung to announce the beginning and end of the work day. Life in the fort was notoriously boring for Europeans, and alcoholism was rampant; the most commonly found items in archaeological excavations at Ghana's forts are bottles of schnapps, gin, wine, and smoking pipes.[16] With few white women available, it was common for European men to form relationships with local women.

It was during this period, in the mid-1700s, that my sixth great-grandfather arrived at Elmina. A man named Welzing, he probably came from a family of Mennonites, and travelled to Elmina under the auspices of the Dutch West Indische Compagnie, almost certainly to trade in slaves. His relationship with a woman from the local Fante ethnic group – we know nothing more about her – produced a son, Pieter, born in Elmina around 1780.[17]

By the late eighteenth century an entire community of mixed-race Afro-European people existed in and around Elmina. English speakers called them 'mulatto', but in Dutch, they were known as *tapoeyer*. It's not a flattering term; some speculate it comes from the Portuguese *tapear* which means 'to cheat'.[18] These Afro-Europeans had the additional advantage of being entitled to recourse under Dutch law. They were traders and middlemen, the crucial link in the trade between Africans and Europeans, and interpreters who assisted Europeans with translations into Fante and other local languages.[19]

I've always been fascinated by the Welzing family history. It horrified me that we were descended from a Dutch slave trader; it tormented me that nothing could be learned about the woman who fathered his child. My sixth great-grandmother remains a nameless, faceless, Ghanaian woman – what were the circumstances of her union with this Dutchman, during the depraved, greedy days when men like Welzing drank and smoked their way through their tropical orgy of trading in black lives?

And then her son – Pieter Welzing; mixed heritage like me. It intrigues me that these Afro-European *tapoeyer* traders had not just their own name, and their own distinctive racial mix, but their own sociopolitical structure. They even had their own district in Elmina's town – known to locals as Garden Side, because it had been the site of a Dutch vegetable garden since the seventeenth century. It's hard to reconcile their comfortable suburb with the fact that this was Ground Zero – Elmina – the place where a million human tragedies unfolded, where the modern world's economy was harvested, where the African diaspora was born.

The Welzings moved with the times. When the British acquired Elmina from the Dutch in 1872, they strategically anglicised their name to 'Welsing' – which remains the family name today. Pieter Welzing had a son, Pieter Welsing Junior – less prudent than his father, piling up large debts with a firm in Rotterdam in the 1840s – and two daughters, Elizabeth and Betsy, who built their own properties near the Elmina fort in 1846. Pieter Junior's son, Johannes Welsing, my third great-grandfather, became a colonial official in the new British protectorate. They moved to Sekondi, a prosperous port seventy kilometres away from Elmina, due west along the coast, and set about acquiring land. Johannes married a Fante woman named Yaa Tereba – they were the first generation to be photographed.

Stories of Yaa Tereba have always had a special kind of hold over me. Bad eyesight had plagued her as a young mother, and when her youngest daughter, Betty – or Maama, who would become the baker of Aburi – was old enough to travel, she left the coast and went in search of a white doctor, who, she'd heard, could do magical things. The white doctor was based in Aburi, no longer Fante country, but the home of the Akuapim to the east. Aburi was by then the favourite destination of Europeans seeking respite from the coast. The botanical gardens were being planted, and the town was prospering with its perennially abundant agriculture and, now, influx of colonial missionaries, officials and spa-seekers. Yaa Tereba and Maama liked Aburi too; they stayed there, finding new enterprise in trading palm oil with their relatives and contacts in Sekondi. My grandmother told the story, each time we mounted the zigzag roads from the Akuapim suburbs at the edge of Accra up the steep mountains to Aburi, of how Yaa Tereba and Betty would carry their heavy barrels of palm oil on foot, rolling them downhill to the coast, and there board boats heading west. It was arduous work, but they were strong.

Maama, my second great-grandmother, fell in love with an Aburi man, a goldsmith named Adae, whose jewellery of exquisite gold beads is still remembered proudly. They had four children, including twins, Martha and Mary. Mary was my great-grandmother, we knew her as 'Obuom', meaning 'there's another one inside'. The discovery of a second twin may have come as a bit of a shock in the time before antenatal scans. Obuom lived between Sekondi and Aburi, and, like her mother Maama before her, fell in love with an Aburi man. She was only fourteen when she gave birth to my grandmother, Ophelia Joyce, so Ophelia Joyce was raised by various relatives, shuttled between the coast and the mountains – she spent part of her childhood growing up in Sekondi and was then sent to school in Aburi, where she lived with her grandmother, helping out with the bakery after school. Set up with P.K. at the wedding in Aburi's botanical gardens, she ended up falling in love with the Cambridge scholar from Konkonuru – the little village just south of Aburi. My grandfather – in my mother's words – a 'pure Aburi man'.

Then, in my family's case, this link was broken. P.K. was driven out of Ghana by the downfall of the country's democracy and the collapse of Kwame Nkrumah's government. For my grandmother, even more toxic than the political situation, was the persecution she experienced at the hands of her in-laws, who blamed her for my grandfather's adoption of a more Western way of family life. By moving to London, her children would be freed from this nightmare, she decided, they would benefit instead from the security and more straightforward family structures that life in the UK can offer. For her *grandchildren*, born in the UK and total strangers to Ghana, this was virtually guaranteed.

When I met Sam – a total stranger – through a chance encounter in the Houses of Parliament, I could not, not ever, have imagined that I was unpicking a project my grandmother began long before I was born. As far as I was concerned, Sam was a random, though remarkable, man from Tottenham, a part of north London I had never visited, from a community into which I had almost no insight. I did know that Sam's parents had come from Ghana – a country of 20 million people – but Sam, who had only been there once, overtly wore an identity that was more black British than it was Ghanaian. He had an American-sounding name, he did not speak Twi, but he *was* a master and product of black London's influential subculture, and that was easy to see. When I later met his family, it seemed much closer to Ghanaian trad-ition than anything I had ever experienced – but this too was mostly unfamiliar to me.

There is nothing therefore that could have prepared me for the shock my grandmother expressed when she first found out about Sam. Sam's mother is the queen of Konkonuru, not just part of Aburi, where Ophelia Joyce spent part of her childhood living with her grandmother Maama, but the same *exact* village that my grandfather P.K. comes from. The two families have been neighbours for genera-tions. The rationale for my grandmother bringing her children up in the UK, immersing them in British social circles, was to avoid encoun-ters like this. By the time it came to my generation, so anglicised, unable to speak Twi, all but strangers to the Ghanaian community, the risk was so minimal, it had not been factored in as a possibility. And there I was. The fifth generation of women from my grandmother's Welsing line, to come from another land, and fall in love with – to use the words my mother still utters sometimes, with a great deal of astonishment, and a little wonder – a pure Aburi man.

Sam and I named our daughter after his grandmother, an Aburi woman like my grandmother, both of whom, not surprisingly, have known of each other for decades. Over the years the extent of our over-lapping heritage has become clear – we are, precisely, chillingly, uncan-nily, from exactly the same place. It simply confirms what I have learned throughout my life – there is no escaping your identity. And identity – in order for it to have any sense, or internal legitimacy – has to be, in some way, shaped by something you believe to be true in your past.

Ironically, in breaking the link between her own cultural heritage and her descendants, I think my grandmother created, completely unwittingly, a void. It manifested in me as a crisis, as a desperate need to know about my past, my family, and my cultural and political inheritance, and as a result, that need defined my adult life. It shaped my tastes, my academic and career choices, and my friendships around them. I pursued it across the African continent, looking for information, understanding and a place to fit in. Is it any surprise, really, that the man I was most attracted to, who drew me magnetically to him across the cold, clinical spaces of the Palace of Westminster, was from the same small village as the grandfather I knew so little about? Some things, I believe, do not happen by chance.

Aburi makes me emotional. These deep green mountains, rising above the dusty cacophony, bathe me in something calming, as if the trees are exhaling over me in a long, oxygen-rich, ancient breath. While we live in Ghana, I visit often with Sam – after all, both our families are from there. As we climb and leave the city sprawling beneath, I drink in the cool air and feel the memories of my grandmother's childhood, selling bread on her head after school, in an age I'll never know. Of P.K.'s great-grandmother, who fled Baden-Powell's offensive, seeking refuge in this town after weary weeks trekking through the forest. Maama and her mother Yaa Tereba, rolling palm oil down the hill in barrels in an even more distant page of history, whose picture I have seen, dressed up in stiff, starched Victorian clothes, like prim German missionaries. I love to fill the gap between that cold, frigid appearance and the hectic warmth of life under this fragrant sky, the life that I have always yearned for.

On these visits to Aburi, we take our little daughter, and I sit with her, wrapping my arms around her car seat, whispering in her ear that we are going home, to the place where she is truly from. She has Aburi on both sides of her parentage – it's as if subconsciously I was trying to bring uniformity back to my disparate identity, and give my child coherence where I had confusion, and knowledge where I had ignorance.

That's not to say I could ever know how she will craft her own identity. She is British. She has spent more of her life now in London than anywhere else. She has Jewish and English heritage from my father, and the Afro-European Welsing line from my mother, as well as Ashanti heritage from the Kumasi refugees and from Sam's father too, along with a strong dose of Konkonuru inheritance from both sides. I can't help but think that, subconsciously, I gravitated towards Aburi, like my maternal ancestors; in some ways, she is the manifestation of that journey. But that's my journey, not hers. She will begin where I left off. If there is one lesson I have learned from my own life, it's that her identity will matter to her, but – like mine – it won't be what others necessarily expect.

Moving to Ghana in 2012 with my mother and grandmother in tow, my greatest hope was that this was a homecoming. A return that could bridge a divide that had been yawning across the ocean, ever since my family had left fifty years earlier. But my greatest anxiety was that, when Sam arrived, living there would expose the extent of our difference, causing a rift that could only grow. If in the UK Sam and I have grown up at opposite ends of the social spectrum, in Ghana the spectrums are completely reversed. In Aburi, my family are ordinary people, commoners, people who went abroad and, for all intents and purposes, did not come back. Sam's mother, on the other hand, is the queen. Sam's grandmother – from whom our daughter takes her name – is notorious in our and surrounding villages. His family have status, royal status, a place on the council of elders, and a ten-bedroom house which Sam's mother has been building, brick by brick, with her hard-earned pounds and pence, and where it's likely, in my estimation, that at least triple that number of relatives will end up living. In Ghana my family, by contrast, are rootless. We rely on friends to put us up in their home, or we stay in a hotel, like tourists – the ultimate indicator of non-Ghanaianness.

I feared that being in Ghana would reveal the extent to which I was not Ghanaian enough in Sam's eyes. His privilege, in Ghanaian social and cultural terms, would set his life there on a trajectory where I would not be able to follow. Through discipline and dedication, he had caught up with the head start my privilege had given me in London, but in Ghana, I'd never catch up with his.

It's true that Sam blended in – physically, at least – in a way that I could only dream of. But in other ways, surprising ways, Ghana was like a flood, sweeping away the differences that exist between Sam and me. What difference did it make, in Ghana, whether you came from Tottenham or from Wimbledon? We were both from a place where a different kind of order prevailed, where grey skies focused the mind, where the 'system' was something we were equipping ourselves to navigate, where sophistication could unlock every door. In Ghana, we were both British.

When we first moved into our house in Diamond Hill, a vinegary regret lingered on my tongue in the mornings. My favourite things in Ghana had always congregated in the stirring of morning, the sounds and smells of day breaking. I would lie in crumpled sheets and strain, over the sound of the fan, to hear the rowdy birds, the cocks crowing, the people rising at dawn, fetching their buckets and shouting at their children, the FanMilk boy tooting his rubber horn, the bread, oats and pineapples passing your window on a wooden tray on someone's head. These things were shut out of Diamond Hill, with its guarded gates and its secure location, tucked far back from the main road. It could have been an American suburb in Virginia, or a smart English housing estate among the golf clubs of Surrey, with its row upon row of identical red-roofed houses, each with its own tall gates, bars on the windows, its pristine garden. There was no stray person wandering the street, hawking or haggling, in sight. In Diamond Hill, as in all developments like it, each lived behind their high wall, the doors closed to keep the air conditioning in. But the attack changed everything.

Sam and I were walking on the beach at Krokobite – a Ga fishing village just on the outskirts of Accra. We'd been sitting at Big Milly's – a gap-year joint on the beach that catered to weed-smoking American girls and hefty German vegans, with reggae in the evening and trans-racial love on tap. They had Wi-Fi and cold drinks, and we worked on our laptops at a quiet table in the corner, the ravenous waves behind us, until dusk. Before we went home, we locked our phones, computers, wallets, bags and everything else in the car, and went for a walk on the beach. We were heading east – my idea – so that when we headed back west to the car we'd get to walk right into the sunset. We held hands, and dangled our shoes with the hand that was free. It was a moment whose loveliness we grasped in real time, talking, laughing at the fact this dream had become a reality, comparing it to past adventures in Clacton or Canterbury. We ran away from the waves, and even though we were straying further and further away from the touristy track of Big Milly's, this was a touristy beach, right? We only vaguely noticed that the only people we were seeing now were fishermen putting away their nets for the night, and some children cleaning their baskets in a stream. One man we passed, unkempt and uninterested, was standing by a little beach stall that had just been boarded up.

His was one of the faces that thrust onto us from nowhere, pulling us, touching me, holding us down. I saw the attack unfolding through the expressions on Sam's face. From the urgent fury I saw there, I realised that we might die. We had just been turning round, to head back into the raging sky, when three men came up to Sam, surrounding him with terrifying speed. I saw a look of panic cloud over him, someone I have never truly seen lose control before. Sam was overreacting, I told myself desperately, they had just come to ask him something. 'We've got nothing!' he was shouting, and his shout seemed so violent, so unnecessary, in my desperation to believe this was an innocent approach by curious locals. It wasn't. 'We've got nothing!' – they held him down then, one on each arm, the third holding a knife to his throat.

What broke me was the sight of Sam, powerless. I have never seen him helpless, not even close. I realised then how much he makes me feel safe. And now his life was in the jittering, deranged hands of this jumpy, murderous fisherman, the knife already grazing his skin. It trapped me in mesmerising terror, so much so that I barely noticed the other three men seizing me, pulling me away from Sam. They began to undress me, lifting up my top, searching my body. They were sure there was some stash of money, some phone, and they became increasingly angry that we had nothing of value. At first when they took me a strange sound emerged from the dregs of my lungs – something between a scream and a low, low moan. But then there was no point in screaming – there was no one to hear. I feared hysterics would panic them further and they would slash Sam's throat. Inside I was bracing myself for the fact that they were going to kill him and then rape me. I could envisage no other ending, I had to find the strength to protect myself from what was about to happen. So when I suddenly found myself next to Sam, sprinting along the sand, him leading me by the hand as I stumbled, it was sheer relief that made me weep. I could not believe we were free.

They had ripped the earrings from my earlobes, and the ring I had worn since Senegal from my finger. That was the extent of the damage. We had had nothing else to give, and by some utter miracle, Sam had spotted a moment of distraction where they caught their surprise that we had no stash of notes, jewellery or gadgets to offer, and pulled himself free, whipping me up in the speed of his getaway until we were both sprinting. We were free, we were alive, we were unharmed. It felt like a miracle. Sam looked back as we ran; I couldn't, ever. I was too afraid I would see them running after us, and I would have died running to outpace them.

Afterwards, I became permanently jumpy. I was terrified for our daughter, torn between fear and grateful relief that she had not been with us that afternoon. I felt afraid, threatened and vulnerable in Ghana. It didn't even feel like Ghana any more – 'Ghana' was fading from my sentiment like a dream. I know there is violent crime everywhere, but in London, New York or Paris, it has a different relationship to me. I don't look wealthy at home. I don't look like a lucrative target. But in Ghana my skin colour alone is enough to function like a big 'rob me' slogan tattooed across my forehead. Things I used to detest as excessive status symbols now became invaluable. I had hated the fact that we live in a gated community, but now I wouldn't live anywhere else, and I became so grateful for our guards. I used to leave doors and windows open to let in the rich air, but now I began to lock everything. I couldn't fathom why I had once thought it was OK to leave our gate swung wide, scornfully watching my neighbours with their bolts and keys. Sam wanted to buy a gun. He began obsessively researching crime in Ghana, and what he found were home invasions, armed gangs holding up public buses on remote rural roads and shooting everyone on board, men with AK-47s crossing the border and causing havoc. 'This isn't Ghana,' he would say, 'this is West Africa.' Arms flowed through the region freely. Our neighbours – Côte d'Ivoire, Mali, Liberia, Nigeria – were unstable on all sides.

Almost as disturbing as the incident itself was what happened when we reported it to the police. We went straight from the beach to Krokobite Police Station. When we got there, there were two police officers and no lights. We had to come back the next day to give our statements, when they hoped the power would be back.

We did come back, twice. The first time to give our statements – in daylight, so the absence of electricity mattered less – and then a second time, when they had arrested the suspects. They were holding them in a cell just behind the front desk – I recognised the one who had been standing at the beach hut, who had been the first to grab Sam and pull him down. The officers read out our names and address right in front of the prisoners, to our alarm, and from that point on, Sam wanted to deal with the case alone. The police could not protect us. And they had no vehicle. On the morning of the first court appearance, they called Sam and asked him to come to the station, pick up the suspects, and drive them to court on our back seat.

Sam persevered, giving evidence at their trial. He was joined by Belinda and Jan, the couple whose guest house, beloved by German men of a certain age, I'd stayed in during my first week in Accra. It turned out the elderly couple had been robbed by the exact same gang, walking along the same beach with a group of their German 'tourists'. In the eyes of locals, hungry and resentful at the wealthy outsiders coming to stroll along their beach, we were all the same.

The attack was a wake-up call I needed, probably – before, in my naive belief that I was somehow welcome in Ghana, I wandered into an even more dangerous situation. We had lost only a few bits of jewellery and, though shaken up, come to no harm. It changed me, and the way I looked at my environment. The look I had seen in the robbers' eyes that day – a wild hunger, full of hate – I began to see everywhere. It had always been there – in the carpenter by the roadside, the plantain-chip vendor at the car window, the man on the building site, with no protective equipment – I just hadn't been able to interpret it. Now I knew what it meant. I felt pain for Ghana, which is always described as a model of how developing countries can progress, but which has so far not really changed for the lives of the majority, who are poor. I also knew that living there would mean locking myself and my family away from hostility, everywhere. What role could we play, if we didn't feel safe? All my romantic ideas; the bridge-building, the circle-closing, the time-healing of this return to Ghana, fifty years after my family left, filling the void that had gripped my identity . . . all this meant nothing to the man in Ghana, poor, hungry, who saw, as far as he was concerned, a British couple, and knew that robbing us could bring him food.

I had my own reasons for needing to attempt life in Ghana. Maybe my grandmother's painful separation from her country furrowed its way into my psyche somehow, compelling me to the very people and places she worked so hard to evade. Maybe I just needed to explore competing versions of the future I saw for myself. Maybe I just needed to get better at pronouncing my name.

Nevertheless, I can't help but reflect on the lengths I've gone to in the search for an identity that would allow the two sides of my heritage – British and Ghanaian – to peacefully coexist. I am proud of my African heritage, it has shaped me, given me a history and a sense of continuity that enriches the contours of my world. At the same time, I really am very British, as Ghanaians have often taken great pains to point out. I was born with these two sets of cultural and ethnic inheritance, but the conflict between them is something I had to grow into understanding – a tension that maybe my fifth great-grandfather Pieter Welzing, the *tapoeyer*, might have recognised, so ancient are its roots.

For me, living in Ghana ultimately created more problems of belonging than it was able to solve. But I can't resolve these problems by falling back on my British identity either, because Britishness has not yet fully rejected its roots in ideological whiteness, and the pain that has inflicted on blackness. For someone like me, Britishness contains the threat of exclusion. An exclusion only made more sinister by discovering – after so many years of searching – that there is nowhere else to go.

6. CLASS

Alexander Paul, speaking at the Conservative Party Conference in 2014, aged 18.

I don't really believe in race. I don't really believe in colour. But I do know what I see.

– James Baldwin, *Baldwin's Nigger*[1]

After growing up in Wimbledon, eleven years of private school and three of Oxford University, I thought that nothing about race, class and privilege in the UK could shock me. And then I decided to become a barrister.

It began with a secret world. A cloistered world, hidden away behind its Tudor walls, a large, spacious and gloriously ancient campus. I remember feeling a childish wonder as I ducked away from the claustrophobic clutter of the concrete, stone and glass law firms on Chancery Lane, the heartland of legal London, and found the Great Lawn of Lincoln's Inn – a neat expanse of striped green, and a majestic red-brick library like a palace on the other side. Beyond that, the gateway to Lincoln's Inn Fields, a hidden gem of a park built during the reign of Henry VII. My first encounter with this oasis reminds me of a scene in the *Sex and the City* movie, when Carrie and Mr Big walk into the ridiculously luxurious penthouse apartment they're viewing in New York, and she says, 'So *this* is where they keep the light.'

I lived in the Inn during my year of Bar vocational training, thanks to the generosity of its scholarship programme, which boosted my chances and my ability to devote time to studying and temping to pay back the bank loans that began where my bursary ended. It was a scene lacking in diversity in every way. Even the clothes people wore were all the same – dark suits, dull uniform. The only colour you were likely to see was a horsehair wig, or the occasional postbox red of a tax barrister's Ferrari.

Then there were all the cultural aspects of life at the Bar to contend with. Dining in Lincoln's Inn – which was compulsory – was like experiencing Oxford on steroids. An intimidating medieval hall, lined with grand paintings of dead white men, working out which of several sets of cutlery to use, and which of the side plates is for your walnut rye and butter. 'There are ghosts in this hall,' Sam would say, even less used to both this environment and the port that was served in it, which saw him become both drunk and haunted for the very first time. At the end of that year I read about how William Murray, 1st Earl of Mansfield, had been tasked with ruling on the legal status of slaves after heated discussions in this very hall in 1772. And how a fellow 'bencher' – or senior member of the Inn elected in recognition of their services to law – the famous jurist William Blackstone, had amended his authoritative reference book *Commentaries on the Laws of England* to suggest Mansfield should find against the slaves' case. In the end, the judge championed the underdog, declaring slavery 'odious'. News of the ruling swept through Georgian London's black community with the speed and impact of a virus. Now it was us students seated at the table, spread out so that each was next to a barrister or judge.

Lincoln's Inn is one of the great hidden centres of British power – at one point Margaret Thatcher, when she was prime minister, her Lord Chancellor Lord Hailsham, the Lord Chief Justice Lord Widgery, the Master of the Rolls Lord Denning, and the head of the High Court's Chancery Division, Sir Robert Megarry, were all benchers of Lincoln's Inn at the same time.[2] Denning – whom like most other law students I had greatly admired at law school because his judgments were so funny, a welcome soap-opera-like break from the usual, dry legalese – eventually fell from grace dogged by race allegations. His 1982 book *What Next in the Law* argued that the fact that 'the English are no longer a homogeneous race' was a threat to the system of trial by jury. These dark-skinned people could not be trusted with the responsibility of determining guilt or innocence, Denning wrote. 'They are white and black, coloured and brown . . . Some of them come from countries where bribery and graft are accepted and where stealing is a virtue so long as you are not found out. They no longer share the same code of morals or religious beliefs.'

It wasn't just bluster to sell books. The legal system was something that was run by white men to dispatch justice to dark-skinned deviants. Around the same time that Denning doubted the integrity of immigrants, my uncle was arrested and detained by the police for simply being in the Inn. He'd turned off Chancery Lane towards Old Buildings, where I lived all those years later, when he was stopped by the police and asked what he was doing. He replied that he was a barrister – he was wearing a suit and carrying his papers so it seemed obvious enough – and this was his Inn. They arrested him anyway, unable to fathom that this black man could have been on the site of such an important institution for any legitimate reason.

As a young black person in the Inn in 2006, I certainly still felt like an impostor, even if I was never arrested for being one. I felt both awe and resentment towards the institution. Its history was rich and fascinating, plus it had used some of its endless wealth to finance my own studies, for which I was extremely grateful. On the other hand, the self-importance of its history, the Englishness of its protocol, the exclusivity of its attitude, its system and function of elite self-congratulation were all alienating to me.

As a pupil barrister, I had my share of unreal experiences. I was asked to do some book research for a QC from another chambers. When I consulted colleagues as to whether I should take on the task – significant extra work on top of my existing workload – they told me that it would be a good thing to do. They also thought it was appropriate to add that he had form for groping black women. 'He has a thing for them.' It was an unproven allegation, and I didn't think there were enough black women at the Bar to develop a taste for groping them, but that was the least of my concerns. I did the book research, but ensured I was never alone with him with the door closed.

A male member of my own chambers googled me and, reading that old teenage interview about identity and body-image angst, began an incessant and completely inappropriate email campaign to find out why I'd said I didn't date white men. This forty-year-old man had taken personally something I'd said when I was eighteen, about the fact white boys at school called me 'thunder thighs'. It was not a conversation I wanted to have with a senior man in the chambers at which

I was working hard to make a good impression. The identity angst of my past was following me around; it was my own fault, I suppose, for speaking about it publicly. Thank God the Internet hadn't arrived until the tail end of my adolescence.

But on the whole mine was an enlightened chambers. Going to court was another matter. There was a notorious male judge at a busy London crown court, who had a reputation for making pupils cry, whom I seemed to have an uncanny knack of appearing before. And the whole time I was at the Bar, I was conscious of resembling the clients I was defending from criminal charges much more closely than almost any of my colleagues. There was, and still is, a movement to abolish the wearing of wigs and gowns by barristers – a tradition which is often regarded as outdated and unhelpful in reinforcing the archaic reputation of the profession. And it was a movement I empathised with. I even had to begin straightening my hair, so that it could be smoothed down underneath my wig – laying it on top of a head of Afro curls would only have made me look more absurd than I already did. But I surprised myself by defending the tradition. In a world where no one thought the way I looked was what a barrister was *meant* to look like, this uniform gave me legitimacy, and let everyone know that I was a professional just like all the others. If it seems absurd that I needed to put on a wig and gown to make this point, it just tells you how bad perceptions are.

When I later joined the *Guardian* newspaper as legal affairs correspondent, it was important to me that this was a role that had nothing to do with gender or race. Coming as I did from a world of bundles of paper tied up in pink ribbon, cantankerous public-school boys paid to have a high opinion of their charisma and bravado, and white horsehair wigs, I expected the newspaper to be enlightenment personified. But there, too, diversity was conspicuous by its absence.

When Howard W. French, the distinguished black *New York Times* columnist, was posted to Japan as a correspondent, he regarded it as a victory far beyond the implications of actually reporting news from the country. He had broken outside the walled city of reporting 'urban' and 'black' places and stories to which black reporters are usually confined. 'Howard has reached the river!' French reported his colleagues as saying. 'Someone had escaped, or so it seemed, what we sometimes called the "corporate negro calculus", the careful tending of our presence, never dramatically expanding our numbers but also never letting them fall too low, all the while keeping us employed in predictable roles . . .'[3]

The world French described is one I still recognise, characterised by what he calls the 'persistent problem of typecasting' – a deeply embedded view that regards certain topics as 'black' and the rest as 'white'. It's impossible not to notice a similar phenomenon in the British media. As far back as 2002, a report supported by a number of organisations including the BBC acknowledged that 'the pattern of minority ethnic participation shows less contribution to heavyweight roles and subjects of a serious nature, while minority ethnic contributions cluster around vox pop interviews or stereotypical topics of minority group issues, sport, music and sex'.[4]

To me, it's non-negotiable that newsrooms should reflect the cultural, racial, class, religious and gender make-up of the nation. I can think of no other profession where the personal contacts and perspective of an employee have such a blatant impact on their output. The playwright Kwame Kwei-Armah tells a story about how, growing up in west London in the 1970s, his mother would – very occasionally – shout up the stairs saying 'Come quick! There's a black man on the telly!' Things were not all that different by 2001, when BBC Director General Greg Dyke famously described the corporation as 'hideously white'. I was in my second year at university then, and painfully aware at the paucity of black people – especially senior or visible black people – in all of the professions I was considering entering. Dyke was speaking just a few years after the Metropolitan Police were judged to be affected by 'institutional racism'; it was as if the 'R' word, as the professor and broadcaster Kurt Barling has called it, was finally coming out of the closet and into the open for public analysis and dissection. It was a relief.[5]

Collecting examples of blatant racism in the mainstream press is one of my hobbies. It's too much work for one person, so I often rely on members of another WhatsApp group, this time a group of female journalists, which includes all races, the only requirement being that everyone involved is committed to increasing diversity in the profession. My phone buzzes endlessly with the constant stream of offensive examples, but some stand out. A *Daily Mail* cartoon from November 2015 in particular had special significance because of its timing. The newspaper published a drawing by its long-standing cartoonist Stanley McMurtry satirising the fact that the singer Tom Jones was exploring the possibility that he could have African ancestry. The cartoon, which I imagine would have caused offence in 1915 let alone 2015, showed a white explorer in colonial-era dress, in a black-as-night jungle, approaching a pot-bellied black tribesman with a test tube. The caption has the explorer telling the tribesman, 'The DNA matches – now just one more question . . . can you sing Delilah?'

What singled this incident out was the fact that, on the very same day that the newspaper published it, the *Mail* was playing host to a 'special celebratory reception to mark 10 years of the Journalism Diversity Fund' – a fund that dispenses bursaries to talented journalism students from 'diverse backgrounds'. Joseph, the Hull-born mixed-race *Guardian* journalist who shared his experiences of childhood with me for this book, was at the reception, and listened to a speech by one of the *Mail*'s senior editors, in which he praised efforts to increase diversity in the industry and stressed how important it was that more was done. After the speech, Joseph made a point of showing the cartoon to some of the *Mail* grandees present at the reception, asking how depicting black people in this way was compatible with encouraging diversity. 'Stop being a troublemaker,' he reports being told.

It's too easy to implement corporate diversity schemes and social responsibility checklists, without any actual thought about why our society excludes people of colour. Shonda Rhimes, the American screenwriter and producer – creator of multiple hit US shows including *Grey's Anatomy* and *Scandal* – is often asked why she's so invested in 'diversity' on television, in the sense that she has created lead characters who are from different minority backgrounds, who are women

and who are gay. 'I really hate the word *diversity*,' Rhimes says. 'It suggests something other . . . As if there is something unusual about telling stories involving women and people of color and LGBTQ characters
on TV. I have a different word: NORMALIZING. I'm normalizing TV.
I am making TV look like the world looks. Women, people of color,
LGBTQ people equal WAY more than 50 per cent of the population.
Which means it ain't out of the ordinary.'[6]

The problem is, things have been so skewed for so long, that
tampering with the old 'normal' creates instant enemies. For many
people, 'diversity' feels like discrimination against them; they see it as
a zero-sum game. On my first day at Sky News, a senior female colleague gave me a dressing-down for my audacity in getting my job,
saying, 'Don't take this personally, but you can't get a promotion
around here if you're white these days. You should know that. I'm just
telling you, as if people are less than pleased to see you, it might explain
why.' There was always this lingering suspicion that I managed to get
the job as a result of some sophisticated scam or, worse, affirmative
action. At the *Guardian*, people kept asking me how I did it, as if there
was some kind of story to tell. 'I applied to the job ad in the *Guardian*,
did two rounds of interview, and wrote three sample articles,' I said.
'How did you get yours?' The fact is that until a few years before I
joined the newspaper, jobs weren't even advertised as standard
practice – in some cases, editors simply appointed people they knew.
Privileged, straight, white men who lived in affluent areas tended to
appoint – guess what – other people like themselves.

The media is changing, with streaming services like Netflix, online
news platforms like Vice, and social media news services like *The
Young Turks* disrupting the market and stealing the loyalties of a generation, who would never dream of waiting for the BBC *News at Six* to
find out what's going on in the world, as my parents used to when I
was growing up. But the fact remains that the decisions made in the
newsrooms and commissioning offices of our major TV studios still
have enormous influence over public opinion and sentiment. Public
service broadcasters in particular are among the first to acknowledge

that their content is creating a narrative of the nation, to 'enrich and challenge the assumptions of modern Britain, and connect its past and future', for example,[7] or to 'increase social cohesion and tolerance by enabling the UK's many communities to talk to themselves and each other about what they hold in common and how they differ'.[8]

But diversity in TV is actually falling. The latest figures at the time of writing show that for the creative sector – which includes film, advertising, radio, gaming and TV – representation of minorities declined from 7.4 per cent to 5.4 per cent between 2006 and 2012.[9] Relatively speaking, it's a significant change, one in the wrong direction. The BBC's director for England described it as 'deeply shocking', pointing out, in a familiar refrain, decades old, that 'the creative industries have historically used friends and family recruitment. If you don't know anybody, it's very difficult to find your way in.' One producer said the talk around diversity was nothing more than 'warm and fuzzy language'.[10]

The film industry mirrors or perhaps trumps TV in its failure to recruit, retain and promote non-white talent. You notice this, if you are a black child in a white world, searching desperately for stories of people who look like you, or have names like you, or come from countries like the ones in your own family background. Hollywood has been quite happy to appropriate the places or the themes that have most significance for black people, as I discovered watching *Zulu*, *Ashanti* and *Out of Africa*, but hasn't seen fit to dignify the actual black people involved with a backstory or a character worth developing.

There have been black actors in Hollywood movies for as long as there have been Hollywood movies. Hattie McDaniel, whose performance as Mammy in *Gone With the Wind* won her the Oscar for Best Supporting Actress, the first ever Academy Award won by a black person (and the last for almost a quarter of a century after), succeeded because she was – to all intents and purposes – playing a slave. The introduction to the novel on which the film is based sets out the context, the 'Old South', perfectly. 'Here was the last ever to be seen of the

Knights and their ladies Fair, of Master and of Slave . . . it is no more than a dream remembered.'

In this 'dream', the material life of white Southerners is the focus, while black people amount to little more than furniture.[11] In *Gone With the Wind* particularly, a popular black character transitioned onto the silver screen as the 'ideal black nanny', a woman who is 'asexual and consequently she had to be fat (preferably obese); she also had to give the impression of not being clean so she was the wearer of a greasy dirty head rag; her too tight shoes from which emerged her large feet were further confirmation of her bestial cow-like quality. Her greatest virtue was of course her love for white folk whom she willingly and passively served.'[12]

When I read that description by bell hooks, I felt it could equally have been written about almost all the most successful films – and the books on which many are based – that have depicted black people in recent years; *The Help* – a story told from the perspective of a white Southerner who decides to help empower downtrodden black nannies – is a case in point. As a child, the few films I did see with black characters included Whoopi Goldberg in *Ghost*, in which she plays a strange, asexual, voodoo-like medium who lives in the projects, and *The Nutty Professor*, in which Eddie Murphy cross-dresses and caricatures black family members in a manner so unflattering, it makes Hattie McDaniel's Mammy an almost attractive representation of black womanhood by comparison. It's not that there is no place for mockery, or the depiction of unflattering or subservient roles for black people, or for black characters to make audiences laugh. It's that, for the last century of cinema, they have been the *only* roles. There have been so few other kinds of depictions of black people to put that in realistic context. As Zoë Kravitz, the young actor who's played significant roles in movies including *Mad Max*, the *Divergent* series and *X-Men*, said candidly, the best role a black actor like her can hope for is 'best friend of the white girl'.[13] Kravitz relayed her attempt to audition for Christopher Nolan's Batman film *The Dark Knight Rises*, which she said was blocked because, she reports being told, the film-makers 'weren't going urban'.

Above all, the role of the black characters that have appeared in films is to be saved by a white hero. Think *Dangerous Minds*, in which Michelle Pfeiffer rescues 'tough' inner-city kids; Hilary Swank's similarly themed 'save a thug' film *Freedom Writers*; Sam Worthington as messiah to an endangered alien species, the Na'vi, in *Avatar*. And if it's not about a white saviour rescuing a black victim, he's being assisted by a 'Magical Negro' – whose only role is to give special wisdom to the white saviour; think Laurence Fishburne's Morpheus in *The Matrix*, or his role as a spaceship captain in the 2016 sci-fi film *Passengers*, in which his character's role is to appear briefly, save everyone, and promptly die.

One-dimensional black characters are in part a symptom of a lack of diversity behind the scenes. The more black directors there are in the film industry, the more films will be made which deviate from the usual single black character narrative. The rise of black British director Amma Asante has seen stories like that of Dido Elizabeth Belle, the mixed-race girl raised by Lord Mansfield, of Lincoln's Inn and slavery judgment fame, in the second half of the eighteenth century, told to a mass audience for the first time; and her 2017 film *Where Hands Touch* is about a mixed-race teenager in Berlin in 1944. 'I'm here to disrupt expectations,' Asante has said.[14]

Yet there are no signs of things changing radically yet. Steve McQueen, who became the first black director to win an Oscar for best picture for *Twelve Years a Slave* in 2014, and won numerous awards for a previous film, *Hunger*, set in Northern Ireland, has said that his own success did not necessarily represent wider change. 'We need more hope, to be quite honest,' he said in 2015. 'When I look behind me, I don't see anyone else. When I shot *Hunger*, I didn't see any black people, on any set. We have to fix this. It's kind of crazy.'[15]

Another film produced by Brits and released to acclaim on both sides of the Atlantic was *Loving* – the beautifully shot story of Mildred and Richard Loving, a black woman and white man who were arrested for breaking the anti-miscegenation laws, or laws against interracial relationships, which still existed well into the 1960s. Their Supreme Court petition against the state of Virginia finally ended the last of these slavery-era laws in 1967. I watched the film at the US Embassy in London at the end of 2016, in the final days before power was handed over from the Obama administration to Trump. There was a distinct sense that the Obama-era confidence that America would stride greatly towards race equality was wavering.

After the screening, Ged Doherty, former chair of Sony Records, and Colin Firth, the actor seen as something of a British national treasure – whose production company Raindog Films was behind the movie – answered a question about why, as white men, they had such passionate interest in the story. 'I was in an interracial relationship, so I was familiar with some of the themes,' Doherty explained. 'And I discovered that the Lovings were married the week I was born. So there were a few things that drew me to the story – I became obsessed by it.' Firth, in turn, described his childhood in other parts of the world, including India and Nigeria, which he said had sensitised him to the existence of other stories. Both made it abundantly clear that irrespective of their race, they had reasons for being able to relate to the story, and their personal experiences had made them committed to a narrative that is rarely heard in film. Without that personal connection, I wonder, would others in their position have backed a film such as this?

The narratives that you see on the television, in film and at the theatre shape nothing less than your sense of your own life, your very perception of yourself. My first exposure to the notion that there were other black people in the world, and that some of them lived in nice houses and had happy marriages, was watching American sitcoms like *The Cosby Show* and *Fresh Prince of Bel Air* as a child. Books like *Song of Solomon* and *The Bluest Eye* by Toni Morrison, *The Color Purple* by Alice Walker, and *Cry, the Beloved Country* by Alan Paton awoke me to the struggle that people suffering under systems of oppression based on race were going through in places I had never been, but which resonated with what I saw in the UK too.

The comedian Lenny Henry, who shocked many at the 2014 BAFTAs with a no-holds-barred speech about the 'appalling' percentage of black and Asian people in the creative industries,[16] has spoken about the effect of the 1970s televised version of Alex Haley's book *Roots* on his life as a young man growing up in the West Midlands. '*Roots* profoundly affected the image of African Americans, both in the US and here at home,' Henry said, speaking in a series about race in the arts on Radio 4 in 2016. 'When *Roots* was on TV, that Monday was a very different Monday to any other Monday that had ever been,' the comedian explained. 'Little [black] kids were like *"what?! We made the middle passage, fool!"*'[17]

For black actors, being cast in non-race-specific roles is half of the problem, but once they do land the parts, a whole other world of challenges rears its ugly head. 'Try and get a haircut on set – it's crazy! There is no provision for a black artist,' the actor David Harewood tells me. 'If you talk about it, it's like you are causing trouble. I've done four shows here in America, and each time, I have had to have a discussion with make-up about them getting what I need.' The problem, from Harewood's perspective, is the fact that barbering Afro hair is a skilled art, and getting it wrong has consequences. 'After a few weeks my hairline gets further and further back!' Harewood says. 'Every time I work in the States, I have had to have my haircut outside of the set. And I think to myself *surely this is wrong – why am I having to go and drive half an hour up the road to a black barber?* It's not just the principle, but a business case – think of the time I'm losing!'

Harewood has resorted to legal measures to solve the problem, getting black barber requirements written into his contract. 'Welcome to the crazy world of black hair and television,' Harewood laughs. 'I'm learning what Denzel does, and what Jamie Foxx does – they will say, "No fifty-year-old white lady from Texas is going to cut my hair. Get my man Tyrone to come and cut my hair. I'm not being racist – I just want a black barber."'

It might sound like a superficial thing, but for Harewood it's a metaphor for the whole business. 'That is the way that the business itself will diversify – by black people advancing in the business, and making sure they have the people that they want and they need around them.'

Harewood is one of the small but growing number of famous black British actors willing to speak openly about the prejudice they face. It began in 1997 when he played Othello, becoming the first black actor to do so at the National Theatre. At the time, even the liberal press was scathing. 'One of the most famous works in the English language has become a victim of political correctness,' complained the director of Birmingham University's Shakespeare Institute, cited in the *Independent*. 'It's a great shame to deprive white actors of one of the most demanding roles in the repertoire.'[18] As is still so often the case, his assumption that Harewood was given the role only because of his race, not because of his talent as an actor, was both patronising and also proved wrong – the production went on to receive critical acclaim, and Harewood went on to find fame and recognition with starring roles in hit US TV series including *Homeland* and *Supergirl*.

It's becoming a familiar pattern that black British actors have to go to the US before their talent is recognised at home. Hollywood – for all its well-documented racism – is still more willing to give black actors a chance than their own country. Chiwetel Ejiofor became a household name in film only when he was cast in *Twelve Years a Slave*, and David Oyelowo was courted seriously in the UK only after *Selma*. Idris Elba would arguably never have become a leading man without his role in *The Wire*. Landing big US roles, however, is not the end of their problems, as Harewood knows from intimate experience. Breaking his silence about his overall frustrations with the state of diversity in film in the UK, Elba gave a rare public speech in Parliament in 2016 explaining just how this affects actors like him.

'I was busy, I was getting lots of work, but I realised I could only play so many "best friends" or "gang leaders",' Elba told MPs. 'I knew I wasn't going to land a lead role. I knew there wasn't enough imagination in the industry for me to be seen as a lead. In other words, if I wanted to star in a British drama like *Luther*, then I'd have to go to a country like America.'

Conversely, Harewood says, in the UK, a lack of diversity breeds a lack of diversity. 'In the UK, you feel like a member of the revolutionary guard the minute you even mention race. Television in England, for example, is made by a very small group of upper-middle-class people. For them to have the balls or the foresight to see drama in a different way, it's going to take change. They will have to diversify their lifestyle – they probably don't know any black people.'

In 1992, in the lush, volcanic hills near the northern shore of Lake Kivu, a small, old-fashioned turboprop plane crashed, killing everyone on board. It was a tragedy, not least for the pilot, who didn't even usually fly this plane, but was covering for the main pilot who was away on holiday. For the main pilot, Armand Diangienda, being off work that day saved his life, but it still cost him his job. The airline he worked for owned only that one plane, and when it crashed, he found himself at home in the Congolese capital Kinshasa, out of work.

It's safe to say no one would have predicted what he did next. Diangienda decided not to find another job as a pilot. Instead he started an orchestra. The day we meet, as I interview him before an audience at London's Africa Utopia festival, he is wearing a pink pinstriped shirt with a necktie and smart trousers – a checked jumper slung loosely over his shoulders. It's a classic French look, but he wears it with a little sprinkle of Congolese swag – a bit like his orchestra, L'Orchestre Symphonique Kimbanguiste (OSK), or Kimbanguist Symphony Orchestra, a fusion of Western and African influences, which he has mashed up in a way never seen before in the classical world. The result is a transcendent experience that has attracted dozens of musicians and an entirely new audience of Congolese classical music fans, but which has also touched audiences globally. In 2013, Diangienda was made an honorary member of the Royal Philharmonic Society, and his orchestra – of professional musicians, market vendors, doctors and ordinary Kinshasans – now tours the world. His next symphony, he tells me, which he is composing as we speak, will be called *My Identity*.

The next day, the OSK performs at the Royal Festival Hall on London's South Bank, with Britain's National Youth Orchestra. It's a Sunday in September swelling with the warmth of late summer, and the first time my then four-year-old daughter has navigated the levels of London's great concert space, begging to be allowed to press the lift buttons, and meandering joyfully to the right row and the right seat, with whispered instructions about keeping quiet and sitting still. As the concert got under way, I looked up, and felt a strange sense of disorientation. On stage before me, the vision of a choir almost one hundred strong, and a full orchestra – swept up by a conductor in the rising and falling of a symphony, then weaving their song with classical Congolese melodies – and half of them were black Africans. It was beautiful, and mesmerising. I didn't realise how limited my own expectations of classical music were, until this scene disrupted them.

I share this story with Chi-chi Nwanoku, and she nods in recognition. Nwanoku created the UK's first predominantly ethnic minority orchestra – Chineke! – after a hugely successful career as a double bassist in which she was almost always the only black person playing. 'When people see a group of black people together, they instinctively think there's going to be trouble – don't they? Stereotypical character profiling that we have been brainwashed into thinking. I've said this to a few people and they've actually admitted it. So how wonderful will it be when the Chineke! orchestra walks on the stage, and plays incredible music.'

Nwanoku describes growing up conscious of race, but not seeing it as something that held her back. Although being black wasn't without its hazards. 'Growing up, we were the only black family as far as the eye could see in Kent,' she tells me, relaying the story of how her Nigerian father met her Irish mother in London, then the family moved to a small town near Canterbury, where life in general was good. But when they moved to the outskirts of Reading, things were very different. 'The racism in the police there was unbelievable; it was terrible. My brothers and sisters were frequently targeted by police as they made their way home innocently from anywhere, even from school, and my mother would go to retrieve them from the police station like a whirling dervish, leaving the police regretting they had dared to arrest her mixed-race children, for nothing as it always turned out.'

Nwanoku tells a harrowing story of her brother Gus, who was best man at his mixed-race friend's wedding aged nineteen. 'They didn't have a stag night – couldn't afford it. They just met at a pub in Reading, had a beer each – they weren't big drinkers – and said *see you tomorrow at the wedding*.' Gus and the groom-to-be walked to their respective bus stops, when a police car pulled up and arrested the groom, accusing him of some misdemeanour. The groom had an alibi. 'I've just been at the pub with my best man, I'm getting married tomorrow,' he explained. Nkwanoku recounts what happened next in a matter-of-fact tone that somehow amplifies its horror. '[The police] did not check his alibi, but rather shoved him into the police car, took him to the station, and threw him out a few hours later when they had finished with him. He was unrecognisable the following day, his wedding day; teeth . . . gone, eyes out here. They just beat the shit out of him. That's what used to happen to some of our friends. And the thing is there was nothing anyone could do about it. It was your word against the police's, which counted for nothing. This was the early 1970s – it was really, really bad.'

Nwanoku – a serious 100-metre sprinter who was already competing at national level when an injury ended her career aged seventeen and a half – is riled by the low numbers of ethnic minority children taking up classical music. She thinks the explanation is fairly straightforward: a combination of the prohibitive cost of playing instruments, and the cuts to music programmes in schools. Nwanoku says her eyes were opened when she discovered the composer Joseph Boulogne, Chevalier de Saint-Georges, who was born a slave and whose work was copied by Mozart. Like Nwanoku, Saint-Georges was both a brilliant musician and an athlete; he performed his own composed violin concertos for high society, and was the music teacher and a favourite of Marie Antoinette. The second president of America, John Adams, described Chevalier de Saint-Georges as 'the most accomplished man in Europe'.

Saint-Georges has been largely forgotten by history. So when Nwanoku was asked to direct a chamber orchestra for the two hundredth anniversary of the abolition of the slave trade in Westminster Abbey, in the presence of the Queen, Tony Blair and many leading Cabinet ministers, she intended to change that. 'I put together a small twenty-piece multicoloured, multiracial chamber orchestra, and [I had] vowed that I would do so on one condition – that we play music by Joseph Boulogne, Chevalier de Saint-Georges. The establishment who had invited me were concerned that because none of them had heard of him that therefore his music would not be good enough. But when they heard it, they joyfully exclaimed, "Oh, he sounds like Mozart." And of course I said, "Well, in actual fact, it's the other way round . . . Mozart sounds just like *him* . . . " '

Musical genres are losing their hard edges, with black people no longer intimidated – as I was growing up – by the idea that classical music should be white. Meanwhile, music which has traditionally been regarded as 'black' music is appealing to wider audiences like never before.

But even the 'urban' scene – to borrow the euphemism so often used to describe black music – is still failing to recognise black talent. One of the UK's most recognisable rappers, Akala, has spoken about the hostility towards his brand of highly educated, intelligent, conscious and political lyricism from the music industry. '*You write raps, I write history / On the page and quite literally / An elder statesman to my own generation,*' he refrains in *Fire in the Booth* – a series of performances for the BBC's 1Xtra station that went viral on social media with several million views on YouTube. In the same performance, Akala describes his style as:

> . . . *the knowledge of Timbuktu*
> *Mixed with the slang of a London youth*
> *Adding in the heart and the soul of blues*

My youth, now how can I not go true?
Half of a cracker, plus half of a coon
Half of a Celt, plus half a Maroon
If I'm feeling anything that's close to half-hearted
You're half more than half doomed
Half of my tune
Contains more content than every single thing you'd ever do . . . [19]

Akala tours regularly and packs out the same venues as some of the best-known artists in the industry, yet has never had a record deal with a major label or been given any airtime on daytime radio. 'Mainstream music is still controlled by the same people it was always controlled by. It's true the Internet has provided a certain level of democratisation – certainly I wouldn't have been able to tour the world the way I have twenty years ago,' Akala says. He talks like he raps – rapidly, intelligently, with a sense of urgency. 'The music industry is like "we just don't want clever people full stop".'

Just as the film industry has been reeling from accusations of racism – when 2016 became the second consecutive year in which not a single black actor was nominated for an Academy Award, the hashtag #OscarsSoWhite was born – so the music industry has been similarly criticised. In 2016 the Brit Awards faced an outcry when not a single black recording artist was nominated in a major category – a year that had seen a boom in grime music with wildly popular artists like Stormzy and acclaimed albums by singer-songwriters like Lianne La Havas – propelling the industry to address its diversity standards.[20] Even the MOBOs – which were originally created specifically for what they termed 'Music of Black Origin' – have faced accusations of whitewashing genres that originated and continue to be innovated primarily by black artists.

Around the same time, white artist Ed Sheeran was nominated the 'most important person in black music' by the BBC 1Xtra power list, and, defending his nomination, told audiences to 'listen with their ears, not their eyes'.

'Clearly it hadn't occurred to him that it was precisely the fact that people "listen with their eyes" that saw him top the farcical list in the first place,' protested Yomi Adegoke, a young journalist, representing the fresh anger of a new generation at an age-old trend. 'I know the world would like to believe that Britain's biggest soul exports over the decade – Duffy, Amy Winehouse, Adele, Sam Smith, Jack Garratt and others – are so because they're the best, but we've all seen enough black teens perfecting Mariah Carey's falsetto highs on *The X Factor* to know it's simply not the case.'[21] 'White artists have not thrived within a predominantly black genre in spite of being white, they have thrived because of it ... It's white privilege at its most dizzying.'

Music is one of the most powerful signifiers of identity. When I was a teenager, the music scene was the closest I ever came to a glimpse of a post-racial society. British genres like drum'n'bass, garage, jungle and grime have helped create a sense of belonging for a generation of British people and been unifying to an extent that makes their 'urban' tag redundant. With their reggae and soul origins in inner-city areas, they fused with dance, trance, punk and pop, through heavy production and turntabling which made stars out of black girls from Birmingham, Asian teenagers in Hertfordshire and posh white boys in the Home Counties, given as much credibility as anyone else, if they could make or play the tunes. These fusions were and still are a British sound – full of the subversion, rebelliousness and darkness of life in a grey council estate through long, rainy winters, sometimes soaring with the light of the soul, calypso and jazz that immigrants had brought with them. Everything was in the mix. No one else could replicate it. But when it became popular, and artists began to get signed, and release albums and win awards ... for only the *white* artists to be recognised and rewarded – it felt like a betrayal.

Some white artists have confronted this sense of betrayal directly, like the white American rapper Macklemore whose track 'White Privilege II' is a nine-minute ode to white American guilt. '*You've exploited and stolen the music, the moment / The magic, the passion, the*

fashion, you toy with / The culture was never yours to make better /
You're Miley, you're Elvis, you're Iggy Azalea,[22] he opined, reeling off a
familiar list of white artists who have found fame and fortune from
making black music without – their critics say – any discernible benefit to the artists or community whose shoulders they stood on.

As well as partying to its soundtrack, I used to write about the
British music scene for the *Voice* in the late 90s. Back then, the existential dilemma for UK hip hop was whether it was OK for rappers to
use (fake) American accents, or whether the genre could stand on its
own two feet, and should stop trying to be an imitation of the better-
known genre from across the Atlantic. Things changed in just a few
years, with bold young artists like Ms Dynamite – Akala's big sister –
whose conscious lyrics about everything from blood diamonds to
abusive relationships made us think while we raved, and So Solid
Crew, who described themselves as '30 black guys mobbing the music
industry'.[23] And then came grime, a genre that started in London and
spread to cities around the UK, gaining recognition all over the country and the world. A uniquely British blend of brutally honest lyrics
built on a tradition of garage, jungle and hip hop beats, grime moved
away from the party vibe of other genres, capturing instead the reality
of young black people growing up on some of the toughest council
estates in the country. 'We're writing to escape. If you listen deep
into the lyrics, there's probably a lot of cries for help in there,' said
Wiley, often called the godfather of grime. But despite his early success,
and other artists like Kano, Lethal Bizzle and Dizzee Rascal – who
won a Mercury Prize in 2003 for his album *Boy In Da Corner* – it was
thirteen years before the genre would be recognised again by the
mainstream awards, when Skepta won the 2016 Mercury Prize for
his album *Konnichiwa*. It took just as long for grime to gain official
acceptance by music giants like Apple, with its software iTunes only
recognising grime as a category unto itself in 2016. Prior to that, the
company had slotted it into dance, electronic music and rap – none of
which really came close.

But it would be an exaggeration, even now, to say that grime has been truly embraced by the mainstream. In 2016, David Cameron alienated a whole generation by telling a room full of mainly white editors that he didn't think the BBC should even play the music. 'I would say to Radio 1, do you realise that some of the stuff you play on Saturday nights encourages people to carry guns and knives?' he said, singling out the DJ Tim Westwood's long-running show.

What Cameron doesn't seem to have understood is that grime artists don't deny their proximity to crime, nor is it fair to say they encourage it – they explore it. The music is a symptom of the violence, pressure and struggles they grow up experiencing on London's unrelenting streets, not the cause. They are struggles rooted in poverty, low pay, poor schools, struggling parents, government neglect, realities that fall heavily on black children in this society, something political leaders have been slower to condemn.

The association of grime – the sound of today's black youth culture – with crime is only a micro-scale version of the larger association that links all black people with crime in the popular imagination. Black and brown people are at best 'urban', which always makes me wonder what happens if we move to the countryside – do we spontaneously combust? At worst, and so commonly, we are inextricably linked to inner-city criminal underworlds, to gangs, violence, baby mothers, prison and deprivation. You are reminded of this, moving into a new area as a black family – you expect hostility from the neighbours, you know you will have to prove to them that you are a trouble-free zone.

I know that black people look like criminals, because of my own experience of being treated like a suspect by shop security guards. This happens to anyone who is black, even if – like Leona Lewis, the pop star who told her story of being kicked out of a shop because the way she and her father looked offended the owner – they are very fair-skinned, glamorous and famous.[24] It happened to me, it still does now – a black woman, wearing a tracksuit on a Saturday morning, little black child in tow. How much worse would this be if I were a black boy, jeans hung low, hood up, going about my business?

In 2014, the then Home Secretary Theresa May developed a surprising reputation for speaking candidly about the discrimination facing black people, condemning the fact that police officers had attempted to smear the family of Stephen Lawrence, while failing to pursue those accused of the crime.[25] Just a few months later, she stunned officers by accusing them of displaying 'contempt for the public' in their handling of sensitive cases and in the excessive use of stop and search in the black community.[26]

That autumn, May invited Alexander Paul, a young black man from south London, to introduce her keynote speech at the Conservative Party Conference. May had met Alexander, then eighteen, at his sixth form college, where she'd held a focus group of young black people to hear their concerns about the criminal justice system. He had impressed her. He was exceptionally smart and articulate, and though there was nothing unusual about the fact that as a young black man he had grown up living with continual police harassment, what was surprising was that he had documented it. He'd been stopped and searched forty-five times in his young life, and he'd kept every single police slip as evidence.

'The first time I got stopped and searched was when I was thirteen. That wasn't a bad experience, in fact it was the best stop and search I've ever had,' Alexander told me. 'It was done properly, correctly. When you are stopped and searched they are supposed to tell you what they are doing. They give you a slip so that no other police officer can stop and search you that day, [stating] that you have no illegal drugs or weapons on you. But even though it was done properly, I still felt vilified. The officer said I looked suspicious. I asked him why – bear in mind I was thirteen years old – and I was in my area. It was a weekend, I was wearing trousers and a jumper, coming back from the shop. I had milk in one bag and eggs in the other, and I was stopped and searched.

'Subsequent stop-and-search routines have never been the same,' Alexander continued. 'There are times when I've been mishandled.

There are times when I've been in a stop-and-search routine and I was in a suit and I was on my way to work experience with a law firm. And for me to get stopped and searched in a suit, it kind of broke my heart. It made me feel like even when I'm wearing their uniform, the uniform of the corporate, of the upper class, going to a law firm, I still cannot get away from injustice just because I'm a black person.'

It is heartbreaking. Here was a young person who had done everything right; done well at school, had chosen and was pursuing an ambitious career, excelled in the arts and sport, even managed to impress the future prime minister so much that she chose him to introduce her to her party, and the country. But when you look at the figures around stop and search, it's like taking Alexander's experience, and multiplying it by 70,000, which is the number of times ethnic minority people were stopped and searched by the police in England in 2015, a rate two to four times higher than the white population.[27]

On 13 July 2016, two years after Alexander introduced her conference speech, Theresa May became prime minister. Standing on the steps of 10 Downing Street, she made her first speech as the nation's leader. Her party, the Conservatives, she told the nation, stood for social justice. 'That means fighting against the burning injustice that, if you're born poor, you will die on average nine years earlier than others. If you're black, you're treated more harshly by the criminal justice system than if you're white.'[28]

On the same day, 220 miles away, as the new prime minister was speaking, a young man was on the move. An eighteen-year-old named Mzee Mohammed, with full cheeks and a multi-watt smile, was living out his last moments.

Mzee's was a quintessential tale of Liverpool – the town that had had one of the earliest black and mixed-race populations in the country. His mother Karla is half Kenyan, half white British. Some of her siblings are white, and Mzee grew up close to his white cousins. He was also close to his father – whom everyone calls 'Blacks' – who came more recently from Jamaica, and whose family are spread out through the UK, and – as is so often the case with the Jamaican diaspora – the world. While Theresa May had been at Buckingham Palace receiving the Queen's blessing to form a new government, Mzee had been heading to his dad's house in a cab to 'pree his father's pot', as they say in Liverpool, or to see what was cooking.

Mzee didn't have a lot of money, but he still preferred to take taxis. He disliked crowds, having suffered from autism and ADHD, conditions which his family say he was good at managing, in part by avoiding triggers like large groups and crowded shopping centres. Two years earlier Mzee had been stabbed fourteen times in a racist attack by a group of white lads in the rough Kensington neighbourhood where he lived, which made him even less comfortable with being out and about.

But that afternoon – for reasons that have never become clear – Mzee ended up at Liverpool One, the city's busiest shopping centre. His cousin Kalum was working there, as a supervisor at the Subway fast-food outlet, and heard security guards from the private firm contracted by the shopping centre discussing an incident on the internal comms.

'I heard the security saying there was a "big black male with dreads running around barefoot with a knife",' said Kalum, who was close to Mzee. His initial impression of the threat, seen through the eyes of security guards relaying it on the intercom, echoes some of the first reports in the press, which claimed that Mzee had been threatening shoppers with a twelve-inch blade.[29] Those claims were later retracted. But Kalum was concerned enough that he asked his manager whether he should close up the shop until the incident was over. It did not occur to him, not even remotely, that the 'big black male with dreads' he was hearing about over the intercom was his beloved cousin Mzee. He continued following the intercom anyway.

'I heard the command for the security guards to call the police, and at that point, they already had the person detained,' said Kalum. Video footage filmed on a mobile phone later emerged showing Mzee lying face down, his hands handcuffed behind his back as a medic takes his blood pressure.[30] An ambulance was called, and at 7.53 p.m., he was pronounced dead.

The family were initially told that Mzee, having run through Liverpool One with security guards in pursuit, bounded down a flight of stairs six at a time, falling over and hitting his head. The autopsy, however, revealed no sign of the kind of head injuries they believe would be consistent with such a fall. The family accept that something was wrong. Mzee was clearly in distress, and needed help, they believe, but was instead met with a lethal show of force. 'Knowing that [Mzee was already being detained], they still sent eighteen police officers. So there were eight security guards, eighteen police officers, a police dog and a helicopter,' Kalum added. 'All for one lad who was already hand-cuffed and on the ground.'

An inquest and an independent police complaints commission began investigating what happened that day. Since July 2016, the family have found tragic common ground with the families of other young black men who died after coming into contact with the authorities, many of them suffering from mental illness and in need of help. Patterns emerge. Families like Mzee's, and campaign groups like Inquest that represent them, believe when black men are vulnerable and in need of some kind of intervention, they are much more likely to be seen instead as a threat that needs to be put down with a massive show of force.

'You see racial profiling and perceptions which inform how those officers responded, which is the idea of black men being inherently "big, black and dangerous" – those kind of stereotypes which I do think seep into police consciousness and inform the way individuals are then treated,' said Deborah Coles, chair of Inquest. 'It's the explanation I think about why it is that black men are disproportionately represented amongst those who are most likely to die following the use of force. Then we have the way in which misinformation seeps into the media and the police narrative of events, which appears to blame the deceased for their own death and deflect attention from the force that was used. That's a kind of toxic combination.'

On 10 July, just three days before Mzee died, the Black Lives Matter movement had had its first ever protest in Liverpool.[31] The movement had begun in America, after a spate of shocking deaths of young black people at the hands of the police – twelve-year-old Tamar Rice shot dead by officers in Ohio, a seventeen-year-old unarmed black boy shot dead by a neighbourhood watch volunteer, and Eric Garner, a man placed in a stranglehold by police for selling cigarettes without the correct tax stamp, where he suffocated to death, memorably exclaiming, 'I can't breathe.'

What angered African Americans was not just that children and adults were dying at the hands of the authorities, but also the fact that those responsible were frequently acquitted or not charged in the first place. The sense of unfairness that the system did not punish those who unfairly killed them contributed to the belief that America's justice system – which only fifty years ago officially treated African Americans as of inferior status – continued to disregard their rights. All lives in America would not matter, they chanted, until black lives matter.

The week Black Lives Matter was coming to Liverpool, Mzee asked his mother Karla if she was going, and when she lacked enthusiasm, he made fun of her for being more interested in bingo. He was cheeky like that, everybody said. 'We laughed about it,' Karla says, a bewildered expression on her face. 'How could we have known that the next Black Lives Matter march in Liverpool would be for him?'

Yet that is exactly what happened. The weekend after Mzee's death, several hundred friends, family members and activists marched through Liverpool demanding answers. They suspected that the nature of the police response was disproportionate, and ultimately lethal. It's a suspicion that merges uncomfortably with memories the family has inherited from the era of slavery of the very real abuse at the hands of the British in Jamaica, where Mzee now lies buried. His tomb is on land passed down from his third great-grandfather, who had been born a slave. But the path to burying their beloved boy was far from straightforward, and during the funeral, his relatives struggled to ignore the smell seeping from the coffin. The authorities had held on to Mzee's body for weeks and, when they released it, it seemed to have been improperly stored. 'First they killed him, and then they gave the family a rotting body to bring back here – it's just very unfortunate,' muttered Karen Williams, a cousin of Mzee's who had travelled from Philadelphia for the funeral. 'Even after he was dying, Mzee was still not being treated as if he was human.'

The continuities with slavery are striking. The night before the funeral, the family gathered on the gentle, stony hillside at the foot of their land, under a night sky made smoky by the jerk chicken BBQ, for a ritual that some call 'Nine Night' – a name handed down by African slaves who believed it took nine days for the deceased's spirit to return home to Africa. At the funeral itself, which I was reporting on for the *Observer*, many mourners were wearing black and red clothes – colours I recognised immediately from Ghana's Ashanti funeral tradition. *Why are people wearing black and red?* I asked. 'It's just what we do,' I was told. Like a memory half forgotten, no one could provide an explanation, but they kept doing it anyway. In her moving eulogy to Mzee during the funeral service, Mzee's friend Roxanne summed up the feeling. 'You died handcuffed on the floor like a slave,' she said, quietly swallowing rage. 'We can't bring you back ... I make you a promise, we will fight to the end. We will find out who killed you, my friend.'

Black people are disproportionately likely to come into contact with law enforcement. For example, in 2016, one-third of all people stopped by the police in England and Wales under 'stop and search' were from ethnic minority backgrounds,[32] more than double the number you would expect if it was representative of the make-up of society.[33] This overrepresentation is consistent throughout the criminal justice system, not least in deaths at the hands of the state. Between 1990 and 2017, one in seven deaths in custody, and one in five deaths after being shot by police, were people from black and ethnic minority backgrounds, while they only make up one-tenth of the population as a whole.[34] Some caution that the numbers of people dying are too small to draw big, statistical conclusions, and the figures are less dramatic than those in the US.

Mzee's death came at a time when Black Lives Matter was gaining real traction in the UK. But the British movement differs from its American counterpart in its very Britishness. Attending protests in Sheffield, Liverpool and London in 2016, I realised that the movement here is, in part, a demand to claim being black. Unlike the African American identities that all Americans acknowledge exist, in the UK, a new generation of black people are defiantly describing themselves as black, and claiming it as an identity bound up with pride. It's also striking how multiracial the marches are – there are middle-class white mums with babies in expensive slings (one is worried about an on-camera interview in case it comes across as another example of 'white privilege'), interracial families, students of all skin colours and sexual orientations. It seems like a powerful assertion of identity, to me, that in this country, all of these people are embracing the existence of black British identities, and saying that yes, they matter. I wonder if, were I growing up now in this atmosphere, I would have felt able to find a place for my sense of identity in Britain more easily, rather than gazing always at the African continent as the only place I felt I could be myself.

This is not to say that the issues at stake are unique to the black or any other ethnic minority community. In 2016, prison suicides in England and Wales rose to the highest levels since records began, a fact that conceals the tragedies of many predominantly young white men whose cries for help, and vulnerabilities, have been ignored by a prison system bursting to capacity, understaffed and underfunded.[35]

In 2011, a small-scale protest in Tottenham, metres from the house where Sam grew up, turned into three days of rioting across English cities, the worst civil disorder in the country in a generation. Millions of words have been written about the root causes of the 2011 riots. Some pronounce that they originated with so-called thugs in Tottenham's black community, and were then spread around the country by criminals – as the government claimed – a view which had real consequences when jail terms were inflated by as much as 25 per cent to punish those who were caught inciting and looting. Others insist that these communities on the brink, hammered by austerity, numbed by poverty, alienated from the political system and furious at their treatment by the police, seized a voice in the most immediately available manner.

'The riots had nothing to do with gangs, or feral youth,' Kenny Imafadon told me. Kenny is something of an anathema – a young black man from south London who was sent to jail in his final year of A levels, while awaiting trial for a total of seven serious charges including murder, along with four of his closest friends. He became the first person to sit his A levels in Feltham, a notorious young offenders' institution in London, and after being acquitted, launched himself into politics. He was in Feltham when London erupted in rioting, and understood what was happening immediately. 'The interesting thing about the riots is that it wasn't a youth issue – there were a lot of people involved across the generations,' Kenny said. 'What they showed was frustration across the political system, and poverty. The biggest places to be hit by the riots were clothing stores and food stores. I think that sends a big message. We have one million people [relying] on food banks in one of the fastest growing G7 economies. And we are surprised they are rioting?'

Poverty affects British people from all racial, cultural and religious backgrounds. The top ten parts of England most affected by what the government calls 'multiple deprivation', for example, include mainly white Hastings and Hull, Bradford – where one-fifth of the population is Asian – and multicultural Manchester, Birmingham and Liverpool.[36]

But many white working-class people have a sense of identity as British people independent from poverty. *Black* British identities, on the other hand, seem inextricably bound up with poverty. This is why, for example, when we speak of crime committed in poor, black areas, we describe it as 'black-on-black crime'. As the journalist and writer Gary Younge points out in his book *Another Day in the Death of America*, about fatal shootings of children on one randomly chosen day in the US, 'Black-on-black crime' is a nonsense term. America is very segregated, and its criminality conforms to that fact. The victims of most crimes are of the same race as those who commit them. Eighty-four per cent of whites killed every year, are killed by whites. White people who buy illegal drugs are most likely to buy them from other white people. So the fact that black people are killing each other conforms to, rather than contradicts, America's criminal patterns where race is concerned.'[37] The same could be said of the UK, where there is equally no such thing as *white-on-white crime*, even though crime by white perpetrators against white victims accounts for by far the greatest majority of cases in the criminal justice system.[38]

Our idea of ethnic minority people is why, when I visited a state school on a notorious London council estate that had become an unlikely success story, the head teacher, a black man who was highly decorated for his services to education, asked me, 'What kind of black person are you? You're not a proper black person!' In his mind, to be black was to have the speech and manner of someone from a poor area, someone 'hood', someone 'street', not someone middle class and professional. If someone like this headmaster, who was himself black, middle class and professional, thought like this, I said to myself, how much lower the expectations must be of others as to what is possible for black people. It's a common accusation, that middle-class-sounding black people – some of whom are actually from working-class backgrounds but got scholarships or whose parents worked two jobs to fund private education – are not 'proper black' people.

I was at that particular school to take on mentoring for four young black pupils. They were talented, their teacher told me, and could go far, but they suffered from uncooperative families, chaotic homes and low aspiration. In this respect, they were typical of the intake – at this school, obtaining average GCSE results is seen as an 'outstanding achievement', that's how low their starting point is.

He was right. The four girls were exceptionally bright, but their lack of opportunity shocked me. When I was fifteen, my school arranged post-GCSE work experience for me at a major global advertising agency. Others in my class had gone to magic circle law firms, the House of Commons and investment banks. These girls had done theirs at Superdrug, Primark and KFC. This made me angry. Work experience is a chance to see the peak of what's possible, not the worst-case scenario, I complained to the head. When I took my four mentees to see the Houses of Parliament, the Inns of Court and the *Guardian* on a kind of tour of the establishment in 2008, it emerged that three out of the four had never been into central London before. One had never before been on an escalator.

In 2016, 45 per cent of black children in the UK were growing up in poverty, compared with 25 per cent of white children. This affects their chances at school; a poor child's vocabulary lags one whole year behind that of a child growing up in an affluent household. Only 4 per cent of black students obtained the three As at A level needed for a top university, compared to 10 per cent of white pupils. The UK has never had a black prime minister, but in 2016, the actor David Harewood conducted an exercise for the BBC, analysing data on previous prime ministers to calculate the odds of children from different backgrounds becoming one in the future. He found that the odds of the average white child becoming prime minister is 1 in 1.4 million. For a privileged, private-school-educated white child who goes to Oxbridge and obtains a top profession, the odds of becoming prime minister are slashed to just 1 in 200,000. But for the average black child, the odds of becoming the UK's prime minister currently stand at a staggering 1 in 17 million.[39]

It's not because black children are less intelligent or capable. Talk to the ones who have proven their potential – against the odds – and this becomes abundantly clear. Akala talks about his experiences at school in north London when it emerged that he was academically gifted. 'Adults were uncomfortable with the fact that I was a very bright little kid,' he tells me. 'If I was a middle-class kid I probably would have never started playing football or rapping. I'd have been a physicist. I wanted to be an astronaut. But I learned from the society very quickly. I was discouraged from pursuing those things.

'Ironically the people who actually encouraged me were all supposedly bad,' Akala continues. 'Drug dealers, bank robbers – the bad people in the local area. Other than my godfather and my dad who were both, you know, upstanding working men, you know, they encouraged my intelligence too. But the road man – they could see I was smart. And they made me feel really special because I was clever. Whereas schoolteachers . . . my first primary schoolteacher said I had a magic button on my chest and I couldn't speak unless he poked me, he said I had too much to say for myself. Another teacher when I was seven used to hit me. My mum came into the school because of that, and because they hadn't read with me for nine months. I had a GCSE reading age when I was seven, I wanted to read *The Man with the Golden Gun*. A supply teacher came in, and without even checking, she said "you can't read this". I felt, in the tone of her derision, I couldn't read that.'

Akala ended up in a special needs class, along with children who couldn't speak English. 'There was a boy from Indonesia, a girl who had just arrived from Uganda, they couldn't speak good English,' he explains. 'They didn't tell my parents they were doing it, so you know they were doing something funny. I believe that my teacher was made to feel so uncomfortable by the fact that I was top of the class.'

It's remarkable how many of the black people I know who are successful – whether they went to failing state schools or elite private schools – have this experience in common. Baroness Patricia Scotland, in 1991 the first black woman to be made a QC, the first black and female attorney general since the role was created in 1315, has many stories in this vein. As legal affairs correspondent for the *Guardian*, I used to spend a good deal of time with Scotland, the tenth of twelve children, born in Dominica, raised in east London and state-school educated. She tells me how, when she saw a school careers adviser, she said she wanted to be a lawyer. She was told that it would be more realistic to consider working in a supermarket like Sainsbury's instead.

Maggie Aderin-Pocock, the renowned space scientist and science communicator, also tells me how when she mentioned to teachers that she wanted to be a scientist, she was told to aspire to become a nurse. And like Akala and so many other black children from all points on the social spectrum, she was put in a class with children who had special needs, where expectations were even lower. She went on to gain a degree in physics from Imperial College and a PhD in mechanical engineering, but not before that experience left a permanent mark of low expectation she believes is linked to race.

These experiences – getting stopped and harassed by the police, being perceived as a troublemaker in school or a low achiever, being told you won't amount to anything – add up. There's evidence that exposure to racial discrimination, from schools, the media and the police, leads to decreased self-efficacy, anger, poor health and lower levels of empathy, characteristics which in turn lead to an increase in risky behaviours such as drug use and aggression, and increased risk of chronic illness.[40] For all the success stories I have referred to in this chapter, I have equally met scores of people whose lives have been shaped by these problems, who are in and out of secure psychiatric detention for example, who have a string of failed relationships and abandoned children of their own. Such is the profile of many of the people I defended in criminal cases at the Bar. They are the stories behind the statistics – some of the 12 per cent of black people with mental illness,[41] the 10 per cent of the prison population which is black, the 43 per cent of NEETs (young people 'not in education, employment or training') who are from ethnic minority backgrounds.[42]

This is what I found uniquely depressing about being a defence lawyer. There appeared to be no good outcome for the seemingly endless stream of young black men being represented in court by inexperienced, naively idealistic lawyers like me. Many of them had made various cries for help – to their parents, to their school, to their friends. They were growing up surrounded by violence and an asphyxiating version of masculinity, the law of the streets, in which to show fear or weakness is to subscribe to a death sentence.

One young man I represented, Lamar, was a case in point. He was fifteen, and he had stabbed another boy in the playground. It was my first ever full trial. Lamar was extremely quiet, shy and seemed vulnerable. He was small for his age – a skinny black boy whose eyes were deep and contemplative. His father had died when he was nine, and ever since, his mother told me, he had suffered from nightmares, bedwetting and prolonged periods of silence. A plump woman with silvery brown skin, originally from Nigeria, she had been doing her best for Lamar and her younger son, working as a cleaner and attending night school to get a BTEC and then a degree. She wanted to be a social worker herself. She had repeatedly approached social services for help with Lamar, who had become so withdrawn, he barely communicated with her at all, but she had been told that her son did not meet the threshold for care, since there was no evidence of life-threatening behaviour. 'Do I have to wait for my baby to take his own life, or someone else's, before someone will help him?' she asked me, tears running down her full cheeks.

That's what Lamar had done. He had gone up to another boy in the playground, taken a knife out from his sock, and stabbed the other child in the side of his stomach and in the leg. The injuries were not life-threatening, but the victim, who was only fourteen, was badly hurt, and traumatised. The assault had been witnessed in person by the headmaster, who had intervened, and the entire attack had been caught on CCTV. Yet Lamar insisted on pleading not guilty. I did everything in my power to convince him that an admission of guilt was in his interests; his conviction was inevitable, and he would get a longer sentence for dragging the case out and putting the victim through the ordeal of a trial. But he insisted on his innocence. It was as if he wanted to go to jail, and for as long as possible.

Perversely – it seemed to me – the time and expense of a legal team, the youth offending team, the statements taken from teachers and friends, the court time, the psychologist who prepared his pre-sentence report, and then the cost of incarcerating Lamar for twenty-four months in a young offenders' institution, were many times what it would have cost to simply give this child the attention he had so badly needed months and years earlier. But that is not how the criminal justice system works. Resources kick in after the fact, when a crime has been committed, and investigating, understanding and contextualising become bound up in the duty to provide a fair hearing. It costs taxpayers more, and it costs children like Lamar the most. The cost of sending a young offender to prison is just under £100,000 per year.[43] The cost of sending a child to Eton is around one-third of that amount.[44] During the trial I discovered that Lamar – who had been going to school every single day of term for eight years – could neither read nor write.

By the time kids like Lamar came to me, what could I do? The best-case scenario, from their perspective, was that my advocacy could secure them an acquittal – probably on some technicality. This would help them escape jail time, but mean sending them straight back to the environment that had got them here in the first place. And in almost all cases, that world was a violent one. One which had seen them succumb to the pressures of the street and their own, unattended inner demons, and which would, in the absence of other opportunities, see them succumb again. Or they would be convicted, and sent to a young offenders' institution or an adult prison, where violence, drugs and mental illness were far more accessible than books or education. With a full immersion in that environment, and a criminal conviction to their name, their chances of changing their lives were even slimmer. Lamar was not, I knew, going to come out in two years' time a happier, more nurtured child. I never forgot him, and how vulnerable he seemed.

Sam and I were both doing criminal defence work at the time, and often used to share stories of the craziness we were seeing. But it was only when I was interviewing other people for this book that he shared his own experiences of stop and search with me. His first happened aged twelve, when he was walking with a friend near Alexandra Palace, a grand Victorian entertainment venue and public park in north London. When they heard a police siren, Sam – who'd never been in any trouble with the police – found himself ducking, as if by reflex. He had, even at that age, an instinctive sense of seeming guilty, because he was black, even though he'd done nothing wrong. His attempt to hide then obviously attracted the police's attention, in a perfectly self-fulfilling cycle. The officers searched Sam and his friend, and finding nothing, one officer jabbed him hard in the chest. 'I'll see you,' he said menacingly, 'when you're older.' That was the day Sam decided that if the officer was going to see him again when he was older, it was not going to be as a suspect, but in a suit, representing one of his clients in court.

7. THE NEW BLACK

'Strange Fruit', Mata-Marielle, 2016.

He wrote his dreams in the present tense. He kept his suit-
case full of clothes in the cupboard to stop it from flying
back by itself. He never actually unpacked. He slowed down
his speech to be better understood. He was never better
understood.

– Roger Robinson,
The Butterfly Hotel

When I take off my uniform,
Will I be safe from harm –
Or will you do me
As the Germans did the Jews?
When I've helped this world to save,
Shall I still be color's slave?
Or will Victory change
Your antiquated views?

– Langston Hughes,
'Will V-Day Be Me-Day Too?'

If someone were to look for a textbook definition of the 'Good Immigrant', they could do worse than describe the story of my father's father, and his family.

Born Hans Hirsch in 1920, my grandfather was the first of two sons to Regina and Ismar Hirsch – an affluent family of German Jews, who lived in Schöneberg, near Berlin's fashionable Bayerischer Platz. These days, the former glory of this neighbourhood – whose residents included Albert Einstein, Gisèle Freund, the art historian Carl Einstein and the great political theorist Hannah Arendt[1] – is mostly remembered for the abrupt and traumatic manner of its ending. Memorials dotted subtly around the Bayerischer Platz recall the many petty and sinister assaults on the humanity of the Jewish families who lived here in the 1930s. My grandfather – like so many Jews who survived life under the atrocities of Nazi rule – spoke of these times rarely, and only with persuasion. His memories are of a child's world closing slowly in, suffocating him. His father, a cloth buyer, lost his shop to a long-time employee who took advantage of a government policy encouraging 'Aryans' to seize Jewish businesses. Ismar died not long after. Curfews prevented young Hans from riding his bike outside. His best friend at school stopped speaking to him. Then he was not allowed to attend school at all. Posters of the Nazi tabloid *Der Stürmer* ('The Attacker') began appearing in the square, with crude caricatures of devilish Jewish figures from the Middle Ages. '*Disaster broods in their wombs*,' stated one. Another, chillingly, '*The End of Judah*'.

By 1938, my great-grandmother, Regina, had resolved that the family must leave their home and seek refuge in the UK. Isaac Schoenberg, a German Jew at the London-based electronics and record company EMI, was willing to take on young German Jews who were good at physics or engineering, and my grandfather, then seventeen, fitted the bill. He travelled to London alone in October 1938, and Regina followed weeks later. The socialite from the Bayerischer Platz, who not long before had busied herself instructing architects to install a modern bar in the living room of the family's grand apartment, found work as a domestic servant at a house in Chelsea. My grandfather's younger brother, Kurt, arrived next, travelling alone on the Kindertransport – a formal scheme in which an estimated 10,000 unaccompanied, mainly Jewish children from Central and Eastern Europe were sent to the UK to live with host families on the eve of the Second World War. The boys' stepfather, Herbert Meyersohn – a dentist – came last, Regina having pulled innumerable strings to secure him a visa and a job at a Fulham taxi company, with the same family that had taken in Kurt.

Hans and Kurt, aged seventeen and thirteen, had never left Germany before, and now they were alone – Hans at lodgings in Hayes, Kurt with an English family in Fulham, who had graciously taken him in. They changed their names – Hans became 'John', and Kurt became 'Peter'. They learned English. My grandfather's main priority, he told me decades later, was to join the RAF, to bomb the Nazis. Not surprisingly, being German, he was rejected by the British military, so instead John Hirsch had to content himself with making light bulbs and radar, hoping that this was still doing his bit towards bringing down his mortal enemy.

The presence of so many Jews like my grandfather in the electronics industry, working under Isaac Schoenberg at EMI, was, it's now believed, a significant reason for the success of British radar during the war.[2] And once the war was over, this formidable group of immigrant scientists 'helped place Britain at the forefront of the development of electronic television'.[3] My grandfather dedicated his life to physics, and worked as a professor at Birkbeck College, University of London, well into his eighties. His little brother Kurt, having become 'Peter', later became Sir 'Peter' Hirsch, knighted for his services to metallurgy.

You could not have asked for a more loyal, grateful or aspirational group of immigrants. For all four of them, moving to the UK was not a question of 'integrating' or 'assimilating', although they did both, it was a matter of life or death. My grandfather and his brother both married Englishwomen, and let go of even the minimalistic practice of Judaism with which they were raised. They spoke rarely of what had gone before in Berlin. My grandfather was a committed member of the British left. They opposed tyranny in all its forms for the rest of their lives. They worked, paid taxes, raised their children, in a world free from the kind of terror that had touched their early lives. They did these things not to prove that they subscribed to 'British values' but because they were human beings, given a chance in life, following their own version of a British Dream they created for themselves. And for that, I think they were grateful.

Gratitude, hard work, assimilation – this is very much the kind of behaviour we now require of immigrants in order to find them worthy. And there are few who, all these decades later, would lament the fact that Britain offered sanctuary to those escaping the Holocaust; Britain's decision – not without reluctance – to accept so many unaccompanied child refugees fleeing the Nazis from 1938 is a matter of national pride.

But who could have foreseen the true horror of the Holocaust that was to come? And, not knowing that was the danger that faced these refugees, who could have fallen back on the certainty which we have now, with the benefit of hindsight, that these refugees would carve incredibly successful new lives in Britain? There are grand lists now, of the accomplishments and contributions that Britain's Jewish refugees have made to the nation – Nobel prizes, in scientific advancement, literature, technology, music and art – but at the time, people like my grandfather were the most unwelcome kind of arrival – almost penniless, with no belongings and barely a word of English – the kind the British public has never rejoiced in receiving. And the tabloids, in a grand tradition so recognisable today, did their best to ensure those refugees were not welcome, either.

'Britain becomes Dump for Nazi Exiles,' exclaimed the *Daily Mirror* in 1938.[4] 'The way stateless Jews from Germany are pouring in from every port of this country is becoming an outrage,' the *Daily Mail* reported a magistrate as saying the same year, adding its own reference to 'the number of aliens entering the country through the "back door"'.[5] The hostility was more than just rhetoric to sell newspapers. Although there were many British people who personally offered sanctuary to Jewish refugees, others had, by 1940, been roused into feverish xenophobia. My grandfather's stepfather, Herbert Meyersohn – the last of the family to escape Germany in the spring of 1939, thinking he had found safety in Britain – was rounded up alongside 27,000 other German-speaking Jewish refugees, many in terrifying dawn raids. Some were given the option of joining the war effort. But many were interned for three years, in his case near Bideford in Devon, as a so-called 'enemy alien'.

By then, anti-immigration feeling in Britain was already well established, and Jews in fact had a long history of being the main targets. The UK's first real immigration law, the 1905 Aliens Act, was primarily intended to stem the flow of European Jews. Otherwise, one newspaper editor warned, 'the debilitated sickly and vicious products of Europe' could be 'grafted onto the English stock'.[6] Prime Minister Arthur Balfour argued at the time, British 'nationality would not be the same and would not be the nationality we should desire to be our heirs through the ages yet to come'.[7]

But what Balfour and so many British leaders after him have failed to grasp is that the 'English stock' or 'British nationality' in their imaginary notion of Britain was both untrue and irrelevant. Untrue because Britain has always been an immigrant nation. The dark hair and eyes still romanticised in Britain as 'Celtic' features are, it's now believed, much more likely to have come from the Mediterranean.[8] There were Africans in Britain before there were English people in Britain; Africans were making this their home, when the marauding tribes of Jutes, Angles and Saxons – all Germanic tribes from what is now Denmark and Germany – and their violent invasions were little more than a distant nightmare. The tribes who gave their name to the supposedly indigenous 'Anglo-Saxon' race invaded in the dying days of the Roman Empire, destroying all trace of civilisation in their wake.[9] Yet it is they who are considered the UK's true inhabitants. 'Britain has an amnesiac streak when it comes to acknowledging the immigrant blood in her veins,' writes the historian Robert Winder in *Bloody Foreigners*,[10] pointing out how mixed a race the Brits were even a millennium ago. 'By the so-called Dark Ages – a period many regard as archetypically British – there were Mediterranean, Celtic, Saxon, Roman, Jute, Angle, Danish and Norwegian immigrant invaders happily mingling their DNA with the pre-existing population.'[11]

By 1500, 6 per cent of the population of London were immigrants, and when Queen Elizabeth I polled seven thousand foreigners in 1573, she found that a third or more had come 'onlie to seeke woorck for theire living' as – in the modern, and often deeply unflattering, phrase – 'economic migrants'. 'Tottenham,' one Londoner complained during Henry VIII's reign, 'has turned French.'[12] As the slave trade commenced in Queen Elizabeth's day, thousands of Africans began to be brought to Britain, a population which had 'disappeared' by the end of the Victorian era. The only explanation for this 'disappearance' is assimilation. They married and had children with white British people, with two consequences. The first is that generations of 'racial dilution' means that their descendants' black heritage is no longer visible. The second is that their genes remain spread far and wide, in even the most seemingly ethnically un-diverse of places.[13]

As well as being wrong, the idea that there were no immigrants in the nostalgic Britain of old is also irrelevant, because while it claims to be about foreigners coming to the UK, it's really about something else. The true purpose of modern claims about immigration is to create a scapegoat for society's deeper, more intractable problems. Jewish refugees fleeing the Nazis were interned not when they first arrived in the 1930s, but in the summer of 1940, as France and the Low Countries fell to the Nazis and the prospect of invasion became real. 'Civilization has shrunk,' wrote Virginia Woolf on the eve of the war, capturing the fears about the decline of the British Empire and the nation's sense of existential threat.[14]

In times of fear and suffering, people look for visible others to blame. So even though Enoch Powell was sacked from the Cabinet after his infamous 'Rivers of Blood' speech, his language was echoed by Margaret Thatcher in 1978, when she told Granada Television's *World in Action* that 'this country might be rather swamped by people with a different culture',[15] and again by David Cameron in 2015, when he warned that Britain had to protect its borders amid the Syrian refugee crisis because 'you have got a swarm of people coming across the Mediterranean'.

But ideas of who is 'alien' are constructed; it is just as easy to turn on people with a long history within a country, as it is on those newly arriving. Post-revolutionary France, for example, had huge anxieties about the diversity of its population, only about half of which even spoke French, and the lowest of whom were still regarded, by the mid nineteenth century, as 'so miserable, inferior and bastardised that they may be classed as below the most inferior savage races, for their inferiority is sometimes beyond cure'. These interminable 'races' were not African or Asian immigrants, but simply the French rural poor.[16]

Vilification of the working classes is something that the British establishment also perfected. The working-class white population of east London, now often eulogised as a symbol of a lost past of strong communities and old-fashioned values, was not always so loved. 'The Bethnal Green poor', an 1864 article in a popular magazine said, are 'a caste apart, a race of whom we know nothing, whose lives are of quite different complexion from ours, persons with whom we have no point of contact'. Differences between the middle classes and the urban and agricultural poor were so profound, the article went on, that they prevented 'anything like association or companionship'.[17] The journalist Owen Jones devotes an entire book, *Chavs*, to the continuing demonisation of the working class. 'I genuinely think that there are people out there in the middle classes, in the church and the judiciary and politics and the media, who actually fear, physically fear the idea of this great, gold bling-dripping, lumpen proletariat that might one day kick their front door in and eat their au pair,' Labour MP Stephen Pound told Jones.[18]

When people create nostalgic narratives of Britain's past, a long history of pervasive class prejudice is rarely what they choose to recall. They sell a version of Britain in which white, British people had greater opportunity, until immigration ruined it all. Immigration – and immigration alone – has become the source of Britain's problems. A brief tour of political rhetoric since mass immigration began after the Second World War makes the point. Immigration first became a salient political issue at a time when there was actually net *emigration* from the UK, with numbers of Brits leaving exceeding numbers of primarily Commonwealth citizens coming in.[19] The two main political parties have competed over appeasing anti-immigration feeling in the electorate ever since. In 1961 then Home Secretary Richard Austin 'Rab' Butler passed an act to restrict immigration from the Commonwealth, against the advice of a parliamentary committee, justifying the law with the claim that 'a sizeable part of the entire population of the earth is at present legally entitled to come and stay in this already densely populated country' – a reference to the 800 million Commonwealth citizens theoretically entitled to move to Britain.[20] In 1964 the Conservative Smethwick candidate Peter Griffiths' slogan 'If you want a nigger for a neighbour, vote Liberal or Labour' won him the seat. The Labour government of 1964 restricted immigration, as did the Labour government of 1968, limiting the number of East African Asians able to flee to the UK from persecution in Kenya and Uganda. Edward Heath, Margaret Thatcher, Tony Blair, Gordon Brown, David Cameron and Theresa May all attempted to give voice to voters' concerns that immigration and asylum were responsible for the problems and grievances among the electorate.

The hardening of immigration rhetoric can be traced in the phrases used by politicians in the 2000s and 2010s, which were regarded as offensive and racist at the time, but accepted as mainstream only a few years later. When Gordon Brown said in 2007 that his government would provide 'British jobs for British workers', for example, he was accused of promoting 'employment apartheid', and accused of having borrowed the phrase from the BNP.[21] But by 2016, Conservative Theresa May's government had gone even further, pledging to make businesses disclose how many foreign workers they employ, to discourage employment of other nationals. And whereas Labour Home Secretary David Blunkett faced fierce criticism in 2002 for stating that immigrants should be required to learn English,[22] by 2015 it was a key part of Labour leader Ed Miliband's immigration stance.[23] That Miliband 'forgot' to mention immigration in his party conference speech in 2014 was seized upon as a fatal error. One year later, his party was selling red mugs emblazoned with the words *Controls on Immigration. I'm voting Labour*.[24] The idea that immigration was both bad and out of control had become an almost unchallengeable political fact. Of the four biggest parties contesting the 2015 election – the Conservatives, Labour, the Liberal Democrats and UKIP – only the Liberal Democrats did not support restrictions on the number of non-EU migrants and other measures to discourage those from within the EU.[25]

The problem with the political discussion of immigration is twofold. First, when voters who express anger at immigration are pressed for the root causes of their unhappiness, they often describe things which have nothing to do with immigration per se. As a journalist covering social affairs, many of the people I've interviewed about seemingly unrelated subjects, often refer to immigration as a component of the struggles they face. I spent time with a family in Hertfordshire in 2014, for example, forced to rent a home in the private sector which they struggled to afford – an example of a trend affecting many low-income families across the UK because of the chronic shortage of social housing. These two parents, in their late twenties, talked about unmanageable levels of immigration, which they said made it impossible for people like them to obtain a council home. The same year, in east London, I spent time at a school leasing an industrial estate to create capacity for several hundred new children – a drop in the ocean of the potential shortfall of 80,000 new school places needed by 2020. Parents I spoke to at parents' evening that day, many of them immigrants themselves, expressed their concern that the country was 'full'.[26] In 2015, I spent a day with a single mother in Kent, who broke down in tears when asked about how impending cuts to working tax credits would affect her. She would be hard hit financially by a Conservative policy, and vowed to vote in the next election for UKIP, with a sense that the country 'is not what it was'. In Stoke-on-Trent in 2017, voters told me that one of the reasons they had voted to leave the European Union, was to curb levels of immigration. But the actual problems they spoke of related to the decline of industry since the closure of the potteries, the local steel industry and the coal pits, and a sense of being 'left behind' by regeneration projects elsewhere, and by infrastructure programmes like the high-speed rail line 'HS2', which they pointed out would simply pass Stoke-on-Trent by.

The frustration and fear affecting these people was clearly justified – they faced uncertainty in key areas of their and their family's future. But it was equally obvious to me that the root causes of these problems had relatively little to do with immigration. The family unable to access social housing in Hertfordshire were experiencing the repercussions of successive government decisions not to build or replenish anywhere near enough social housing stock to meet demand. The mother in Kent was struggling with the high cost of childcare, which made it unaffordable for her to work, inadequate benefits and the high cost of housing – with rents across Britain having risen by 14 per cent between 2011 and 2017.[27] This was only exacerbated by the government's policy of 'austerity' – a policy of public-spend belt-tightening which the spending watchdog warned could last decades. Economists have suggested these cuts may have to be even deeper if political promises to reduce immigration are kept. Britain's economy benefits from – the Office for Budget Responsibility has said – working, taxpaying migrants in order to offset the ageing population. The sense that de-industrialised towns like Stoke-on-Trent have been left behind may be aggravated by the presence of upwardly mobile immigrant communities, but those communities are not the cause of the problem.

A further problem with the rhetoric that places immigration front and centre of promises to improve life for 'hard-working British families' in future, is that it promotes a politics of demonisation. The promise of less tolerance to those seeking to enter the UK dishonestly endorses the view that immigration is necessarily bad, and that the individual human beings who make up the phenomenon are the source of British people's hardship, personified. Politicians – some have tried – find it difficult to maintain the political stance that accepts immigration as a negative on the one hand, appealing to what they think voters want to hear, and acknowledges the contribution that immigrants have made to Britain's economy and public services on the other.

The New Labour government of Tony Blair stands slightly apart from the history of post-war, anti-immigration political rhetoric. Even though New Labour took a series of draconian measures to curb the number of 'asylum seekers' – a phrase which became a pejorative term in the 2000s – it also saw immigration as conferring some advantages. Immigration was regarded as both a social good and a process with a desirable end – it was, the Labour speechwriter Andrew Neather infamously put it in 2009, 'the way that the government was going to make the UK truly multicultural'. Between 1997 and 2010, annual net migration quadrupled from 48,000 people, to 198,000.

But this top-down, social engineering approach to immigration arguably did even more damage. Immigrants were still political footballs, only this time they were a tool of a particular kind of social engineering. The result was to cement, in the eyes of many British people, the idea of immigration as a cultural assault. In the words of one commentator, immigration had now become 'weaponised'.[28]

On 23 June 2016, 33.6 million British people voted in the EU referendum. At 72 per cent, turnout was significantly higher than in recent general elections, when it has hovered around 60 per cent over the last fifteen years. Fifty-two per cent – 17.4 million people – voted to leave the EU, while 48 per cent, 16 million, voted to remain. It sounds like a narrow margin, but it was far less close than many predicted.[29] Almost

nothing about the result had really been anticipated by the mainstream press, or indeed those campaigning to leave, many of whom
could be seen looking dazed and confused the following day. Both
sides in a campaign dominated by threats, lies and attempts to appeal
to people's deepest fears underestimated the strength of feeling that
lay beneath the political nuances of their strategy.

I was among those who did not foresee that the majority of voters
would want to leave the EU. British people are a practical and risk-
averse bunch, I thought, when it comes to matters of great consequence; plus we are, at heart, a tolerant nation that has always looked
outward as well as in. That turned out to be optimistic, and – if the
critics on social media who regularly hurl insults at my TV appear-
ances are to be believed – symptomatic of the fact that I belong to the
'liberal metropolitan elite'.

It's true that class and geographic trends did emerge in the analysis of voter behaviour. A survey of more than 12,000 voters by the
pollster Lord Ashcroft revealed, for example, that two-thirds of people
living in social housing voted to leave. Analysis by the political website
the Conversation which compared data from the Electoral Commission
with economic data from the Labour Force Survey, and population
data from the 2011 Census, found that the towns which voted most
strongly in favour of Brexit were English constituencies with significant deprivation, including East Lindsey in the Midlands and Thanet
in Kent, and former mining districts, such as Mansfield in
Nottinghamshire and Bolster in Derbyshire, affected by long-term
post-industrial decline.[30] They were also – ironically, given their
apparently anti-immigration motivation for voting leave – areas with
relatively low levels of immigration. But at the same time, it would be
wrong to characterise Brexit along straightforward class, race or
regional lines, and an oversimplification to regard Brexit as a vote of
protest by the white working class. According to the Ashcroft poll, the
majority of homeowners voted Brexit,[31] and while the majority of
people in the AB social group (those in professional or senior managerial occupations) voted remain, C1 (junior professionals and

clerical workers) and C2 (skilled manual labourers) voted leave. Other data shows that, although London was pro-remain, the majority of voters in the south-east voted to leave.[32]

On the other hand, working-class identities did have a significant role to play in Britain's decision to leave the European Union. These identities are generally so little understood across Europe that the Soros Foundation – the large non-profit organisation I worked for on improving prospects for the poor in West Africa – is now devoting more and more resources to studying the white working class in places such as Manchester.[33] Many of Scotland's identities, so fiercely debated during the independence referendum of 2014, have the advantage of perceiving the English with hostility, which I have observed as a unifying factor across other divides. For example, I have found Scottish people of black, Sikh or mixed-heritage descent much quicker to call themselves 'Scottish' than people living in England with similar heritage would be to call themselves English.[34] In the EU referendum result, the Scottish were united in voting to remain in the EU by a significant majority. In Northern Ireland, where identities are specific and unequivocally defined along sectarian lines, voters also wanted to remain – albeit by a smaller majority than in Scotland. It was the Welsh and the English who were marginally in favour of leaving the EU; the referendum results for Wales showed that the outcome there was representative of the UK as a whole, with 52 per cent voting leave.

So England stands apart. Because there is a greater gap in England than any other UK nation between those who live in England on the one hand, and those who perceive themselves as 'English' on the other. 'Englishness' is an identity that is still regarded as exclusive. And according to one poll, two-thirds of voters who see themselves as 'English' voted to leave, while almost two-thirds of those, in England, who see themselves as British not English, voted to remain.[35] Englishness is not an identity that many English people feel is open to immigrants. 'We're the English people,' an elderly lady in Purfleet, southern England, told *Channel 4 News* when asked about Brexit. 'I'm not saying "Britain" because everyone can be British. I'm English, and we voted out.'[36]

On the surface, the EU referendum vote was about sovereignty and European bureaucracy, and had nothing to do with ethnic diversity. But in reality, it had everything to do with identity. The polls show the distance between those with 'English' identities – which are so often framed as excluding those who are not white – and people who define themselves as members of ethnic minorities. The same poll which showed the correlation of perceived 'English' identities with being pro-Brexit, showed that those who see themselves as 'British' voted to remain. It's further evidence of the fact that 'British' as an identity is more capable of being inclusive than 'Englishness', even for people who live in England. It's an identity that overlaps more with those describing themselves as Asian, black or Muslim, the majority of whom voted Remain.

One man I interviewed at an event in east London, intended to encourage British Africans to vote in the EU referendum, summarised the position. 'They are talking about going back to 1973,' he said, referring to the date when Britain originally opted to join the EU, known then as the European Economic Community. 'I remember 1973. As a black man, it was not unusual to have Teddy boys chasing you down the street, calling you names. We were not safe. The EU has given us more protection – not just from racists, but from right-wing British governments as well. What black person in their right *mind* wants to go back to 1973?'

What makes those with perceived 'English' identities different from others in the United Kingdom? One answer is that, unlike Wales, Northern Ireland and Scotland, with their devolved legislatures, separate languages, and tangible and distinct culture, England's identity as distinct from the rest of the UK is less secure. In post-war Britain, one theory goes, 'ethnic English' identities in particular were reformed in a way inextricably linked with the social contract of the welfare state, or 'welfare citizenship'. It was a sense of belonging bound up with a reciprocal deal; a willingness to pay for the needs of strangers in exchange for the protection of the state for one's own social and health needs. The deterioration of this contract, due to the state scaling back

on welfare, the decline of traditional social classes and the rise of indi-
vidualist consumerism, have corresponded with a newly threatened
sense of identity.[37]

Threatened identities don't disappear – my life has been a lesson
in that reality. I have always been infinitely more interested in my
identity than others I know – whether white Brits or black Ghanaians –
whose identity is clear and secure. Threatened identities fight back.
'Expect to see a rebirth of the English tribe,' the futurist Patrick Dixon
said in 2015, in his renowned book *The Future of Almost Everything*,
accurately predicting the Brexit vote a year before it happened, 'a
fresh energy in a new generation who want to be as English as the
Scots are Scottish, or the French are French . . . Tribalism is a very
strong force, and the global trend is firmly set towards autonomy and
self-government.'[38]

People who have experienced a downward class trajectory for the
past few decades are those most energetically swept up in this force,
which manifests in Britain as a kind of resentful nationalism.[39] This is
the case not just in the UK, but all over the world, where the rise in
income inequality and the march of globalisation have corresponded
remarkably to the rise in nationalism and 'tribalism'.[40] This applies
to a staggering range of nations, from India to Turkey, from Sweden to
the US.[41] The America that elected Donald Trump was the country in
which, a few years earlier in 2013, the wealthiest 3 per cent increased
their share of the pie to 54.4 per cent, while the bottom 90 per cent
saw theirs decline to just 25 per cent.[42] In the UK net household
incomes for the average person now are on a par with their share of
the economy twenty years ago, but the top 1 per cent have increased
their share from 6 per cent to 8 per cent.[43]

The period after the Second World War in Britain was accompanied by an expansion of the welfare state, with unprecedented new
levels of welfare benefits, unemployment compensation and free,
universal health care. Some have described this as the price that had to
be paid to compensate Britons for their involvement in the 'total war'
of the preceding years. The new welfare state extended the privileges

of citizenship to Britain's working classes in new ways, forging new, twentieth-century identities. Now that those privileges are being stripped back, the identities they gave rise to are threatened.[44]

There is a lot of mileage in this argument. The principle, and expectation, of free, high-quality health care on the NHS has become part and parcel of what living in Britain is about. Unlike the US, where the political tug of war over the extension of free health care is among the most contentious of all political issues, no mainstream political party in the UK dares suggest privatising the NHS. Those that do face severe consequences, such as the former UKIP leader Paul Nuttall, who failed to win a parliamentary seat after a number of controversies, including past support for privatising the NHS. The obsession with people 'cheating' the benefit system provokes an equally emotive discussion, with television shows such as *Benefit Street* sparking unusual levels of naval gazing and introspection.[45] Debates about the future of the welfare state are more than just questions of government policy or public spending; they go to the heart of the way we see ourselves as a nation.

It's often remarked that the solidarity of Britain's wartime society, and the sense of entitlement which followed, has given way to a consumption-orientated individualism.[46] 'Benefits cheats' has become a euphemism for the idea that welfare recipients are taking advantage of the middle mass of working people, a group who in political shorthand are now referred to as 'hard-working British families'. The perceived loss of solidarity is knotted up with the sense of cultural assault from immigrant communities, the experiences of communities changing and losing the camaraderie once present in everyday life. The weakening of security and civility compound the grievance, and are seen as 'national failings' in narratives of decline.

If the post-war welfare-citizenship foundations for English national identity are slipping away, what will the reborn tribal identity that replaces it actually look like? If the EU referendum debate is anything to go by, it looks a lot like an imagined version of the past. And there is plenty of ambivalence towards Europe in Britain's past from which to draw inspiration. There is the geography of being an island. There is the peculiarity of a royal family that is European but has rebranded itself as British since time immemorial, and whose legitimacy has long derived from its own Church, severed from the Catholic Church in Rome. There is the suspicion that the EU is really about the Germans and the French, and their ages-old 'psychodrama'. The birth of the EU was, after all, at its heart an effort to prevent a repeat of the catastrophic, genocidal war born in Western Europe.[47]

Echoes of that drama were audible when former London Mayor Boris Johnson came out in favour of Brexit, saying Britain would contribute to, rather than be inside, Europe, drawing on a 1953 speech by Winston Churchill.[48] It was the same speech in which Churchill had also said, 'We are with them, but not of them. We have our own Commonwealth and Empire.'[49]

Churchill's rhetoric in 1953 betrayed no clue as to how close the empire was to disintegrating altogether in just a few years. But the empire was never mourned or buried. Neither its problematic life nor its sudden death has ever been truly acknowledged. It's hardly surprising, therefore, that the ghosts of the British Empire are everywhere in modern Britain, and nowhere more so than in the dream of Brexit. 'I am running towards the dawn,' said prominent leave campaigner and former Conservative Party leader Iain Duncan Smith. 'It is the great dawn of Britain's independence and the chance to be a power in the world again.'[50] The nostalgic idea that the Commonwealth would rise out of the ashes of Britain's trading relationship with Europe and carry the nation back to this greatness was powerfully compelling, and not just in the rhetoric of politicians, but among voters too.

One of the best examples I heard was on the BBC current affairs discussion programme, *Question Time*, when an A-level student conveyed his reasons for wanting to leave the EU. 'My stepfather is from the Caribbean. I had the pleasure to go and visit the country of St Vincent,' the teenager told the panel on live TV. 'We have a Commonwealth. They are loyal to our queen . . . they understand how we act as a nation. We should feel fine about leaving the EU because

the Commonwealth countries understand us. They will look after us.'
I was half expecting him to add on the end, 'They serve us.' This sentiment was impossible to escape when leave campaigners called in 2016
for an end to EU migration, in favour of attracting newcomers from
Australia, for example, implicitly reviving the imperial fantasy of the
'White Dominions' – British territories with significant settler
populations.[51]

It's a British thing, this nostalgia for empire. Unlike other countries, such as Germany, Spain or Portugal, our nostalgia afflicts not
only the white working class, but unites elite politicians and the middle
classes as well. And while income inequality fuels a rise in nationalism,
for those at the top as well as the bottom, the globalised reality of melt-
ing borders has made micro belongings more important than ever.
Those belongings need substance to underpin them, and in the
question to make Britishness an identity to believe in, politicians
appealed to the need to 'make Britain great again'. And in the search
for a time when Britain was 'great', the gaze settled naturally on the
era of empire.

The role of nostalgia in our current political discourse is beginning
to be recognised for the potent force it is – a sentiment, as one academic has said, 'at the very core of the modern condition'. These days
it's treated with an appeal to an imperial past and an immigration-free
future, a fantasy that never did, and never will, exist. Few who invoke the
history of imperial greatness realise that the British Empire was the reason for post-war mass immigration from Africa, Asia and the Caribbean
in the first place. In envisaging Britain as the great power, they rarely
appreciate that immigration and open borders are now regarded as
key characteristics of the successful economies of the future. They rarely
explain the success of Silicon Valley, say, or the NHS, as due to their
ability to quite literally brain-drain the most able people with the most
in-demand skills from a global pool of available talent.[52]

Instead, they imagine Britain in a pre-globalised age when having
the biggest navy or the greatest number of sugar plantations determined who was king. 'The UK will continue to nurse a fading fantasy of

being a global power, the second police force of the world after America – but this already looks absurd in the light of dwindling armed forces,' wrote Dixon. 'In the 1940s, Britain still ruled over 25 per cent of the world's land area from London. It is hard for this independent-minded, island nation to cope with the thought of being ruled by the EU from Brussels.'[53]

It's hard to take out your frustration on declining international might, globalisation or the bureaucratisation of trade and regulation. The presence of large numbers of immigrants, on the other hand, is a tangible symptom of these changes, so naturally it gets the hit. My teenage grandfather, growing up in 1930s Berlin, saw his people, in horrible caricatures scrawled across billboards in the Bayerischer Platz, blamed for everything wrong with Germany – from recession to the quality of the school curriculum.[54] It's no coincidence that the now notorious Enoch Powell speech was focused as much on the humiliations of the past as it was on the immigration of the present. 'Our history of the last 20 years seems to have been one long series of retreats and humiliations, from Suez to Aden, from Cyprus to Rhodesia,' he lamented, in a mournful ode to the symbols of Britain's faded power.[55]

The accusations hurled at immigrants in the years and months leading up to the 2016 EU referendum campaign ranged from the horrific to the ridiculous. Immigrants continue to be held responsible for the shortage of social housing – even though the major political parties all reluctantly admit social housing is in long-term and unstoppable decline. Immigrants are blamed for the squeeze on the welfare state, even though figures show that EU migrants, and especially those arriving since 2000, have paid billions more in tax than they took out in benefits.[56] Immigrants have even been blamed for traffic jams – most notably when UKIP leader Nigel Farage claimed he'd arrived late for a UKIP event because 'the population is going through the roof, chiefly because of open-door immigration . . . the M4 is not as navigable as it used to be'.[57] With its roots in Euro-scepticism rather than neo-fascism, UKIP took full advantage of what has been described as a 'reputational shield' over other anti-immigration parties like the BNP to make a number of openly racist and xenophobic claims, including to call for the repatriation of a British-born TV actor, and to claim – as Farage did – that he would not like to live next door to a Romanian.[58]

Immigration has become weaponised as a political issue like never before. But what does this have to do with race? It's one of the more bitter ironies that although most black and other minority Brits voted remain, some – themselves either immigrants or the recent descendants of immigrants – fell for this combination of nostalgia and immigrant-blaming. The £4 billon curry industry, for example, which campaigned for Brexit, believing it would ease immigration for their chefs from Bangladesh,[59] or a Ghanaian relative of mine frustrated at the number of European midwives on her ward, whom she believes are usurping opportunities for African midwives to join the NHS. It's painful because it seemed to me a betrayal of the tolerance towards immigration that facilitated their *own* ability to come to the UK and improve their lot. There is no obligation on immigrants to feel grateful – I don't believe the fact of having migrated to the UK imposes some duty to adopt a particular political orientation. And even if there were, this would become meaningless as second- and third-generation descendants of immigrants had less and less personal connection to the experience of their forebears. But having a personal immigration background is an asset that broadens your perspective, and should add a sophistication to your understanding of the way immigration works, the ability to see through the simplified depiction of it so often portrayed in the media.

And whatever your political opinion of immigration, there is another reason to challenge the views that saw a significant minority of African and Asian British voters supporting Brexit. I was highly suspicious that promises of easing Commonwealth immigration rules would ever materialise. Predictably, it wasn't long before voters who had believed it began crying betrayal. One of Theresa May's first moves in office was to rule out the kind of points system, easing immigration from the Commonwealth, that they believed Brexit would facilitate. The official line is still immigrants bad, curbing immigration good.[60]

A further irony is that, just as my great-grandfather Ismar Hirsch found that the Iron Cross he had earned for risking his life for his country offered no sanctuary from the Nazis in 1930s Germany, being an immigrant who voted Brexit in 2016 did not reduce your chances of being personally attacked by racists during the horrifying and indiscriminate wave of violence and abuse that swept the country in the days after the vote. I personally experienced only the mildest end. 'You'll be going home soon then?' a taxi driver asked me, that June Friday morning, as I was scrambling to package a story for Sky News on the backlash against immigrants following the vote. That evening, I saw an African man, sweeping the road outside Wimbledon station in his Merton council uniform and high-vis vest, shoved by a young white man, flanked by two friends, beer cans in hand. 'Time for your lot to fuck off!' he shouted. I had never before seen anything like this in Wimbledon, home usually to far more polite acts of microaggression, yet this was twice in one day, within twenty-four hours of the result.

When official figures were finally released four months after the vote, they showed the scale of these incidents. There was a 41 per cent increase in racially and religiously aggravated crimes in the month after the referendum, and in the week following the vote, a 58 per cent rise. There were even deaths. Two months after the referendum, on 27 August 2016, Arek Jóźwik – a forty-year-old Polish man – died in Harlow, after a group of teenagers heard him speaking Polish to friends, and a 31-year-old Czech man, Zdenek Makar, was killed in Poplar, east London, on 21 September. The Czech prime minister called Theresa May to say he was 'disturbed by the increase in hateful attacks in Britain aimed at the citizens of EU member states', and demanded greater protection for his citizens.[61] Who knows how many more people were simply abused? A database records the nature of some of the attacks, including dog excrement being thrown at doors or shoved through letter boxes.

This in particular made me think of my grandmother, Ophelia Joyce. In the early 2000s, well into her seventies then, she lived in a semi-detached house in a once down-at-heel part of south-east

London, from where she still took the bus across London to work overnight shifts as a nurse in a psychiatric hospital. Almost every single day, her neighbours would walk out of their front door with their dog, heading to a nearby park, but not before stopping on her doorstep to let their dog shit. It went on for years. Not at any other house, just hers. Finally, my mother called the police, and informed the neighbours she was installing CCTV. Only then did they stop.

What was different after the Brexit vote was that acts of open hostility towards immigrants were no longer confined to vulnerable old black ladies living in areas with a history of racist aggression. Now white Europeans realised they were 'immigrants' too – French bankers, Italian architects and Portuguese beauticians suddenly felt vulnerable. The parents of friends at my daughter's posh Wimbledon school began questioning their decision to build their career and buy their house in the UK, to confer its citizenship on their children, even while theirs belonged to Germany or Spain. At the time, investing in a future in Britain had seemed certain to offer the opportunities of an open part of an open continent. Now, for the first time, they were beginning to feel unwelcome. 'Everybody speaking a "funny language", or with a foreign accent is now at risk,' wrote one Belgian academic, alarmed by reports of attacks, including in his relatively middle-class neighbourhood.[62]

To say that Britain is a racist country, or that the majority of people who voted Brexit did so motivated by racism, unhelpfully oversimplifies the dynamic at work. It feeds into caricatures of the white working class – who, as I've already pointed out, were far from the only ones voting Brexit, but who are themselves often depicted as 'half-witted racist scroungers in tracksuits milking the welfare state from their sofas'.[63]

The British Africans I know who voted Brexit would certainly not consider themselves racist, although some quite openly display the same kind of prejudice towards Eastern Europeans that racist Brits have at times displayed towards them. Working-class white people I've interviewed have, as I said, spoken of their concern that 'immigration is out of control' – a slogan they have been repeatedly fed by politicians and the media – although in many cases they have close ties to, including through marriages or friendships, immigrants.

At the same time, if my comparison between the Nazi treatment of my great-grandfather in 1930s Germany and the racist abuse of immigrants in the post-Brexit Britain of 2016 sounds too hyperbolic, consider the rhetoric about Turkey during the referendum campaign. Then Justice Secretary Michael Gove claimed that Turkey and four other countries could join the EU as soon as 2020 and lead to 5.2 million extra people moving to the UK, a population 'the size of Scotland', despite the fact that there is no remotely real prospect of Turkey joining the EU in the foreseeable future. Fellow leave campaigner Penny Mordaunt claimed that Turkey's membership, totally improbable as it was, would cost the NHS £400 million in ten years and put lives at risk.[64] But the most chilling echo of a time when fascism was in its lethal ascent came from a UKIP poster, depicting a column of non-white refugees crossing the Croatia–Slovenia border in 2015, along with the slogan 'Breaking Point'. The poster was strikingly reminiscent of Nazi propaganda footage of migrants that had been shown in a BBC documentary in 2005. It was so offensive it was reported to the police, prompting high-profile leave politicians like Boris Johnson to officially distance themselves from UKIP's campaign.[65]

The Brexit campaign took people's fears – about housing shortages, austerity and cultural change – and harvested them. It didn't overly concern itself with the facts – making among other things the patently false claim that £350 million per week spent on the EU would, in a post-Brexit Britain, be ploughed into the NHS. Instead it wove those fears into an identity – an identity where 'welfare citizenship' would go hand in hand with 'British jobs for British workers', a phrase that caused great offence when it was first introduced,[66] but is now commonplace in politics.[67]

For white Europeans, the feeling of discrimination may have been a new, post-Brexit sense of threat. But the descendants of imperial subjects had been feeling the hate long before. My friend, the writer

Musa Okwonga, didn't wait for the result to leave the UK, the build-up was bad enough. Musa, who went to school at Eton, where he was at times the only black pupil, and whom I met at Oxford, found his country unrecognisable.

'I left the UK because I got sick of all the immigration stuff. My mum came to this country from Uganda as a refugee, we did our thing. And now they are still saying this stuff years later. It's not like it's a balanced conversation. I now call myself British Ugandan, not black British. I feel less British than I did ten years ago. When you read the headlines, you feel like, Jesus, that's us they're talking about,' Musa told me on the phone from Berlin, where he now lives. 'They really hate us.'

In July 1981, the Liverpool neighbourhood where generations of Mzee Mohammed's family had lived was plunged into chaos. Coming almost exactly thirty years before the riots of 2011 sent the acrid smell of burning metal and plastic across England's skies, the Toxteth riots were just one of a series that swept across the country over the course of a year, beginning in St Paul's – the heart of Bristol's black community – in 1980. Next was Brixton, historic centre of London's black community, then Southall, where there were violent clashes between Asian youths and racist skinheads. A police station was attacked in Moss Side, Manchester, and disturbances and riots reported from Leeds and Hull.

Toxteth was home to a historically black community of Liverpudlians, whose heritage dated back to the era of African seamen and slave trading. Black men had children with local women – raising the profound racial alarm I described earlier – and the population included many mixed-race people, before there were words for mixed race. Black, mixed race and white, and immigrants from other backgrounds, lived and worked side by side in Toxteth, formed relationships and had children across racial divides. Yet Toxteth was rarely championed as an example of 'integration'. In fact, the town would have damaged integration's brand. It was a community out of work – 40 per cent of the male population was unemployed, and some estimate that the black youth unemployment figure was as much as 80 per cent.[68] Its inhabitants were on the whole poor, and continually harassed by the police, not least under 'sus' laws which effectively criminalised hanging around in the street, by giving the police broad powers to arrest anyone they claimed looked suspicious.[69] Those who could had left Toxteth altogether – the population of the area had fallen by one-third in a decade.[70]

Beginning on 3 July 1981, the neighbourhood tipped over the edge. This was no ordinary riot. Young men hot-wired bulldozers and excavators and used them as weapons, they raided schools for javelins, broke off metal spikes from railings, and even commandeered milk floats.[71] Missiles and petrol bombs flew, killing one, injuring 470 police officers and incinerating seventy buildings. Five hundred people were arrested over nine nights of violence, still regarded as the most virulent single riot on the British mainland within living memory, and the most far-reaching. They were not 'race riots', even though Toxteth had a historic black community and such a high incidence of unemployed black men; deprivation in the area transcended the racial divide, and young white people joined in the violence. No one called this a triumph of integration. They called it a 'riot', but the locals still prefer to describe it as an 'uprising'.[72]

The Thatcher government had seen it coming. A secret file released in 2011 under the 'thirty-year rule' now reveals in black and white its belief that 'There is potential for serious disorder by members of ethnic minorities. Increased militancy and large numbers of bored, unemployed youths may spark off disturbances in almost any large town, with the police a main target. Tension is aggravated by the fact that racial issues and immigrant areas have become the battlegrounds of the (predominantly white) extremists of right and left.'[73] A handwritten note on the front of the report – which anticipated all the potential causes of civil disturbance in the coming year – summarised its contents for the prime minister: 'ethnic minorities are the likeliest flashpoint'.

Toxteth's eruption in 1981 cannot, therefore, have come as a massive surprise. The whole of Liverpool was seen as one, potentially irredeemable, problem. After Toxteth had finished burning, Thatcher considered writing off the city altogether, evacuating its residents and recognising that it was a hopeless case. But instead she dispatched Michael Heseltine, then environment secretary, to investigate. His recommendations in the report 'It Took a Riot' are now considered the godfather of modern 'regeneration', and the beginnings of an industry of urban renewal in Britain. It recognised poverty and alienation as the root causes of violent unrest, and recommended new housing, infrastructure, public spaces and planned communities as the solution.

What Heseltine had correctly diagnosed is that there were identifiable physical manifestations of inner-city unrest. The picture he painted of Liverpool was bleak. 'The river is an open sewer,' he wrote. 'Among the people who have left the area have been middle managers who have gone to the suburbs for better homes, schools and surroundings. More significant still has been the loss to Liverpool of the headquarters of its major firms. There are hardly any left ... Local government ... is remote, and much of its housing indescribable. There are 38,000 outstanding repair notices for the city's 78,000 dwellings ... One has to talk to the people day after day to understand just what hopelessness means. Young people expect to be unemployed and they are being brought up by parents who expect them to be unemployed. We have to realise the hollowness of the phrase "parental responsibility" when unemployed parents – many of them single – live cooped up with energetic kids with nothing to do, and nowhere to go. Many parents have lost their sense of purpose, they cannot command their children's respect.'[74]

Toxteth, Heseltine pointed out, was particularly troubled – 'the only black community on Merseyside – Liverpool people of several generations' standing. The crime rate is high, education attainments low. The reputation of the area is a barrier when applying for work.'[75]

Heseltine ultimately advocated a model which was new at the time but so familiar now – public-private partnerships and the involvement of for-profit corporations in building new housing and creating new jobs. But he recognised that it would take a central government intervention before the area was even viable for private investment, estimating a bill of £100 million a year – a huge amount in 1981. 'There is a whole range of projects that the private sector will never tackle,' he said. 'But until they are tackled, the inner-city opportunities for the private sector are prejudiced in favour of the suburbs.'

Heseltine's ideas, many of which were implemented, did not solve Liverpool's problems. Thirty-four years later, in 2015, the city was ranked the fourth most deprived part of England, with almost half of its neighbourhoods in the top 10 per cent of most deprived neighbourhoods in England.[76] That hasn't stopped the model being replicated. The government's only concrete policy response to the 2011 riots was to announce that one hundred of the worst 'sink estates' would be demolished and replaced by a mix of private and social housing,[77] a plan which critics have claimed amounts to nothing less than using the riots as an excuse for 'social cleansing'. But perhaps Heseltine's greatest insight was one for which he had no solution at all.

It's June 2016, and I'm sitting down with Michael Heseltine, in a room in a new Home Office building deliberately, it seems, channelling the bright plastic of Google headquarters. His broad-shouldered, tall and intimidatingly upright gait and dash of wavy blond hair bring the 1980s House of Commons to life. We talk Brexit – just a few days before the referendum vote will take place – and how the anti-immigration rhetoric of the leave campaign is impacting people of colour. 'It's nothing compared to Enoch Powell,' he says. 'I was the first Conservative to challenge Powell . . . it was the most immoral speech.'

Heseltine sees himself as something of a champion of race equality. He tells me that, in his exactly five decades in British politics, the single thing of which he is most proud is a speech he made at the Conservative Party conference in Blackpool, October 1981. He repeats the relevant part of the speech, in which he said, 'We now have large immigrant communities in British cities. Let this party's position be absolutely clear. They are British. They live here. They vote here.'[78]

What he understood was that these riots of the 1980s were expressions of identity. The people rioting, treated like foreigners in their own country, with inferior rights and inherently suspicious faces, had had enough. 'It was very bold to say that at the time,' Heseltine tells me. 'It was very confrontational. It was very moving.'

It's hard to appreciate, in 2016, that this could have been a revolutionary thing to say. *Of course* black people like those who rioted in Toxteth are British, I thought. What else would they be? We *know* that 'black' and 'British' are not mutually exclusive identities. The obviousness of this makes me reflect on how much we – the vast majority of British people who now understand this – have gained, how much my generation now takes for granted.

On the other hand, how much have we gained? We still get asked The Question – our Britishness questioned every day, regardless of our officially British status. Many of us choose not to identify ourselves as British, despite having – on Heseltine's interpretation at least – earned the right. Alexander Paul, addressing that same gathering of the Conservative Party faithful thirty years after Heseltine's speech, was born in Britain, was deemed British enough to be the symbolic precursor to Theresa May, introducing her speech as home secretary before her own party. And yet he tells me . . . 'I feel that I am British in the sense that I have the citizenship, I live here, this is who I know, but when I think about it critically, and see how accepted I am as a British person, as a black British person, it makes me question how British I feel.' All these years later, Britain has still not made itself a place where we can unreservedly belong.

Who gets to be British? In 1990, the Tory MP Norman Tebbit suggested it's those immigrants who can pass 'the cricket test' – cheering for the England side in a match in which England is playing one's country of origin, so that people of Pakistani heritage would cheer for England over Pakistan, people with Caribbean roots would cheer for England over the West Indies, and so on. 'When people come to a new country, they should be prepared to immerse themselves totally and utterly in that country,' he declared. 'Split loyalties' could not be tolerated.

I wonder if Tebbit would have been quite so dismissive of the identities of British settlers who made their homes in South Africa or Zimbabwe, retaining ties with Britain and many gaining seats in both Houses of Parliament. I doubt it somehow. White British people who live abroad are 'expatriates' – a lovely word that allows the bearer to retain their British nationality and identity while settling – even permanently – in another country. Asian and African people who leave their countries and move to the UK are not expatriates, they are 'immigrants'. 'Europeans are expats because they can't be at the same level as other ethnicities. They are superior. Immigrants is a term set aside for "inferior races",' one young African entrepreneur observed.[79] And 'immigrants' have to behave well.

It's 2015 and I'm on a Virgin train to Leeds. The land feels cold and hard-boiled in the weak sunshine – bright, crisp and slightly barren. I'm sitting at a table, opposite a businessman in a creaseless navy suit and blue-and-white-checked shirt, who thumbs messages onto his iPhone, occasionally nursing his Pret coffee cup. Across the aisle is another table, occupied by a Nigerian man holding his phone; it's plugged into the socket, providing life support for his calls. There are a lot of calls. From 0935 when the train departs from the Harry Potter notoriety of its King's Cross platform, to 1148 when we arrive in Leeds, he speaks on the phone, non-stop. Sometimes in a thick Nigerian accent, coupled with London street slang.

First, he is apologising to someone who is clearly annoyed he didn't call them yesterday, explaining that he was under a lot of stress because the police had shown up with a warrant for his arrest – he had had to urgently get hold of his solicitor. They discuss this at length. A woman called 'Esi' calls him and he greets her with audible affection – *Esi! My first wife!* Then laughs loudly. Next he is on the phone to a friend or business associate, saying he needs a new passport, how much will that cost? He is getting the money together. And then it seems someone has crossed him. He tells someone else, 'I'm don with him. Don for good. Don't ever pick his head again. Eeehhh. I don't want him there again any more. *Yu unerstan?'*

The white businessman sitting opposite me is visibly uncomfortable. He squirms in his seat. I want to look at him in sympathetic annoyance – I'm tapping away on my laptop, working on the way to this interview with a victim of trafficking in Leeds. But siding obviously with the businessman whose table I'm sharing would make me feel complicit in his judgement, which I imagine to be *'Why are people like this being let into my country?'* Much as I relate to his annoyance, I can't choose his side.

This is the dilemma of the 'Good Immigrant'. I am not an immigrant – I was born to two British parents, entitled from birth to British citizenship. It is only because of my ethnicity, the fact that my skin is not white and my name is African, that I am associated with immigration, my actions – whether I'm deemed to have contributed to or detracted from society – counted as a side effect of immigration. The inherent prejudice in our attitude towards immigration means that of my immigrant grandparents, my father's father ceased to be counted that way. My mother's mother, on the other hand, will always be seen as an immigrant in this country. She, like I, feels the burden that this carries. We must be good, we must be grateful – legally we are entitled to remain here unconditionally, but psychologically, in the perceptions of others, our right to be here is somehow conditional upon good behaviour, gratitude and adequate displays of the intention to assimilate.

People like me, raised to believe that living out our lives in the UK is a privilege, for which those before us made considerable sacrifices, have always strived to be good, grateful citizens. Musa Okwonga, who made the, he says 'heartbreaking', decision to leave the UK after anti-immigrant fever became too much to bear, took this sentiment to the maximum. As a black boy from a single-parent family in the alienating environment of Eton, Musa saw himself as 'an unofficial ambassador for black people'. He took this sense of responsibility so far that he didn't touch alcohol until he was twenty-two years old, feeling that 'my white peers had grown up seeing so many negative stereotypes of black people their entire lives, I had a duty to counteract as many of them as possible. That meant never getting drunk, never getting that Afro I had long wanted, never taking the joint when it was offered.'[80] It was only coming out as bisexual – an incredibly difficult experience for many black people from communities that are less than accepting of sexual diversity – that released Musa from this burden. 'It was so life-altering an event that it forced me no longer to see myself as some sort of diplomat for my people, but instead to live for myself.'

This is I think exactly what my grandfather was conveying in one of his last letters to his tutor at Queens' College, written a year after he'd left Cambridge and was back in the Gold Coast. He had not got the grades he had hoped in his final exams, but instead of taking this as a personal failure, he saw it as a failure of his diplomacy in representing an entire continent. 'I am looking forward to the time when some of my pupils will come up and redeem the good name of Africa, which some of us let down by failing to acquire ourselves creditably,' he wrote. It's a similar diplomacy I am trying to unpick in my seat on the train to Leeds. I am embarrassed by the behaviour of my Nigerian neighbour because he is breaking the rules. Good Immigrants do not speak loudly in public, and especially not in an African language. Good Immigrants do not have any dealings with the police, and they do not talk about dodgy-sounding business deals, and it goes without saying that bragging about polygamous/adulterous or whatever relationships is a total no.

The Good Immigrant dynamic is everywhere. It's what the organisers of a petition were referencing when they appealed to the Home Office on behalf of May Brown, a young mum battling a fatal form of leukaemia, whose only chance of survival rested on her sister getting a visa to donate her own bone marrow, but that visa to travel from Nigeria had been denied. 'It is heartbreaking to see unfair bureaucratic red tape being put in the way of saving a young mum's life,' the petition states, underneath a poignant image of a smiling, pretty black woman, surrounded by medical equipment. 'She's 23 years old, married to a British ex soldier, she's the mum of two-year-old Selina May.' The subtext was clear. Married to a British man: check. Patriotic links to British military: check. Responsible mother of small child: check. May Brown: good immigrant, and on this basis, she deserves to live.[81]

The classic Good Immigrant is Nadiya Hussain – 2015 winner of quintessentially British TV series, *The Great British Bake Off*. A practising Muslim, Hussain became one of the first ever hijab-wearing brown British women to appear on the front cover of the British papers in a flattering context, or to be described on the cover of *Hello!* magazine as 'the nation's new sweetheart'.[82] This is not to say her victory was met without resistance at the time. *Daily Mail* columnist Amanda Platell accused the *Bake Off* team of being too politically correct, saying a white contestant had no hope with her chocolate carousel and that 'if she'd made a chocolate mosque, she'd have stood a better chance'.[83] The *Radio Times* felt the need to explain to readers that for Hussain 'her headscarf doesn't stop her loving tea and bunting'.[84] The general reaction, however, was one of self-congratulation, the media praising itself for how tolerant a society Britain has become, as if it were an act of editorial benevolence to allow Hussain to win.

It therefore came as an unwelcome surprise for many when Hussain – interviewed on Radio 4's *Desert Island Discs* in 2016 – revealed that racism was 'a part of my life now'. She went on to say that racist experiences were so frequent, 'I expect it . . . I expect to be shoved or pushed or verbally abused, because it happens, it's happened for years.' For some commentators, her Good Immigrant status had come to a swift end. 'We've all been there, we've all been "pushed and shoved",' claimed *Daily Mail* columnist Liz Jones. 'Why are we worshipping at this woman's altar?' Jones continued, pointing out that Nadiya had 'an arranged marriage' and had been 'at home with her three kids for ten years'.[85] Jones's reaction stood out, but elsewhere the media coverage revealed the deep uncertainty with which many British people appear to regard their fellow Muslim citizens. 'The way you can become a Good Immigrant is to transcend opinion in the public eye by winning the *Great British Bake Off*,' said Nikesh Shukla, who edited *The Good Immigrant*, a book on the experiences of ethnic minority Brits which explores this issue in unprecedented depth. 'As an aside if you then admit that you have experienced casual racism on *Desert Island Discs*, then you will immediately become a Bad Immigrant again.'[86]

Winning Olympic medals for Great Britain makes you a Good Immigrant, putting athletes Mo Farrah and Jessica Ennis-Hill very firmly in this category. So does becoming a Tory MP, raising money for charity, showing deference to the royal family, marrying a white British person, abstaining from drunken or excessive behaviour – as Musa so valiantly attempted for his entire youth – or distancing oneself from Bad Immigrants, as I was so tempted to do on the train. But you never get any thanks for all this effort. Being a Good Immigrant doesn't stop you from being evicted from a local shop for 'looking like a criminal', as I was in Wimbledon Village as a teenager, or from being thrown out of a friend's home, as Musa was when his friend's father realised his son had invited a black boy to spend the night.[87] It doesn't stop you being stopped and searched by the police forty-five times during your childhood, as Alexander Paul was. The reward for being a Good Immigrant is being grudgingly acknowledged as someone worthy of living in their own country – a privilege that white British people seem to acquire without any effort at all.

Of course politicians don't speak about ethnic minority people in terms of 'good' and 'bad' immigrants. The language they use is more subtle, and coded. When they speak of 'bad immigrants', they tend to be referring to the failures of multiculturalism. And when they speak of 'good immigrants', it's usually in the context of the ultimate hallmark of what the Good Immigrant achieves: integration.

Although the United Kingdom is a set of islands populated by immigrants, the mass immigration that is so hotly debated now did not begin until after the war. In the late 1940s, and throughout the 50s and 60s, large numbers of people from the Caribbean, India and Pakistan came to the United Kingdom to fill labour shortages. Their arrival presented British government officials with an existential fear. 'A large coloured community as a noticeable feature of our social life would weaken ... the concept of England or Britain to which people of British stock throughout the Commonwealth are attached,' one warned in 1953.[88] The official response was to reduce colonial and Commonwealth entitlement to British citizenship, rather than any attempt to ensure opportunity and equality for those who were already here. Influxes of West Africans (including Ghanaians like my mother's family), Nigerians, and East African Asians would follow into the 1970s and 80s, and people from Somalia, Sudan and Zimbabwe – many of them refugees – after those.[89]

The same fears have surfaced repeatedly and consistently – and for these immigrants and their descendants, being associated with these fears is simply a fact of life. 'We must be mad, literally mad, as a nation to be permitting the annual inflow of some 50,000 dependants, who are for the most part the material of the future growth of the immigrant-descended population,' said Enoch Powell in 1968.[90] 'It is like watching a nation busily engaged in heaping up its own funeral pyre.' It was as if Powell had been lurking in the green room at the BBC in 2011, when the popular historian David Starkey delivered a rant on *Newsnight* confirming the Rivers of Blood predictions had indeed come to fruition. 'The whites have become black!' declared Starkey. 'A particular sort of violent, destructive, nihilistic gangster culture has become the fashion . . . Black and white, boy and girl, operate in this language together. This language, which is wholly false, which is this Jamaican patois that has intruded in England. This is why so many of us have this sense of literally a foreign country.' Starkey concluded his outburst by praising the black MP David Lammy, a Good Immigrant, an 'archetypal successful black man', as Starkey called him, because 'if you turn the screen off, so you were listening to him on radio, you would think he was white'.

It would be easier to dismiss this perspective if it were just the stream of consciousness of an attention-seeking TV historian. Theresa May, as home secretary, famously commissioned a set of vans which read 'In the UK Illegally? GO HOME OR FACE ARREST.' The vans were withdrawn after groups representing refugees threatened legal action.[91] It was later reported that the vans resulted in a grand total of eleven immigrants leaving the country. An unquantifiable number felt threatened, demonised and faced with the prospect that the government was adopting the favourite slogan of the neo-Nazi far right, who have always been fond of saying 'Fuck off back home'.[92]

The Home Office defended the vans by saying that they were only intended to target those who were in the country illegally; immigrants who were lawfully abiding here had nothing to fear. But anyone visibly connected with immigration knows it doesn't work like this. So many of us – of all races – have immigration in our background, but if it's manifest in your skin colour, your faith or your name, you are tainted. You are often asked The Question. You are considered part of the 'social impact' of immigration on the country, by the *Daily Mail* complaining for example that government immigration figures fail to record its true impact because they do not include immigrants' British-born children.[93] People born in the UK but descended from immigrants are to be set aside and counted as part of a problem. This does not, of course, apply to everyone. Prince Charles, Prince William and Prince Harry, second- and third-generation descendants of immigrants, are exempt.[94]

The facts about immigration in the UK have become increasingly irrelevant – views about immigration and its benefits are highly subjective. As the Brexit vote made clear – with areas with relatively little immigration most concerned about its impact – it's the perception of immigration that matters. This has always been the case. It seems absurd, now, for Queen Elizabeth I to have felt the concern about the presence of a few thousand migrants that drove her to the intolerance I described earlier, but no doubt it felt to her like a 'swarm' at the time. These days, immigrants planning to stay a year or more arrive at the rate of about 1,700 per day.[95] There is a perception that this is either an unmanageable rate, or that it is not being managed properly, which is hardly surprising given the laissez-faire approach of governments in introducing policies proactively supporting and coordinating immigration.

There is no overarching government strategy to ensure immigrants are able to participate in society, to ensure they are able to speak English and form the wide networks that are so essential for getting access to jobs and generally thriving in this country.[96] There has been no coordinated plan to manage the distribution of immigration flows through the country, leading some areas to experience high levels of immigration which existing residents feel are unsustainable, and others to miss out on the opportunities that immigrant communities create for society and the economy.[97] To the extent that immigrant communities have been on the receiving end of government policies designed to facilitate their continuing presence in the UK, these have often been unsophisticated.

Many can be characterised under the umbrella concept of 'multi-culturalism' – an ideology that accepted minority groups had their own ethnic, religious and cultural identities, and tolerated their expression in distinct communities. As a political policy, 'multiculturalism' boiled down to funding the development of these separate identities, actively promoting their needs with public funds, and allocating resources to separate minority communities.

This 'hard' multiculturalism has no political friends now, and stands accused of multiple crimes. In some local authorities, the way multiculturalist policies were implemented amounted to little more than corrupt patronage, through self-styled 'community leaders' who extracted funding and favours in return for delivering their commu-nity's votes en masse. From a socialist perspective, multiculturalism is accused of serving a capitalist 'divide and rule' conspiracy – protecting the interests of a white elite, which remains separated from the masses in taste and value, while the masses are divided among themselves along racial lines.[98] Owen Jones in his book *Chavs* accuses multicul-turalism of fanning the flames of white English nationalism. 'Liberal multiculturalism has understood inequality purely through the prism of race, disregarding that of class,' he writes. 'Taken together, this has encouraged white working-class people to develop similar notions of ethnic pride, and to build an identity based on race so as to gain acceptance in multicultural society. The BNP has made the most of this disastrous redefinition of white working-class people as, effectively, another marginalised ethnic minority.'[99] In its crude imple-mentation by governments with little real grasp of immigrant identities, multiculturalism has been lampooned as 'the 3 S's – saris, samosas and steelbands'.[100]

While politicians have argued over the theory of multiculturalism, racial and economic exclusion for immigrants and their descendants has remained a reality. Fifty per cent of families from black African backgrounds live in low-income households, compared to 20 per cent of white households. Twenty-five per cent of young black people and 28 per cent of young Bangladeshi and Pakistani young people are unemployed, more than double white jobseekers of the same age.[101] Civic engagement is low; staggering numbers of ethnic minority people are not even registered to vote – more than one-quarter of British Africans, compared to 7 per cent of white people – before counting those who actually show up on polling day.[102] No one minds the fact that people who live in places like Tottenham clean up after them, or provide overnight security for their shops and offices. But the fact that you are as likely to hear Twi or Polish spoken on the high street, and shops offering cheap phone-unlocking and to send money to a list of far-off countries marked by colourful flags – *it doesn't even feel like Britain any more*. Too many immigrants crowded into one place together, with shops selling their food, and churches and mosques offering their versions of faith – says the unwritten rule of identity – and they become Bad Immigrants.

The answer, supposedly, is integration. 'Integration' is a strange word in Britain. Its definition here is not the same as in other countries. In segregated America, for example, where laws kept the races apart and black people in a position of institutionalised inferiority until the 1960s, 'integration' was simply the end of 'segregation'. It meant busing black children into previously all-white schools; it meant outlawing the provision of separate public toilets and carriages on trains. It meant ending the official ban on relationships between people of different races. 'Integration' meant a new legal regime, albeit another highly imperfect one, enforceable by the courts.

Although Britain had plenty to rival this in its colonies, on home soil 'integration' has always meant something vaguer, something closer to social mixing and assimilation. The Labour MP Chuka Umunna, who chairs a parliamentary committee that delivered a report on social integration in January 2017, says, 'My definition is that there is a difference between *diversity* and *integration*. Diversity is where you have different people from different backgrounds living in an area. Integration is the extent to which different groups have a relationship with each other.'

The social integration inquiry chaired by Umunna is one of a slew of reports between 2015 and 2017 looking at integration. One high-profile government report by Dame Louise Casey in 2016 singled out Pakistani and Bangladeshi communities as particularly failing to integrate. The report found that people with this ethnicity live in more residentially segregated communities than other ethnic groups, and have particular practices – such as transnational marriage – creating 'a first generation in every generation'.[103] But of the three main reasons for segregation, the report found, only one – the desire to live near and have the support of a community of people from similar backgrounds – had anything to do with personal choice. The others were the pull of the labour market, which has sought immigrants to fill its gaps, and the poverty trap. Once living in these areas – all of them poor – it was hard to get out. 'Rates of social mobility among Pakistani and Bangladeshi ethnic groups . . . who are the groups most concentrated in deprived areas,' the report found, 'are significantly lower than rates for White groups.'

There is plenty of evidence to support the fact that this segregation does exist. But there is also an incredible amount of hypocrisy around it. Segregation is presented as something minority communities do – the crimes of the Bad Immigrant – with little analysis of its root causes. It's rarely associated with highly discriminatory practices in the private housing sector, and a state school system that rewards the savviest middle-class parents adept at manipulating the system – it defeated me when I tried, and failed, to get my daughter into the nearby outstanding local state school that I went to until I was seven – leaving those less equipped to navigate the system, or buy a house in the right catchment area, stuck with what the others leave behind. As a result, half of all children on free school meals – taken as an indication of deprivation – are educated in 20 per cent of schools, while British schools are the fourth most segregated for recent migrants in the OECD.[104] Faith schools have institutionalised discrimination against children from the 'wrong' background, with report after report identifying their role in cementing segregation.[104] But no major political party is seriously willing to criticise a tradition that includes the many Church of England and Catholic schools that provide the high-quality, free education their voters rely on.

In this respect, reports on social integration tend to raise more questions than they answer. African and Caribbean communities, which are regarded as better performing when it comes to integration, still suffer from the highest rates of young unemployment and household poverty. The mixed-race children of Caribbean men and white women – products of ethnic integration – suffer, as I've explained earlier, an 'ethnic penalty', placing them further down the socioeconomic ladder than their parents. 'Integration' has not been the answer to the barriers they face.

In this context, 'integration' is a concept that needs to be handled with care. It seems to me at risk of becoming the default aspiration, only partially thought through, and predicated on the idea that through mixing and assimilating, minority identities and cultures will be toned down and made palatable. At its most reductive, 'integration' represents the unspoken hope that eventually these visible others will have their otherness neutralised by British culture. They will eventually disappear, leaving nothing more than a trace of curly hair, a splash of extra freckles, a liberal, harmless version of a foreign faith, or the memory of a funny-sounding name, their culture blending seamlessly into the mainstream British experience.

This view of integration already has popular resonance; it's a bit of jerk seasoning on your Sunday roast, or vindaloo after a heavy night drinking. It's the Notting Hill Carnival, whose roots are inherently bound up in protest at the treatment of black immigrants in west

London, but which is now a reason to enjoy a pattie and a coconut, without letting social injustice get in the way of having some fun.[105] It's a 'spray-on beard', as some Muslims disparagingly describe those who have toned down their heritage to give themselves mainstream appeal. It's downplaying perceived cultural differences, as Nadiya Hussain did on *Desert Island Discs*, when she claimed the reason she wears a hijab is not because of any profound attachment to Islam, something that Radio 4 listeners might feel a bit uncomfortable about, but to cover up her 'bad hair more than anything else' because her father 'cut it really badly'.[105] It's public figures with Ghanaian names mispronouncing them themselves to make them less intimidating. It's my all-white school friends telling me I shouldn't worry, as they don't really see me as black anyway, and me taking that as a compliment. This is not integration, or assimilation, it's fear. Identities have been formed, and lost, under the intense fear of being held back by associating with a race or culture that is perceived as inferior – a legacy from the recent past when that was official British thinking. 'Success', so aptly articulated by David Starkey's comments about David Lammy, is the suppression of any sign of difference, of alien culture or outward appearance.

The whole debate around integration often overlooks the fact that many immigrants to the UK do not come with a headful of plans to live separately, or some kind of agenda as to how to avoid assimilation at all costs. They come with the ambition to create a better life than the one they had before. They bring with them their culture and traditions – mild attempts to preserve an element of their heritage, which pale in comparison to the behaviour of the British, who swept across the globe leaving Christianity, the English language, common law and Victorian education in their wake, and who are still busy re-creating towns in Spain's Costa del Sol, for example, in the image of the places they left behind in the UK. Immigrants who come to the UK are not looking for segregation, nor do they *desire* to be treated differently. What they desire is to be treated the same.

'Most new arrivals *want* to become English or British – my dad certainly did,' Umunna tells me. It's clear he is personally invested in questions of immigration, integration and British identities in no small part because of the influence of his father – a self-made man who migrated to the UK from Nigeria's Niger Delta in the 1960s. Umunna thinks that it is crucial for immigrant communities to integrate. 'But,' he adds, 'we don't want people to leave their culture at the border. We want them to bring it into our country and it help enrich us, and make Britain even more interesting than it is already ... I've always been brought up to feel very comfortable with all the different facets of my heritage.' And he is keen to point out that segregation is caused not only by immigrants *arriving*, but by existing populations *leaving*. 'We are very clear that it is a two-way street,' Umunna says. 'It's not just an issue of new arrivals congregating and living next to each other, it's also an issue of white flight and why that is happening.'

The departure of white residents, through the phenomenon that has come to be known as 'white flight', is rarely given much attention. It's the reaction of the white working-class community in Southall – a part of London where more than half of the population now is of Indian or Pakistani heritage – and where Greg Dyke told me of his childhood in the 1950s, describing how the white residents attempted to club together to stop the new arrivals from buying houses, and then left the area altogether when they failed. 'A lack of integration is an issue for all groups,' a report into integration by the Social Integration Commission pointed out. 'White Britons are as likely to have unrepresentative social networks as people from other ethnic backgrounds, and Londoners' networks are amongst the furthest away from reflecting the makeup of the communities in which they live.'[106]

Looking at the way the debate around immigration has been handled in the UK is depressing, not just because of what is said, but because of what is thought but left unsaid. The muddled thinking that links immigration with race – casting my maternal but not my paternal ancestors as immigrants – and links the legacy of the empire with its economic wealth but not its people, has been allowed to take root, so much so that it has become received wisdom in the political mainstream. Yet it's a suppressed narrative, full of dog-whistle appeals to the need to scapegoat, based on the prejudice that comes with visible difference, but not fully spoken and aired enough for it to be challenged in the light of day.

Immigration could have been managed differently, truthfully – with a frank acknowledgement of why it was happening, what it was adding to the country, and how and where its limits should be. Instead it became a toxic scapegoat for the nation's problems, which sympathetic politicians were too cowardly to unpick, and far-right politicians too quick to exploit. The casualties have been British identities, with a hardening of white identities, hell-bent on nationalism, insularity and the closing of borders and minds on the one hand, and a crisis of non-white identities on the other, which feel alienated and confused about belonging.

At the same time, it's equally clear that there is no essential truth about immigration. Sure there are facts on both sides – immigrants making net contributions to the economy, enriching cultural life in ways that people welcome, doing jobs that the labour market needs them to do, living in areas where they are not necessarily welcome, bringing ways of dressing, eating, worshipping and talking that are unfamiliar to those already there. But what can be claimed about immigration is that it's a debate shaped by politics. What is currently a poisonous and blame-filled narrative will not necessarily be so in the future.

In the meantime, you can't please public opinion by being a Good Immigrant. There's no better example of this than Umunna. The chair of the cross-party group looking into integration is in many ways a poster child for it – a mixed-heritage black Brit, who represents a constituency in Parliament and has clear political aspirations. Yet the media constantly tries to pigeonhole him into one of its segregated categories.

'It's hard being second or third generation [descendant of immigrants] because you have multiple identities in a world which is desperate to put you into a pigeonhole, and is reluctant to allow you to associate in multiple ways with different groups,' Umunna says. 'I have felt it acutely since becoming an MP. The Westminster media village finds it very difficult to get its head around the fact that you can be of a particular class background and multiple ethnicities. They cannot understand that. They have to assign you a category.'

Umunna's version of 'integration' is an attractive one – a kind of halfway house that recognises distinct identities, and seeks connectedness between different groups rather than the erasure of their differences. And at the same time acknowledges that this doesn't just happen by itself without enlightened government policy. It really does sound good.

The problem is, we don't seem politically mature enough to grapple with this debate. Just as there has never been an apartheid system of segregation in the UK, so there has also never been a British civil rights movement to end it. The American civil rights movement of the 1960s forced the US into a painful confrontation over the state of racial oppression and injustice. But the UK has never had an open or organised dialogue about the predicament of its ethnic minority communities. It has never faced up to the long history behind their presence in the country, the way they were treated in the past, or the new British identities their presence in the country entails. A sensible debate about immigration and integration is something that has to be earned.

A new generation is not going to sit about waiting for that to happen – they are taking British identity into their own hands. The descendants of immigrants – whose parents were under such intense pressure to assimilate, and to be grateful – are ripping up the rule book. Grime artist Bashy captured this in his classic song 'Black Boys' (*'Yo look, no we ain't hooligans / Just young and talented Nubians / With potential and promise / Innovative young masterminds like Sean Wallace'*). An entire movement that dominated the UK music scene was based on this confident assertion of African identity by British-born black artists; they named it 'TINA' or 'This is New Africa'. Multicultural London English (MLE) – the dialect that originated on the diverse council estates of Tottenham and other inner London areas, merging West Indian and South Asian, cockney and Estuary slang – is now, we are told, 'sweeping across the country'.[107]

This new generation is grasping social media by the thread-load, defining itself with pride in its ethnic heritage, flaunting natural hair, defying mainstream images of beauty, supporting each other's businesses, and speaking out against prejudiced rhetoric or oppressive policy. It's an exciting time, a time where subversion can happen on a viral scale, a time ripe for shaking things up.

This same generation is rejecting the current thinking around immigration. A 2017 poll of 18- to 34-year-old voters found that they regarded immigration as the least important issue, ranking it bottom of twenty-two policy areas on a list.[108] Around 70 per cent of the same group voted to remain in the EU in the 2016 referendum.

The debate around immigration affected all four of my grandparents. My paternal grandfather, conscious of both anti-Jewish and anti-German feeling, and the Englishwoman he married, my grandmother, faced their own prejudice and hostility in their time. As did my maternal grandfather, with his experiences of racism, and my grandmother, living with the neighbours' regular gift of dog shit on the doorstep. It has been ticking on back and forth for my entire adult life. I was sixteen when New Labour was voted in, promising 'multiculturalism' – the politicians' social tool for building Britain into something that pleased them. I was in my early twenties when the EU underwent its largest expansion so far, admitting the Eastern European states whose migrants – though on the whole not visibly members of an ethnic minority – brought their own culture, languages and shops, just as my mother's generation of African immigrants had done before them, a perceived onslaught that helped make immigration the political issue of our time. At thirty-five, I watched a slim majority of British voters choose to take Britain out of the EU – a decision which will have profound consequences for decades to come – one-third saying they had done so because they wanted to 'regain control of immigration'.[109] There has been racism on the anti-immigration side, just as there has been elite naivety on the pro-immigration side, reflecting the views of affluent Londoners who neither live nor interact with immigrants but appreciate the contribution low-paid migrant workers make to their own bank balances. There is everything in between.

What's important are not the specifics of whatever immigration policy our political leaders enforce. It's the sentiment that lurks beneath it. The tone of the debate around immigration is, in so many ways, a window into Britain's deepest view of itself. If it weren't for the strongly held belief that 'indigenous' Brits are a white race, with a pristine culture stemming from time immemorial, then the debate around immigration could conceivably be a rational one, based on economic needs, public resources, historical facts and geopolitical realities. Instead what we have is an emotional, and emotive, story of threat and invasion, the undertones as old and as global as Britain itself – a delicate, white nation facing a black, brown, Muslim, Eastern and African swarm. It's a narrative so strong that even members and descendants of previous 'swarms', when settled and conditioned into the British world view, begin adopting the same mentality; the Huguenot heritage of former UKIP leader Nigel Farage is a case in point. At times what we have is nonsensical. The idea that Britain can somehow revive its imperial might, by trading with the former colonies now grouped in the Commonwealth, while at the same time barring their citizens from living, working or even studying in the UK. Deepening trade, while erecting ever higher barriers to immigration, is a puzzling circle to square.

What's being lost in the meantime is a version of Britishness that is capable of absorbing the millions of British people for whom immigration is part of their identity. I felt the tragedy of this in Ghana, meeting young British people of Ghanaian heritage who were seeking out new lives there. The tragedy was not that they were moving to Ghana; I know first-hand that getting to know, and contributing to, a country of your heritage, especially an African country that can so benefit from its diaspora, is a positive thing. The tragedy was that they were doing it not just from a sense of Ghanaian opportunity, but also from a sense of British rejection. Britain did not want them, they believed, even though they *were* British, born here, raised here, educated, socialised, conditioned here, speaking no other language than the one spoken here. Bound up with my own sense of Ghanaianness, this sense of rejection was also alive and well. A nation that singles out the youngest, brightest, most energetic and enthusiastic among them, and tells them they do not belong, is a nation that is getting something badly wrong.

8. THE DOOR OF NO RETURN

A British postcard produced in support of the anti-slavery movement,
which also reveals Victorian attitudes to race and power.

You are beyond. Broken-off, like limbs from a tree. But not lost, for you carry within your bodies the seeds of new trees. Sinking your hopeful roots into difficult soil.

– Caryl Phillips, *Crossing the River*

Britain can be difficult soil. I only have the luxury of writing this book because of the battles that were fought here before me. Because all except one of my grandparents found sanctuary here, and the one who was from here – my father's mother – faced her own ostracism for marrying someone who wasn't. They weren't thinking about identity, they were thinking about survival, about opportunity, about their children being safer, and more prosperous, than they were.

I wonder what they would think of this book. Only my Ghanaian grandmother, Ophelia Joyce, is still alive and she has been at the book's core. She tolerates my endless fascination with my heritage and identity, albeit with a degree of alarm. Through my searching she has often felt compelled to go back – not trusting me to go alone – to the parts of Ghana she had decided to leave. I'm humbled by the sacrifices of my parents, their parents and grandparents, and those before them. Sometimes, when people tell me to 'get over' the questions of race and identity that so preoccupy me, I think how carefree that would be. I would conjure thoughts of my forebears, I imagine, with gratitude and a bit of curiosity, not dwelling too deeply on their legacy and what it means today, I would thank them politely and just carry on.

But the struggle of *my* life has been to come to terms with my identity. It's been a personal struggle – not one I chose, but one that chose me, beginning, I reckon, with my name. My parents were wise to give me this name, I think, because it never let me forget where I was from, nor did it let me off any of the work required to actually understand it. It was not so much a name as a project.

This struggle of mine – one that I've come to discover is shared by so many others – found me because I was marked from birth, in British society, as other. Years of my life were devoted to establishing that this is what happened. Then I needed to understand how it happened. Then I needed to understand why. There is no manual that provides an explanation for your lived experience as a brown child growing up in this society. A lot of the time, there is not even an acknowledgement that there is anything *to* explain. You have to work it out for yourself. I think I have. And I've written about what I have learned in this book, so that I can hold on to it. And so that others don't have to start from scratch.

Like mine, my daughter's journey began with her name. Ghanaian culture dictates that the father chooses the first child's name, and – being a sucker for the few traditions from my heritage that I actually understand – I was willing to give in to that one. She's named after Sam's grandmother, the cantankerous old lady, known in her Aburi village for splitting whatever money she has a hundred ways, among an endless number of needy, distant relatives.

Her surname, though, was more complicated. In choosing which of our names she would take, Sam and I shared a common, primary objective – giving our daughter the best chance in life. But we had conflicting perspectives on what this actually meant. For Sam, who grew up sensing that opportunities were closed to people who looked and sounded like him, a perception confirmed by listening to school-teachers and observing older children, his main priority was to shield our little girl from the prejudice he had faced. He knew that his daughter would not experience the material deprivation he did. But deprivation of opportunity was a risk he took just as seriously. Sam's surname – obviously African, double-barrelled and, for some British people, therefore doubly intimidating – might place, he worried, an unnecessary obstacle in her way. My surname, *Hirsch*, on the other hand, he reasoned, sounded less remarkable, less baggage-laden and frankly less black, to the admissions tutor or the prospective employer of her future. And that meant a whole lot easier a life.

From my perspective, though, Sam's Ghanaian surname was a precious gift that would help guard our daughter against the threat of rootlessness. A name can't do that *alone*, obviously, but it might help. It would be a gift entailing cultural certainty, and signifying her membership of a clearly denoted tribe. Not a 'tribe' in the colonial sense of the word, the propaganda term used to demean and demote Africans to primitive idiots, but 'tribe' in the modern sense of the word – her people, their subculture – whether in Britain, or in Ghana, where a river bears the same name, a river that nourished Sam's family over generations. In my eyes, bearing Sam's name will make that place a little less distant and its legacy a little more real. Others with the same name would not look at my daughter the way other Hirsches look at me – surprised by the mismatch of the name to the face, hoping for an explanation. They will look at my daughter and say, she is one of us. She may choose to reject that identity, that belonging, that heritage. My greatest wish for her is that she will define her own identity and find her own sense of purpose. But whatever she chooses, that she *will* have a choice.

So we gave our daughter her Ghanaian names. Partly, I like to think, because I won the argument and persuaded Sam that, when other more immediate battles against poverty and hardship are won, identity remains. But partly because, we realised, we can't endorse a vision which expects us to, or accepts the fact that we, inhabit a world as prejudiced as the one we grew up in. I have to believe in a future world in which a name like hers, with its rich West African intonation, and Britishness will not be mutually exclusive, as I so often felt my Ghanaian first name and my British identity were when I was growing up. I have to hold on to the belief that she will experience a Britain where she can be British, while bearing a name whose history and culture unequivocally belong to an African nation of which she can be equally proud.

Sometimes it's hard to be optimistic. When my daughter was three months old, England erupted into riots. The disproportionately poor, young black people identified as responsible – had he been fifteen years younger, Sam could easily have been among them – were described as a stain on society, tried and sentenced to unusually long sentences. If the riots were a cry for help, it felt as if no one was listening.

In the years that followed, the far right tightened their grip on a disillusioned electorate throughout Europe. By the time my daughter was five, Nigel Farage was celebrating changing the course of British history, having started a movement which resulted in Britain voting to leave the EU. I felt scared for our safety in my own home town for the first time. Later that year, Farage was celebrating with an even more right-wing president. America's first black president handed over power to America's first orange president – a reality-TV star who used open racism, misogyny and hate to win enough votes to enter the White House. I had to mute the news, to avoid her hearing how the leader of the free world liked to 'grab [a woman] by the pussy'.

There are two things my daughter has said to me that confirm what it's like to be her growing up in this world. Once, when she was three, watching a movie on TV together, she asked, 'Mummy, is everyone in that town white?' I can't now remember which film it was, but it could have been almost any of those on our on-demand TV box. Through her eyes I realised that normal, and by extension magical, beautiful and interesting – since these are qualities in which children's stories trade – still does not look like us. It seemed different somehow, away from the Twitter rage of #OscarsSoWhite or the sanitised reports on the state of diversity in the creative industries, to hear a small child, with no agenda, only curiosity and wonder, trying to make sense of this world.

The second remark came when she was five, a few months after the Brexit vote. She and Sam were messing about in the living room, and he had wrapped himself up in blankets on a cold winter evening, the boiler still chugging into action to warm up our flat. He had one blanket draped from his shoulders to the floor, and another covering his head. I think he was trying to pretend to be a monster, but in fact the effect was closer to a kind of Ikea-fabric burka. 'You can't dress like that in this country, Daddy!' she said sternly. 'If you want to dress like that, you'll have to leave.'

Identities are formed in relation to others. My daughter sees herself as someone who is brown. She has none of the baggage that tells us that blackness is loaded with threatening meaning; it's simply a colour and a rich heritage of which she has been taught to be proud. She draws pictures of herself, meticulously colouring her skin and her arms with her favourite glittery brown pen, then tracing the outline of a mass of curls that spiral outward from her head in jet black, in a glorious chaos of squiggles. Her mixed-heritage friend also gets curls – she applies a little more gravity to those. And her blonde friend gets sleek shoulder-length straight yellow lines. Each is immediately identifiable. There are no complexes, there's no agenda, no anxiety. These are her friends, whom she loves. We go to church only occasionally, and none of us are baptised, but when she is with her Muslim friend, she sees herself as Christian. When she plays with boys she is very firm in the view that she is a girl. When we met a white British family on holiday in Italy, who asked us where we were from, I told them that we too were British. My daughter interrupted, correcting me loudly. 'We are from Ghana, Mummy,' she said.

This inspired mixed emotions in me. On the one hand, she was articulating what distinguished our Britishness from theirs. It was an expression of fact; we looked different from this family, we probably ate different food much of the time, we had lived in and identified with a country that these British holidaymakers, in all likelihood, had not visited, and perhaps would not have been able to locate on a map. On the other hand, her insistence that we were not British, in the way this other family were British, suggested I had passed my own ambivalence about my identity on to her. Had I conveyed to her the idea that Britishness somehow excluded her? Or did Britain do that all by itself?

I don't know the answer. But because she is already expressing this, it's something we can discuss. I sometimes wish that everyone had the wisdom, and honesty, of my five-year-old daughter. 'I don't see race,' people say, 'I am genuinely colour-blind.' What this turns out to mean, when you probe it, is that they have never experienced the disadvantages of being a visible other. And they have especially not experienced an otherness to which the old baggage of inferiority is attached. This gives them the luxury of effectively ignoring the impact of race in

British life, while patting themselves on the back for their tolerance. Colour blindness denies the reality of a world that – whether we like it or not – is highly racialised. The motive for rejecting this reality is often well meaning – an attempt to distance oneself from racism. But in doing so it also assumes that recognising difference is inherently negative. It assumes there is nothing to be proud of in having a different identity, or cultural heritage, it invalidates other perspectives.[1]

Part of the problem here is whiteness. When Claudia Rankine's book *Citizen* won her a MacArthur Genius grant of $625,000, the American poet decided to spend it on studying 'whiteness'. It began in a bookstore, when she asked for books on whiteness, which she translated to the confused shop assistant as 'the ways in which white contemporary artists deal with whiteness, interrogate it, analyse it, work in ways that push up with constructions of whiteness'. No one in that or subsequent bookshops understood what she meant. Unlike 'blackness', 'whiteness' is an invisible construct. In the sense that its presence has become regarded as invisible, normal, neutral even. 'I think we've seen whiteness centralised forever, so they're no longer interested in making it the subject, putting it in the subject position,' said Rankine.

Critics might object that in a country where white people are in the majority, there is nothing wrong with normalising whiteness. But that misses the point. Whiteness has a history – it's an identity that was invented in order to provide the superior identity to blackness's inferior one. It's an identity that continues to operate on a political and economic level in the UK, only without anyone acknowledging it.

If this sounds like an invention that is good for white people, it isn't. Failing to acknowledge that whiteness exists, means ignoring the burden for a white child born into a culture that tells them they are innately superior, that they are entitled. And that if others – black and brown – find themselves in the same position as them, they have been conditioned to believe that's because something dodgy is going on. *How did you get this job anyway?* people ask me. I must have pulled some trick. Or perhaps it was affirmative action. Whiteness has set white children up to believe in a complex web of interconnecting myths, the most pernicious of which is that a free market naturally results in white people taking their rightful place at the top. A world without this myth is a place where everyone knows they must compete with others on a meritocratic footing. This should be straightforward for anyone who believes in capitalism to understand. Ever since whiteness was invented, we have not had a free market. What we have had is a massive intervention in the market in favour of white people.

I first became aware that whiteness exists, as opposed to the received wisdom that whiteness is normal and neutral, while everyone else is some*thing* else, when I began learning about things in my heritage that I was proud of. I went out of my way – since it was not ever offered in anything I learned at school – to find out about the contribution of black civilisations to humanity; the inventions, the libraries, the economies, the architecture of pre-colonial sub-Saharan Africa. As I've said in previous chapters, I'm not a fan of a 'celebratory' approach to history, I'm simply interested in facts. There were plenty of despotic features in ancient African societies – misogyny, war and pillage, arbitrary criminal justice systems – as there were in all societies. Rape in marriage was not a criminal offence in England until the 1990s, for example; and the abuse of young boys has not stopped anyone studying the philosophy or literature of ancient Athens. Similarly, the absence of the kind of universal, inalienable human rights – fundamental to my values now – in Songhai, the ancient kingdom of Ghana or Ashanti, has not stopped me being interested in their accomplishments either.

It's not seen as radical to immerse oneself in understanding the legacy of Isaac Newton, Winston Churchill or David Hume – all of whom incidentally directly supported racism one way or another.[2] But as a mixed-race person, I've found that concerning myself with the other side of my heritage is regarded as exactly that. It's not normal, it's not what's expected, it *is* even radical. White history is seen as 'history', black history is seen as 'black history' – a specialist subject for those who wish to opt out of the mainstream. It's a subcategory, added to the syllabus in the interests of political correctness.

Discussing race, in contemporary Britain, is still a radical act. Mention it in a positive context, and people visibly squirm. Good Immigrant status is placed in jeopardy. Sometimes, it feels wiser to stay silent. The film-maker Munsur Ali told me that when people ask him where he is from, he says, 'My parents are from Bangladesh.' But he *wants* to say more. 'I can almost see the connotations, the images in their mind. They visualise a deprived state, a corrupt state, that's as far as they think. And what I really want to say is, *My name is Munsur. I'm from Bangladesh, which used to have the largest, richest port in the world, which was then in 1757 ravaged by the British because of its riches, and suffered two great famines, because of the British.* Otherwise, when you say your name and where you're from, there's no content.'

I'm not saying that people should feel obliged to introduce themselves with reference to whatever atrocities Britain has committed against the country of their heritage. Nor am I suggesting that we stop recognising the contributions of Isaac Newton to science, the leadership and vision of Winston Churchill, or the philosophy of David Hume, which I have long admired – something I now have to reconcile with the fact that he helped create the racist ideology that black people are an inherently inferior subcategory of human. We have to separate the call for an honest appraisal of Britain's history from demands for statues to be knocked down, chickens repatriated – as a Cambridge college contemplated when it emerged that its bronze cockerel was actually an *okukor* looted from Benin – or books removed from the syllabus. These claims are often written off as hysteria from 'snowflake' students. We shouldn't dismiss these demands out of hand. These students are responding to centuries of our colonial legacy, a legacy which is utterly incompatible with the values Britain now claims as part of the national identity.

But we do need to find a British response to our uniquely British history. The debate over what version of history should be preserved and taught only goes to show how important, and powerful, narratives of history are in shaping identity. I've yet to find a British person who has no pride or interest in British history; in Shakespeare, in the engineering feats of the Victorians, in the Beatles or David Bowie. So I find it remarkable when people assume that the worst excesses of racism are in the past now, and it is time to move on. No one says 'get over the Second World War', because, even as increasingly there are fewer people alive who remember it, it shaped our national identity as well as our geopolitical reality. No one says 'Shakespeare is in the past', because his work is part of Britain's narrative, it has become part of what Britain *is*. Even if you wanted to 'put Shakespeare behind you', it would be virtually impossible, since his legacy is embedded into every corner of British literature, language, drama and culture. And if it's impractical to put Shakespeare behind you, then it's even *more* difficult to get over the ideas, enshrined by monarchs, governments, businesses, banks and even some of our favourite brands, that black people are inferior, that they have to prove their worth, or their beauty, their intellect or their honesty, that only Good Immigrants are acceptable, and that white British people get to be the judge. It's harder to get over those ideas because not only are they pervasive, but we still won't face up to them.

Any sensible person would, I think, like to see a post-racial future. In my particular version, heritage would be preserved and identity recognised as an emotional bedrock for all the members of our species, and we would have the right to self-define our personal identities, and yet not be defined by them. But we cannot achieve this, or any post-racial future, until we confront the fact that this *is* a racial present. We can't just let time and procreation do its work. The fact that by 2050, if the figures are right, more than one-third of the British population will be non-white, doesn't solve anything by itself, it just massively expands the number of people who will be affected by the problem. A problem about which we are in complete denial. To paraphrase the poet Dan Chiasson, 'post-racial' Britain is like Elsinore, in *Hamlet*, celebrating its renewal as a way of covering up its crimes.[3] There's Shakespeare's influence again.

These themes are universal, but this being the United Kingdom, our version has some quirks. There are the identities of our four nations, England, Wales, Scotland and Northern Ireland. Each has a different relationship with itself, with its ethnic minority members, and with its sense of Britishness. Some black people in England have told me that they relate more to Britishness than any other national identity because a parent or grandparent was born in a former colony which is now part of the Commonwealth, something that they associate more with 'Britain' than, say, England or Scotland. At the same time it's been well documented that the 'English' national identity is more affected by the loss of empire and a sense of insecurity about Britain's place in the world. So the 'English' long for empire, but the descendants of imperial subjects want to be 'British'. No one ever said identity was a straightforward thing.

And then there's the monarchy. As an undergraduate, when a staunchly Conservative, pro-monarchist, semi-aristocratic housemate and I were having an argument about the royal family, I expressed republican sentiments. These I held more out of default than anything else. The royal family to me, growing up, was just another of many examples of why Britishness was white, and not something that belonged to people who looked like me. It belonged to people who thought they should buy, sell or rule over people who looked like me, whose literal and cultural descendants happened to be, at that moment, enjoying themselves in Buckingham Palace, while things hadn't played out so well for my ancestors. 'How would you feel,' this friend asked, 'if I went to Ghana, and said that the king of Ashanti should be abolished? Isn't that part of your identity? Can't you see how important it is to British people to have theirs?'

The British did actually do that, incidentally, in the war in which Baden-Powell helped destroy the Ashanti capital, exile its king and turn my family into refugees. It's a shame I didn't know the history, or my personal connection to it, at the time. But putting that to one side, I actually agreed with him, and I still do. The symbols and traditions that anchor our identities – whatever those may be – are a fundamental human need. In the early nineteenth century, it was popular to believe that as people became better educated, the rituals surrounding the monarchy would be rejected as 'nothing more than primitive magic, a hollow sham'. Precisely the opposite has happened. 'The mass of the population may indeed have become better educated,' wrote the historian David Cannadine, 'but they have not, as a result, lost their liking for the secular magic of monarchy.'[4]

The monarchy may have magic on their side, but the challenge they face is one of sustainability. In a country that has redefined itself since the end of the empire as one wedded to fairness, equality, free markets and meritocratic principles, and – in theory at least – multiculturalism, how could it be sustainable to have a monarchy that ostensibly embodies none of those things? For a generation forced to create new British identities – since the ones we inherited were never intended to accommodate people with our history or appearance – how can we relate to such a monarchy?

The royal family have sought to answer this question by presiding over a system that makes black and brown people Members and Officers of the British Empire by awarding them MBEs and OBEs, and occasionally knighthoods,[5] by energetically sponsoring charities that help disadvantaged young people, and by engaging with organisations like the Stephen Lawrence Foundation, established to honour the legacy of the murdered teenager, and create opportunities for future generations of young black British people.

These efforts are having an impact. The actor Idris Elba recalled the support he had had from Prince Charles's Prince's Trust. 'Yeah, the good old Prince Charles stepped straight up for me, right in there, well done!' said Elba, telling a packed-out committee room in the House of Commons how the charity had subsidised his first ever audition, then given him £1,500 in cash support because his parents didn't have the money. 'Back then obviously I never met Prince Charles,' he continued, 'but we had one thing in common: we both fell into the same line of work as our parents. Yeah, it just sort of happens . . . My dad worked in a car factory, so before I could get work as an actor, I ended up doing night shifts at Ford Dagenham. Historically in Britain, you never escaped. If you started at the bottom of the heap, you most likely died at the bottom of the heap.'[6]

Multiculturalism is sometimes conceived as manipulative power play, cynically designed to keep the masses separated along racial lines while an all-white elite enjoy the spoils of land ownership, capital and power, without showing any interest in diversity, while the monarchy and the aristocracy remain all white. The term 'blue-blooded', which we still use to refer to the aristocracy, comes after all from the Spanish *sagre azul*, coined in the late 1500s to distinguish between the racially superior white Christian nobility, and the Jews, Muslims and West Africans whom Europeans were increasingly ousting from Europe and encountering in Africa and the New World.[7]

I used to think it was a question of the royal family, clinging on to their 'blue blood' and all the white supremacist notions that embodies, resisting the 'integration' that is now preached at everyone else. Putting the history of the slave trade and colonialism, both projects significantly implicating the royals, to the side for a moment, our contemporary royals have a formidable list of racial faux pas in their résumés. Prince Philip, known for indiscretions that are by no means limited to people of colour, once said to the then Nigerian president Olusegun Obasanjo, dressed in traditional Yoruba *agbada* cap and *dashiki*, 'You look like you're ready for bed!'[8] Prince Harry dressed up as a Nazi, and told the black British comedian Stephen Amos he 'didn't sound like a black chap'.[9] Apart from Princess Diana's ill-fated attempt to build a relationship with Egyptian heir Dodi Fayed in the lead-up to her death, and notwithstanding the theory that the 'famously ugly' Queen Charlotte of Mecklenburg-Strelitz may well have actually been black,[10] plus the odd colonial ward like Dido Elizabeth Belle and Sophia Duleep Singh – the mixed-heritage Punjabi princess and god-daughter of Queen Victoria – there have been very few 'Aristoblacks', as they're known these days. Emma McQuiston, the mixed-heritage socialite who married the heir to the sixteenth-century Longleat estate Viscount Weymouth, faced blatant racism, with the viscount's mother asking him, 'Are you sure about what you're doing to 400 years of bloodline?'[11] 'There's class, and then there's the racial thing,' McQuiston said.

When Prince Harry began a relationship with the mixed-race American actor Meghan Markle in 2016, I realised that the picture was more complicated than simply royal hostility to racial diversity. A significant body of public opinion was, it turned out, even more invested in the idea of the royal family remaining white. Meghan Markle is, the newspapers warned when she first appeared on the scene, a 'saucy brunette', 'something of a departure from Prince Harry's usual type', and 'not in the society blonde style of previous girlfriends'. Her mother, even more alarmingly, comes 'complete with dreadlocks and a nose stud', the *Daily Mail* declared.[12] It was classic British racism – only half said, and half implied, a kind of polite prejudice that is only more pernicious for its subtlety. For the avoidance of doubt, though, the *Mail* told readers that Markle was '(almost) straight outta Compton', a poor Los Angeles neighbourhood which it described as 'gang-scarred', asking 'will [Harry] be dropping by for tea?'[13]

The experience rocked Prince Harry sufficiently that he was temporarily turned into a racism awareness campaigner, taking the unprecedented step of issuing a statement calling out the press coverage for what it was: racist. It's easy to be oblivious to how prejudiced our society is, until it happens to you.[14]

There are some things you can do in Britain, other than begin a relationship with an heir to the throne, to get your identity taken seriously. One of them is to become a suspected terrorist. The only time I have ever, in my lifetime, heard questions of dual identity discussed at the senior levels of the British establishment is in connection to Islamist extremism and terrorist attacks. The fact that British-born and -educated people of Muslim faith could be capable of launching suicide bomb attacks on British soil has prompted an unprecedented level of soul-searching, which always, inevitably comes back to identity.

'For all our successes as a multi-racial, multi-faith democracy,' said David Cameron in 2015, 'we have to confront a tragic truth that there are people born and raised in this country who don't really identify with Britain – and who feel little or no attachment to other people here.'[15]

What caused young Brits to have this alienation, even hostility, towards their own country? Without exception, dozens of young British Muslims I have interviewed while reporting radicalisation, socially conservative Islam, recruitment to the war in Syria, and so on, have expressed a sense that Britain does not accept them. 'I'm not British, British people won't accept me as British,' a young man in Blackburn told me. 'But I've never even been to Pakistan, I'm not really from Pakistan either. What I do have, is Islam. That's the only identity I've got, it's everything to me.' The problem is not, I think, that a young generation of British people from ethnic minority backgrounds tend to place a higher value on their faith than their white counterparts. There is nothing wrong with that and it should be respected. The problem, to me, is the *reason* they choose an extreme version of their faith and use it to craft all-encompassing identities. In many cases it seems less like the result of a proactive decision, and more the result of finding doors to other identities in Britain closed in their face.

What's the solution? Overcoming the uniquely British combination of convenient ignorance and awkward squeamishness that prevents us from confronting the past. Facing up to the fact that whiteness is not the only civilisation, letting go of intractable ideas of white superiority and genuinely embracing the meritocracy we claim to already stand for. It's not good enough to launch projects on 'diversity', to do inspirational talks in schools, to introduce quotas or targets on appointing people from different backgrounds – although all of these things do have a role to play. There is so much well-intentioned, hard work carried out by people who want to see change – I do my best to be among them – but without addressing the root causes of prejudice and the unfairness at the heart of our national identity, it's simply tinkering.

We might hope that technology and social media will solve all our problems. But we can't leave shaping our dialogue and our sense of ourselves to Silicon Valley, which by the way is one of the most un-diverse industries of all. At both Twitter and Facebook, for example, 1 per cent of the employees are black men, and at Twitter 0 per cent are black women.[16]

I'm committed to confronting the most un-British awkwardness this project involves, because I have no choice. Like many of my generation, I'm truly sickened by the hypocrisy of the ongoing and undeniably racially skewed limits on opportunity, accompanied by a complacent official rhetoric about diversity that is crowned occasionally with open racism. I tried to leave the country. I genuinely believed that the solution to my frustration was to move to an African nation where, surely, racial injustice on an industrial scale was one problem they didn't have. But identity can't be created out of insecurity. The fact that there are gaps in my sense of Britishness ultimately did not mean there were equal and equivalent pools of belonging in my sense of Ghanaianness. Ghana will always be part of who I am. But so much of my purpose is here, in the society I know, the textures of whose wrongs, and opportunities, I feel intimately and intuitively. And the number of younger versions of me, confused, floating in a mystery, with no knowledge of the past, but a lingering sense of suspicion towards the future, is proliferating. It's not something I or anyone else can escape. What we can do, instead, is begin to be honest.

Our identities are not diktats that can be dreamed up in Whitehall, dismissed by the self-styled 'post-racial' and 'colour-blind' commentators who so often hog the debate in the media; they cannot be policed by anyone at all. My parents never expected me to look them in the eye one day and tell them that I was black. They didn't see me that way; to them it made no sense. But it makes sense to me. My identity started from a place of feeling 'other' and alien, it evolved in conditions of prejudice and unfairness, and then grew and blossomed into something that I cherish, that enriches my relationship with Britain, my country, that helps me to see nuances, truths and opportunities here that I would perhaps have been blind to otherwise.

Now I feel privileged to have had these problems thrust upon my most vulnerable inner world as a child, because it removed the option of ignoring them – something in reality no one really does have the luxury of doing. Britain's solution has too often been colour blindness, with the familiar ripostes, *I don't see race*, or *black brown white yellow green purple blue – it's all the same to me.* Blindness, it seems fairly obvious to point out, is not a good strategy for seeing what is there. Race *is* there, as lived experience, as the basis for the most dramatic economic and human shifts in history. Colour is there, and while people work on their myopia to avoid confronting awkward truths, others are finding their identities shaped by it. Identities are not becoming less important in our globalised world, they are becoming more important than ever. And Britishness is an identity that is excluding a growing number of people who, like me, should be among its core constituents.

This conversation is long overdue: a conversation begun in a spirit of honesty, not defensiveness, or fear, or blindness. I don't know when a conversation like this would end, but I hope this book will be part of the beginning.

ACKNOWLEDGEMENTS

I owe the greatest debt in writing this book to my parents, Peter Hirsch and Mary Owusu Hirsch: for raising and supporting me; encouraging me (I suspect at times unintentionally) to question everything; for endless grandparental contributions; and for hands-on research. My sister, Dr Ama Quarshie-Collison, has been on the journey with me the whole way, a loyal and lovely companion. In addition to all this, all three of you also have to tolerate me writing about you. I don't know how you put up with it.

My grandmother, Ophelia Joyce Owusu, has always been the link between my life in Britain and my Ghanaian heritage, through food, wisdom, stories and attempts – sometimes futile – to educate me. Thank you for your patience, love and schooling. Thank you to Kes, my big sister and WhatsApp group enactor extraordinaire, whose own research helped me greatly with this book. Thank you also to the generous staff at Queens' College, Cambridge: Revd Dr Jonathan Holmes, who was the first to retrieve our grandfather's documents and kindly wrote a detailed summary of them, and Becky Heath, who provided documents for a second time, and the space and photocopying needed. My aunt Elsie Owusu has also conducted impressive research, gathering photos, and archives, and speaking to distant relatives, for which I'm incredibly grateful.

My grandfather John Hirsch was patient and kind, sharing memories that ranged from the traumatic to the comedic, until the very end of his life. His brother, my great uncle Sir Peter Hirsch, continues to be incredibly generous with his time and energy. His son Paul Kellar has done invaluable work organising and sharing photos. So many other family members came to my rescue with memories, facts and research. Kofi Owusu, Kwabena Owusu, Adjoa Owusu, Penny Peckham, Ann Linden and Stella Hirsch, Carmen John, Nancy Christina Welsing-Ross, Helen Eno Welsing, and Graham Roderick Laurence Oliphant of Oliphant, younger.

Some aspects of family history I have drawn on in this book are contested and others handed down by oral, and at times conflicting, versions of events. I have been as accurate as possible and where possible drawn on written and historical records that do exist.

I am grateful to the friends who ventured way beyond the call of duty in supporting my work. Miranda Quammie was by my side in Ghana, Dunstable and Jamaica (I hope the good balanced out the bad!) and offered reassurance, companionship when I needed it most, and trademark genius. Christina Lyons has been an advocate and connector, Amaki Sogbodjor was a generous travel companion. Feyi Rodway let me write about experiences we shared, and provided much inspiration. Matthew Ryder was helpful in probing and questioning, Tony Tagoe never, ever said no to any of my unreasonable requests. Omega Douglas shared thoughts and research. I'm incredibly lucky to have writers in my life whom I hugely admire – Gary Younge and Ben Okri both provided mentoring and guidance during my writing process, for which I thank you. Trevor Faure was a huge support during difficult times. Marcus Ryder has never yet been known to run out of ideas. Naomie Harris was always a ray of light, Matthew Kay gave me books and ideas.

I owe the idea for this book in no small part to Bill Hamilton, who never gave up, not even over three different manifestations of this book, once we had settled that question, dozens of different drafts. Becky Brown, whose changes improved the idea beyond measure and Florence Rees, who has had so much enthusiasm for my work. Michal Shavit, whose genius, confidence and insight turned this into something way better than it would otherwise have been, Bea Hemming, who is patient and thoughtful beyond measure, and Clare Bullock, for diligent problem solving. Thank you to Candice Carty-Williams for being a publishing wind beneath my wings, and to Joe Pickering.

I'm indebted to everyone who gave me their time for interviews: Lee Pinkerton, Joseph Harker, Lola Fadare, David Harewood, Armand Diangiande, Chichi Nwanoku, Simon Frederick, Michael Heseltine, Greg Dyke, Chuka Umunna, Musa Okwonga, David Olusoga, Gus Casely-Hayford, Reggie Yates, Dominic Proctor, Maddii Town, Faisa Qureshi, Rachel Kasuija, Adrian Lester, Stafford Scott, Deedee Banks, Evita Robinson, Dennis Owusu-Sem, Mallence Bart-Williams, Jasmine Cameron-Chileshe, Melissa Bashiri, Munsur Ali, June Givanni, Robert Beckford, Kenny Imafidon, Cypren Edmunds, Eric Kaufmann, Simon Wooley, Miri Song, Robert Beckford, Onyekachi Wambu. Akala and Roger Robinson lent me both their ideas and their words. The family of Mzee Mohammed, especially Karla Mohammed, Clement Daley, Kalum Rigley, Roxanne Tagoe, and the many members of the Daley family, opened their homes and hearts at a horrendously painful time.

Many more people agreed to speak to me anonymously and so while I won't name them here, I'm incredibly grateful to them for taking time to speak to me about often sensitive personal experiences, and for believing in the project of this book.

The staff at the British Library, the Liverpool Maritime Archives and the Codrington Library were unfailingly helpful and kind. Jonathan Levy, David Mapstone, Liz Lane, Baruch Ben-Chorin and Michael Blair provided ideas and encouragement that made a real difference. The Royal Society of Literature and the Jerwood Foundation gave me a huge boost, which had very practical as well as psychological benefits. My friends at the Migration Museum Project, the Movement for Justice and Reconciliation and AFRUCA all supported and contributed to my work in different ways.

A number of young people helped me with interviews, research and ideas. Cleo Tsivadnis let me draw on her impressive research. I had help with interviews and transcripts from Ella Sackville-Adjei, Gena Barrett, and Alexander Paul, in whose memory this book is dedicated. I never could have imagined he would not be here to read it for himself.

Being a full time working parent is not easily combined with writing a book, although so many others make it look easier than it is, and the team of people who allowed me to claw away time is vast. As well as family members, whose help and support was far beyond the call of duty, thanks to Emilia Zienkiewicz-Milewska, Beverley Gadsden, Cherie McClymont, Lauren Jeffries, and Faye Hamilton Nash for all your help and support.

Last but not least, I'm grateful to my best friend, whose ravenous reading meant there was rarely a relevant book that passed me by, who challenged every single one of my ideas – and if I couldn't convince him at least helped me convince myself in the process. Thank you for teaching me how to be militant in making full use of my time, and for inspiring me to never give up.

PLAYLIST

I grew up just before the era of social media, reality TV, online forums and the virtual subcultures that are such a big part of life now. Living in an area that didn't reflect the parts of my heritage I intuitively sensed but didn't fully understand, music opened windows to voices, causes and communities that I wouldn't otherwise have known existed. The music on this list is more than just a collection of songs; it is the story of who I am. These songs are a kind of soundtrack to my personal sense of identity. I hope you enjoy them too.

Nina Simone, 'Four Women' / 'Mississippi Goddam'
Desmond Dekker, 'Pretty Africa'
Prince Nico Mbarga, 'Sweet Mother'
Bob Marley, 'Redemption Song'
Apache Indian & Shy FX, 'Original Nuttah'
Oumou Sangaré, 'Voix du Mali'
Lady of Rage, 'Afro Puffs'
Alpha Blondy, 'Peace in Liberia'
General Levy, 'Incredible'
Goldie, 'Inner City Life'
Bashy, 'Black Boys'
Sway, 'Black Stars'
Les Nubians, 'Makeda'
Erykah Badu, 'Soldier'
Jill Scott, 'Do You Remember' (Experience 826 Live Version)
Jaguar Wright, 'Self Love'

Nas, 'Black President'
Angie Stone, 'Brother'
Fuse ODG, 'Azonto'
Nas, 'Moment of Silence'
Apache Indian, 'Election Crisis'
Fuse ODG, 'Azonto'
Amel Larrieux, 'Congo'
Beyoncé, 'Formation'
Akala, 'Fire in the Booth, Part 4'
Kendrick Lamar, 'The Blacker the Berry'
Jhené Aiko, 'To Love & Die (feat. Cocaine 80s)'
India Arie, 'Brown Skin'
Solange, 'For Us, By Us'

CREDITS

NOTES

INTRODUCTION

1. See for example the photographic series 'You Get Me' by Mahtab Hussain, exploring Asian working-class masculinity and the impact of black urban culture on Asian men and boys, http://autograph-abp.co.uk/exhibitions/you-get-me.

2. The Scottish grime scene has been heavily influenced by artists from Tottenham; Ian McQuaid, 'Skepta on grime: "People are catching on. There's a revolution happening"', *Guardian*, 10.09.16, https://www.theguardian.com/global/2016/sep/10/skepta-konnichiwa-boy-better-know-mercurys; and Kamila Rymajdo, 'Inside Scottish grime, the genre you never knew existed', *Dazed*, 2016, http://www.dazeddigital.com/music/article/33460/1/inside-scottish-grime-the-genre-you-never-knew-existed.

3. *Top Boy*, the television series chronicling the lives of a group of young black people on the streets of north-east London's Hackney, was acquired by the Canadian rap superstar Drake in 2017.

4. Maya Angelou (1986), *All God's Children Need Travelling Shoes*, Vintage, 196.

5. I wrote about the impact Maya Angelou had had on my life when she died in 2014; 'Maya Angelou Appreciation – The ache for home lives in all of us', *Observer*, 01.06.14, https://www.theguardian.com/books/2014/jun/01/maya-angelou-appreciation-afua-hirsch.

6. Watching the Dreamworks *Trolls* movie in 2016, giving the little characters with vertical hair the Hollywood treatment, was a bitter-sweet experience for me!

7. 'School League Tables 1997', *Independent*, 18.11.97, http://www.independent.co.uk/life-style/school-league-tables-1997-1294716.html.

8. Chimamanda Ngozi Adichie and Trevor Noah were in conversation at PEN America 2017; the video can be streamed at https://pen.org/trevor-noah-chimamanda-adichie-live/. See also Matt Grant, 'Chimamanda Ngozi Adichie and Trevor Noah on Racial Identity', Book Riot, 19.05.17, http://bookriot.com/2017/05/19/chimamanda-ngozi-adichie-and-trevor-noah-on-racial-identity/.

9. See for example Philip Gleason, whose observation is often still cited. 'The meaning of "identity" as we currently use it is not well captured by dictionary definitions, which reflect older uses of the word. Our present idea of "identity" is a fairly recent social construct, and a rather complicated one at that . . .', Philip Gleason (1983), 'Identifying Identity: A Semantic History', *Journal of American History*, 6:910–13.

10. Ralph Ellison (2016), *Invisible Man*, Penguin.

11. Eduardo Bonilla-Silva (2006), *Racism without Racists: Color-Blind Racism and the Persistence of Racial Inequality in America*, Rowman & Littlefield, 2–3.

1. WHERE ARE YOU FROM?

1. On 13 May 2000, *The Economist* ran with a front cover depicting an image of the African continent, a child soldier, and the headline, 'The Hopeless Continent', http://www.economist.com/printedition/2000-05-13.

2. Even Britain's foreign secretary in 2016 referred to Africa as 'that country'. 'Boris Johnson refers to Africa as "that country"', Adam Withnall, *Independent*, 02.10.16, http://www.independent.co.uk/news/uk/politics/boris-johnson-africa-country-conservative-tory-conference-speech-foreign-secretary-a7341936.html.

3. Tim Jeal (1989), *Baden-Powell*, London, Hutchinson, 162.

4. Ibid.

5. Barack Obama (2008), *Dreams from My Father: A Story of Race and Inheritance*, Canongate, 302.

2. ORIGINS

1. It later transpired that many of these images had been displayed at the National Portrait Gallery and Autograph Gallery in London as part of an exhibition entitled *Black Chronicles* in 2016 and *Black Chronicles II*, in 2014, http://autograph-abp.co.uk/exhibitions/black-chronicles-ii.

2. Junius P. Rodriguez (1997), *Historical Encyclopaedia of World Slavery*, ABC-CLIO, 557.

3. Peter Fryer (2010), *Staying Power*, Pluto Press, 14.

4. Ibid.

5. Brian Dyde (2005), *Out of the Crowded Vagueness: A History of the Islands of St Kitts, Nevis & Anguilla*, Macmillan Caribbean, 15.

6. Benjamin F. Carr (1994), *Nelson, Nisbet and Nevis*, Nevis Historical and Conservation Society, 8.

7. *Calendar of State Papers Colonial, America and West Indies, 1677–1680*, 573, cited in Fryer, 1.

8. Osei-Tutu, 'Growth of the Atlantic Slave Trade: Racial Slavery in the New World', in Julius O. Adekunle and Hettie V. Williams, eds (2010), *Color Struck: Essays on Race and Ethnicity in Global Perspective*, University Press of America, 98.

9. Paul Lovejoy, 'Volume of the Atlantic slave trade: A synthesis', in *Journal of African History* 23 (1982), 483, 497.

10. Sylvia R. Frey & Betty Wood, 'The Americas: The Survival of African Religions', in Gad J. Heuman (2003), *The Slavery Reader*, Routledge, 388.

11. Mark Juergensmeyer, ed. (2014), 'Thinking Globally: A Global Studies Reader', University of California, 60.

12. Christer Petley, 'Nelson, the Caribbean, and Visions of the British Atlantic Empire', Slavery and Revolution – Jamaica and Slavery in the Age of Revolution, lecture posted 25.06.14, https://blog.soton.ac.uk/slaveryandrevolution/2014/06/25/659/.

13. William Hague (2008), *William Wilberforce: The Life of the Great Anti-Slave Trade Campaigner*, Harper, 122.

14. Ibid., 47–8.

15. Jerry White (2013), *London in the Eighteenth Century: A Great and Monstrous Thing*, Harvard University Press, 22.

16. Cardinal Wiseman (1850), *An Appeal to the Reason and Good Feeling of the English People on the Subject of the Catholic Hierarchy*, Thomas Richardson & Son, 30.

17. Vincent Carretta, 'Three West Indian Writers of the 1780s Revisited and Revised', *Research in African Literatures*, Vol. 29, No. 4 (Winter, 1998), *The African Diaspora and Its Origins*, Indiana University Press, 76.

18. J. T. Smith (1828), *Nollekens and his Times*, I, 28–9, cited in Fryer, 95.

19. Carretta, 77–9.

20. Ibid., 75.

21. Fryer, 107

22. Junius P. Rodriguez (2015), *Encyclopedia of Emancipation and Abolition in the Transatlantic World*, Routledge, 492.

23. Hakim Adi, 'Quick History and Definition of Pan Africanism', Center of Pan African Thought, https://www.youtube.com/watch?v=VgMUXe3ctkA.

24. Fryer, 108.

25. Ibid., 109.

26. Andrew Hough, 'Revealed: David Cameron's favourite childhood book is Our Island Story', 29.10.10, *Telegraph*, http://www.telegraph.co.uk/culture/books/booknews/8094333/Revealed-David-Camerons-favourite-childhood-book-is-Our-Island-Story.html.

27. Tom Holland, 'Our Island Story: Not as Conservative as David Cameron imagines', *Guardian*, 07.02.14, https://www.theguardian.com/books/booksblog/2014/feb/07/our-island-story-conservative-david-cameron.

28. David Conway, 'Our Island Story triumphant!', 20.07.07, Civitas, http://www.civitas.org.uk/2007/07/20/our-island-story-triumphant/.

29 H. E. Marshall (1905), *Our Island Story: A History of England for Boys and Girls*, T. C. & E. C. Jack, 467.

30. G. M. Trevelyan (1952), *Illustrated English Social History*, I, D. McKay, 20.

31. Ibid., 42.

32. Manisha Sinha, 'The U.N. Is Commemorating Haiti's Role in Ending the Slave Trade. Here's Why', *Time*, 23.08.16, http://time.com/4452232/unesco-haitian-abolition/. According to the *Encyclopaedia of Slave Resistance and Rebellion*, 'historians estimate that insurrections took place on about one of every ten slave ship voyages in the transatlantic trade'. Junius P. Rodriguez (2007), *Encyclopedia of Slave Resistance and Rebellion*, Greenwood, Vol. 1, 324.

33. C. L. R. James (1938), *The Black Jacobins: Toussaint L'ouverture and the San Domingo Revolution*, Secker & Warburg, 311.

34. Eric Williams (1944), *Capitalism & Slavery*, University of North Carolina Press, 149.

35. David Ryden (2009), *West Indian Slavery and British Abolition, 1783–1807*, Cambridge University Press, 237–62.

36. Richard Hart (2002), *Slaves Who Abolished Slavery: Blacks in Rebellion*, University of the West Indies, 335.

37. Harold Drayton, in *New Scientist & Science Journal* (1971), Vol. 51, 26.

38. Sian Rees (2009), *Sweet Water and Bitter*, Chatto & Windus, 239.

39. Ibid., 215.

40. Ibid, 230.

41. Hague, 510.

42. W. E. B. Du Bois (1935), *Black Reconstruction in America 1860–1880*, Simon & Schuster (1999 edn), 5.

43. David Olusoga (2017), *Black and British: A Forgotten History*, Macmillan, 285, 356–9.

44. See for example David Cameron's trip to Jamaica in September 2015, or Tony Blair in 2006, who stopped short of offering a formal apology on behalf of Britain for enslaving millions of Africans.

45. See for example the open letter by former Jamaican Prime Minister P. J. Patterson to David Cameron: 'What PJ Patterson told David Cameron: Open Letter', *Jamaica Observer*, 11.11.15., http://www.jamaicaobserver.com/columns/What-PJ-Patterson-told-David-Cameron_19233022.

46. Chinua Achebe (2009), *The Education of a British-Protected Child*, Penguin, 56.

47. Richard Benjamin and David Fleming (2010), *Transatlantic Slavery: An Introduction*, Liverpool University Press, 22.

48. Ibid.

49. Decca Aitkenhead, 'Steve McQueen: My Hidden Shame', *Guardian*, 04.01.14, https://www.theguardian.com/film/2014/jan/04/steve-mcqueen-my-painful-childhood-shame.

50. Richard Suchet, 'McQueen Slams Hollywood For "Ignoring Slavery" ', Sky News, 03.01.14, https://uk.news.yahoo.com/news/steve-mcqueen-hits-hollywood-slavery-snub-050241357.html.

51. Frantz Fanon (1963), *The Wretched of the Earth*, Grove Press, 251.

52. Benjamin and Fleming, 43.

53. Fryer, 7–8.

54. Will Dahlgreen, 'The British Empire is something to be proud of', YouGov, 26.07.14, https://yougov.co.uk/news/2014/07/26/britain-proud-its-empire/.

55. Salman Rushdie, 'Outside the Whale', *Granta*, 01.03.84, https://granta.com/outside-the-whale/.

56. Harlan Kennedy, 'The Brits Have Gone Nuts: A Romantic Schism', *American Cinema Papers Print Archive*, 1985, <http://www.americancinemapapers.com/files/BRITS_HAVE_GONE_NUTS.htm>.

57. Ekwa Msangi, 'From An Independent African Filmmaker: We're Not Just Today's Griots, We're Your Freedom Fighters', 13.05.16, http://www.okayafrica.com/op-ed-2/ekwa-msangi-african-filmmakers-freedom-fighters/.

58. Fryer, 7.

59. 'The British Empire Exhibition, 1924/25', London Borough of Brent, https://www.brent.gov.uk/media/387533/The%20British%20Empire%20Exhibition.pdf.

60. Jinny Kathleen Prais (2008), *Imperial Travelers: The Formation of West African Urban Culture, Identity, and Citizenship in London and Accra, 1925–1935*, University of Michigan, 56.

61. Jan Morris (2012), *Farewell the Trumpets: An Imperial Retreat*, Faber, 300.

62. Prais, 54.

63. Ibid., 56.

64. Frederick John Dealtry Lugard (1922), *The Dual Mandate in British Tropical Africa*, W. Blackwood and Sons, 1.

65. Max de Haldevang, 'Why do we still use the term "sub-Saharan Africa"?', Quartz Africa, 01.09.16, http://qz.com/770350/why-do-we-still-say-subsaharan-africa/?utm_source=qzfbarchive.

66. Jessica Shepherd, 'The word on Oxford University's All Souls fellows exam is: axed', 14.05.10, *Guardian*, https://www.theguardian.com/education/2010/may/14/oxford-university-all-souls-college-exam.

67. Morris, 54.

68. See for example his obituary in the *Guardian* in 1902 which describes his views as 'vulgar'.

69. Justin Parkinson, 'Why is Cecil Rhodes such a controversial figure?', BBC News, 01.04.15, http://www.bbc.co.uk/news/magazine-32131829.

70. Theresa Richardson, 'John Locke and the Myth of Race in America', *Philosophical Studies in Education*, 2011, Vol. 42, 105.

71. Derek Bell, 'Race, Racism and American Law', *Aspen Law and Business* (1992), 2, 115.

72. David Hume (1735), 'Of National Characters', *Essays* (1906 edn), Routledge, 152 n1.

73. Hume, 153.

74. 'Patten criticism of Cecil Rhodes campaign "scandalous"', BBC Radio 4 *Today*, 14.01.16, http://www.bbc.co.uk/programmes/p03fgfxg.

75. House of Commons, Parliamentary Business, Michael Gove MP, answer to parliamentary question by Philip Davies MP, 15.11.10, col 634, https://www.publications.parliament.uk/pa/cm201011/cmhansrd/cm101115/debtext/101115-0001.htm.

76. Open Letter, 'Gove's plans contravene Education Acts', *Independent*, 13.06.13.

77. Toni Morrison, 'A Humanist View', part of the Public Dialogue on the American Dream Theme, Portland State University Library, 30 May 1975, accessed on 20.03.15, http://bit.ly/1q8HG3h.

78. Fryer, 107.

79. Ibid., 106.

80. Ibid., 215.

81. Ibid., 222–3.

82. Ibid., 320.

83. For example, Indian women who marched with the suffragettes were encouraged to do so on the basis that if women were among the white voters in Britain, then they would better be able to take care of the needs of Indian women within the empire. See A. Burton (1994), *Burdens of History: British Feminists, Indian Women and Imperial Culture*, Chapel Hill, chapters 1 and 7.

84. Tweet by @CharleneWhite posted 09.11.16, https://twitter.com/CharleneWhite/status/796473091337650180.

85. Salman Rushdie (1988), *The Satanic Verses*, Vintage, 343.

86. Steven Swinford, 'Millions of African migrants threaten standard of living, Philip Hammond says', *Telegraph*, 09.08.15, http://www.telegraph.co.uk/news/uknews/immigration/ 11792798/Millions-of-African-migrants-threaten-standard-of-living-Philip-Hammond-says.html.

3. BODIES

1. Evan Bleier and Richard Spillett, 'Our disappearing High Streets: Once thriving Dunstable now a ghost town with 43 boarded-up shops', Mail Online, 14.01.15, http://www.dailymail. co.uk/news/article-2908559/Once-thriving-Dunstable-ghost-town-43-boarded-shops. html#ixzz4QNhmOPPo.

2. 'Sex Stereotypes of African Americans Have Long History', NPR, 07.05.07, http://www. npr.org/templates/story/story.php?storyId=10057104.

3. Peter Fryer (2010), *Staying Power*, Pluto Press, 6.

4. Ibid., 7.

5. 'A description and historical declaration of the golden Kingdom of Guinea', in Purchas (1625), II, 927, in Fryer, 140.

6. S. Speed (1665), *The Golden Coast, or A Description of Guinney*, 76, in Fryer, 140.

7. R. Jobson (1623), *The Golden Trade*, 153, in Fryer, 140.

8. William Shakespeare, *Othello*, I, i, 122, Longman (1996 edn), 7.

9. Philip Kadish, 'Pharaohs, Mandingos, and Saxons: The Afrocentric Auto-Ethnologies of Frederick Douglass and Martin Delany, and the Counter-Auto-Ethnology of Harriet Beecher Stowe', CUNY Graduate Center, 6.

10. Fryer, 317.

11. *Daily Herald*, no. 1,313 (10 April 1920), [1], 4, in Fryer, 317.

12. Oliver Laughland, 'Donald Trump and the Central Park Five: the racially charged rise of a demagogue', *Guardian*, 17.02.16, https://www.theguardian.com/us-news/2016/feb/17/central-park-five-donald-trump-jogger-rape-case-new-york.

13. William Smith (1744), *A New Voyage to Guinea*, John Nourse, in Fryer, 140.

14. Charles Page Smith (1970), *Daughters of the Promised Land*, Little Brown, 219.

15. David Olusoga (2017), *Black and British: A Forgotten History*, Macmillan, 88.

16. Edward Long (1774), *The History of Jamaica*, Lowndes, 22.

17. Ben Arogundade (2000), *Black Beauty*, Pavilion, 22.

18. Richard Hakluyt (1598–1600), *The principal naviagations, voiages, traffiques and discouveries of the English Nation*, II, ii, 25, in Fryer, 142.

19. bell hooks (1981), *Ain't I a Woman: Black Women and Feminism*, Pluto Press, 37.

20. Ibid., 52.

21. Jenée Desmond-Harris, 'Seeking My Race-Based Valentine Online', *Time*, 22.02.10, http:// content.time.com/time/magazine/article/0,9171,1963768,00.html. Reports in 2016 suggest relatively little has changed. For example Dominique Mosbergen, 'Online Dating Is Rife With Sexual Racism, "The Daily Show" Discovers', Huffington Post, 15.04.16, http://www.huffingtonpost.com/entry/sexual-racism-the-daily-show_us_5710aa9ce4b0060ccda2e97d.

22. Frantz Fanon (1998), *Black Skin, White Masks*, Pluto Press, 88.

23. Omega Douglas, 'Watching You, Watching Me', *Guardian*, 12.08.99, https://www.the-guardian.com/uk/1999/aug/12/race.world.

24. The most conservative estimates seem to be that black women spend three times more on their hair than white women; other estimates suggest the figure is six times more. See for example 'The growth of UK Afro-Caribbean Hair Care and Beauty Market', Think Ethnic, 07.10.14, http://www.thinkethnic.com/growth-uk-afro-caribbean-hair-care-beauty-market/.

25. Google search conducted on 07.06.17.

26. www.menshealth.com/sex-women/hottest-women-2015. Of the six black women chosen out of a hundred, the only dark-skinned woman was actress Janelle Monáe.

27. Leigh Alexander, 'Facebook's censorship of Aboriginal bodies raises troubling ideas of "decency"', *Guardian*, 23.03.16, https://www.theguardian.com/technology/2016/mar/23/facebook-censorship-topless-aboriginal-women.

28. 'Woman "lost job chance" over hairstyle', *BBC London News*, 16.03.15, http://www.bbc.co.uk/news/uk-england-london-31914177.

29. Yesha Callahan, 'UK Retailer Asos Thanks Cara Delevingne for Making Microbraids a "Thing"', *The Root*, 21.04.16, http://www.theroot.com/blog/the-grapevine/uk_retailer_asos_thanks_cara_delevingne_for_making_microbraids_a_thing/.

30. *Cambridge English Dictionary* definition.

31. In *G v St Gregory's Catholic Science College* (Rev 1) [2011] EWHC 1452 (Admin) (17 June 2011) the High Court of England and Wales ruled that a school's policy, responsible for sending a black pupil home on his first day of secondary school for wearing his hair in cornrows, constituted indirect racial discrimination. International examples include the Butler Traditional High School in Louisville, Kentucky, which in 2016 distributed a dress code banning students from 'dreadlocks, cornrows and twists', and Pretoria High School for Girls whose policy states 'all styles should be conservative, neat and in keeping with school uniform', which has been used to disapprove of natural Afro hairstyles, http://www.phsg.org.za/uploads/cms/files/code_of_conduct_leaners.pdf.

32. Amandla Stenberg, 'Don't Cash Crop on my Cornrows', 15.04.15, https://www.youtube.com/watch?v=O1KJRRSB_XA.

33. Antonia Opiah, 'Why the Conversation About Cultural Appropriation Needs to Go Further', *Teen Vogue*, 24.05.17, http://www.teenvogue.com/story/why-the-cultural-appropriation-conversation-needs-to-go-further.

34. See for example Italian designer Valentino's Spring 2016 collection, which featured African prints but few black models, and described its African-inspired clothes as 'primitive' and 'wild'.

35. Eva Wiseman, 'I want to talk about what goes on', *Guardian*, 20.09.13, https://www.theguardian.com/fashion/interactive/2013/sep/20/twiggy-cara-delevingne-25-years-supermodels.

36. Lester Davids, 'Skin lightening: The beauty industry's ugly billion dollar secret', *International Business Times*, 02.09.16, http://www.ibtimes.co.uk/skin-lightening-beauty-industrys-ugly-billion-dollar-secret-1579218.

37. Rebecca Ley, 'As Holland & Barrett come under fire for selling a controversial skin lightening cream … The women who'll do anything to have whiter skin', *Daily Mail*, 26.11.14, http://www.dailymail.co.uk/femail/article-2850927/As-Holland-Barrett-come-fire-selling-controversial-skin-lightening-cream-women-wholl-whiter-skin.html.

38. Image from the Brussels World Fair 1958, see for example 'Human Zoos: A Shocking History of Shame and Exploitation', CBC, June 2017, http://www.cbc.ca/natureofthings/features/human-zoos-a-shocking-history-of-shame-and-exploitation.

39. Arogundade, 216.

40. Mary Jo Festle, 'Members Only: Class, Race, and Amateur Tennis for Women in the 1950s', in Mary Jo Festle, *Playing Nice: Politics and Apologies in Women's Sports* (1996), Columbia University Press, 54.

41. David J. Leonard, 'Dilemmas and Contradictions: Black Female Athletes', in Lori Latrice Martin, ed. (2014), *Out of Bounds: Racism and the Black Athlete*, ABC-CLIO, 218.

42. Nick McDermott, 'I was that cheeky tennis girl says 52-year-old mother of three', *Daily Mail*, 23.03.11, http://www.dailymail.co.uk/femail/article-1368795/Athenas-iconic-Tennis-Girl-Fiona-Walker-revealed-35-years-on.html#ixzz4R0kRc5Vy.

43. *Daily Mail* reporter, 'Ooh la la! Venus Williams reveals a little too much in lacy burlesque dress at French Open', *Daily Mail*, 24.05.10.

44. Oliver Brown, 'It's not racist, but Caroline Wozniacki's impersonation of Serena Williams is a crime against comedy', *Telegraph*, 13.12.12, http://www.telegraph.co.uk/sport/tennis/9741118/Its-not-racist-but-Caroline-Wozniackis-impersonation-of-Serena-Williams-is-a-crime-against-comedy.html.

45. Charles Sale, 'Croft gets to the bottom of Serena', 28.06.13, *Daily Mail*, http://www.dailymail.co.uk/sport/article-2351341/Charles-Sale-Annabel-Croft-gets-Serena-Williams.html.

46. Martin Jacques, 'Tennis is racist – it's time we did something about it', 25.06.03, *Guardian*, https://www.theguardian.com/sport/2003/jun/25/wimbledon2003.tennis11.

47. Stephen Rodrick, 'Serena Williams: The Great One', *Rolling Stone*, 18.06.13, http://www.rollingstone.com/culture/news/serena-williams-the-great-one-20130618.

48. Ben Carrington (2002), *Fear of a black athlete: Masculinity, politics and the body*, Lawrence & Wishart, 91.

49. BBC reporter, 'Williams "hurt" by jeers', BBC News, 06.06.03, http://news.bbc.co.uk/sport1/hi/tennis/french_open_2003/2967190.stm.

50. Nicola Rollock, 'The invisibility of race: intersectional reflections on the liminal space of alterity', in *Race Ethnicity and Education*, Vol. 15, 2012 – Issue 1, *Critical race theory in England*.

51. Jasper Jackson, 'ITV News apologises for using footage of Ainsley Harriott instead of Lenny Henry', *Guardian*, 04.12.15, https://www.theguardian.com/media/2015/dec/04/itv-ainsley-harriott-lenny-henry-knighthood.

52. 'Against the odds: ethnic minority students are excelling at school', University of Leicester, 01.02.16, http://www2.le.ac.uk/offices/press/think-leicester/education/2016/against-the-odds-ethnic-minority-students-are-excelling-at-school.

53. Haroon Siddique, 'Figures show extent of NHS reliance on foreign nationals', *Guardian*, 26.01.14 https://www.theguardian.com/society/2014/jan/26/nhs-foreign-nationals-immigration-health-service.

54. John Harris and John Domokos, 'Hospital cleaners stage one-day strike for London living wage', *Guardian*, 21.03.16, https://www.theguardian.com/society/commentisfree/2016/mar/21/hospital-cleaners-stage-one-day-strike-for-london-living-wage.

55. 'Life Expectancy at Birth and at Age 65 by Local Areas in the United Kingdom: 2006–08 to 2010–12', Office for National Statistics, https://www.ons.gov.uk/peoplepopulationand-community/birthsdeathsandmarriages/lifeexpectancies/bulletins/lifeexpectancyatbirt-handatage65bylocalareasintheunitedkingdom/2014-04-16.

4. HERITAGE

1. Ged Martin, 'Nostalgia: Elm Park – A Garden City', *Romford Recorder*, 31.03.13, http://www.romfordrecorder.co.uk/news/heritage/nostalgia_elm_park_a_garden_city_1_1996222.
2. Elm Park falls in the parliamentary constituency of Dagenham and Rainham Constituency, whose 2015 election results can be found here: http://www.bbc.co.uk/news/politics/constituencies/E14000657.
3. David Parker and Miri Song (2001), *Rethinking 'Mixed Race'*, Pluto Press, 5.
4. Martin Narey, 'THE NAREY REPORT: A blueprint for the nation's lost children', *The Times*, 05.07.11, http://www.thetimes.co.uk/tto/life/families/article3083832.ece.
5. 'Michael Gove speech on adoption', Department for Education, 23.02.12, https://www.gov.uk/government/speeches/michael-gove-speech-on-adoption.
6. 'Adoption: Pre-Legislative Scrutiny Report', House of Lords, 19.12.12, http://www.publications.parliament.uk/pa/ld201213/ldselect/ldadopt/94/94.pdf, par. 64.
7. 'Right on time: Exploring delays in adoption,' Ofsted, April 2012, https://www.gov.uk/government/uploads/system/uploads/attachment_data/file/419066/Right_on_time_exploring_delays_in_adoption.pdf.
8. 'Breaking Down Barriers to Adoption', Department for Education, 22.02.11, https://www.gov.uk/government/news/breaking-down-barriers-to-adoption.
9. Narey.
10. Parker and Song, 3.
11. F. Nietzsche (1881), *Daybreak: Thoughts on the Prejudices of Morality*, Cambridge University Press (2006 edn), IV, 274.
12. Julie K. Ward and Sam L. Lott (2002), *Philosophers on Race: Critical Essays*, John Wiley & Sons, 159.
13. Frank Furedi, 'How Sociology Imagined "Mixed Race"', in Parker and Song, 23–41.
14. Mark Christian, 'The Fletcher Report 1930: A Historical Case Study of Contested Black Mixed Heritage Britishness', *Journal of Historical Sociology*, Vol. 21, No. 2/3, June/September 2008.
15. Furedi, 26.
16. Ibid.
17. Lucy Bland, 'Race, nation and gender in inter-war Britain', in Black and Asian Studies Association, Newsletter 33, April 2002, 14.
18. *Sunday Express*, 15 June 1919, in Bland, 15.
19. Bland, 13.
20. M. Kohn (1992), *Dope Girls: the Birth of the British Drug Culture*, Oxford University Press, 2.
21. Christian, 215.

22. M. E. Fletcher (1930), *Report on an Investigation into the Colour Problem in Liverpool and Other Ports*, Association for the Welfare of Half-Caste Children, 27.

23. Ibid., 28–9.

24. Christian, 219.

25. Jayne O. Ifekwunigwe (2015), *Mixed Race Studies: A Reader*, Routledge, 77–8.

26. Phyllis Young, 'Report on Investigation into Condition of the Coloured Population in a Stepney Area', March 1944, quoted in Furedi, 26.

27. Rosalind Edwards (2012), *International Perspectives on Racial and Ethnic Mixedness and Mixing*, Routledge, 38.

28. Christian, 236.

29. Oscar Wilde (1891), *The Picture of Dorian Gray*, Penguin (1949 edn), 208.

30. Bland, 14.

31. Christian, 218.

32. Full text of Enoch Powell's 'Rivers of Blood' speech, *Telegraph*, 06.11.07, http://www.telegraph.co.uk/comment/3643823/Enoch-Powells-Rivers-of-Blood-speech.html

33. Rick Dewsbury, 'The NHS did not deserve to be so disgracefully glorified in this bonanza of left-wing propaganda', *Daily Mail*, 28.07.12.

34. Sayeeda Warsi (2017), *The Enemy Within*, Allen Lane, 23.

35. Parker and Song, 2.

36. '2011 Census analysis: What does the 2011 Census tell us about Inter-ethnic Relationships?', Office of National Statistics, http://www.ons.gov.uk/peoplepopulationandcommunity/birthsdeathsandmarriages/marriagecohabitationandcivilpartnerships/articles/whatdoesthe-2011censustellusaboutinterethnicrelationships/2014-07-03.

37. 'Ethnic group statistics: A guide for the collection and classification of ethnicity data', Office for National Statistics, 2003, http://www.ons.gov.uk/ons/guide-method/measuring-equality/equality/measuring-equality--a-guide/ethnic-group-statistics--a-guide-for-the-collection-and-classification-of-ethnicity-data.pdf, 2–3.

38. Parker and Song, 2.

39. Miri Song, 'What happens after segmented assimilation? An exploration of intermarriage and "mixed race" young people in Britain', in *Ethnic and Racial Studies* (2010), 33 (7), 1194–1213.

40. Ibid., 6–7.

41. Ibid., 6.

42. Stephen Jivraj, 'The Dynamics of Diversity: evidence from the 2011 Census', Joseph Rowntree Foundation and University of Manchester Centre on Dynamics of Ethnicity (CoDE), December 2012, http://www.ethnicity.ac.uk/medialibrary/briefings/dynamicsofdiversity/how-has-ethnic-diversity-grown-1991-2001-2011.pdf.

43. Joseph Harker, 'This rush to downplay race ignores the truth of inter-racial adoption', *Guardian*, 02.11.10, https://www.theguardian.com/commentisfree/2010/nov/02/transracial-adoption-race-is-crucial.

44. 2011 Census Analysis, ONS.

45. Jivraj.

46. Song, 'What happens after segmented assimilation?', 9.

47. Peter J. Aspinall and Miri Song (2013), *Mixed Race Identities*, Palgrave Macmillan, 218.

48. Ibid.

49. Song, 'What happens after segmented assimilation?', 9.

50. Ibid., 12.

51. Miri Song, 'Does "race" matter? A study of "mixed race" siblings' identifications', *Sociological Review*, 58:2, 2010, 274.

52. Steve Bradt, ' "One-drop rule" persists', *Harvard Gazette*, 09.12.10, http://news.harvard.edu/gazette/story/2010/12/one-drop-rule-persists/.

53. Aspinall and Song, 94.

54. 'The colour black, mixed-race people', BBC Radio 4, *Thinking Allowed*, 27.07.15, http://www.bbc.co.uk/programmes/b062kx4g. See also Miri Song and Caitlin O'Neill Gutierrez, ' "Keeping the story alive": is ethnic and racial dilution inevitable for multiracial people and their children?', *Sociological Review*, http://dx.doi.org/10.1111/1467-954X.12308.

55. Ifekwunigwe, 3.

56. Jackie Hogan (2008), *Gender, Race and National Identity: Nations of Flesh and Blood*, Routledge, 60.

57. David Graham, 'European Jewish Identity at the Dawn of the 21st Century: A Working Paper', Institute for Jewish Policy Research, 2004, http://www.jpr.org.uk/documents/European%20Jewish%20identity%20at%20the%20dawn%20of%20the%2021%20century.pdf, 9.

58. Warsi, 91–4.

59. Kurt Barling (2015), *The 'R' Word*, Biteback Publishing, xvi.

60. 'DC2101EW – Ethnic group by sex by age', 2011 Census, http://www.nomisweb.co.uk/census/2011/DC2101EW/view/2013265927?rows=c_age&cols=c_ethpuk11.

61. James R. Gaines, 'From the Managing Editor', *Time*, 18.11.93, http://content.time.com/time/magazine/article/0,9171,979727,00.html.

62. Ifekwunigwe, 2.

63. 'Ethnicity and National Identity in England and Wales: 2011', Office for National Statistics, https://www.ons.gov.uk/peoplepopulationandcommunity/culturalidentity/ethnicity/articles/ethnicityandnationalidentityinenglandandwales/2012-12-11.

64. David Robson, 'There really are 50 Eskimo words for "snow" ', *Washington Post*, 14.01.13, https://www.washingtonpost.com/national/health-science/there-really-are-50-eskimo-words-for-snow/2013/01/14/e0e3f4e0-59a0-11e2-beee-6e38f5215402_story.html?utm_term=.022d930ab6d0.

65. Data from 2010 showed that 28 per cent of eligible people with black African heritage were not registered to vote, for example, compared to 7 per cent of white people. 'Race and Elections', Runnymede Trust, http://www.runnymedetrust.org/uploads/RaceandElections-FINAL_interactive.pdf, 24.

66. 'A Humanist View', Toni Morrison, part of the Public Dialogue on the American Dream Theme, Portland State University Library, 30 May 1975, accessed on 20.03.15, http://bit.ly/1q8HG3h.

5. PLACES

1. 'Senegal: New Steps to Protect Talibés, Street Children', Human Rights Watch, 28.07.16, https://www.hrw.org/news/2016/07/28/senegal-new-steps-protect-talibes-street-children.

2. P. N. Davies (1973), *The Trade Makers: Elder Dempster in West Africa, 1852–1972*, Allen & Unwin Ltd, 303.

3. Ibid., 305.

4. James E. Cowden and John O. C. Duffy (1986), *Elder Dempster: Fleet History 1852–1985*, Mallett & Bell, 284–6.

5. University of Oxford, undergraduate admission statistics, 2013, https://www.ox.ac.uk/media/global/wwwoxacuk/localsites/gazette/documents/statisticalinformation/admissionsstatistics/Admissions_Statistics_2013.pdf, 9.

6. Jeevan Vasagar, Rowenna Davis and Tom Meltzer, 'Oxford University diversity row: "Grades aren't enough"', *Guardian*, 12.04.11, https://www.theguardian.com/education/2011/apr/12/oxford-university-diversity-row-students.

7. Emily Lawford, 'Oxford has introduced a compulsory exam on ethnic minority history to diversify its overly "white" curriculum', *The Tab*, 30.05.17, https://thetab.com/uk/oxford/2017/05/29/oxford-introduced-new-compulsory-exam-paper-black-asian-ethnic-minority-history-diversify-overly-white-curriculum-28215.

8. Jinny Kathleen Prais (2008), *Imperial Travelers: The Formation of West African Urban Culture, Identity, and Citizenship in London and Accra, 1925–1935*, University of Michigan, 8.

9. Ibid.

10. Basil Davidson (1973), *Black Star: A View of the Life and Times of Kwame Nkrumah*, Boydell & Brewer, 54.

11. Ama Biney (2011), *The Political and Social Thought of Kwame Nkrumah*, Palgrave Macmillan, 1.

12. Ibid., 104, and Godfrey Mwakikagile (2015), *Western Involvement in Nkrumah's Downfall*, New Africa Press, 14.

13. Boni Yao Gebe, 'Ghana's Foreign Policy at Independence and Implications for the 1966 Coup D'état' (PDF), *Journal of Pan African Studies*, 2 (3), March 2008.

14. See for example: 'Bye Bye Britain' on the Asian blog Banana Writers, http://www.banana-writers.com/racistuk, http://www.dailymail.co.uk/news/article-2046962/Thousands-British-Indians-heading-land-ancestors.html; Edna Fernandes, 'Return of the British Rajas: It's 60 years since the end of the Empire, but thousands of British Indians are heading to the land of their ancestors', *Daily Mail*, 09.10.11, http://www.dailymail.co.uk/news/article-2046962/Thousands-British-Indians-heading-land-ancestors.html#ixzz4iam6sYdI; and Sara Wajid, 'Going back to my roots. A growing number of Pakistani women brought up in the UK are leaving to live in their mother country – despite its oppressive image. Sara Wajid reports', *Guardian*, 23.10.06, https://www.theguardian.com/world/2006/oct/23/pakistan.familyandrelationships.

15. Kwesi J. Anquandah (1999), *Castles & Forts of Ghana*, Atalante, 8.

16. Ibid., 12

17. Notes from the *Elmina Journal*, 4 August 1835 (NBKG 362), retrieved by Dr Larry Yarak.

18. Mary Esther Kropp Dakubu, 'The Portuguese Language on the Gold Coast, 1471–1807', *Ghana Journal of Linguistics*, 1.1, 2012, 20.

19. Larry W. Yarak, 'West African Coastal Slavery in the Nineteenth Century: The Case of the Afro-European Slaveowners of Elmina', *Ethnohistory*, Vol. 36, No. 1 (Winter, 1989), Duke University, 44–60.

6. CLASS

1. A 1969 documentary film featuring a discussion between the civil rights commentators and authors James Baldwin and Dick Gregory, directed by Horace Ové.

2. 'Paintings', The Honourable Society of Lincoln's Inn, http://www.lincolnsinn.org.uk/index.php/history-of-the-inn/paintings.

3. Howard French, 'The Enduring Whiteness of the American Media', *Guardian*, 25.05.16, http://www.theguardian.com/world/2016/may/25/enduring-whiteness-of-american-journalism?CMP=share_btn_tw.

4. Andrea Millwood Hargrave, 'Multicultural Broadcasting: concept and reality', Broadcasting Standards Commission and Independent Television Commission, November 2002, http://downloads.bbc.co.uk/guidelines/editorialguidelines/research/multicultural-broadcasting.pdf.

5. Kurt Barling (2015), *The 'R' Word*, Biteback Publishing.

6. Shonda Rhimes (2015), *Year of Yes: How to Dance It Out, Stand in the Sun and Be Your Own Person*, Simon & Schuster, 235.

7. Channel 4 Programme Policy, http://www.channel4.com/about_c4/programme_policy_2003/policy_home.html.

8. Mukti Jain Campion, 'Look Who's Talking: Cultural Diversity, Public Service Broadcasting and the National Conversation', Nuffield College, Oxford, 2005, 3.

9. Creative Skillset Employment Survey 2014, cited in Matthew Bell, 'Quotas unfair? So is the status quo', July/August 2014, *RTS* magazine, https://rts.org.uk/article/quotas-unfair-so-status-quo.

10. Bell.

11. Stephen Marche, 'The Racism of Gone With the Wind is still with us', *Esquire*, 24.09.14, http://www.esquire.com/entertainment/movies/a30109/gone-with-the-wind-racism/.

12. bell hooks (1981), *Ain't I a Woman: Black Women and Feminism*, Pluto Press, 84.

13. Henry Barnes, Zoë Kravitz: 'Why do stories happen to white people and everyone else is a punchline?', *Guardian*, 20.08.15, http://www.theguardian.com/culture/2015/aug/20/zoe-kravitz-why-do-stories-happen-to-white-people-and-everyone-else-is-a-punchline.

14. Alex Clark, 'Amma Asante: I'm here to disrupt expectations', 02.10.16, *Guardian*, https://www.theguardian.com/film/2016/oct/02/amma-assante-interview-a-united-kingdom-london-film-festival.

15. *Raising the Bar: 100 Years of Black British Theatre and Screen*, episode 1 'The Big Time', BBC Radio 4, 09.11.15, http://www.bbc.co.uk/programmes/b06nnbwl.

16. Tara Conlan, 'Lenny Henry calls for law to boost low numbers of black people in TV industry', *Guardian*, 18.04.14, https://www.theguardian.com/media/2014/mar/18/lenny-henry-black-asian-television.

17. *Raising the Bar*.

18. David Lister, 'Can it be wrong to "black up" for Othello?', *Independent*, 06.08.97.

19. Akala, 'Fire in the Booth', Part 4, published on 4 June 2016, https://www.youtube.com/watch?v=J8umCijRdnQ.

20. Jess Denham, 'Brit Awards 2016: Organisers promise to improve diversity after nominations shun leading grime artists', *Independent*, 24.02.16, http://www.independent.co.uk/arts-entertainment/music/news/brit-awards-2016-organisers-promise-to-improve-diversity-after-nominations-shut-out-leading-grime-a6892751.html.

21. Yomi Adegoke, '#BritsSoWhite: why this year's nominees need to take a stand', *Guardian*, 24.02.16, https://www.theguardian.com/music/2016/feb/24/brits-so-white-why-this-years-nominees-need-to-take-a-stand.

22. Macklemore, 'White Privilege II', 2016.

23. Hattie Collins and Olivia Rose (2016), *This Is Grime*, Hodder & Stoughton, 35.

24. Rebecca Hardy, ' "Fame's taking a cruel toll on me": Leona Lewis on the vicious attack that shook her to the core', *Daily Mail*, 31.10.09, http://www.dailymail.co.uk/femail/article-1223512/Fames-taking-cruel-toll-Leona-Lewis-vicious-attack-shook-core.html.

25. 'Oral statement to Parliament: The Ellison Review', Home Office and the Rt Hon. Theresa May MP, delivered 06.03.14, House of Commons, https://www.gov.uk/government/speeches/the-ellison-review.

26. Vikram Dodd, 'Theresa May stuns Police Federation with vow to break its power', 21.05.14, *Guardian*, https://www.theguardian.com/uk-news/2014/may/21/theresa-may-police-federation-power.

27. Home Office, 'Police powers and procedures England and Wales year ending 31 March 2015', Table 4.01, Ethnic breakdowns of persons stopped under section 1 PACE and section 60 of the Criminal Justice and Public Order Act 1994, England and Wales, year ending March 2015, https://www.gov.uk/government/publications/police-powers-and-procedures-england-and-wales-year-ending-31-march-2015/police-powers-and-procedures-england-and-wales-year-ending-31-march-2015#stop-and-search-1.

28. Transcript of speech, Prime Minister's Office, 10 Downing Street and the Rt Hon. Theresa May MP, delivered on 13 July 2016, https://www.gov.uk/government/speeches/statement-from-the-new-prime-minister-theresa-may.

29. Eleanor Barlow, 'Mzee Mohammed threatened teenage girls at knifepoint before his death', *Liverpool Echo*, 14.07.16, http://www.liverpoolecho.co.uk/news/liverpool-news/mzee-mohammed-threatened-teenage-girls-11615386.

30. Frances Perraudin, 'Liverpool Mayor Promises Transparent Inquiry', *Guardian*, 18.07.16, https://www.theguardian.com/uk-news/2016/jul/18/mzee-mohammed-death-liverpool-mayor-transparent-inquiry.

31. Tom Belger, 'Black Lives Matter protest to be held in city centre this weekend', *Liverpool Echo*, 09.07.16, http://www.liverpoolecho.co.uk/news/liverpool-news/black-lives-matter-protest-held-11592755.

32. Home Office statistics, https://www.gov.uk/government/uploads/system/uploads/attachment_data/file/562977/police-powers-procedures-hosb1516.pdf.

33. According to the 2011 Census, BAME people make up 13 per cent of the population, https://www.ons.gov.uk/peoplepopulationandcommunity/culturalidentity/ethnicity/articles/ethnicityandnationalidentityinenglandandwales/2012-12-11.

34. BAME deaths in police custody, 2007–2016, Inquest, http://inquest.org.uk/statistics/bame-deaths-in-police-custody.

35. 'The 3 R's of Prison Reform', Howard League, http://howardleague.org/what-you-can-do/the-3-rs-of-prison-reform/.

36. Department for Local Government and Communities, 'The English Indices of Deprivation 2015', 30.09.15, https://www.gov.uk/government/uploads/system/uploads/attachment_data/file/465791/English_Indices_of_Deprivation_2015_-_Statistical_Release.pdf.

37. Gary Younge (2016), *Another Day in the Death of America*, Guardian Faber, 79.

38. 'Statistics on Race and the Criminal Justice System 2014', Ministry of Justice, 2013, https://www.gov.uk/government/uploads/system/uploads/attachment_data/file/480250/bulletin.pdf.

39. 'David Harewood: Will Britain ever have a black Prime Minister?', 14.11.16, BBC News, http://www.bbc.co.uk/news/magazine-37799305.

40. K. Sanders-Phillips, B. Settles-Reaves, D. Walker and J. Brownlow (2009), 'Social Inequality and Racial Discrimination: Risk Factors for Health Disparities in Children of Color', Washington DC, http://pediatrics.

41. Annie Ferguson, ' "The lowest of the stack": why black women are struggling with mental health', *Guardian*, 08.02.16, https://www.theguardian.com/lifeandstyle/2016/feb/08/black-women-mental-health-high-rates-depression-anxiety.

42. Briefing paper, Number SN 06705, 'NEET: Young People Not in Education, Employment or Training', UK Parliament, 30.11.16.

43. 'Costs per place and costs per prisoner', Table 1, 'National Offender Management Service, Annual Report and Accounts 2013–14', Management Information Addendum, https://www.gov.uk/government/uploads/system/uploads/attachment_data/file/367551/cost-per-place-and-prisoner-2013-14-summary.pdf.

44. 'School Fees 2016/2017', Eton College, http://www.etoncollege.com/currentfees.aspx.

7. THE NEW BLACK

1. Ian Johnson, ' "Jews Aren't Allowed to Use Phones": Berlin's Most Unsettling Memorial', *New York Review of Books*, 15.06.13, http://www.nybooks.com/daily/2013/06/15/jews-arent-allowed-use-telephones-berlin-memorial/.

2. Peter J. Hugill (1999), *Global Communications Since 1844: Geopolitics and Technology*, JHU Press, 188.

3. Ibid., 189.

4. *Daily Mail*, 20 August 1938, in Anne Karpf, 'We've been here before', *Guardian*, 08.06.02, https://www.theguardian.com/uk/2002/jun/08/immigration.immigrationandpublic services.

5. Karpf.

6. J. L. Silver in *Eastern Post and City Chronicle*, 2 November 1901.

7. 2 May 1905, *PDeb*, 4th Series, Vol. 145, col. 796, in Jason Tomes (2002), *Balfour and Foreign Policy: The International Thought of a Conservative Statesman*, Cambridge, 203.

8. Robert Winder (2013), *Bloody Foreigners: The Story of Immigration to Britain*, Abacus, 20.

9. Ibid., 22.

10. Ibid., 12.

11. Ibid., 28.

12. Ibid., 57.

13. See for example Cedric Barber, descendant of Francis Barber, a freed slave once owned by Dr Samuel Johnson in the eighteenth century: Richard Brooks, 'Dr Johnson's kindness to ex-slave repaid, 250 years on', *Sunday Times*, 10.05.15, http://www.thesundaytimes.co.uk/sto/news/uk_news/Arts/article1554348.ece.

14. Elizabeth Podnieks (2000), *Daily Modernism: The Literary Diaries of Virginia Woolf, Antonia White, Elizabeth Smart and Anaïs Nin*, McGill-Queen's University Press, 162.

15. MTF, Speeches, Interviews & Other Statements, Granada Transcript, TV Interview for Granada *World in Action* ('rather swamped'), 27 January 1978 < http://www.margaretthatcher.org/document/103485>, in Cleo Tsivadnis (2016) ' "Post-Colonial?": Britain in the 1980s', University of Leeds dissertation.

16. Kenan Malik (1996), *The Meaning of Race: Race, History and Culture in Western Society*, NYU Press, 82.

17. Malik, 93.

18. Owen Jones (2012), *Chavs: The Demonisation of the Working Class*, Verso, 131.

19. Andrew Geddes and Peter Scholten (2016), *The Politics of Immigration in Europe*, SAGE, 26.

20. House of Commons, 16 December 1961, Series 9, Vol. 649, 687–819.

21. Deborah Summers, 'Gordon Brown's "British jobs" pledge has caused controversy before', *Guardian*, 30.01.09, https://www.theguardian.com/politics/2009/jan/30/british-jobs-british-workers.

22. Arifa Akbar, 'Blunkett: British Asians should speak English at home', *Independent*, 15.09.02, http://www.independent.co.uk/news/uk/politics/blunkett-british-asians-should-speak-english-at-home-177088.html.

23. Rosa Prince, 'Ed Miliband: Labour got it wrong on immigration – it is not prejudiced to be concerned', *Telegraph*, 18.04.15, http://www.telegraph.co.uk/news/general-election-2015/11547241/Ed-Miliband-Labour-got-it-wrong-on-immigration-it-is-not-prejudiced-to-be-concerned.html.

24. Christopher Hope, 'Ed Miliband's "shameful" immigration mug attacked by Diane Abbott', *Telegraph*, 29.03.15, http://www.telegraph.co.uk/news/general-election-2015/11502577/Ed-Milibands-shameful-immigration-mug-attacked-by-Diane-Abbott.html.

25. In their election manifesto in 2015 the Conservatives proposed limiting net migration to the tens of thousands, and restricting benefits or social housing to EU migrants for four years. Labour proposed a cap on non-EU workers, making it illegal for employers to undercut British workers with lower-paid migrant workers, and restricting out-of-work benefits for EU migrants for two years. UKIP wanted a points system to select only skilled migrants for entry, immigration capped at 50,000 for skilled workers only, a five-year ban on unskilled workers, and restrictions on migrant benefits for five years.

26. Afua Hirsch, 'Secondary Schools Face 80,000-Place Black Hole', Sky News, 14.03.14, http://news.sky.com/story/secondary-schools-face-80000-place-black-hole-10413796.

27. Index of private housing rental prices (IPHRP) in Great Britain, Office for National Statistics, 21.03.17, https://www.ons.gov.uk/economy/inflationandpriceindices/bulletins/index ofprivatehousingrentalprices/feb2017.

28. Tim Black, 'How the Elite Weaponised Immigration', Spiked, 30.06.16, http://www.spiked-online.com/newsite/article/how-the-elite-weaponised-immigration-eu-referendum-brexit/18519#.WOPShhIrLVo.

29. 'EU Referendum Results', Electoral Commission, http://www.electoralcommission.org.uk/find-information-by-subject/elections-and-referendums/past-elections-and-referendums/eu-referendum/electorate-and-count-information.

30. Chris Lawton and Robert Ackrill, 'Hard Evidence: how areas with low immigration voted mainly for Brexit', The Conversation, http://theconversation.com/hard-evidence-how-areas-with-low-immigration-voted-mainly-for-brexit-62138.

31. Lord Ashcroft, 'How the United Kingdom voted on Thursday ... and why', 24.06.16, http://lordashcroftpolls.com/2016/06/how-the-united-kingdom-voted-and-why/.

32. EU referendum: The result in maps and charts, BBC News, 24.06.16, http://www.bbc.co.uk/news/uk-politics-36616028.

33. Simon Kuper, 'A Portrait of Europe's White Working Class', *Financial Times*, 14.06.13, https://www.ft.com/content/4139381a-f1bb-11e3-a2da-00144feabdc0.

34. See for example my interview with Charandeep Singh in 'Ethnic minorities could swing EU ref outcome', 28.05.16, Sky News, http://news.sky.com/story/ethnic-minorities-could-swing-eu-ref-outcome-10297938.

35. Ashcroft, http://lordashcroftpolls.com/2016/06/how-the-united-kingdom-voted-and-why/.

36. Channel 4 News Democracy, 'Today the Supreme Court ruled Parliament has to vote on the triggering of Article 50, the mechanism for leaving the European Union. Here's how voters in Purfleet, who overwhelmingly opted to leave, reacted.' Facebook, 24 January 2017, at 12.34 p.m., https://www.facebook.com/Channel4News/posts/10154479096561939.

37. Steve Fenton, 'Resentment, class and social sentiments about the nation: The ethnic majority in England', 14.08.12, *Ethnicities* 12 (4) 465-83, 467.

38. Patrick Dixon (2015), *The Future of Almost Everything*, Profile Books, 122.

39. Fenton, 465-83.

40. Thomas Piketty, trans. Arthur Goldhammer (2014), *Capital in the Twenty-First Century*, Harvard University Press, 539.

41. Jonathan Freedland, 'Welcome to the age of Trump', *Guardian*, 19.05.16, https://www.theguardian.com/us-news/2016/may/19/welcome-to-the-age-of-trump.

42. 'Changes in US Family Finances from 2010 to 2013: Evidence from the survey of Consumer Finances', Federal Reserve Bulletin, September 2014, 10, Figure A.

43. 'Dramatic rise in the proportion of low-paid men working part-time', IFS, 13.01.17, https://www.ifs.org.uk/publications/8850.

44. For a summary of these arguments by different political theorists, see Fenton.

45. A *Guardian* headline explained 'How Britain was divided by a television show', when *Benefit Street* – which documented life in a street where the majority of residents live on benefits – was aired. See Gareth Price, 'Decoding Benefits Street: how Britain was divided by a television show', *Guardian*, 22.02.14, https://www.theguardian.com/commentisfree/2014/feb/22/benefits-street-tv-programme-divided-the-nation.

46. B. Williamson (1998), 'Memories, visions and hope: Themes in the historical sociology of Britain since the Second World War', *Journal of Historical Sociology*, 1(2): 161-83, 177.

47. Harold James, 'Britain and Europe, what ways forward?', 2016 Harold Wincott Memorial Lecture, http://www.wincott.co.uk/lectures/Harold_James.docx.

48. Boris Johnson, 'Boris Johnson exclusive: There is only one way to get the change we want – vote to leave the EU', *Telegraph*, 16.03.16, http://www.telegraph.co.uk/opinion/2016/03/16/boris-johnson-exclusive-there-is-only-one-way-to-get-the-change/.

49. Speech by Winston Churchill, Hansard, FOREIGN AFFAIRS, HC Deb, 11 May 1953, Vol. 515, cols 883-1004, http://hansard.millbanksystems.com/commons/1953/may/11/foreign-affairs, 891.

50. Tim Ross, 'EU referendum: Iain Duncan Smith interview – Tory veteran says vote to leave on June 23 will make Britain great again', *Telegraph*, 30.04.16, http://www.telegraph.co.uk/news/2016/04/30/eu-referendum-iain-duncan-smith-interview--a-vote-to-leave-on-ju/.

51. See for example Chloe Westley, 'How Brexit will bring Australia and the UK closer together', Conservative Home, 11.02.17, http://www.conservativehome.com/platform/2017/02/chloe-westley-how-brexit-will-bring-australia-and-the-uk-closer-together.html.

52. Dixon, and Farhad Manjoo, 'Why Silicon Valley Wouldn't Work Without Immigrants', *New York Times*, 08.02.17, https://www.nytimes.com/2017/02/08/technology/personaltech/why-silicon-valley-wouldnt-work-without-immigrants.html.

53. Patrick Dixon (2015), *The Future of Almost Everything*, Profile Books, 122.

54. *Der Stürmer*, Issue 44, October 1936.

55. Wendy Webster, '"There'll Always Be an England"', in Stephen Howe, ed. (2010), *The New Imperial Histories Reader*, Routledge, 300.

56. Immigrants who arrived in the UK between 2000 and 2011 contributed more in taxes than they received in benefits and other state assistance; EU migrants contributed £1.34 for every £1 they took out, non-EU migrants £1.02 for every £1. Between 1995 and 2000 EU migrants contributed £1.05 for every £1 received, non-EU migrants, 85p for every £1. Christina Dustmann and Tommaso Frattini, 'The Fiscal Effects of Immigration to the UK', Centre for Research and Analysis of Migration (CREAM), http://www.cream-migration.org/publ_uploads/CDP_22_13.pdf#page=41, 41.

57. Kevin Rawlinson, 'Farage blames immigration for traffic on M4 after no-show at Ukip reception', *Guardian*, 07.12.14, https://www.theguardian.com/politics/2014/dec/07/nigel-farage-blames-immigration-m4-traffic-ukip-reception.

58. Geddes and Scholten, 31.

59. Zlata Rodionova, 'Brexit-backing curry industry says it feels "betrayed" by Theresa May's immigration clampdown', *Independent*, 04.11.16, http://www.independent.co.uk/news/business/news/brexit-latest-immigration-curry-industry-theresa-may-betrayal-a7398196.html.

60. Ibid.

61. Katie Forster, 'Hate crimes soared by 41% after Brexit vote, official figures reveal', *Independent*, 13.10.16, http://www.independent.co.uk/news/uk/crime/brexit-hate-crimes-racism-eu-referendum-vote-attacks-increase-police-figures-official-a7358866.html.

62. Stijn Smismans, 'Brexit, Identity, and the Value of EU Citizenship: the Insider-Outsider Perspective', 06.12.16, *Eutopialaw*, https://eutopialaw.com/2016/12/06/brexit-identity-and-the-value-of-eu-citizenship-the-insider-outsider-perspective/.

63. Simon Kuper, 'A Portrait of Europe's White Working Class', *Financial Times*, 14.06.13, https://www.ft.com/content/4139381a-f1bb-11e3-a2da-00144feabdc0.

64. Tom Parfitt, '"Turkish migrants to CRIPPLE the NHS" Brexit minister's stark WARNING about EU ascension', *Daily Express*, 22.05.16, http://www.express.co.uk/news/politics/672611/Turkey-migration-NHS-Brexit-EU-referendum-Penny-Mordaunt.

65. Heather Stewart and Rowena Mason, 'Nigel Farage's anti-migrant poster reported to police', *Guardian*, 16.06.16, https://www.theguardian.com/politics/2016/jun/16/nigel-farage-defends-ukip-breaking-point-poster-queue-of-migrants.

66. When then prime minister Gordon Brown referred to 'British jobs for British workers' in his first party conference speech in 2007, he was accused of borrowing a phrase from the extreme far-right parties the National Front and the British National Party. See for example Deborah Summers, 'Gordon Brown's "British Jobs" pledge has caused controversy before', *Guardian*, 30.01.09, https://www.theguardian.com/politics/2009/jan/30/british-jobs-british-workers.

67. See for example the language of high-profile Brexit campaigner and former Conservative Party leader Iain Duncan Smith in an interview with the *Sunday Telegraph* in 2016: Kate McCann, 'Brexit is our chance to ensure British jobs go to Britons, says Iain Duncan Smith', *Sunday Telegraph*, 27.08.16, http://www.telegraph.co.uk/news/2016/08/27/brexit-is-our-chance-to-ensure-british-jobs-go-to-britons-says-i/.

68. Andy Beckett, 'Toxteth, 1981: the summer Liverpool burned – by the rioter and economist on opposite sides', 14.05.15, *Guardian*, https://www.theguardian.com/cities/2015/sep/14/toxteth-riots-1981-summer-liverpool-burned-patrick-minford-jimi-jagne.

69. James Proctor (2003), *Dwelling Places: Postwar Black British Writing*, Manchester University Press, 78.

70. 'SECRET: IT TOOK A RIOT', Report by Michael Heseltine to Margaret Thatcher, 1981, http://fc95d419f4478b3b6e5f-3f71d0fe2b653c4f00f32175760e96e7.r87.cf1.rackcdn.com/810813%20Heseltine%20to%20MT%20(578-278).pdf, 1.

71. Beckett.

72. Ed Vulliamy, 'Toxteth revisited, 30 years after the riots', *Guardian*, 03.07.11, http://www.theguardian.com/uk/2011/jul/03/toxteth-liverpool-riot-30-years.

73. 'SECRET: REVIEW OF POTENTIAL FOR CIVIL DISTURBANCE IN 1981 27.04.81', National Archives, cached, http://discovery.nationalarchives.gov.uk/details/r/C11918934#imageViewerLink.

74. Ibid., 3–4.

75. Ibid., 4.

76. 'The English Indices of Deprivation 2015', Department for Communities and Local Government, 30.09.15, https://www.gov.uk/government/uploads/system/uploads/attachment_data/file/465791/English_Indices_of_Deprivation_2015_-_Statistical_Release.pdf.

77. Colin Wiles, 'Cameron will not be able to redevelop "sink estates" without a fight', *Guardian*, 27.01.16, https://www.theguardian.com/housing-network/2016/jan/27/david-cameron-redevelop-sink-estates-social-cleansing

78. Brian MacArthur (2012), *The Penguin Book of Political Speeches*, Penguin.

79. Mawuna Remarque Koutonin, 'Why are white people expats when the rest of us are immigrants?', *Guardian* global development professionals network, 13.03.15, http://www.theguardian.com/global-development-professionals-network/2015/mar/13/white-people-expats-immigrants-migration.

80. Musa Okwonga, 'The Ungrateful Country', in Nikesh Shukla, ed. (2016), *The Good Immigrant*, Unbound, 229.

81. Ronke Oke, 'Home Office: Grant this visa to save a young mum's life', change.org https://www.change.org/p/home-office-grant-this-visa-to-save-a-young-mum-s-life?utm_source=action_

alert&utm_medium=email&utm_campaign=668534&alert_id=gaJpxJWHVH_hI1ahBfTdVjgY2
D7Sb6m98l3FPCICOhqAuogXVGa%2BB%2BjN5Hv0Vo%2FAIFz2OW63jOB.

82. 'Nadiya Hussain tells HELLO! about her Bake Off win, her "dreamboat" hubby and how life has changed', *Hello!* magazine, 19.10.15, http://www.hellomagazine.com/cuisine/2015101927751/nadiya-hussain-gbbo-hello-exclusive/.

83. Amanda Platell, 'Why Womb Transplants Make Me Shudder', *Daily Mail*, 30.10.15, http://www.dailymail.co.uk/femail/article-3258338/AMANDA-PLATELL-womb-transplants-make-shudder.html.

84. Rosie Millard, 'Bake Off's Nadiya on her baking inspiration, coping with fame and why her headscarf doesn't stop her loving tea and bunting', *Radio Times*, 07.10.15, http://www.radiotimes.com/news/2015-10-07/bake-offs-nadiya-on-her-baking-inspiration-coping-with-fame-and-why-her-headscarf-doesnt-stop-her-loving-tea-and-bunting.

85. Liz Jones, 'LIZ JONES on Nadiya Hussain: Why are we so bewitched by a sweet-guzzling bun baker?', *Daily Mail*, 21.08.16, http://www.dailymail.co.uk/femail/article-3751041/LIZ-JONES-Nadiya-Hussain-bewitched-sweet-guzzling-bun-baker.html.

86. Recording of Royal Society of Literature (RSL) event 'The Good Immigrant', 22.11.16, Soundcloud, https://soundcloud.com/rsl/the-good-immigrant; event information, https://rsliterature.org/rsl-event/the-good-immigrant/?page=CiviCRM&q=civicrm/event/info&page=CiviCRM&id=307&snippet=2.

87. Okwonga, 228.

88. Kenan Malik, 'The Failure of Multiculturalism: Community Versus Society in Europe', *Foreign Affairs*, March/April 2015, https://www.foreignaffairs.com/articles/western-europe/failure-multiculturalism.

89. David Olusoga (2017) *Black and British*, Macmillan, 524.

90. Full text of Enoch Powell's 'Rivers of Blood' speech, *Telegraph*, 06.11.07, http://www.telegraph.co.uk/comment/3643823/Enoch-Powells-Rivers-of-Blood-speech.html.

91. Rowena Mason, 'Home Office backs down over "Go Home" vans after legal complaint', *Guardian*, 12.08.13, https://www.theguardian.com/uk-news/2013/aug/12/home-office-backs-down-go-home-vans.

92. Alan Travis, '"Go Home" vans resulted in 11 people leaving Britain', *Guardian*, 31.10.13, https://www.theguardian.com/uk-news/2013/oct/31/go-home-vans-11-leave-britain.

93. That article – which could be found at http://www.dailymail.co.uk/news/article-1153928/One-people-living-Britain-born-overseas-300-000-foreigners-settle-UK.html – has since been removed.

94. Sunny Hundal, 'So, who does the Mail think is British?', 25.02.09, *Liberal Conspiracy*, http://liberalconspiracy.org/2009/02/25/so-who-does-the-mail-think-is-british/.

95. 'Interim Report into Integration of Immigrants', All Party Parliamentary Group (APPG) on Social Integration, January 2017, http://d3n8a8pro7vhmx.cloudfront.net/themes/570513f1b504f500db000001/attachments/original/1483958173/TC0012_AAPG_Interim_Report_Screen.pdf?1483958173, 17.

96. Ibid., 8.

97. Ibid., 14.

98. Timothy D. Taylor (2007), *Beyond Exoticism: Western Music and the World*, Duke University Press, 125.

99. Jones, 225.

100. Tariq Modood, 'Multiculturalism and education in Britain: an internally contested debate', Stephen May Centre for the Study of Ethnicity and Citizenship, University of Bristol, http://www.tariqmodood.com/uploads/1/2/3/9/12392325/multiculturalism_education_britain.pdf.

101. House of Commons briefing paper, 'Unemployment by ethnic background', June 2017, http://researchbriefings.files.parliament.uk/documents/SN06385/SN06385.pdf, 2.

102. Lester Holloway, 'Power of the Black Vote in 2015: The Changing Face of England and Wales', Operation Black Vote, August 2013, https://www.obv.org.uk/sites/default/files/images/downloads/Powerofthe%20BlackVotev3.pdf.

103. Dame Louise Casey, 'The Casey Review: A review into opportunity and integration', December 2016, https://www.gov.uk/government/uploads/system/uploads/attachment_data/file/575973/The_Casey_Review_Report.pdf, 9.

104. 'Interim Report into Integration of Immigrants', 8.

105. See for example the Social Integration Commission's 'Kingdom United', 2015, 12, which called on the government to insist that faith schools have a 'clear plan for pupils to meet and mix with children from different faith backgrounds and communities', and 'The Casey Review', 12, which found that attempts to introduce admissions criteria for faith-based free schools were not reducing segregation.

106. Daniel Khalili-Tari, 'Black culture is popular, but everyone should remember why Carnival started when partying this weekend', *Independent*, 29.08.16.

107. Radhika Sanghani, 'Nadiya Hussain's "bad hair", - and the other reasons why Muslim women wear headscarves', *Telegraph*, 10.08.16, http://www.telegraph.co.uk/women/life/nadiya-hussains-bad-hair---and-the-other-reasons-why-muslim-women/.

108. 'Social integration: A wake-up call', Social Integration Commission, http://socialintegrationcommission.org.uk/a-wake-up-call-social-integration-commission.pdf, 3.

109. Emine Sinmaz, 'Is this the end of Cockney? Hybrid dialect dubbed "Multicultural London English" sweeps across the country', *Daily Mail*, 10.10.13, http://www.dailymail.co.uk/news/article-2498152/Is-end-Cockney-Hybrid-dialect-dubbed-Multicultural-London-English-sweeps-country.html#ixzz4Y0aBe6qn.

110. Toby Helm, 'Immigration is lowest concern on young voters' Brexit list', *Observer*, 22.01.17, https://www.theguardian.com/uk-news/2017/jan/21/immigration-lowest-priority-young-people-brexit-poll.

111. Ashcroft, http://lordashcroftpolls.com/2016/06/how-the-united-kingdom-voted-and-why/.

8. THE DOOR OF NO RETURN

1. Monnica T. Williams, 'Culturally Speaking', *Psychology Today*, www.psychologytoday.com/blog/culturally-speaking/201112/colorblind-ideology-is-form-racism.

2. Isaac Newton was a shareholder in the notorious South Sea Company that traded in enslaved Africans, among other commodities. Winston Churchill bragged about killing 'savages' in colonial wars and said that the wrongs done to Australian Aborigines and Native Americans were in the context of 'a stronger race, a higher-grade race, a more worldly wise race' replacing them. David Hume helped invent racism: 'I am apt to suspect the Negroes, and in general all other species of men to be naturally inferior to the whites. There never was any civilized nation of any other complection than white, nor even any individual eminent in action or speculation.'

3. Dan Chiasson, 'COLOR CODES: A poet examines race in America', *New Yorker*, 27.10.14, http://www.newyorker.com/magazine/2014/10/27/color-codes.

4. E. Hobsbawm and T. Ranger, eds (2000), *The Invention of Tradition*, Cambridge, 102.

5. In 2017, 9.3 per cent of those acknowledged in the Queen's New Year's honours list came from black and minority ethnic backgrounds, the highest proportion in history so far, https://www.gov.uk/government/news/new-years-honours-2017.

6. 'Idris Elba's Keynote speech to Parliament on Diversity in the Media', Channel4.com, 18.01.16, http://www.channel4.com/info/press/news/idris-elba-s-keynote-speech-on-diversity-in-the-media.

7. Editors of the American Heritage Dictionaries (2007), *Spanish Word Histories and Mysteries: English Words That Come From Spanish*, Houghton Mifflin Harcourt, 29.

8. Andrew Hough, 'Prince Philip's Best Gaffes', *Telegraph*, 17.07.15, http://www.telegraph.co.uk/news/uknews/prince-philip/9883276/Duke-of-Edinburghs-best-gaffes.html.

9. Lucy Cockcroft, 'Prince Harry in new race row after telling comedian Stephen K. Amos "you don't sound black"', *Telegraph*, 11.02.09, http://www.telegraph.co.uk/news/uknews/theroyalfamily/4586296/Prince-Harry-in-new-race-row-after-telling-comedian-Stephen-K-Amos-you-dont-sound-black.html.

10. Stuart Jeffries, 'Was this Britain's first black queen?', *Guardian*, 12.03.09, https://www.theguardian.com/world/2009/mar/12/race-monarchy.

11. Amy Oliver, 'Lady Bath? She's a ghastly racist b***h', Mail Online, 12.09.15, http://www.dailymail.co.uk/femail/article-3232291/Lady-Bath-s-ghastly-racist-b-read-mud-slinging-Longleat-comes-stinging-non-PC-riposte-all.html#ixzz4Og9XJu00.

12. Beth Hale, Claire Ellicott, Rebecca English, 'Meet the Los Angeles-born divorcee rumoured to be Prince Harry's new lover', Mail Online, 31.10.16, http://www.dailymail.co.uk/femail/article-3888052/Prince-Harry-s-rumoured-new-love-ambitious-star-s-battled-prejudice-mixed-race-heritage.html#ixzz4Y7KdSmCY.

13. Ruth Styles and Shekhar Bhatia, 'EXCLUSIVE: Harry's girl is (almost) straight outta Compton: Gang-scarred home of her mother revealed – so will he be dropping by for tea?', Mail Online, 02.11.16, http://www.dailymail.co.uk/news/article-3896180/Prince-Harry-s-girlfriend-actress-Meghan-Markles.html.

14. 'A Statement by the Communications Secretary to Prince Harry', 08.11.16, https://www.royal.uk/statement-communications-secretary-prince-harry.

15. 'Extremism: PM speech', Prime Minister's Office, 20.07.15, https://www.gov.uk/government/speeches/extremism-pm-speech.

16. Thomas Ricker, 'How do tech's biggest companies compare on diversity?', The Verge, 20.08.15, http://www.theverge.com/2015/8/20/9179853/tech-diversity-scorecard-apple-google-microsoft-facebook-intel-twitter-amazon.

INDEX

Westminster, London, 12, 56–7

Westwood, Tim, 237

Weymouth, Viscount, *see* Thynn,
    Alexander

What Next in the Law (Denning), 218

WhatsApp, 49–50, 106, 222

Where Hands Touch, 226

white flight, 294

White Hart Lane, Tottenham, 4

'White Privilege II' (Macklemore),
    235

white supremacy, 23, 24

White, Charlene, 85

Whitechapel, London, 129

whiteness, 308–9

WhyIsMyCurriculumWhite, 80, 184

Widgery, John, Baron Widgery, 218

Wilberforce, William, 51, 55, 59

Wilde, Oscar, 149

Wiley, 236

'Will V-Day Be Me-Day Too?'
    (Hughes), 254

William IV, 59

William, duke of Cambridge, 288

Williams, Eric, 60

Williams, Francis, 79

Williams, Karen, 243

Williams, Ralph, 146

Williams, Venus and Serena, 112–16

Wimbledon, London, 5–6, 7, 10–11, 12,
    16, 19, 30, 37, 176
    black people, 40, 41, 71
    Common, 37
    Laurel Grove, 55
    racism, 117, 274, 276, 286
    Tennis Championships, 112–16

Winder, Robert, 259

Winehouse, Amy, 235

Winfrey, Oprah, 116

Wire, The, 229

Wolof, 170, 176

women's rights, 85

Woolf, Virginia, 259–60

work experience, 246–7

Workers' Dreadnought, 85

working class
    and Brexit, 266
    and multiculturalism, 289
    vilification of, 260–61, 275
    and welfare state, 267–9

World Bank, 75, 197

World in Action, 260

Worthington, Samuel, 226

Wozniacki, Caroline, 114

Wright, Richard, 168

Wu Tang Clan, 9

X Factor, The, 235

X-Men, 225

Yahoo! Personals, 101–2

Yorkshire, 8, 23, 142–4

Yoruba, 314

YouGov, 67

Young Turks, The, 223

Younge, Gary, 245–6

YouTube, 233

Zambia, 76

zebras, 68

Zephaniah, Benjamin, 119

Zimbabwe, 40, 77, 282, 287

Zulu, 67, 224

Zurich, Switzerland, 197